S0-DZO-980

Comparative Politics 10/11
Twenty-Eighth Edition

EDITOR

O. Fiona Yap
University of Kansas

O. Fiona Yap is an Associate Professor of Political Science and the Director of Undergraduate Studies at the University of Kansas. Her research work is available through journals such as the *British Journal of Political Science, Journal of East Asian Studies, Japanese Journal of Political Science,* and *Journal of Theoretical Politics* as well as chapter contributions in edited volumes. Her book, *Citizen Power, Politics, and the "Asian Miracle"* (2005) was widely reviewed. Prior to assuming the editorship, she served as an Academic Advisory Board member for *Annual Editions: Comparative Politics.* She is also a reviewer for numerous journals, including *American Journal of Political Science, Journal of Politics, British Journal of Political Science, Comparative Politics, International Studies Quarterly, International Studies Perspective, Social Science Quarterly, Governance, Asian Survey,* and *Journal of East Asian Studies.*

McGraw Hill

Connect
Learn
Succeed™

ANNUAL EDITIONS: COMPARATIVE POLITICS, TWENTY-EIGHTH EDITION

1 2 3 4 5 6 7 8 9 0 WDQ/WDQ 1 0 9 8 7 6 5 4 3 2 1 0

ISBN 978–0–07–805055–8
MHID 0–07–805055–3
ISSN 0741–7233

Managing Editor: *Larry Loeppke*
Developmental Editor: *Debra A. Henricks*
Editorial Coordinator: *Mary Foust*
Editorial Assistant: *Cindy Hedley*
Production Service Assistant: *Rita Hingtgen*
Permissions Coordinator: *DeAnna Dausner*
Senior Marketing Manager: *Julie Keck*
Senior Marketing Communications Specialist: *Mary Klein*
Marketing Coordinator: *Alice Link*
Director Specialized Production: *Faye Schilling*
Senior Project Manager: *Joyce Watters*
Design Coordinator: *Margarite Reynolds*
Production Supervisor: *Sue Culbertson*
Cover Graphics: *Kristine Jubeck*

Compositor: Laserwords Private Limited
Cover Images: Official White House Photo by Pete Souza; The McGraw-Hill Companies, Inc./Christopher Kerrigan, photographer; The McGraw-Hill Companies, Inc./Andrew Resek, photographer; Copyright Thomas Hartwell/2003 (inset from upper left, clockwise); © The Studio Dog/Getty Images (background)

Library in Congress Cataloging-in-Publication Data
Main entry under title: Annual Editions: Comparative Politics. 2010/2011.
  1. Comparative Politics—Periodicals. I. Yap, O. Fiona, *comp.* II. Title: Comparative Politics.
658'.05

Editors/Academic Advisory Board

Members of the Academic Advisory Board are instrumental in the final selection of articles for each edition of ANNUAL EDITIONS. Their review of articles for content, level, and appropriateness provides critical direction to the editors and staff. We think that you will find their careful consideration well reflected in this volume.

ANNUAL EDITIONS: Comparative Politics 10/11
28th Edition

EDITOR

O. Fiona Yap
University of Kansas

ACADEMIC ADVISORY BOARD MEMBERS

Preface

Comparative politics focuses on the empirical study of political behaviors, institutions, and rules to facilitate explanations, predictions, and theory-building. This book sets as its task the presentation of information based on systematic study of such behaviors, institutions, and rules.

To complete this task, the volume is organized to emphasize political behaviors, institutions, and rules from a comparative perspective. Current comparative politics texts make similar arguments regarding the need for such a focus and probably support it. However, few are able to depart from a presentation that is country specific.

This book makes that departure. Instead of providing information on a country basis, each unit presents information about how people and governments behave and interact politically, given the rules and institutions that are in place, across a range of countries and political systems. The point I emphasize is this: Systematic generalizations that address the questions of "why, what, and how" regarding political behaviors and institutions apply across countries and political systems.

This is articulated in all the units, beginning with Unit 1. For those new to comparative politics, it is probably intriguing that people and governments across different countries and systems aim for political balance over the same issues—stability, change, security, and freedom—and try to achieve them the same way. I do not dispute that country-relevant information contextualizes behavior and interactions. Rather, I consider it necessary to clarify the generalizations that provide baseline knowledge regarding why, what, and how of political behaviors and institutions. With this baseline in place, particularities that are observed become even more interesting or unusual.

Each unit begins with an overview that introduces students to the systematic questions of why, what, and how regarding political behaviors and institutions. Often, the first readings in the units introduce students to debates and discussions regarding these systematic questions in the discipline. Subsequent readings provide the empirical "flesh," drawn from the news, public press, or academic studies. They also show that the answers to the systematic questions apply across different countries. This structure—the questions in the discipline and the answers from real-world studies—ensures that students see how the discipline connects with the real world.

Unit 1 introduces comparative politics as a vigorous and important subfield in political science, and compares how other disciplines study governments and politics to showcase the significance of the comparative political science approach. To all those who see that the comparison highlights how comparative political science compares—focusing on why, how, and what—we say "Bravo!" Unit 1 also describes citizen participation and its effects on the stability and change of institutions, processes, and political systems of nations. The unit surveys citizen participation in Western industrialized countries, Africa, and the Middle East to show that citizen participation underlies the procedures that realize democracy.

Unit 2 builds upon the discussion of citizen participation in Unit 1 to address systematically why and how citizen participation is organized and in what forms. The emphasis in Unit 2 is on the relevance of interest groups and political parties as outlets of political behavior that, if repressed or ignored, may lead people to find less democratic ways to participate.

Units 3 through 5 consider the institutions of government to address questions regarding the roles they play in the political process, how they affect political behaviors, and, perhaps most important, how their successes or failures are evaluated. Unit 3 looks at the executive, noting that accountability and responsiveness to the public is the performance bar for the position. Unit 4 looks at legislative representation and accountability and show how legislatures across Rwanda, India, and Zimbabwe embody representation to their constituencies rather than the party or government. This foreshadows the discussion and debate over the lack of minority and women representation in government and how electoral systems influence that representativeness. Unit 5 examines the bureaucracy and the judiciary—the unelected policymakers—to consider the bases of popular resentment against these unelected officials.

Unit 6 focuses on public policy, that is, the outcome of the foregoing discussions of comparative behaviors and institutions. I use this unit to showcase how different countries tackle the same public policy—such as economic development, the environment, or education. This provides the opportunity for a truly comparative review of public policy. In the 10/11 edition, the focus is health care policy. The unit begins with an article on how successful policies are achieved: through a coalition of politicians and citizen-groups. This must come as no surprise; however, the fact that such coalitions are not more frequent should be surprising. The reason why they are not predominant is because of the debate over what is public versus what is private, which snags almost all discussions over the "right" policies to put in place. As the unit overview states, this debate means that there are few easy answers related to policy-making. It makes clear the importance of the roles of citizens and interest groups in clarifying their policy preferences and mobilizing for their causes. It also underscores the need for executive accountability and responsiveness, and the legislature's representation to ensure that policy-making captures the willingness of the citizenry to make the necessary trade-offs.

Unit 7 completes the volume by considering how institutional changes occur. The relationship between institutions and political behaviors is clearly reciprocal, so the question of how institutional changes occur is timely and important. The readings describe three trends—capitalism, globalization, and supra-national governments—to show that domestic demand and new pressures initiate institutional changes. The readings also note that while culture is frequently cited as an explanation for institutional change, a narrower focus—such as on tolerance—is more useful because it is more specific and facilitates systematic evaluation. Aspiring comparativists may take heart in that knowledge: It means that there are no "cultures" that are beyond accountability, responsiveness, representation, and civic participation.

There are several individuals to thank for this current volume. Thanks go to the editorial staff at McGraw-Hill, particularly Debra Henricks, Developmental Editor, for her immense patience. I am also grateful to Larry Loeppke, Managing Editor for the *McGraw-Hill Contemporary Learning Series,* for his support. My colleagues at the University of Kansas—particularly Gary Reich, Hannah Britton, Allan Cigler, Donald Haider-Markel, and Dorothy Daley—must be acknowledged for their support, advice, and critiques that helped with the construction and completion of this volume. The responses of the advisory board members in critiquing and suggesting selections in this edition are instrumental; I am indebted to their painstaking efforts and commitment to see an improved, accessible, and academically rigorous edition. Finally, thanks to the readers, whose comments helped with the selection of readings. I hope that you will continue to help improve future editions by keeping me informed of your reactions and suggestions for change. Please complete and return the article rating form in the back of the book.

O. Fiona Yap
Editor

Contents

UNIT 1
Citizen Participation: The Foundation of Political Stability and Impetus for Change

The concepts in bold italics are developed in the article. For further expansion, please refer to the Topic Guide.

UNIT 2
Political Parties and Interest Groups:
From Preferences to Policies

The concepts in bold italics are developed in the article. For further expansion, please refer to the Topic Guide.

UNIT 3
The Executive: Instituting Accountability and Responsiveness

The concepts in bold italics are developed in the article. For further expansion, please refer to the Topic Guide.

UNIT 4
The Legislature: Representation and the Effects of Electoral Systems

The concepts in bold italics are developed in the article. For further expansion, please refer to the Topic Guide.

UNIT 5
The Bureaucracy and Judiciary: Unelected Policy Thugs or Expert Policymakers?

The concepts in bold italics are developed in the article. For further expansion, please refer to the Topic Guide.

UNIT 6
Public Policy: Defining Public, Effects and Trade-Offs

The concepts in bold italics are developed in the article. For further expansion, please refer to the Topic Guide.

The concepts in bold italics are developed in the article. For further expansion, please refer to the Topic Guide.

UNIT 7
Trends and Challenges: Institutional Change through Capitalism, Globalization or Supra-National Government?

The concepts in bold italics are developed in the article. For further expansion, please refer to the Topic Guide.

Correlation Guide

The *Annual Editions* series provides students with convenient, inexpensive access to current, carefully selected articles from the public press. **Annual Editions: Comparative Politics 10/11** is an easy-to-use reader that presents articles on important topics such as *citizen participation, the economy, social change,* and many more. For more information on *Annual Editions* and other *McGraw-Hill Contemporary Learning Series* titles, visit www.mhhe.com/cls.

This convenient guide matches the units in **Annual Editions: Comparative Politics 10/11** with the corresponding chapters in one of our best-selling McGraw-Hill Political Science textbooks by Sodaro.

Annual Editions: Comparative Politics 10/11	Comparative Politics: A Global Introduction, 3/e by Sodaro
Unit 1: Citizen Participation: The Foundation of Political Stability and Impetus for Change	**Chapter 7:** Democracy: What Is It? **Chapter 8:** Democracy: How Does It Work? State Institutions and Electoral Systems **Chapter 9:** Democracy: What Does It Take? Ten Conditions **Chapter 10:** Conditions for Democracy in Afghanistan and Iraq **Chapter 11:** People and Politics: Participation in Democracies and Nondemocracies **Chapter 23:** Nigeria and South Africa
Unit 2: Political Parties and Interest Groups: From Preferences to Policies	**Chapter 8:** Democracy: How Does It Work? State Institutions and Electoral Systems **Chapter 11:** People and Politics: Participation in Democracies and Nondemocracies **Chapter 16:** The United Kingdom of Great Britain and Northern Ireland **Chapter 18:** Germany **Chapter 19:** Japan
Unit 3: The Executive: Instituting Accountability and Responsiveness	**Chapter 4:** Power **Chapter 5:** The State and Its Institutions **Chapter 16:** The United Kingdom of Great Britain and Northern Ireland **Chapter 18:** Germany **Chapter 20:** Russia **Chapter 21:** China **Chapter 22:** Mexico and Brazil
Unit 4: The Legislature: Representation and the Effects of Electoral Systems	**Chapter 5:** The State and Its Institutions **Chapter 16:** The United Kingdom of Great Britain and Northern Ireland **Chapter 17:** France **Chapter 18:** Germany **Chapter 19:** Japan
Unit 5: The Bureaucracy and Judiciary: Unelected Policy Thugs or Expert Policymakers?	**Chapter 4:** Power **Chapter 5:** The State and Its Institutions
Unit 6: Public Policy: Defining Public, Effects and Trade-Offs	**Chapter 3:** Critical Thinking About Politics: Analytical Techniques of Political Science—The Logic of Hypothesis Testing **Chapter 14:** Political Economy: Laissez-Faire—Central Planning—Mixed Economies—Welfare States **Chapter 15:** The Politics of Development
Unit 7: Trends and Challenges: Institutional Change through Capitalism, Globalization, or Supra-National Government?	**Chapter 2:** Major Topics of Comparative Politics **Chapter 4:** Power **Chapter 6:** States and Nations: Nationalism-Nation Building-Supranationalism **Chapter 12:** Political Culture **Chapter 14:** Political Economy: Laissez-Faire—Central Planning—Mixed Economies—Welfare States **Chapter 15:** The Politics of Development

Topic Guide

This topic guide suggests how the selections in this book relate to the subjects covered in your course. You may want to use the topics listed on these pages to search the Web more easily.

On the following pages a number of websites have been gathered specifically for this book. They are arranged to reflect the units of this Annual Editions reader. You can link to these sites by going to *http://www.mhhe.com/cls*.

All the articles that relate to each topic are listed below the bold-faced term.

Internet References

The following Internet sites have been selected to support the articles found in this reader. These sites were available at the time of publication. However, because websites often change their structure and content, the information listed may no longer be available. We invite you to visit http://www.mhhe.com/cls for easy access to these sites.

Annual Editions: Comparative Politics 10/11

General Sources

Central Intelligence Agency
http://www.odci.gov

Use this official home page to get connections to *The CIA Factbook,* which provides extensive statistical and political information about every country in the world.

National Geographic Society
http://www.nationalgeographic.com

This site provides links to National Geographic's archive of maps, articles, and documents. There is a great deal of material related to political cultures around the world.

U.S. Information Agency
http://usinfo.state.gov

This USIA page provides definitions, related documentation, and discussion of topics on global issues. Many Web links are provided.

UNIT 1: Citizen Participation: The Foundation of Political Stability and Impetus for Change

Africa News Online
http://allafrica.com

Open this site for extensive, up-to-date information on all of Africa, with reports from Africa's leading newspapers, magazines, and news agencies. Coverage is country-by-country and regional. Background documents and Internet links are among the resource pages.

BBC World News
http://news.bbc.co.uk/2/hi/africa/default.stm

This page of the British Broadcasting Corporation provides an up-to-date online resource for Africa and contains links to the news in the Middle East and other regions.

Inter-American Dialogue (IAD)
http://www.thedialogue.org

This is the website for IAD, a premier U.S. center for policy analysis, communication, and exchange in Western Hemisphere affairs. The 100-member organization has helped to shape the agenda of issues and choices in hemispheric relations.

The North American Institute (NAMI)
http://www.northamericaninstitute.org

NAMI, a trinational public-affairs organization concerned with the emerging "regional space" of Canada, the United States, and Mexico, provides links for study of trade, the environment, and institutional developments.

The United Nations
http://un.org/members

This United Nations webpage provides brief profiles of member countries and links to the individual countries. The country links include websites to news agencies and sources.

UNIT 2: Political Parties and Interest Groups: From Preferences to Policies

Human Rights Watch
http://www.hrw.org

This official website of Human Rights Watch describes its beginnings in 1978 as Helsinki Watch. It is the largest human rights organization based in the United States that investigates human rights abuses in all regions of the world and publishes those findings in dozens of books and reports to draw attention to them.

National Geographic Society
http://www.nationalgeographic.com

This site provides links to National Geographic's archive of maps, articles, and documents. There is a great deal of material related to political cultures around the world.

Research and Reference (Library of Congress)
http://www.loc.gov/rr

This massive research and reference site of the Library of Congress will lead you to invaluable area studies information on politics and changes across the globe. It also provides links to bibliographies for those interested in delving more deeply into a topic.

Sun SITE Singapore
http://sunsite.nus.edu.sg/noframe.html

These South East Asia Information pages provide information and point to other online resources about the region's 10 countries, including Vietnam, Indonesia, and Brunei.

UN Interactive Database
http://cyberschoolbus.un.org/infonation/index.asp

This is a United Nations interactive database, InfoNation, to provide official and up-to-date information and statistics regarding UN member countries.

UNIT 3: The Executive: Instituting Accountability and Responsiveness

Asian Development Bank
http://www.adb.org/Countries

The website provides up-to-date information on 44 developing member countries in Asia regarding political, social, and economic policies to reduce poverty and improve the quality of life of the people.

Internet References

BBC World News
http://news.bbc.co.uk/2/hi/middle_east/default.stm

This page of the British Broadcasting Corporation provides an up-to-date online resource for the Middle East and contains links to news in Africa and other regions.

Germany Chancellor's website
http://www.bundesregierung.de/Webs/Breg/EN/Homepage/home.html

This official website of the German Chancellor provides links to executive offices and furnishes up-to-date policy and news releases from the office of the executive.

Latin American Network Information Center, University of Texas at Austin
http://lanic.utexas.edu/la/region/government

The Latin American Network Information Center (LANIC) provides Internet-based information on Latin America and includes source-links to other websites that provide information on Latin American countries.

Russian and East European Network Information Center, University of Texas at Austin
http://reenic.utexas.edu

This is the website for information on Russia and the former Soviet Union. The site also contains links to research a topic in greater depth.

U.S. White House and Cabinet
http://www.whitehouse.gov/government/cabinet.html

The official White House website for the United States government with links to each of the cabinet members as well as cabinet-ranked members that also provides statements on the executive's stance regarding topical domestic and foreign policies.

UNIT 4: The Legislature: Representation and the Effects of Electoral Systems

Asian Development Bank
http://www.adb.org/Countries

The website provides up-to-date information on 44 developing member countries in Asia regarding political, social, and economic policies to reduce poverty and improve the quality of life of the people.

Inter-Parliamentary Union
http://www.ipu.org/wmn-e/world.htm

This website of the IPU comprises data for women representatives in national parliaments and some regional assemblies. The IPU is the international organization of Parliaments of sovereign States (Article 1 of the Statutes of the Inter-Parliamentary Union), established in 1889.

Latin American Network Information Center, University of Texas at Austin
http://lanic.utexas.edu/la/region/government

The Latin American Network Information Center (LANIC) provides Internet-based information on Latin America and includes source-links to other websites that provide information on Latin American countries.

U.S. Information Agency
http://www.america.gov

This USIA page provides definitions, related documentation, and discussion of topics on issues across the globe. Many Web links are provided.

World Bank
http://www.worldbank.org

News (press releases, summaries of new projects, speeches) and coverage of numerous topics regarding development, countries, and regions are provided at this site.

UNIT 5: The Bureaucracy and Judiciary: Unelected Policy Thugs or Expert Policymakers?

Carnegie Endowment for International Peace
http://www.carnegieendowment.org

This organization's goal is to stimulate discussion and learning among both experts and the public at large on a wide range of international issues. The site provides links to the journal *Foreign Policy*, to the Moscow Center, to descriptions of various programs, and much more.

Central Intelligence Agency
www.cia.gov

Use this official home page to get to *The CIA Factbook*, which provides extensive statistical and political information about every country in the world.

Research and Reference (Library of Congress)
http://www.loc.gov/rr

This massive research and reference site of the Library of Congress will lead you to invaluable area studies information on politics and changes across the globe. It also provides links to bibliographies for those interested in delving more deeply into a topic.

U.S. Executive offices
http://www.usa.gov/Agencies/Federal/Executive.shtml#vgn-executiveoffice-of-the-president-vgn

The website lists 15 executive departments with links to each of the departments that, in turn, lists the key bureaucratic agencies that report to the respective departments.

World Wide Web Virtual Library: International Affairs Resources
http://www.etown.edu/vl

Surf this site and its extensive links to learn about specific countries and regions, to research international organizations, and to study such vital topics as international law, development, the international economy, and human rights.

UNIT 6: Public Policy: Defining Public, Effects and Trade-Offs

International Institute for Sustainable Development
http://www.iisd.org/default.asp

This site of the International Institute for Sustainable Development, a Canadian organization, presents information through links on business and sustainable development, developing ideas, and Hot Topics. Linkages is its multimedia resource for environment and development policy makers.

The Commonwealth Fund
http://www.commonwealthfund.org

The Commonwealth Fund is a private organization that supports independent research on health care and policies with the aim of improving access and quality of health care. The site contains publications, surveys, research findings and more related to health care.

Internet References

The World Health Organization
http://www.who.int/en

The World Health Organization coordinates the responses of national and international governmental authorities on health issues and pandemics. The site contains updated information on the organization's ongoing efforts to control disease and improve mortality.

United Nations Environment Program
http://www.unep.ch

Consult this home page of UNEP for links to critical topics about global issues, including decertification and the impact of trade on the environment. The site leads to useful databases and global resource information.
http://www.amenetwork.org

U.S. Information Agency
http://www.america.gov

This USIA page provides definitions, related documentation, and discussion of topics on issues across the globe. Many Web links are provided.

World Bank
http://www.worldbank.org

News (press releases, summaries of new projects, speeches) and coverage of numerous topics regarding development, countries, and regions are provided at this site.

UNIT 7: Trends and Challenges: Institutional Change through Capitalism, Globalization or Supra-National Government?

Carnegie Endowment for International Peace
http://www.ceip.org

This organization's goal is to stimulate discussion and learning among both experts and the public at large on a wide range of international issues. The site provides links to the journal *Foreign Policy,* to the Moscow Center, to descriptions of various programs, and much more.

Europa: European Union
http://europa.eu/index_en.htm

This server site of the European Union will lead you to the history of the EU; descriptions of EU policies, institutions, and goals; discussion of monetary union; and documentation of treaties and other materials.

Freedom House
http://freedomhouse.org/template.cfm?page=1

The organization documents and provides access to annual reports tracking democratic and political developments in about 180 countries.

ISN International Relations and Security Network
http://www.isn.ethz.ch

This site, maintained by the Center for Security Studies and Conflict Research, is a clearinghouse for extensive information on international relations and security policy. Topics are listed by category (Traditional Dimensions of Security, New Dimensions of Security) and by major world regions.

NATO Integrated Data Service (NIDS)
http://www.nato.int/structur/nids/nids.htm

NIDS was created to bring information on security-related matters to the widest possible audience. Check out this website to review North Atlantic Treaty Organization documentation of all kinds, to read *NATO Review,* and to explore key issues in the field of European security.

UNIT 1

Citizen Participation: The Foundation of Political Stability and Impetus for Change

Unit Selections

1. **What Democracy Is . . . and Is Not,** Philippe C. Schmitter and Terry Lynn Karl
2. **Public Opinion: Is There a Crisis?,** *The Economist*
3. **Advanced Democracies and the New Politics,** Russell J. Dalton, Susan E. Scarrow, and Bruce E. Cain
4. **Referendums: The People's Voice,** *The Economist*
5. **Facing the Challenge of Semi-Authoritarian States,** Marina Ottaway
6. **People Power: In Africa, Democracy Gains Amid Turmoil,** Sarah Childress
7. **Bin Laden, the Arab "Street," and the Middle East's Democracy Deficit,** Dale F. Eickelman

Key Points to Consider

- How does citizen participation buttress democracy?

- What does it mean that Western democracies focus on how to "help" other countries "catch-up"?

- Is democracy in the Western countries in jeopardy? What evidence suggests that? What evidence suggests otherwise?

- Is a liberal democracy always more efficient and productive than an authoritarian society? Is a liberal democracy always more affluent and harmonious than an authoritarian one?

- What are the concerns regarding citizen participation through the referendum?

- What does it mean that Western democracies fear the "most democratic of devices" (the referendum)?

- What lessons do Western democracies have to offer other countries?

- What lessons do Western democracies have to learn?

- Why do political hybrids, or semi-authoritarian regimes, exist?

Student Website

www.mhhe.com/cls

Internet References

Africa News Online
  http://allafrica.com
BBC World News
  http://news.bbc.co.uk/2/hi/africa/default.stm
Inter-American Dialogue (IAD)
  http://www.thedialogue.org

The North American Institute (NAMI)
  http://www.northamericaninstitute.org
The United Nations
  http://un.org/members

© The McGraw-Hill Companies

What is comparative politics? What do we compare? How do we compare? Why do we compare? Comparative politics refers to the study of governments. That seems clear. Yet, popular dictionaries such as the Merriam-Webster's Dictionary contain no less than five and as many as ten different ways of conceiving the word "government." They include[1]:

1. The exercise of authority over a state district, or territory
2. A system of ruling, controlling, or administering
3. The executive branch of a government
4. All the people and institutions that exercise control over the affairs of a nation or state
5. The study of such systems, people, and institutions

These definitions emphasize several concepts integral to comparative politics. They are authority, system, people and institutions, and state, district, or territory.

What do we compare? In the broadest sense, comparative politics involves the systematic comparison of authority, systems, people, and institutions across states, districts, or other territories. Its focus is on what Joseph La Palombara once called *Politics Within Nations.*[2] In other words, comparative politics focuses on the patterns of politics within a domestic territory, where political parties, interest groups, civil servants, the public and the press interact under specified laws to influence who gets what, when, how, and why.

How do we compare? Comparative politics emphasizes careful empirical study as the way to gain knowledge about how people and governments behave and interact politically, given rules and institutions that are in place. It is important to note that other disciplines also study how people and governments behave; however, their goals or ends for such study are different. Figure 1 lists six disciplines that study governments and describes what they are, the focus, method, strengths, appeal, and weaknesses of each of these disciplines. For example, the history discipline may also study governments; however, the focus of such study is directed at fact-finding and gathering to enhance interpretation and accuracy. This means that country or area expertise does not necessarily make one a comparative political scholar.

Why do we compare? Two reasons are particularly noteworthy: First, as depicted in the figure and reiterated in the previous paragraph, we compare in order to clarify, explain, derive predictions, and enhance theory-building. Thus, for the political practitioner, analyst, or scholar, comparative politics is applied to explain and, subsequently, predict change or stability. Second, it provides a way to systematically consider how people and institutions across different countries, districts, or systems balance the competing goals of stability, change, security, freedom, growth, accountability and responsiveness.[3]

Here's another way to think about it: How do we learn about countries efficiently? The UN recognizes 192 countries; that does not include several that are not UN members.[4] The U.S. government recognizes 194 autonomous countries in the world.[5] The list easily expands beyond 250 if we include nations that are self-governing as well as those that are not. A nation is defined as "a group of people whose members share a common identity on the basis of distinguishing characteristics and claim to a territorial homeland."[6] Each of these nations or countries has a long history that may bear on the government's behaviors or the responses of its people and also influence what institutions and rules are considered and adopted. Clearly, learning about the particularities of even one country requires considerable time and effort, let alone the more than 100 formally recognized ones.

Comparative politics provides systematic generalizations regarding political behaviors, processes, and institutions to promote learning with greater efficiency. This is not to say that the particularities are not important. Rather, it emphasizes that generalizations provide baseline knowledge from which particularities are observed, described, explained, and predicted. For those new to comparative politics, it is probably intriguing that different countries and systems, nevertheless, share fundamental behaviors, processes, and institutions to achieve the balance

Discipline	History	Sociology	Area Studies	Political Science	Economics	Journalism
What it does	Describes, interprets, or explains individual events or time-related series of events.	Understands what connects the person (personal) to the group (social).	Provides country or region-specific information, particularly on language, customs, religion, or culture.	Identifies systematic patterns over time.	Deduces reasoning from mathematical models.	"Spot" analysis/description of individual events or policy.
Focus	Past events	Groups, relations	City, region, country, area	Institutions, behaviors	Mathematical models	Current events, policies
Method	Akin to fitting a jigsaw—are all the pieces there? The end picture is available.	Solving mystery—what group identities lead people to behave the way they do?	Akin to fitting a jigsaw—are all the pieces there? The end picture is sometimes available.	Solving mystery—what do people do in order to keep/protect what they have?	Solving mystery—how do different incentives lead people to behave differently? (Behaviors are known.)	Uncovering information—through investigation, expert testimony, debate, inference.
Strengths	Uncovers situations, information, motivations, personalities, of the past.	Clarifies racial, ethnic, area, and women's studies. (Probabilistic predictions.)	Rich, detailed knowledge of predispositions.	Prediction, generalization (Probabilistic predictions.)	Prediction, generalization (Probabilistic predictions.)	Details (information, motivations) from spot analysis of situation, event.
Appeal	Intelligence & information to enhance interpretation and accuracy. Story-telling, puzzle-solving approach allows students to improve insights and affirm expectations.	Provides connections between student and larger society. Allows student to investigate personally significant behaviors in larger context.	Intelligence & information to enhance interpretation and accuracy. Story-telling and puzzle-solving approach allows students to improve insights and affirm expectations.	Explains why and how institutions/processes are developed, evolved, changed. Supported by evidence that is methodically culled.	Mathematical modeling, allows for study and theorizing of human behaviors not otherwise possible.	Story-telling, exposé, investigation, debate. Spot analysis provides information, specifics, and may reduce uncertainty surrounding situation/event/policy.
Weaknesses	Focus on interpretation and insights, not predictions. Therefore, theories not always generalizable.	Individual motivations entirely developed from the group.	Focus on interpretation and insights, not predictions. Therefore, theories not always generalizable.	Individual events are low on totem pole of study.	Empiricism not always important.	Not theoretically driven—therefore, cannot explain change or predict (conjecture).

Figure 1 Disciplinary differences in the study of governments.

between stability, change, security, freedom, growth, accountability and responsiveness.

Each of the units in this book introduces some of these generalizations and shows how even nations, institutions, or behaviors that are conventionally presented as particularistic or peculiar are actually consistent with such generalizations. This first unit describes citizen participation and its effects on the stability and change of institutions, processes, political systems, or nations. Citizen participation refers to acts of political involvement. Its most common and basic form is the electoral vote but it includes more complex forms, such as direct policy-making using the referendum.

Citizen participation is fundamental to democracy and political stability. What is interesting, of course, is that most advocates of democracy discuss and debate democracy in normative terms without clarifying how citizen participation relates to democracy. The first article, "What Democracy Is . . . and Is Not," returns the discussion to its roots—citizen participation—and outlines how citizen participation underpins democracy. The set of guidelines on procedural democracy shows that there is "no single set of actual institutions, practices, or values embodying democracy."

The articles in the unit show that no country or nation can lay claim to encompassing the ideal of democracy. Thus, the next set of three articles show that even as the Western industrialized democracies are quick to "help" other countries achieve democracy, their citizens are expressing dissatisfaction and loss of confidence in political leaders and institution. In fact, citizens in Western industrialized democracies are jockeying for greater participation in policy-making in their respective countries. One may think that this is a welcome development among democracy advocates in these countries. Yet, the article, "Referendums: The People's Voice" shows that there are concerns with the use of this "most democratic of devices." Does this seem hypocritical? If it does, it underscores the problem of considering democracy from a moral or normative standpoint.

The alternative, offered in comparative politics, is to consider democracy from the perspective of empirical study. From this viewpoint, democracy is an evolution of practices and procedures that fundamentally encapsulates citizens' preferences as expressed through their participation.

What is to be gained from this perspective? At a minimum, it highlights the importance of increasing citizen participation. Increasing citizen participation allows practices and procedures to evolve and, hence, promotes stability; reducing or dismissing citizen participation leads to potentially dangerous forms of participation to push for change. How dangerous? The article on the African subcontinent highlights how the failure to increase participation led citizens in Zimbabwe to mobilize and challenge Mugabe's regimes.

The article on Bin Laden also shows how citizens are responding to limitations on participation by involvement in extremist activities. And, the article on political hybrids explains how semi-authoritarian regimes that have opened up the participation processes have achieved a level of stability that allows the governments there to remain semi-authoritarian.

There is no question of our responses to the three situations: We are infinitely more impressed by the efforts and determination of the opposition movement in Zimbabwe; unambiguously more disturbed by Bin Laden's appeal; and appalled at the political stasis in the semi-authoritarian states. What we learn from a systematic perspective is that all three situations underscore the same argument: Citizen participation underpins stability, so that the failure to provide for that participation leads potentially to perilous forms of participation to push for change.

Comparative politics, then, shows the problems of letting our own biases dictate who gets to participate, and how or when. In the process, we also learn a fundamental and important lesson about participation: If we provide for citizen participation, the expanded venues provide the release of any bottled up responses that may otherwise find relief through dangerous or extremist appeals.

Notes

1. *Merriam-Webster's Online Dictionary.* Accessed August 7, 2009, from http://www.merriam-webster.com/dictionary/government

2. Joseph La Palombara. 1974. *Politics within Nations.* Englewood Cliffs, N.J. : Prentice Hall.

3. See also Gabriel Almond, G. Bingham Powell, Russell Dalton, and Kaare Strom. 2007. *Comparative Politics Today: A World View.* 9th ed. New York: Pearson Longman Publishers.

4. The United Nations. Accessed August 7, 2009, from http://un.org/News/Press/docs//2007/org1479.doc.htm

5. U.S. Department of State. Accessed August 7, 2009, from http://www.state.gov/s/inr/rls/4250.htm

6. Michael Sodaro. 2007. *Comparative Politics: A Global Introduction,* 3rd edition. New York: McGraw Hill.

What Democracy Is . . . and Is Not

Philippe C. Schmitter and Terry Lynn Karl

For some time, the word democracy has been circulating as a debased currency in the political marketplace. Politicians with a wide range of convictions and practices strove to appropriate the label and attach it to their actions. Scholars, conversely, hesitated to use it—without adding qualifying adjectives—because of the ambiguity that surrounds it. The distinguished American political theorist Robert Dahl even tried to introduce a new term, "polyarchy," in its stead in the (vain) hope of gaining a greater measure of conceptual precision. But for better or worse, we are "stuck" with democracy as the catchword of contemporary political discourse. It is the word that resonates in people's minds and springs from their lips as they struggle for freedom and a better way of life; it is the word whose meaning we must discern if it is to be of any use in guiding political analysis and practice.

The wave of transitions away from autocratic rule that began with Portugal's "Revolution of the Carnations" in 1974 and seems to have crested with the collapse of communist regimes across Eastern Europe in 1989 has produced a welcome convergence toward [a] common definition of democracy.[1] Everywhere there has been a silent abandonment of dubious adjectives like "popular," "guided," "bourgeois," and "formal" to modify "democracy." At the same time, a remarkable consensus has emerged concerning the minimal conditions that polities must meet in order to merit the prestigious appellation of "democratic." Moreover, a number of international organizations now monitor how well these standards are met; indeed, some countries even consider them when formulating foreign policy.[2]

What Democracy Is

Let us begin by broadly defining democracy and the generic *concepts* that distinguish it as a unique system for organizing relations between rulers and the ruled. We will then briefly review *procedures*, the rules and arrangements that are needed if democracy is to endure. Finally, we will discuss two operative *principles* that make democracy work. They are not expressly included among the generic concepts or formal procedures, but the prospect for democracy is grim if their underlying conditioning effects are not present.

One of the major themes of this essay is that democracy does not consist of a single unique set of institutions. There are many types of democracy, and their diverse practices produce a similarly varied set of effects. The specific form democracy takes is contingent upon a country's socioeconomic conditions as well as its entrenched state structures and policy practices.

Modern political democracy is a system of governance in which rulers are held accountable for their actions in the public realm by citizens, acting indirectly through the competition and cooperation of their elected representatives.[3]

A *regime or system of governance* is an ensemble of patterns that determines the methods of access to the principal public offices; the characteristics of the actors admitted to or excluded from such access; the strategies that actors may use to gain access; and the rules that are followed in the making of publicly binding decisions. To work properly, the ensemble must be institutionalized—that is to say, the various patterns must be habitually known, practiced, and accepted by most, if not all, actors. Increasingly, the preferred mechanism of institutionalization is a written body of laws undergirded by a written constitution, though many enduring political norms can have an informal, prudential, or traditional basis.[4]

For the sake of economy and comparison, these forms, characteristics, and rules are usually bundled together and given a generic label. Democratic is one; others are autocratic, authoritarian, despotic, dictatorial, tyrannical, totalitarian, absolutist, traditional, monarchic, obligarchic, plutocratic, aristocratic, and sultanistic.[5] Each of these regime forms may in turn be broken down into subtypes.

Like all regimes, democracies depend upon the presence of *rulers*, persons who occupy specialized authority roles and can give legitimate commands to others. What distinguishes democratic rulers from nondemocratic ones are the norms that condition how the former come to power and the practices that hold them accountable for their actions.

However central to democracy, elections occur intermittently and only allow citizens to choose between the highly aggregated alternatives offered by political parties . . .

The *public realm* encompasses the making of collective norms and choices that are binding on the society and backed by state coercion. Its content can vary a great deal across democracies, depending upon preexisting distinctions between the public and the private, state and society, legitimate coercion and voluntary exchange, and collective needs and individual preferences. The liberal conception of democracy advocates circumscribing the public realm as narrowly as possible, while the socialist or social-democratic approach would extend that realm through regulation, subsidization, and, in some cases, collective ownership of property. Neither is intrinsically more democratic than the other—just *differently* democratic. This implies that measures aimed at "developing the private sector" are no more democratic than those aimed at "developing the public sector." Both, if carried to extremes, could undermine the practice of democracy, the former by destroying the basis for satisfying collective needs and exercising legitimate authority; the latter by destroying the basis for satisfying individual preferences and controlling illegitimate government actions. Differences of opinion over the optimal mix of the two provide much of the substantive content of political conflict within established democracies.

Citizens are the most distinctive element in democracies. All regimes have rulers and a public realm, but only to the extent that they are democratic do they have citizens. Historically, severe restrictions on citizenship were imposed in most emerging or partial democracies according to criteria of age, gender, class, race, literacy, property ownership, tax-paying status, and so on. Only a small part of the total population was eligible to vote or run for office. Only restricted social categories were allowed to form, join, or support political associations. After protracted struggle—in some cases involving violent domestic upheaval or international war—most of these restrictions were lifted. Today, the criteria for inclusion are fairly standard. All native-born adults are eligible, although somewhat higher age limits may still be imposed upon candidates for certain offices. Unlike the early American and European democracies of the nineteenth century, none of the recent democracies in southern Europe, Latin America, Asia, or Eastern Europe has even attempted to impose formal restrictions on the franchise or eligibility to office. When it comes to informal restrictions on the effective exercise of citizenship rights, however, the story can be quite different. This explains the central importance (discussed below) of procedures.

Competition has not always been considered an essential defining condition of democracy. "Classic" democracies presumed decision making based on direct participation leading to consensus. The assembled citizenry was expected to agree on a common course of action after listening to the alternatives and weighing their respective merits and demerits. A tradition of hostility to "faction," and "particular interests" persists in democratic thought, but at least since *The Federalist Papers* it has become widely accepted that competition among factions is a necessary evil in democracies that operate on a more-than-local scale. Since, as James Madison argued, "the latent causes of faction are sown into the nature of man," and the possible remedies for "the mischief of faction" are worse than the disease, the best course is to recognize them and to attempt to control their effects.[6] Yet while democrats may agree on the inevitability of factions, they tend to disagree about the best forms and rules for governing factional competition. Indeed,

differences over the preferred modes and boundaries of competition contribute most to distinguishing one subtype of democracy from another.

The most popular definition of democracy equates it with regular *elections*, fairly conducted and honestly counted. Some even consider the mere fact of elections—even ones from which specific parties or candidates are excluded, or in which substantial portions of the population cannot freely participate—as a sufficient condition for the existence of democracy. This fallacy has been called "electoralism" or "the faith that merely holding elections will channel political action into peaceful contests among elites and accord public legitimacy to the winners"—no matter how they are conducted or what else constrains those who win them.[7] However central to democracy, elections occur intermittently and only allow citizens to choose between the highly aggregated alternatives offered by political parties, which can, especially in the early stages of a democratic transition, proliferate in a bewildering variety. During the intervals between elections, citizens can seek to influence public policy through a wide variety of other intermediaries: interest associations, social movements, locality groupings, clientelistic arrangements, and so forth. *Modern democracy, in other words, offers a variety of competitive processes and channels for the expression of interests and values—associational as well as partisan, functional as well as territorial, collective as well as individual. All are integral to its practice.*

Another commonly accepted image of democracy identifies it with *majority rule*. Any governing body that makes decisions by combining the votes of more than half of those eligible and present is said to be democratic, whether that majority emerges within an electorate, a parliament, a committee, a city council, or a party caucus. For exceptional purposes (e.g., amending the constitution or expelling a member), "qualified majorities" of more than 50 percent may be required, but few would deny that democracy must involve some means of aggregating the equal preferences of individuals.

A problem arises, however, when *numbers* meet *intensities*. What happens when a properly assembled majority (especially a stable, self-perpetuating one) regularly makes decisions that harm some minority (especially a threatened cultural or ethnic group)? In these circumstances, successful democracies tend to qualify the central principle of majority rule in order to protect minority rights. Such qualifications can take the form of constitutional provisions that place certain matters beyond the reach of majorities (bills of rights); requirements for concurrent majorities in several different constituencies (confederalism); guarantees securing the autonomy of local or regional governments against the demands of the central authority (federalism); grand coalition governments that incorporate all parties (consociationalism); or the negotiation of social pacts between major social groups like business and labor (neocorporatism). The most common and effective way of protecting minorities, however, lies in the everyday operation of interest associations and social movements. These reflect (some would say, amplify) the different intensities of preference that exist in the population and bring them to bear on democratically elected decision makers. Another way of putting this intrinsic tension between numbers and intensities would be to say that "in modern democracies, votes may be counted, but influences alone are weighted."

Cooperation has always been a central feature of democracy. Actors must voluntarily make collective decisions binding on the polity as a whole. They must cooperate in order to compete. They must be capable of acting collectively through parties, associations, and movements in order to select candidates, articulate preferences, petition authorities, and influence policies.

But democracy's freedoms should also encourage citizens to deliberate among themselves, to discover their common needs, and to resolve their differences without relying on some supreme central authority. Classical democracy emphasized these qualities, and they are by no means extinct, despite repeated efforts by contemporary theorists to stress the analogy with behavior in the economic marketplace and to reduce all of democracy's operations to competitive interest maximization. Alexis de Tocqueville best described the importance of independent groups for democracy in his *Democracy in America*, a work which remains a major source of inspiration for all those who persist in viewing democracy as something more than a struggle for election and re-election among competing candidates.[8]

In contemporary political discourse, this phenomenon of cooperation and deliberation via autonomous group activity goes under the rubric of "civil society." The diverse units of social identity and interest, by remaining independent of the state (and perhaps even of parties), not only can restrain the arbitrary actions of rulers, but can also contribute to forming better citizens who are more aware of the preferences of others, more self-confident in their actions, and more civic-minded in their willingness to sacrifice for the common good. At its best, civil society provides an intermediate layer of governance between the individual and the state that is capable of resolving conflicts and controlling the behavior of members without public coercion. Rather than overloading decision makers with increased demands and making the system ungovernable,[9] a viable civil society can mitigate conflicts and improve the quality of citizenship—without relying exclusively on the privatism of the marketplace.

Representatives—whether directly or indirectly elected—do most of the real work in modern democracies. Most are professional politicians who orient their careers around the desire to fill key offices. It is doubtful that any democracy could survive without such people. The central question, therefore, is not whether or not there will be a political elite or even a professional political class, but how these representatives are chosen and then held accountable for their actions.

As noted above, there are many channels of representation in modern democracy. The electoral one, based on territorial constituencies, is the most visible and public. It culminates in a parliament or a presidency that is periodically accountable to the citizenry as a whole. Yet the sheer growth of government (in large part as a byproduct of popular demand) has increased the number, variety, and power of agencies charged with making public decisions and not subject to elections. Around these

agencies there has developed a vast apparatus of specialized representation based largely on functional interests, not territorial constituencies. These interest associations, and not political parties, have become the primary expression of civil society in most stable democracies, supplemented by the more sporadic interventions of social movements.

The new and fragile democracies that have sprung up since 1974 must live in "compressed time." They will not resemble the European democracies of the nineteenth and early twentieth centuries, and they cannot expect to acquire the multiple channels of representation in gradual historical progression as did most of their predecessors. A bewildering array of parties, interests, and movements will all simultaneously seek political influence in them, creating challenges to the polity that did not exist in earlier processes of democratization.

Procedures That Make Democracy Possible

The defining components of democracy are necessarily abstract, and may give rise to a considerable variety of institutions and subtypes of democracy. For democracy to thrive, however, specific procedural norms must be followed and civic rights must be respected. Any polity that fails to impose such restrictions upon itself, that fails to follow the "rule of law" with regard to its own procedures, should not be considered democratic. These procedures alone do not define democracy, but their presence is indispensable to its persistence. In essence, they are necessary but not sufficient conditions for its existence.

Robert Dahl has offered the most generally accepted listing of what he terms the "procedural minimal" conditions that must be present for modern political democracy (or as he puts it, "polyarchy") to exist:

1. Control over government decisions about policy is constitutionally vested in elected officials.
2. Elected officials are chosen in frequent and fairly conducted elections in which coercion is comparatively uncommon.
3. Practically all adults have the right to vote in the election of officials.
4. Practically all adults have the right to run for elective offices.
5. Citizens have a right to express themselves without the danger of severe punishment on political matters broadly defined. . . .
6. Citizens have a right to seek out alternative sources of information. Moreover, alternative sources of information exist and are protected by law.
7. . . . Citizens also have the right to form relatively independent associations or organizations, including independent political parties and interest groups.[10]

These seven conditions seem to capture the essence of procedural democracy for many theorists, but we propose to add two others. The first might be thought of as a further refinement of item (1), while the second might be called an implicit prior condition to all seven of the above.

1. Popularly elected officials must be able to exercise their constitutional powers without being subjected to overriding (albeit informal) opposition from unelected officials. Democracy is in jeopardy if military officers, entrenched civil servants, or state managers retain the capacity to act independently of elected civilians or even veto decisions made by the people's representatives. Without this additional caveat, the militarized polities of contemporary Central America, where civilian control over the military does not exist, might be classified by many scholars as democracies, just as they have been (with the exception of Sandinista Nicaragua) by U.S. policy makers. The caveat thus guards against what we earlier called "electoralism"—the tendency to focus on the holding of elections while ignoring other political realities.

2. The polity must be self-governing; it must be able to act independently of constraints imposed by some other overarching political system. Dahl and other contemporary democratic theorists probably took this condition for granted since they referred to formally sovereign nation-states. However, with the development of blocs, alliances, spheres of influence, and a variety of "neocolonial" arrangements, the question of autonomy has been a salient one. Is a system really democratic if its elected officials are unable to make binding decisions without the approval of actors outside their territorial domain? This is significant even if the outsiders are relatively free to alter or even end the encompassing arrangement (as in Puerto Rico), but it becomes especially critical if neither condition obtains (as in the Baltic states).

Principles That Make Democracy Feasible

Lists of component processes and procedural norms help us to specify what democracy is, but they do not tell us much about how it actually functions. The simplest answer is "by the consent of the people"; the more complex one is "by the contingent consent of politicians acting under conditions of bounded uncertainty."

In a democracy, representatives must at least informally agree that those who win greater electoral support or influence over policy will not use their temporary superiority to bar the losers from taking office or exerting influence in the future, and that in exchange for this opportunity to keep competing for power and place, momentary losers will respect the winners' right to make binding decisions. Citizens are expected to obey the decisions ensuing from such a process of competition, provided its outcome remains contingent upon their collective preferences as expressed through fair and regular elections or open and repeated negotiations.

The challenge is not so much to find a set of goals that command widespread consensus as to find a set of rules that embody contingent consent. The precise shape of this "democratic bargain," to use Dahl's expression,[11] can vary a good deal from society to society. It depends on social cleavages and such subjective factors as mutual trust, the standard of fairness, and the willingness to compromise. It may even be compatible with a great deal of dissensus on substantive policy issues.

All democracies involve a degree of uncertainty about who will be elected and what policies they will pursue. Even in those polities where one party persists in winning elections or one policy is consistently implemented, the possibility of change through independent collective action still exists, as in Italy, Japan, and the Scandinavian social democracies. If it does not, the system is not democratic, as in Mexico, Senegal, or Indonesia.

But the uncertainty embedded in the core of all democracies is bounded. Not just any actor can get into the competition and raise any issue he or she pleases—there are previously established rules that must be respected. Not just any policy can be adopted—there are conditions that must be met. Democracy institutionalizes "normal," limited political uncertainty. These boundaries vary from country to country. Constitutional guarantees of property, privacy, expression, and other rights are a part of this, but the most effective boundaries are generated by competition among interest groups and cooperation within civil society. Whatever the rhetoric (and some polities appear to offer their citizens more dramatic alternatives than others), once the rules of contingent consent have been agreed upon, the actual variation is likely to stay within a predictable and generally accepted range.

This emphasis on operative guidelines contrasts with a highly persistent, but misleading theme in recent literature on democracy—namely, the emphasis upon "civic culture." The principles we have suggested here rest on rules of prudence, not on deeply ingrained habits of tolerance, moderation, mutual respect, fair play, readiness to compromise, or trust in public authorities. Waiting for such habits to sink deep and lasting roots implies a very slow process of regime consolidation—one that takes generations—and it would probably condemn most contemporary experiences *ex hypothesi* to failure. Our assertion is that contingent consent and bounded uncertainty can emerge from the interaction between antagonistic and mutually suspicious actors and that the far more benevolent and ingrained norms of a civic culture are better thought of as a *product* and not a producer of democracy.

How Democracies Differ

Several concepts have been deliberately excluded from our generic definition of democracy, despite the fact that they have been frequently associated with it in both everyday practice and scholarly work. They are, nevertheless, especially important when it comes to distinguishing subtypes of democracy. Since no single set of actual institutions, practices, or values embodies democracy, polities moving away from authoritarian rule can mix different components to produce different democracies. It is important to recognize that these do not define points along a single continuum of improving performance, but a matrix of potential combinations that are *differently* democratic.

1. *Consensus*: All citizens may not agree on the substantive goals of political action or on the role of the state (although if they did, it would certainly make governing democracies much easier).

2. *Participation*: All citizens may not take an active and equal part in politics, although it must be legally possible for them to do so.

3. *Access*: Rulers may not weigh equally the preferences of all who come before them, although citizenship implies that individuals and groups should have an equal opportunity to express their preferences if they choose to do so.

4. *Responsiveness*: Rulers may not always follow the course of action preferred by the citizenry. But when they deviate from such a policy, say on grounds of "reason of state" or "overriding national interest," they must ultimately be held accountable for their actions through regular and fair processes.

5. *Majority rule*: Positions may not be allocated or rules may not be decided solely on the basis of assembling the most votes, although deviations from this principle usually must be explicitly defended and previously approved.

6. *Parliamentary sovereignty*: The legislature may not be the only body that can make rules or even the one with final authority in deciding which laws are binding, although where executive, judicial, or other public bodies make that ultimate choice, they too must be accountable for their actions.

7. *Party government*: Rulers may not be nominated, promoted, and disciplined in their activities by well-organized and programmatically coherent political parties, although where they are not, it may prove more difficult to form an effective government.

8. *Pluralism*: The political process may not be based on a multiplicity of overlapping, voluntaristic, and autonomous private groups. However, where there are monopolies of representation, hierarchies of association, and obligatory memberships, it is likely that the interests involved will be more closely linked to the state and the separation between the public and private spheres of action will be much less distinct.

9. *Federalism*: The territorial division of authority may not involve multiple levels and local autonomies, least of all ones enshrined in a constitutional document, although some dispersal of power across territorial and/or functional units is characteristic of all democracies.

10. *Presidentialism*: The chief executive officer may not be a single person and he or she may not be directly elected by the citizenry as a whole, although some concentration of authority is present in all democracies, even if

it is exercised collectively and only held indirectly accountable to the electorate.

11. *Checks and Balances*: It is not necessary that the different branches of government be systematically pitted against one another, although governments by assembly, by executive concentrations, by judicial command, or even by dictatorial fiat (as in time of war) must be ultimately accountable to the citizenry as a whole.

While each of the above has been named as an essential component of democracy, they should instead be seen either as indicators of this or that type of democracy, or else as useful standards for evaluating the performance of particular regimes. To include them as part of the generic definition of democracy itself would be to mistake the American polity for the universal model of democratic governance. Indeed, the parliamentary, consociational, unitary, corporatist, and concentrated arrangements of continental Europe may have some unique virtues for guiding polities through the uncertain transition from autocratic to democratic rule.[12]

What Democracy Is Not

We have attempted to convey the general meaning of modern democracy without identifying it with some particular set of rules and institutions or restricting it to some specific culture or level of development. We have also argued that it cannot be reduced to the regular holding of elections or equated with a particular notion of the role of the state, but we have not said much more about what democracy is not or about what democracy may not be capable of producing.

There is an understandable temptation to load too many expectations on this concept and to imagine that by attaining democracy, a society will have resolved all of its political, social, economic, administrative, and cultural problems. Unfortunately, "all good things do not necessarily go together."

First, democracies are not necessarily more efficient economically than other forms of government. Their rates of aggregate growth, savings, and investment may be no better than those of nondemocracies. This is especially likely during the transition, when propertied groups and administrative elites may respond to real or imagined threats to the "rights" they enjoyed under authoritarian rule by initiating capital flight, disinvestment, or sabotage. In time, depending upon the type of democracy, benevolent long-term effects upon income distribution, aggregate demand, education, productivity, and creativity may eventually combine to improve economic and social performance, but it is certainly too much to expect that these improvements will occur immediately—much less that they will be defining characteristics of democratization.

Second, democracies are not necessarily more efficient administratively. Their capacity to make decisions may even be slower than that of the regimes they replace, if only because more actors must be consulted. The costs of getting things done may be higher, if only because "payoffs" have to be made to a wider and more resourceful set of clients (although one should never underestimate the degree of corruption to be found within autocracies). Popular satisfaction with the new democratic government's performance may not even seem greater, if only because necessary compromises often please no one completely, and because the losers are free to complain.

Third, democracies are not likely to appear more orderly, consensual, stable, or governable than the autocracies they replace. This is partly a byproduct of democratic freedom of expression, but it is also a reflection of the likelihood of continuing disagreement over new rules and institutions. These products of imposition or compromise are often initially quite ambiguous in nature and uncertain in effect until actors have learned how to use them. What is more, they come in the aftermath of serious struggles motivated by high ideals. Groups and individuals with recently acquired autonomy will test certain rules, protest against the actions of certain institutions, and insist on renegotiating their part of the bargain. Thus the presence of antisystem parties should be neither surprising nor seen as a failure of democratic consolidation. What counts is whether such parties are willing, however reluctantly, to play by the general rules of bounded uncertainty and contingent consent.

Governability is a challenge for all regimes, not just democratic ones. Given the political exhaustion and loss of legitimacy that have befallen autocracies from sultanistic Paraguay to totalitarian Albania, it may seem that only democracies can now be expected to govern effectively and legitimately. Experience has shown, however, that democracies too can lose the ability to govern. Mass publics can become disenchanted with their performance. Even more threatening is the temptation for leaders to fiddle with procedures and ultimately undermine the principles of contingent consent and bounded uncertainty. Perhaps the most critical moment comes once the politicians begin to settle into the more predictable roles and relations of a consolidated democracy. Many will find their expectations frustrated; some will discover that the new rules of competition put them at a disadvantage; a few may even feel that their vital interests are threatened by popular majorities.

Finally, democracies will have more open societies and polities than the autocracies they replace, but not necessarily more open economies. Many of today's most successful and well-established democracies have historically resorted to protectionism and closed borders, and have relied extensively upon public institutions to promote economic development. While the long-term compatibility between democracy and capitalism does not seem to be in doubt, despite their continuous tension, it is not clear whether the promotion of such liberal economic goals as the right of individuals to own property and retain profits, the clearing function of markets, the private settlement of disputes, the freedom to produce without government regulation, or the privatization of state-owned enterprises necessarily furthers the consolidation of democracy. After all, democracies do need to levy taxes and regulate certain transactions, especially where private monopolies and oligopolies exist. Citizens or their representatives may decide that it is desirable to protect the rights of collectivities from encroachment by individuals, especially propertied ones, and

they may choose to set aside certain forms of property for public or cooperative ownership. In short, notions of economic liberty that are currently put forward in neoliberal economic models are not synonymous with political freedom—and may even impede it.

Democratization will not necessarily bring in its wake economic growth, social peace, administrative efficiency, political harmony, free markets, or "the end of ideology." Least of all will it bring about "the end of history." No doubt some of these qualities could make the consolidation of democracy easier, but they are neither prerequisites for it nor immediate products of it. Instead, what we should be hoping for is the emergence of political institutions that can peacefully compete to form governments and influence public policy, that can channel social and economic conflicts through regular procedures, and that have sufficient linkages to civil society to represent their constituencies and commit them to collective courses of action. Some types of democracies, especially in developing countries, have been unable to fulfill this promise, perhaps due to the circumstances of their transition from authoritarian rule.[13] The democratic wager is that such a regime, once established, will not only persist by reproducing itself within its initial confining conditions, but will eventually expand beyond them.[14] Unlike authoritarian regimes, democracies have the capacity to modify their rules and institutions consensually in response to changing circumstances. They may not immediately produce all the goods mentioned above, but they stand a better chance of eventually doing so than do autocracies.

Notes

1. For a comparative analysis of the recent regime changes in southern Europe and Latin America, see Guillermo O'Donnell, Philippe C. Schmitter, and Laurence Whitehead, eds., *Transitions from Authoritarian Rule*, 4 vols. (Baltimore: Johns Hopkins University Press, 1986). For another compilation that adopts a more structural approach see Larry Diamond, Juan Linz, and Seymour Martin Lipset, eds., *Democracy in Developing Countries*, vols. 2, 3, and 4 (Boulder, Colo.: Lynne Rienner, 1989).

2. Numerous attempts have been made to codify and quantify the existence of democracy across political systems. The best known is probably Freedom House's *Freedom in the World: Political Rights and Civil Liberties*, published since 1973 by Greenwood Press and since 1988 by University Press of America. Also see Charles Humana, *World Human Rights Guide* (New York: Facts on File, 1986).

3. The definition most commonly used by American social scientists is that of Joseph Schumpeter: "that institutional arrangement for arriving at political decisions in which individuals acquire the power to decide by means of a competitive struggle for the people's vote." *Capitalism, Socialism, and Democracy* (London: George Allen and Unwin, 1943), 269. We accept certain aspects of the classical procedural approach to modern democracy, but differ primarily in our emphasis on the accountability of rulers to citizens and the relevance of mechanisms of competition other than elections.

4. Not only do some countries practice a stable form of democracy without a formal constitution (e.g., Great Britain and Israel), but even more countries have constitutions and legal codes that offer no guarantee of reliable practice. On paper, Stalin's 1936 constitution for the USSR was a virtual model of democratic rights and entitlements.

5. For the most valiant attempt to make some sense out of this thicket of distinctions, see Juan Linz, "Totalitarian and Authoritarian Regimes" in *Handbook of Political Science*, eds. Fred I. Greenstein and Nelson W. Polsby (Reading Mass.: Addison Wesley, 1975), 175–411.

6. "Publius" (Alexander Hamilton, John Jay, and James Madison), *The Federalist Papers* (New York: Anchor Books, 1961). The quote is from Number 10.

7. See Terry Karl, "Imposing Consent? Electoralism versus Democratization in El Salvador," in *Elections and Democratization in Latin America, 1980–1985*, eds. Paul Drake and Eduardo Silva (San Diego: Center for Iberian and Latin American Studies, Center for US/Mexican Studies, University of California, San Diego, 1986), 9–36.

8. Alexis de Tocqueville, *Democracy in America*, 2 vols. (New York: Vintage Books, 1945).

9. This fear of overloaded government and the imminent collapse of democracy is well reflected in the work of Samuel P. Huntington during the 1970s. See especially Michel Crozier, Samuel P. Huntington, and Joji Watanuki, *The Crisis of Democracy* (New York: New York University Press, 1975).

For Huntington's (revised) thoughts about the prospects for democracy, see his "Will More Countries Become Democratic?," *Political Science Quarterly* 99 (Summer 1984): 193–218.

10. Robert Dahl, *Dilemmas of Pluralist Democracy* (New Haven: Yale University Press, 1982), 11.

11. Robert Dahl, *After the Revolution: Authority in a Good Society* (New Haven: Yale University Press, 1970).

12. See Juan Linz, "The Perils of Presidentialism," *Journal of Democracy* 1 (Winter 1990): 51–69, and the ensuing discussion by Donald Horowitz, Seymour Martin Lipset, and Juan Linz in *Journal of Democracy* 1 (Fall 1990): 73–91.

13. Terry Lynn Karl, "Dilemmas of Democratization in Latin America" *Comparative Politics* 23 (October 1990): 1–23.

14. Otto Kirchheimer, "Confining Conditions and Revolutionary Breakthroughs," *American Political Science Review* 59 (1965): 964–974.

PHILIPPE C. SCHMITTER is professor of political science and director of the Center for European Studies at Stanford University. **TERRY LYNN KARL** is associate professor of political science and director of the Center for Latin American Studies at the same institution. The original, longer version of this essay was written at the request of the United States Agency for International Development, which is not responsible for its content.

Public Opinion: Is There a Crisis?

After the collapse of communism, the world saw a surge in the number of new democracies. But why are the citizens of the mature democracies meanwhile losing confidence in their political institutions? This is the first in a series of articles on democracy in transition.

Everyone remembers that Winston Churchill once called democracy the worst form of government— except for all the others. The end of the cold war seemed to prove him right. All but a handful of countries now claim to embrace democratic ideals. Insofar as there is

a debate about democracy, much of it now centers on how to help the "emerging" democracies of Asia, Africa, Latin America and Eastern Europe catch up with the established democratic countries of the West and Japan. The new democracies are used to having well-meaning observers from the

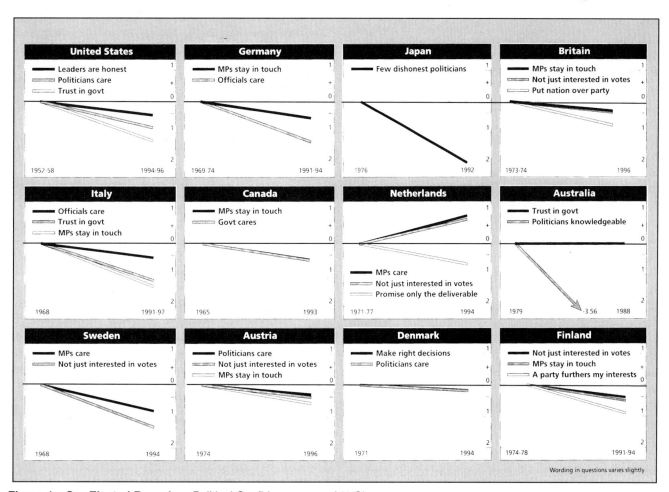

Figure 1   Our Elected Rascals.   Political Confidence, annual % Change.

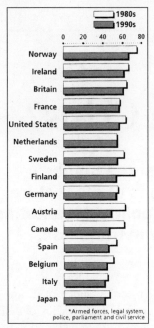

Figure 2   Losing Faith.   Confidence in Political Institutions*, %.
Sources: R. Dalton; World Values Surveys.

mature democracies descend on them at election time to ensure that the voting is free and fair. But is political life in these mature democracies as healthy as it should be?

If opinion research is any guide, the mature democracies have troubles of their own. In the United States in particular, the high opinion which people had of their government has declined steadily over the past four decades. Regular opinion surveys carried out as part of a series of national election studies in America show that the slump set in during the 1960s. The civil-rights conflict and the Vietnam War made this an especially turbulent decade for the United States. But public confidence in politicians and government continued to decline over the next quarter-century. Nor (remember the student unrest in Paris and elsewhere in 1968) was this confined to the United States.

It is hard to compare attitudes toward democracy over time, and across many different countries. Most opinion surveys are carried out nation-by-nation: they are conducted at different times and researchers often ask different sorts of questions. But some generalizations can be made. In their introduction to a forthcoming book "What is Troubling the Trilateral Democracies?", Princeton University Press, 2000) three academics—Robert Putnam, Susan Pharr, and Russell Dalton—have done their best to analyze the results of surveys conducted in most of the rich countries.

Figure 1 summarises some of these findings. The downward slopes show how public confidence in politicians seems to be falling, measured by changes in the answers voters give to questions such as "Do you think that politicians are trustworthy?"; "Do members of parliament (MPs) care about voters like you?"; and "How much do you trust governments of

any party to place the needs of the nation above their own political party?" In most of the mature democracies, the results show a pattern of disillusionment with politicians. Only in the Netherlands is there clear evidence of rising confidence.

Nor is it only politicians who are losing the public's trust. Surveys suggest that confidence in political institutions is in decline as well. In 11 out of 14 countries, for example, confidence in parliament has declined, with especially sharp falls in Canada, Germany, Britain, Sweden and the United States. World-wide polls conducted in 1981 and 1990 measured confidence in five institutions: parliament, the armed services, the judiciary, the police and the civil service. Some institutions gained public trust, but on average confidence in them decreased by 6% over the decade (see figure 2). The only countries to score small increases in confidence were Iceland and Denmark.

Other findings summarised by Mr Putnam and his colleagues make uncomfortable reading:

- In the late 1950s and early 1960s **Americans** had a touching faith in government. When asked "How many times can you trust the government in Washington to do what is right?", three out of four answered "most of the time" or "just about always". By 1998, fewer than four out of ten trusted the government to do what was right. In 1964 only 29% of the American electorate agreed that "the government is pretty much run by a few big interests looking after themselves". By 1984, that figure had risen to 55%, and by 1998 to 63%. In the 1960s, two-thirds of Americans rejected the statement "most elected officials don't care what people like me think". In 1998, nearly two-thirds agreed with it. The proportion of Americans who expressed "a great deal of" confidence in the executive branch fell from 42% in 1966 to 12% in 1997; and trust in Congress fell from 42% to 11%.

- **Canadians** have also been losing faith in their politicians. The proportion of Canadians who felt that "the government doesn't care what people like me think" rose from 45% in 1968 to 67% in 1993. The proportion expressing "a great deal of" confidence in political parties fell from 30% in 1979 to 11% in 1999. Confidence in the House of Commons fell from 49% in 1974 to 21% in 1996. By 1992 only 34% of Canadians were satisfied with their system of government, down from 51% in 1986.

- Less information is available about attitudes in **Japan**. But the findings of the few surveys that have been carried out there match the global pattern. Confidence in political institutions rose in the decades following the smashing of the country's old politics in the second world war. Happily for democracy, the proportion of Japanese voters who agree that "in order

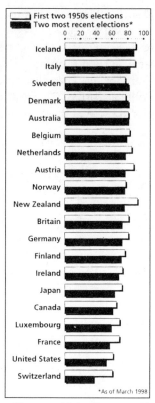

Figure 3   Staying Home.   Voter Turnout, %.
Source: Martin P. Wattenberg, University of California, Irvine.

to make Japan better, it is best to rely on talented politicians, rather than to let the citizens argue among themselves" has been falling for 40 years. However, the proportion who feel that they exert at least "some influence" on national politics through elections or demonstrations also fell steadily between 1973 and 1993.

- Although it is harder to generalize about **Western Europe**, confidence in political institutions is in decline in most countries. In 1985 48% of Britons expressed quite a lot of confidence in the House of Commons. This number had halved by 1995. The proportion of Swedes disagreeing with the statement that "parties are only interested in people's votes, not in their opinions" slumped from 51% in 1968 to 28% in 1994. In 1985 51% expressed confidence in the Rikstad (parliament); by 1996 only 19% did. In Germany, the percentage of people who said they trusted their Bundestag deputy to represent their interests rose from 25% in 1951 to 55% in 1978, but had fallen again to 34% by 1992. The percentage of Italians who say that politicians "don't care what people like me think" increased from 68% in 1968 to 84% in 1997.

Such findings are alarming if you take them at face value. But they should be interpreted with care. Democracy may just be a victim of its own success. It could just be that people nowadays expect more from governments, impose

new demands on the state, and are therefore more likely to be disappointed. After all, the idea that governments ought to do such things as protect or improve the environment, maintain high employment, arbitrate between moral issues, or ensure the equal treatment of women or minorities, is a relatively modern and still controversial one. Or perhaps the disillusionment is a healthy product of rising educational standards and the scepticism that goes with it. Or maybe it is caused by the media's search-light highlighting failures of government that were previously kept in the dark. Whatever the causes, the popularity of governments or politicians ought not to be the only test of democracy's health.

Moreover, there is encouraging evidence to put beside the discouraging findings. However much confidence in government may be declining, this does not seem to have diminished popular support for democratic principles. On average, surveys show, more than three out of four people in rich countries believe that democracy is the best form of government. Even in countries where the performance of particular governments has been so disappointing as to break up the party system itself (such as Japan and Italy in 1993–95), this has brought no serious threat to fundamental democratic principle. It may seem paradoxical for people to express strong support for democracy even while their confidence in politicians and political institutions crumbles. But it hardly amounts to the "crisis of democracy" which political scientists tend to proclaim from time to time.

Nor, though, is it a ringing endorsement, especially given that the evidence of opinion surveys is reinforced by other trends. These include a decline both in the membership of political parties and in the proportion of people who turn out to vote. Numbers compiled by Martin Wattenberg, also at the University of California, show that in 18 out of 20 of the rich established democracies the proportion of the electorate voting has been lower than it was in the early 1950s (see figure 3), with the median change being a decline of 10%. More controversially, some political scientists see the growth of protest movements since the 1960s as a sign of declining faith in the traditional institutions of representative democracy, and an attempt to bypass them. Others reckon that the most serious threat comes from the increasingly professional pressure groups and lobbying organisations that work behind the scenes to influence government policy and defend special interests, often at the expense of the electorate as a whole.

What is to be done? Those who believe that government has over-reached itself call on governments to become smaller and to promise less. Thus, it is hoped, people will come to do more for themselves. But whatever the appropriate size and reach of governments, there is also scope for making the machinery of democracy work better.

Indeed, some commentators see the public's declining confidence in political institutions as an opportunity for democratic renewal. Pippa Norris, at Harvard University's Kennedy School of Government, hails the advent of a new breed of "critical citizens" (in a book of that name, Oxford University Press, 1999) who see that existing channels of participation fall short of democratic ideals and want to reform them.

There are some signs of this. Countries as different as Italy, Japan, Britain and New Zealand have lately considered or introduced changes in their electoral systems. Countries around the world are making growing use of referendums and other forms of direct democracy. Many are reducing the power of parliaments by giving judges new powers to review the decisions that elected politicians make. And governments everywhere are introducing new rules on the financing of politicians and political parties. The rest of the articles in this series will look at some of these changes and the forces shaping them.

Advanced Democracies and the New Politics

RUSSELL J. DALTON, SUSAN E. SCARROW, AND BRUCE E. CAIN

Over the past quarter-century in advanced industrial democracies, citizens, public interest groups, and political elites have shown decreasing confidence in the institutions and processes of representative government. In most of these nations, electoral turnout and party membership have declined, and citizens are increasingly skeptical of politicians and political institutions.[1]

Along with these trends often go louder demands to expand citizen and interest-group access to politics, and to restructure democratic decision-making processes. Fewer people may be voting, but more are signing petitions, joining lobby groups, and engaging in unconventional forms of political action.[2] Referenda and ballot initiatives are growing in popularity; there is growing interest in processes of deliberative or consultative democracy;[3] and there are regular calls for more reliance on citizen advisory committees for policy formation and administration—especially at the local level, where direct involvement is most feasible. Contemporary democracies are facing popular pressures to grant more access, increase the transparency of governance, and make government more accountable.

Amplifying these trends, a chorus of political experts has been calling for democracies to reform and adapt. Mark Warren writes, "Democracy, once again in favor, is in need of conceptual renewal. While the traditional concerns of democratic theory with state-centered institutions remain importantly crucial and ethically central, they are increasingly subject to the limitations we should expect when nineteenth-century concepts meet twenty-first century realities."[4] U.S. political analyst Dick Morris similarly observes, "The fundamental paradigm that dominates our politics is the shift from representative to direct democracy. Voters want to run the show directly and are impatient with all forms of intermediaries between their opinions and public policy."[5] As Ralf Dahrendorf recently summarized the mood of the times, "Representative government is no longer as compelling a proposition as it once was. Instead, a search for new institutional forms to express conflicts of interest has begun."[6]

Many government officials have echoed these sentiments, and the OECD has examined how its member states could reform their governments to create new connections to their publics.[7] Its report testifies:

> New forms of representation and public participation are emerging in all of our countries. These developments have expanded the avenues for citizens to participate more fully in public policy making, within the overall framework of representative democracy in which parliaments continue to play a central role. Citizens are increasingly demanding more transparency and accountability from their governments, and want greater public participation in shaping policies that affect their lives. Educated and well-informed citizens expect governments to take their views and knowledge into account when making decisions on their behalf. Engaging citizens in policy making allows governments to respond to these expectations and, at the same time, design better policies and improve their implementation.[8]

If the pressures for political reform are having real effects, these should show up in changes to the institutional structures of democratic politics. The most avid proponents of such reforms conclude that we may be experiencing the most fundamental democratic transformation since the beginnings of mass democracy in the early twentieth century. Yet cycles of reform are a recurring theme in democratic history, and pressures for change in one direction often wane as new problems and possibilities come to the fore. What is the general track record for democratic institutional reforms in the advanced industrial democracies over the latter half of the twentieth century? And what are the implications of this record for the future of democracy?

Three Modes of Democracy

In a sense, there is nothing new about the call to inject "more democracy" into the institutions of representative government. The history of modern democracies is punctuated by repeated waves of debate about the nature of the democratic process, some of which have produced major institutional reforms. In the early twentieth century, for example, the populist movement in the United States prompted extensive electoral and governing-process reforms, as well as the introduction of new forms of direct democracy.[9] Parallel institutional changes occurred in Europe. By the end of this democratic-reform period in the late 1920s, most Western democracies had become much more "democratic" in the sense of providing citizens with access to the political process and making governments more accountable.

A new wave of democratic rhetoric and debate emerged in the last third of the twentieth century. The stimulus for this first appeared mainly among university students and young professionals contesting the boundaries of conventional representative democracy. Although their dramatic protests subsequently waned, they stimulated new challenges that affect advanced industrial democracies to this day. Citizen interest groups and other public lobbying organizations, which have proliferated since the 1960s, press for more access to government; expanding mass media delve more deeply into the workings of government; and people demand more from government while trusting it less.

The institutional impact of the reform wave of the late twentieth century can be understood in terms of three different modes of democratic politics. One aims at improving the process of *representative democracy* in which citizens elect elites. Much like the populism of the early twentieth century, reforms of this mode seek to improve electoral processes. Second, there are calls for new types of *direct democracy* that bypass (or complement) the processes of representative democracy. A third mode seeks to expand the means of political participation through a new style of *advocacy democracy,* in which citizens participate in policy deliberation and formation—either directly or through surrogates, such as public interest groups—although the final decisions are still made by elites.

1) Representative democracy. A major example of reform in representative democracy can be seen in changes to processes of electing the U.S. president. In a 30-year span, these elections underwent a dramatic transformation, in which citizen influence grew via the spread of state-level primary elections as a means of nominating candidates. In 1968, the Democratic Party had just 17 presidential primaries while the Republicans had only 16; in 2000 there were Democratic primaries in 40 states and Republican primaries in 43. As well, both parties-first the Democrats, then the Republicans—instituted reforms intended to ensure that convention delegates are more representative of the public at large, such as rules on the representation of women. Meanwhile, legislators introduced and expanded public funding for presidential elections in an effort to limit the influence of money and so promote citizen equality. If the 1948 Republican and Democratic candidates, Thomas E. Dewey and Harry S. Truman, were brought back to observe the modern presidential election process, they would hardly recognize the system as the same that nominated them. More recently, reformers have championed such causes as term limits and campaign-finance reform as remedies for restricting the influence of special interests. In Europe, populist electoral reform has been relatively restrained by institutionalized systems of party government, but even so, there are

parallels to what has occurred in the United States in many European countries. On a limited basis, for example, some European political parties have experimented with, or even adopted, closed primaries to select parliamentary candidates.[10]

In recent decades, changes in both attitudes and formal rules have brought about a greater general reliance on mechanisms of direct democracy within the advanced industrial democracies.

Generally, the mechanisms of representative democracy have maintained, and in places slightly increased, citizen access and influence. It is true that, compared with four decades ago, electoral turnout is generally down by about 10 percent in the established democracies.[11] This partially signifies a decrease in political access (or in citizens' use of elections as a means of political access). But at the same time, the "amount of electing" is up to an equal or greater extent. There has been a pattern of reform increasing the number of electoral choices available to voters by changing appointed positions into elected ones.[12] In Europe, citizens now elect members of Parliament for the European Union; regionalization has increased the number of elected subnational governments; directly elected mayors and directly elected local officials are becoming more common; and suffrage now includes younger voters, aged 18 to 20. Moreover, the number of political parties has increased, while parties have largely become more accountable—and the decisions of party elites more transparent—to their supporters. With the general expansion in electoral choices, citizens are traveling to the polls more often and making more electoral decisions.

2) Direct democracy. Initiatives and referenda are the most common means of direct democracy. These allow citizens to decide government policy without relying on the mediating influence of representation. Ballot initiatives in particular allow nongovernmental actors to control the framing of issues and even the timing of policy debates, further empowering the citizens and groups that take up this mode of action. In recent decades, changes in both attitudes and formal rules have brought about a greater general reliance on mechanisms of direct democracy within the advanced industrial democracies. The Initiative and Referendum Institute calculates, for example, that there were 118 statewide referenda in the United States during the 1950s but 378 such referenda during the 1990s. And a number of other nations have amended laws and constitutions to provide greater opportunities for direct democracy at the national and local levels.[13] Britain had its first national referendum in 1975; Sweden introduced the referendum in a constitutional reform of 1980; and Finland adopted the referendum in 1987. In these and other cases, the referendum won new legitimacy as a basis for national decision making, a norm that runs strongly counter to the ethos of representative democracy. There has also been mounting interest in expanding direct democracy through the innovation of new institutional forms, such as methods of deliberative democracy and citizen juries to advise policy makers.[14]

How fundamental are these changes? On the one hand, the political impact of a given referendum is limited, since only a single policy is being decided, so the channels of direct democracy normally provide less access than do the traditional channels of representative democracy. On the other hand, the increasing use of referenda has influenced political discourse—and the principles of political legitimacy in particular—beyond the policy at stake in any single referendum. With Britain's first referendum on European Community membership in 1975, for instance, parliamentary sovereignty was now no longer absolute, and the concept of popular sovereignty was concomitantly legitimized. Accordingly, the legitimacy of subsequent decisions on devolution required additional referenda, and today contentious issues, such as acceptance of the euro, are pervasively considered as matters that "the public should decide." So even though recourse to direct democracy remains relatively limited in Britain, the expansion of this mode of access represents a significant institutional change—and one that we see occurring across most advanced industrial democracies.

3) Advocacy democracy. In this third mode, citizens or public interest groups interact directly with governments and even participate directly in the policy-formation process, although actual decisions remain in the official hands. One might consider this as a form of traditional lobbying, but it is not. Advocacy democracy involves neither traditional interest groups nor standard channels of informal interest-group persuasion. Rather, it empowers individual citizens, citizen groups, or nongovernmental organizations to participate in advisory hearings; attend open government meetings ("government in the sunshine"); consult ombudsmen to redress grievances; demand information from government agencies; and challenge government actions through the courts.

Evidence for the growth of advocacy democracy is less direct and more difficult to quantify than is evidence for other kinds of institutional change. But the overall expansion of advocacy democracy is undeniable. Administrative reforms, decentralization, the growing political influence of courts, and other factors have created new opportunities for access and influence. During the latter 1960s in the United States, "maximum feasible participation" became a watchword for the social-service reforms of President Lyndon Johnson's "Great Society" programs. Following this model, citizen consultations and public hearings have since been embedded in an extensive range of legislation, giving citizens new points of access to policy formation and administration. Congressional hearings and state-government meetings have become public events, and legislation such as the 1972 Federal Advisory Committee Act even extended open-meeting requirements to advisory committees. While only a handful of nations had freedom-of-information laws in 1970, such laws are now almost universal in OECD countries. And there has been a general diffusion of the ombudsman model across advanced industrial democracies.[15] "Sunshine" provisions reflect a fundamental shift in understanding as to the role that elected representatives should play-one which would make Edmund Burke turn in his grave, and which we might characterize as a move away from the *trustee* toward the *delegate* model.

Reforms in this category also include new legal rights augmenting the influence of individuals and citizen groups. A pattern of judicialization in the policy process throughout most Western democracies, for instance, has enabled citizen groups to launch class-action suits on behalf of the environment, women's rights, or other public interests.[16] Now virtually every public interest can be translated into a rights-based appeal, which provides new avenues for action through the courts. Moreover, especially in European democracies, where direct citizen action was initially quite rare, the expansion of public interest groups, *Bürgerinitiativen,* and other kinds of citizen groups has substantially enlarged the public's repertoire for political action. It is worth noting that "unconventional" forms of political action, such as protests and demonstrations, have also grown substantially over this time span.

Citizens and the Democratic State

If the institutional structure of democracy is changing, how does this affect the democratic process? The answer is far from simple and not always positive, for democratic gains in some areas can be offset by losses in others, as when increased access produces new problems of democratic governability. In the following pages, we limit our attention to how these institutional changes affect the relationship between citizens and the state.

Robert A. Dahl's writings are a touchstone in this matter.[17] Like many democratic theorists, Dahl tends to equate democracy with the institutions and processes of representative democracy, paying much less attention to other forms of citizen participation that may actually represent more important means of citizen influence over political elites. Thus, while we draw from Dahl's *On Democracy* to define the essential criteria for a democratic process, we broaden the framework to include not only representative democracy but direct democracy and advocacy democracy also. Dahl suggests five criteria for a genuinely democratic system:[18]

1. **Inclusion:** With minimal exceptions, all permanent adult residents must have full rights of citizenship.
2. **Political equality:** When decisions about policy are made, every citizen must have an equal and effective opportunity to participate.
3. **Enlightened understanding:** Within reasonable limits, citizens must have equal and effective opportunities to learn about relevant policy alternatives and their likely consequences.
4. **Control of the agenda:** Citizens must have the opportunity to decide which matters are placed on the public agenda, and how.
5. **Effective participation:** Before a policy is adopted, all the citizens must have equal and effective opportunities for making their views known to other citizens.

Robert A. Dahl's Democratic Criteria

Democratic Criteria	Representative Democracy	Direct Democracy	Advocacy Democracy
Inclusion	**Universal suffrage provides inclusion**	**Universal suffrage provides inclusion**	Equal citizen access *(Problems of access to nonelectoral arenas)*
Political Equality	**One person, one vote with high turnout maximizes equality.** *(Problems of low turnout, inequality due to campaign finance issues, etc.)*	**One person, one vote with high turnout maximizes equality** *(Problems of equality with low turnout)*	Equal opportunity *(Problems of very unequal use)*
Enlightened Understanding	*(Problems of information access, voter decision processes)*	*(Problems of greater information and higher decision-making costs)*	**Increased public access to information** *(Problems of even greater information and decision-making demands on citizens)*
Control of the Agenda	*(Problems of control of campaign debate, selecting candidates, etc.)* **Control through responsible parties**	**Citizen initiation provides control of agenda** *(Problems of influence by interest groups)*	**Citizens and groups control the locus and focus of activity**
Effective Participation	*(Principal-agent problems: fair elections, responsible party government, etc.)*	**Direct policy impact ensures effective participation**	**Direct access avoids mediated participation**

Note. Criteria that are well addressed are presented in **bold,** criteria that are at issue are presented in *italics* in the shaded cells.

The first column of the Table lists Dahl's five democratic criteria. The second column summarizes the prevailing view on how well representative democracy fulfills these criteria. For example, advanced industrial democracies have met the *inclusion* criterion by expanding the franchise to all adult citizens (by way of a long and at times painful series of reforms). General success in this regard is illustrated by the bold highlighting of "universal suffrage" in the first cell of this column.

Nearly all advanced industrial democracies now meet the *political equality* criterion by having enacted the principle of "one person, one vote" for elections, which we have highlighted in the second cell. In most nations today, a majority of citizens participate in voting, while labor unions, political parties, and other organizations mobilize participation to achieve high levels of engagement. Indeed, that noted democrat, the late Mayor Richard Daley of Chicago, used to say that electoral politics was the only instrument through which a working-class citizen could ever exercise equal influence with the socially advantaged. At the same time, certain problems of equality remain, as contemporary debates about campaign financing and voter registration illustrate, and full equality in political practice is probably unattainable. We note these problems in the shaded area of the second cell. Nevertheless, overall the principle of

equality is now a consensual value for the electoral processes of representative democracy.

At first glance, it may seem that expanding the number of elections amounts to extending these principles. But increasing the number of times that voters go to the polls and the number of items on ballots actually tends to depress turnout. And when voter turnout is less than 50 percent, as it tends to be in, say, EU parliamentary elections-or less than 25 percent, as it tends to be in local mayoral or school-board elections in the United States-then one must question whether the gap between "equality of access" and "equality of usage" has become so wide that it undermines the basic principle of *political equality.* Moreover, second-order elections tend to mobilize a smaller and more ideological electorate than the public at large, and so more second-order elections tend to mean more distortions in the representativeness of the electoral process.

The tension between Dahl's democratic criteria and democratic practice becomes even more obvious when we turn to the criterion of *enlightened understanding.* Although we are fairly sanguine about voters' abilities to make informed choices when it comes to high-visibility (for instance, presidential or parliamentary) elections, we are less so when it comes to lower-visibility elections. How does a typical resident of Houston,

18

Texas, make enlightened choices regarding the dozens of judgeship candidates whose names appeared on the November 2002 ballot, to say nothing of other local office seekers and referenda? In such second- and third-order elections, the means of information that voters can use in first-order elections may be insufficient or even altogether lacking. So the expansion of the electoral marketplace may empower the public in a sense, but in another sense may make it hard for voters to exercise meaningful political judgment.

Another criterion is citizen *control of the political agenda.* Recent reforms in representative democracy have gone some way toward broadening access to the political agenda. Increasing the number of elected offices gives citizens more input and presumably more avenues for raising issues, while reforming political finance to equalize campaign access and party support has made for greater openness in political deliberations. More problematic, though, is performance on the *effectiveness of participation* criterion. Do citizens get what they vote for? Often, this principal-agent problem is solved through the mechanism of party government: Voters select a party, and the party ensures the compliance of individual members of parliament and the translation of electoral mandates into policy outcomes.[19] But the impact of recent reforms on the *effectiveness of participation* is complex. On the one hand, more openness and choice in elections should enable people to express their political preferences more extensively and in more policy areas. On the other hand, as the number of office-holders proliferates, it may become more difficult for voters to assign responsibility for policy outcomes. Fragmented decision making, divided government, and the sheer profusion of elected officials may diminish the political responsiveness of each actor.

How much better do the mechanisms of direct democracy fare when measured against Dahl's five criteria (see column 3 of the Table)? Because referenda and initiatives are effectively mass elections, they seek to ensure inclusion and political equality in much the same way as representative elections do. Most referenda and initiatives use universal suffrage to ensure inclusion and the "one person, one vote" rule to ensure political equality. However, whereas turnout in direct-democracy elections is often lower than in comparable elections for public officials, the question of democratic inclusion becomes more complicated than a simple assessment of equal access. For instance, when Proposition 98—which favored altering the California state constitution to mandate that a specific part of the state budget be directed to primary and secondary education—appeared on the 1996 general election ballot, barely half of all voting-age Californians turned out, and only 51 percent voted for the proposition. But as a consequence, the state's constitution was altered, reshaping state spending and public financing in California. Such votes raise questions about the fairness of elections in which a minority of registered voters can make crucial decisions affecting the public welfare. Equality of opportunity clearly does not mean equality of participation.

Moreover, referenda and initiatives place even greater demands for information and understanding on voters. Many of the heuristics that they can use in party elections or candidate elections are less effective in referenda, and the issues themselves are often more complex than what citizens are typically called upon to consider in electing office-holders. For instance, did the average voter have enough information to make enlightened choices in Italy's multi-referendum ballot of 1997? This ballot asked voters to make choices concerning television-ownership rules, television-broadcasting policy, the hours during which stores could remain open, the commercial activities which municipalities could pursue, labor-union reform proposals, regulations for administrative elections, and residency rules for mafia members. In referenda, voters can still rely on group heuristics and other cues that they use in electing public officials,[20] but obviously the proliferation of policy choices and especially the introduction of less-salient local issues raise questions about the overall effectiveness of such cue-taking.

The real strengths of direct democracy are highlighted by Dahl's fourth and fifth criteria. Referenda and initiatives shift the focus of agenda-setting from elites toward the public, or at least toward public interest groups. Indeed, processes of direct democracy can bring into the political arena issues that elites tend not to want to address: for example, tax reform or term limits in the United States, abortion-law reform in Italy, or the terms of EU membership in Europe generally. Even when referenda fail to reach the ballot or fail to win a majority, they can nevertheless prompt elites to be more sensitive to public interests. By definition, moreover, direct democracy should solve the problem of effective participation that exists with all methods of representative democracy. Direct democracy is unmediated, and so it ensures that participation is effective. Voters make policy choices with their ballot-to enact a new law, to repeal an existing law, or to reform a constitution. Even in instances where the mechanisms of direct democracy require an elite response in passing a law or a revoting in a later election, the link to policy action is more direct than is the case with the channels of representative democracy. Accordingly, direct democracy seems to fulfill Dahl's democratic criteria of agenda control and effective participation.

But direct democracy raises questions in these areas as well. Interest groups may find it easier to manipulate processes of direct democracy than those of representative democracy.[21] The discretion to place a policy initiative on the ballot can be appealing to interest groups, which then have unmediated access to voters during the subsequent referendum campaign. In addition, decisions made by way of direct democracy are less susceptible to bargaining or the checks and balances that occur within the normal legislative process. Some recent referenda in California may illustrate this style of direct democracy: Wealthy backers pay a consulting firm to collect signatures so as to get a proposal on the ballot, and then bankroll a campaign to support their desired legislation. This is not grassroots democracy at work; it is the representation of wealthy interests by other means.

The expansion of direct democracy has the potential to complement traditional forms of representative democracy. It can expand the democratic process by allowing citizens and public interest groups new access to politics, and new control over political agendas and policy outcomes. But direct democracy also raises new questions about equality of actual influence, if not formal access, and the ability of the public to make fair and reasoned judgments about issues. Perhaps the most important question about direct democracy is not whether it is expanding, but *how* it is expanding: Are there ways to increase access and influence without sacrificing inclusion and equality? We return to this question below.

Formal Access and Actual Use

The final column in our Table considers how new forms of advocacy democracy fulfill Dahl's democratic criteria. These new forms of action provide citizens with significant access to politics, but it is also clear that this access is very unevenly used. Nearly everyone can vote, and most do. But very few citizens file lawsuits, file papers under a freedom-of-information act, attend environmental-impact review hearings, or attend local planning meetings. There is no clear equivalent to "one person, one vote" for advocacy democracy. Accordingly, it raises the question of how to address Dahl's criteria of inclusion, political equality, and enlightened understanding.

"Equality of access" is not adequate if "equality of usage" is grossly uneven. For instance, when Europeans were asked in the 1989 European Election Survey whether they voted in the election immediately preceding the survey, differences in participation according to levels of education were very slight (see the Figure, Social-Status Inequality in Participations). A full 73 percent of those in the "low education" category said they had voted in the previous EU parliamentary election (even though it is a second-order election), and an identical percentage of those in the "high education" category claimed to have voted. Differences in campaign activity according to educational levels are somewhat greater, but still modest in overall terms.

A distinctly larger inequality gap emerges when it comes to participation through forms of direct or advocacy democracy. For instance, only 13 percent of those in the "low education" category had participated in a citizen action group, while nearly three times the percentage of those in the "high education" category had participated. Similarly, there are large inequalities when it comes to such activities as signing a petition or participating in a lawful demonstration.

With respect to the criterion of *enlightened understanding,* advocacy democracy has mixed results. On the one hand, it can enhance citizen understanding and make for greater inclusion. Citizens and public interest groups can increase the amount of information that they have about government activities, especially by taking advantage of freedom-of-information laws, attending administrative hearings, and participating in government policy making. And with the assistance of the press in disseminating this information, citizens and public interest groups can better influence political outcomes. By ensuring that the public receives information in a timely fashion, advocacy democracy allows citizens to make informed judgments and hold governments more accountable. And by eliminating the filtering that governments would otherwise apply, advocacy democracy can help citizens to get more accurate pictures of the influences affecting policy decisions, with fewer cover-ups and self-serving distortions. On the other hand, advocacy democracy makes greater cognitive and resource demands on citizens, and thus may generate some of the same inequalities in participation noted above. It requires much more of the citizen to participate in a public hearing or to petition an official than it does simply to cast a vote. The most insightful evidence on this point comes from Jane Mansbridge's study of collective decision making in New England town meetings.[22] She finds that many participants were unprepared or overwhelmed by the deliberative decision-making processes.

Advocacy democracy fares better when it comes to the remaining two criteria. It gives citizens greater control of the political agenda, in part by increasing their opportunity to press their interests outside of the institutionalized time and format constraints of fixed election cycles. By means of advocacy democracy, citizens can often choose when and where to challenge a government directive or pressure policy makers. Similarly, even though advocacy democracy typically leaves final political decisions in the hands of elites, it nevertheless provides direct access to government. Property owners can participate in a local planning hearing; a public interest group can petition government for information on past policies; and dissatisfied citizens can attend a school board session. Such unmediated participation brings citizens into the decision-making process-which ultimately might not be as effective as the efforts of a skilled representative, but greater direct involvement in the democratic process should improve its accountability and transparency (see the bold entries in these last two cells of the Table).

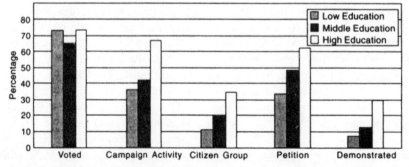

Social-Status Inequality in Participation

Source: Eurobarometers 31 and 31A conducted in connection with the 1989 European Parliament election. Results combine the 12 nations weighted to represent the total EU population.

All in all, advocacy democracy increases the potential for citizen access in important ways. It can give citizens and public interest groups new influence over the agenda-setting process, and it can give them unmediated involvement in the policy-formation process. These are significant extensions of democratic participation. At the same time, advocacy democracy may exacerbate political inequality on account of inequalities in usage. New access points created through advisory panels, consultative hearings, and other institutional reforms empower some citizens to become more involved. But other citizens, relatively lacking in the skills or resources to compete in these new domains, may be left behind. In other words, advocacy democracy may in some ways respond to the strength of the claimants, rather than to the strength of their claims. It can even alter the locus of political expertise. While advocacy democracy values know-how and expertise in the citizenry, it devalues those same characteristics among policy makers.

Environmental policy provides a good illustration of this problem. Here, citizens and public interest groups have gained new rights and new access to the policy process. But these are disproportionately used by relatively affluent and skilled citizens, who are already participating in conventional forms of representative democracy, while the poor, the unskilled, and the otherwise disadvantaged tend to get left behind. So while environmentalism is an example of citizen empowerment, it is also a source of increasing inequality.

No form of democratic action is ideal, each having its advantages and limitations. As democratic practice shifts from a predominant reliance on representation toward a mixed repertoire—including greater use of direct and advocacy democracy—a new balance must be struck among democratic goals. It is possible that new institutional arrangements will maximize the benefits of these new modes while limiting their disadvantages—as, for example, the institutions of representative democracy depend on parties and interest groups. But thus far, the advanced industrialized democracies have not fully recognized the problems generated by the new mixed repertoire of democratic action, and so have yet to find institutional or structural means of addressing them. Democratic reforms create opportunities, but they also create challenges. Our goal should be to ensure that progress on some democratic criteria is not unduly sacrificed for progress on others.

Notes

1. Martin P. Wattenberg, *Where Have All the Voters Gone?* (Cambridge: Harvard University Press, 2002); Susan E. Scarrow, "From Social Integration to Electoral Contestation," in Russell J. Dalton and Martin P. Wattenberg, eds., *Parties Without Partisans: Political Change in Advanced Industrial Democracies* (New York: Oxford University Press, 2000); Russell J. Dalton, *Democratic Challenges, Democratic Choices: The Decline in Political Support in Advanced Industrial Democracies* (Oxford: Oxford University Press, 2004); Susan J. Pharr and Robert D. Putnam, eds., *Disaffected Democracies: What's Troubling the Trilateral Countries?* (Princeton: Princeton University Press, 2000).

2. Russell J. Dalton, *Citizen Politics: Public Opinion and Political Parties in Advanced Industrial Democracies* (New York: Chatham House, 2002), ch. 4; Ronald Inglehart, *Modernization and Postmodernization: Cultural, Economic, and Political Change in 43 Societies* (Princeton: Princeton University Press, 1997); Sidney Verba, Kay Schlozman, and Henry Brady, *Voice and Equality: Civic Volunteerism in American Politics* (Cambridge: Harvard University Press, 1995), 72.

3. James S. Fishkin, *The Voice of the People: Public Opinion and Democracy* (New Haven: Yale University Press, 1995); John Elster, *Deliberative Democracy* (New York: Cambridge University Press, 1998).

4. Mark Warren, *Democracy and Association* (Princeton: Princeton University Press, 2001), 226.

5. Dick Morris, *The New Prince: Machiavelli Updated for the Twenty-First Century* (New York: Renaissance Books, 2000).

6. Ralf Dahrendorf, "Afterword," in Susan J. Pharr and Robert D. Putnam, eds., *Disaffected Democracies: What's Troubling the Trilateral Countries?* 311.

7. OECD, *Government of the Future: Getting from Here to There* (Paris: Organization for Economic Co-operation and Development, 2000).

8. OECD, *Citizens as Partners: OECD Handbook on Information, Consultation and Public Participation in Policy-Making* (Paris: Organization of Economic Cooperation and Development, 2001), 9.

9. Lawrence Goodwyn, *Democratic Promise: The Populist Movement in America* (New York: Oxford University Press, 1976).

10. Susan E. Scarrow, Paul Webb, and David M. Farrell, "From Social Integration to Electoral Contestation," in Russell J. Dalton and Martin P. Wattenberg, eds., *Parties without Partisans: Political Change in Advanced Industrial Democracies;* Jonathan Hopkin, "Bringing the Members Back in: Democratizing Candidate Selection in Britain and Spain," *Party Politics* 7 (May 2001): 343–61.

11. Martin P. Wattenberg, *Where Have All the Voters Gone?*

12. Russell J. Dalton and Mark Gray, "Expanding the Electoral Marketplace," in Bruce E. Cain, Russell J. Dalton, and Susan E. Scarrow, eds., *Democracy Transformed? Expanding Political Opportunities in Advanced Industrial Democracies* (Oxford: Oxford University Press, 2003).

13. Susan E. Scarrow, "Direct Democracy and Institutional Design: A Comparative Investigation," in *Comparative Political Studies* 34 (August 2001): 651–65; also see David Butler and Austin Ranney, eds., *Referenda Around the World* (Washington, D.C.: American Enterprise Institute, 1994); Michael Gallagher and Pier Vincenzo Uleri, eds., *The Referendum Experience in Europe* (Basingstoke: Macmillan, 1996).

14. James S. Fishkin, *The Voice of the People: Public Opinion and Democracy;* Forest David Matthews, *Politics for People: Finding a Responsive Voice,* 2nd ed. (Urbana: University of Illinois Press, 1999).

15. Roy Gregory and Philip Giddings, eds., *Righting Wrongs: The Ombudsman in Six Continents* (Amsterdam: IOS Press, 2000); see also Christopher Ansell and Jane Gingrich, "Reforming the Administrative State," in Bruce E. Cain, Russell J. Dalton, and

Susan E. Scarrow, eds., *Democracy Transformed? Expanding Political Opportunities in Advanced Industrial Democracies.*

16. Alec Stone Sweet, *Governing with Judges: Constitutional Politics in Europe* (New York: Oxford University Press, 2000).

17. Robert A Dahl, *Polyarchy: Participation and Opposition* (New Haven: Yale University Press, 1971); *Democracy and Its Critics* (New Haven: Yale University Press, 1991); *On Democracy* (New Haven: Yale University Press, 1998).

18. Robert A. Dahl, *On Democracy,* 37–38.

19. 1Hans-Dieter Klingemann et al., *Parties, Policies, and Democracy* (Boulder: Westview, 1994).

20. Arthur Lupia, "Shortcuts versus Encyclopedias," *American Political Science Review* 88 (March 1994): 63–76.

21. Elisabeth Gerber, *The Populist Paradox: Interest Group Influence and the Promise of Direct Legislation* (Princeton: Princeton University Press, 1999); see also David S. Broder, *Democracy Derailed: Initiative Campaigns and the Power of Money*

22. Jane Mansbridge, *Beyond Adversary Democracy* (New York: Basic Books, 1980).

RUSSELL J. DALTON is director of the Center for the Study of Democracy at the University of California, Irvine. **SUSAN E. SCARROW** is associate professor of political science at the University of Houston. **BRUCE E. CAIN** is Robson Professor of Political Science at the University of California, Berkeley, and director of the Institute of Governmental Studies. This essay is adapted from their edited volume, *Democracy Transformed? Expanding Political Opportunities in Advanced Industrial Democracies* (2003).

Referendums: The People's Voice

Is the growing use of referendums a threat to democracy or its salvation? The fifth article in our series on changes in mature democracies examines the experience so far, and the arguments for and against letting voters decide political questions directly.

When Winston Churchill proposed a referendum to Clement Attlee in 1945 on whether Britain's wartime coalition should be extended, Attlee growled that the idea was an "instrument of Nazism and fascism". The use by Hitler and Mussolini of bogus referendums to consolidate their power had confirmed the worst fears of sceptics. The most democratic of devices seemed also to be the most dangerous to democracy itself.

Dictators of all stripes have continued to use phony referendums to justify their hold on power. And yet this fact has not stopped a steady growth in the use of genuine referendums, held under free and fair conditions, by both established and aspiring democracies. Referendums have been instrumental in the dismantling of communism and the transition to democracy in countries throughout the former soviet empire. They have also successfully eased democratic transitions in Spain, Greece, South Africa, Brazil and Chile, among other countries.

In most established democracies, direct appeals to voters are now part of the machinery for constitutional change. Their use to resolve the most intractable or divisive public issues has also grown. In the 17 major democracies of Western Europe, only three—Belgium, the Netherlands and Norway—make no provision for referendums in their constitution. Only six major democracies—the Netherlands, the United States, Japan, India, Israel and the Federal Republic of Germany—have never held a nationwide referendum.

The Volatile Voter

Frustrated voters in Italy and New Zealand have in recent years used referendums to force radical changes to voting systems and other political institutions on a reluctant political elite. Referendums have also been used regularly in Australia, where voters go to the polls this November to decide whether to cut their country's formal link with the British crown. In Switzerland and several American states, referendums are a central feature of the political system, rivalling legislatures in significance.

Outside the United States and Switzerland, referendums are most often called by governments only when they are certain of victory, and to win endorsement of a policy they intend to implement in any case. This is how they are currently being used in Britain by Tony Blair's government.

But voters do not always behave as predicted, and they have delivered some notable rebuffs. Charles de Gaulle skillfully used referendums to establish the legitimacy of France's Fifth Republic and to expand his own powers as president, but then felt compelled to resign in 1969 after an unexpected referendum defeat.

Francois Mitterrand's decision to call a referendum on the Maastricht treaty in 1992 brought the European Union to the brink of breakdown when only 51% of those voting backed the treaty. Denmark's voters rejected the same treaty, despite the fact that it was supported by four out of five members of the Danish parliament. The Danish government was able to sign the treaty only after renegotiating its terms and narrowly winning a second referendum. That same year, Canada's government was not so lucky. Canadian voters unexpectedly rejected a painstakingly negotiated constitutional accord designed to placate Quebec.

Referendums come in many different forms. **Advisory referendums** test public opinion on an important issue. Governments or legislators then translate their results into new laws or policies as they see fit. Although advisory referendums can carry great weight in the right circumstances, they are sometimes ignored by politicians. In a 1955 Swedish referendum, 85% of those voting said they wanted to continue driving on the left side of the road. Only 12 years later the government went ahead and made the switch to driving on the right without a second referendum, or much protest.

By contrast, **mandatory referendums** are part of a law-making process or, more commonly, one of the procedures for constitutional amendment.

Both advisory and mandatory referendums can usually be called only by those in office—sometimes by the president, sometimes by parliamentarians, most often by the government of the day. But in a few countries, petitions by voters themselves can put a referendum on the ballot. These are known as **initiatives**. Sometimes these can only repeal an already existing law—so-called "abrogative" initiatives such as those in Italy. Elsewhere, initiatives can also be used to propose and pass new legislation, as in Switzerland and many American states. In this form they can be powerful and unpredictable political tools.

The rules for conducting and winning referendums also vary greatly from country to country. Regulations on the drafting of ballot papers and the financing of Yes and No campaigns are different everywhere, and these exert a great influence over how referendums are used, and how often.

The hurdle required for victory can be a critical feature. A simple majority of those voting is the usual rule. But a low turnout can make such victories seem illegitimate. So a percentage of eligible voters, as well as a majority of those voting, is sometimes required to approve a proposal.

Such hurdles, of course, also make failure more likely. In 1978 Britain's government was forced to abandon plans to set up a Scottish parliament when a referendum victory in Scotland failed to clear a 40% hurdle of eligible voters. Referendums have also failed in Denmark and Italy (most recently in April) because of similar voter-turnout requirements. To ensure a wide geographic consensus, Switzerland and Australia require a "double majority", of individual voters and of cantons or states, for constitutional amendments.

The use of referendums reflects the history and traditions of individual countries. Thus generalising about them is difficult. In some countries referendums have played a central, though peripatetic, role. In others they have been marginal or even irrelevant, despite provisions for their use.

Hot Potatoes

Although referendums (outside Switzerland and the United States) have been most often used to legitimise constitutional change or the redrawing of boundaries, elected politicians have also found them useful for referring to voters those issues they find too hot to handle or which cut across party lines. Often these concern moral or lifestyle choices, such as alcohol prohibition, divorce or abortion. The outcome on such emotive topics can be difficult to predict. In divorce and abortion referendums, for example, Italians have shown themselves more liberal, and the Irish more conservative, than expected.

One of the best single books on referendums—"Referendums Around the World" edited by David Butler and Austin Ranney, published by Macmillan—argues that many assumptions about them are mistaken. They are not usually habit-forming, as those opposed to them claim. Many countries have used them to settle a specific issue, or even engaged in a series of them, and then turned away from referendums for long periods. But this is mostly because politicians decide whether referendums will be held. Where groups of voters can also put initiatives on the ballot, as in Switzerland and the United States, they have become addictive and their use has grown in recent years.

Messrs Butler and Ranney also point out that referendums are not usually vehicles for radical change, as is widely believed. Although they were used in this way in Italy and New Zealand, referendums have more often been used to support

the status quo or to endorse changes already agreed by political parties. Most referendums, even those initiated by voters, fail. In Australia, 34 of 42 proposals to amend the constitution have been rejected by voters. According to an analysis by David Magleby, a professor at Brigham Young University in Utah, 62% of the 1,732 initiatives which reached the ballot in American states between 1898 and 1992 were rejected.

Arguments for and against referendums go to the heart of what is meant by democracy. Proponents of referendums maintain that consulting citizens directly is the only truly democratic way to determine policy. If popular sovereignty is really to mean anything, voters must have the right to set the agenda, discuss the issues and then themselves directly make the final decisions. Delegating these tasks to elected politicians, who have interests of their own, inevitably distorts the wishes of voters.

Referendums, their advocates say, can discipline representatives, and put the stamp of legitimacy on the most important political questions of the day. They also encourage participation by citizens in the governing of their own societies, and political participation is the source of most other civic virtues.

The Case Against

Those sceptical of referendums agree that popular sovereignty, majority rule and consulting voters are the basic building blocks of democracy, but believe that representative democracy achieves these goals much better than referendums. Genuine direct democracy, they say, is feasible only for political groups so small that all citizens can meet face-to-face—a small town perhaps. In large, modern societies, the full participation of every citizen is impossible.

Referendum opponents maintain that representatives, as full-time decision-makers, can weigh conflicting priorities, negotiate compromises among different groups and make well-informed decisions. Citizens voting in single-issue referendums have difficulty in doing any of these things. And as the bluntest of majoritarian devices, referendums encourage voters to brush aside the concerns of minority groups. Finally, the frequent use of referendums can actually undermine democracy by encouraging elected legislators to sidestep difficult issues, thus damaging the prestige and authority of representative institutions, which must continue to perform most of the business of government even if referendums are used frequently.

Testing any of these claims or counter-claims is difficult. Most countries do not, in fact, use referendums regularly enough to bear out either the hopes of proponents or the fears of opponents. The two exceptions are Switzerland and some American states, where citizen initiatives are frequent enough to draw tentative conclusions on some of these points, although both examples fall far short of full-fledged direct democracy.

Voters in both countries seem to believe that referendums do, in fact, lend legitimacy to important decisions. The Swiss are unlikely now to make a big national decision without a referendum. Swiss voters have rejected both UN membership and links with the EU in referendums, against the advice of their political leaders. Similarly, American polls show healthy majorities favouring referendums and believing that they are more likely to produce policies that most people want. Polls also show support for the introduction of referendums on the national level.

The claim that referendums increase citizen participation is more problematic. Some referendum campaigns ignite enormous public interest and media attention. Initiatives also give political outsiders a way to influence the public agenda. But in the United States, much of the activity involved in getting initiatives on the ballot, such as collecting signatures, has been taken over by professional firms, and many referendum campaigns have become slick, expensive affairs far removed from the grassroots (so far, this is much less true in Switzerland). Even more surprising, voter participation in American referendums is well below that of candidate elections, even when these are held at the same time. The average turnout for Swiss referendums has fallen by a third in the past 50 years to about 40%. On big issues, however, turnout can still soar.

Many of the fears of those opposed to referendums have not been realised in either country. Initiatives have not usually been used to oppress minorities. A proposal to limit the number of foreigners allowed to live in Switzerland was rejected by two-thirds of voters in 1988. In 1992 Colorado's voters did approve an initiative overturning local ordinances protecting gays from discrimination, but more extreme anti-gay initiatives in Colorado and California have been defeated by large majorities. Since 1990 voters have consistently upheld certain abortion rights in initiative ballots. Minorities and immigrants have been the targets of initiatives in some states, but voters have generally rejected extreme measures and have often proven themselves no more illiberal than legislators. Most initiatives are, in fact, about tax and economic questions, not civil liberties or social issues, although the latter often gain more attention.

While the frequent use of initiatives has not destroyed representative government, as some feared, it has changed it. Party loyalty among Swiss voters is strong at general elections, but evaporates when it comes to referendum voting. Initiatives, and the threat of mounting one, have become an integral part of the legislative process in Switzerland, as they have in California, Oregon and the other American states where they are most used. Referendums now often set the political agenda in both countries. In the United States they are frequently seen, rightly or wrongly, as a barometer of the national mood. And they can occasionally spark a political revolution. California's Proposition 13, for example, a 1978 initiative lowering local property taxes, set off a tax revolt across America. Elected officials themselves are often active in launching initiatives, and relatively successful in getting their proposals approved, which hardly indicates that voters have lost all faith in their politicians. Initiatives have made legislating more complicated, but also more responsive to the public's concerns.

There is some evidence that American voters, at least, are sometimes overwhelmed by the volume of information coming their way, and cast their vote in ignorance, as critics contend. Mr Magleby cites studies showing that on several ballots, 10–20% of the electorate mistakenly cast their vote the wrong way. Ballot material dropping through the letterboxes of residents in California is now often more than 200 pages long. According to one poll, only one in five Californians believes that the average voter understands most of the propositions put before him. Quite rationally, this has also bred caution. Californians approve only one-third of initiatives.

Hybrid Democracy?

The Swiss and American experience suggests that in the future there is unlikely to be a headlong rush away from representative to direct democracy anywhere, but that, even so, the use of referendums is likely to grow. The Internet and other technological advances have not yet had much impact on referendums, but they should eventually make it easier to hold them, and to inform voters of the issues they are being asked to decide upon.

Representative institutions are likely to survive because of the sheer volume of legislation in modern societies, and the need for full-time officials to run the extensive machinery of government. Nevertheless in an age of mass communication and information, confining the powers of citizens to voting in elections every few years seems a crude approach, a throwback to an earlier era. In a political system based on popular sovereignty, it will become increasingly difficult to justify a failure to consult the voters directly on a wider range of issues.

Facing the Challenge of Semi-Authoritarian States

Marina Ottaway

T he last decade of the 20th century saw the rise of a great number of regimes that cannot be easily classified as either authoritarian or democratic but display some characteristics of both—in short, they are *semi-authoritarian.* They are ambiguous systems that combine rhetorical acceptance of liberal democracy, the existence of some formal democratic institutions, and respect for a limited sphere of civil and political liberties with essentially illiberal or even authoritarian traits. That ambiguous Character, furthermore, is deliberate. Semi-authoritarian systems are not imperfect democracies struggling toward improvement and consolidation but regimes determined to maintain the appearance of democracy without exposing themselves to the political risks that free competition entails.

Political hybrids, semi-authoritarian regimes allow little real competition for power, thus reducing government accountability. However, they leave enough political space for political parties and organizations of civil society to form, for an independent press to function to some extent, and for some political debate to take place. Such regimes abound in the Soviet successor states: In countries like Kazakhstan and Azerbaijan, for example, former Communist Party bosses have transformed themselves into elected presidents, but in reality remain strongmen whose power is barely checked by weak democratic institutions.

Semi-authoritarian regimes are also numerous in sub-Saharan Africa, where most of the multiparty elections of the 1990s failed to produce working parliaments or other institutions capable of holding the executive even remotely accountable. In the Arab world, tentative political openings in Algeria, Morocco, and Yemen appear to be leading to the modernization of semi-authoritarianism rather than to democracy, in keeping with a pattern first established by Egypt. In the Balkans, the Communist regimes have disappeared, but despite much international support most governments are semi-authoritarian, with only Slovenia and—more recently and tentatively—Croatia moving toward democracy.

Even more worrisome is the case of Latin America, where economic crises and sharply unequal distribution of income create the risk of popular disenchantment with incumbent democratic governments, and even with democratic institutions.

Already in two countries, first Peru and then Venezuela, steady progress toward democracy has been interrupted by the emergence of semi-authoritarian regimes. In Asia, formal democratic processes are accompanied by strong authoritarian features in countries such as Pakistan, Singapore, and Malaysia, putting them in the realm of semi-authoritarianism.

Semi-authoritarianism is not a new phenomenon—many past regimes have paid lip service to democracy while frequently violating its basic tenets. But the number of such regimes was limited because until the end of the cold war many governments, often supported by their countries' leading intellectuals, rejected liberal democracy outright. They did so in the name of people's democracy (that is, socialism), or in the name of communal cultural traditions that precluded the egoistic individualism on which, they claimed, liberal democracy is based. Since the end of the cold war, few governments and even fewer intellectuals are willing to mount an ideological defense of nondemocratic systems of government; most feel they have to at least pretend adherence to the concept of democracy. On the other hand, the number of governments willing to accept the strict limitations on the extent and duration of their power imposed by democratic rule remains small. As a result, semi-authoritarian regimes have become more numerous.

The number of such regimes is likely to increase even further. In many countries that have experienced a political transition since the early 1990s, unfavorable conditions—including weak democratic institutions and political organizations, persistent authoritarian traditions, major socioeconomic problems, and ethnic and religious conflicts—create formidable obstacles to the establishment and, above all, the consolidation of democracy. Nevertheless, citizens everywhere have shown their disillusionment with authoritarian regimes, and a widespread return to the unabashedly top-down forms of government so common in the past is improbable. These conditions, unfavorable to both genuine democracy and overt authoritarianism, further enhance the prospects for the spread of semi-authoritarianism.

With their combination of positive and negative traits, semi-authoritarian regimes pose a considerable challenge to U.S. policy makers. Such regimes often represent a significant improvement over their predecessors or appear to provide a measure of stability that is welcome in troubled regions. But that superficial stability usually masks a host of severe problems and unsatisfied demands that need to be dealt with lest they lead to crises in the future. Despite their growing importance, however, semi-authoritarian regimes have not received systematic attention.

It is tempting to dismiss the problems created by the proliferation of semi-authoritarian regimes with the argument that, all things considered, they are not that bad and should be accepted as yet-imperfect democracies that will eventually mature into the real thing. For instance, compared to the old Communist Yugoslavia, or to a deeply divided Bosnia suffering from the aftermath of civil war and ethnic cleansing, or to a Serbia in a state of economic collapse but still defiant, Croatia under Franjo Tudjman did not appear too badly off; nor did it create insurmountable problems for the international community. Similarly, the semi-authoritarianism of President Heydar Aliyev in oil-rich Azerbaijan poses fewer immediate problems for policy makers and for oil companies than would a protracted power struggle with uncertain outcome. The widespread discontent in at least some semi-authoritarian states, however, suggests that further change is inevitable and that it is not in the interest of the United States to ignore the problem until crises erupt.

Promoting the democratization of semi-authoritarian regimes is a frustrating undertaking, since they are resistant to the arsenal of reform programs on which the United States and other donor countries usually rely. Semi-authoritarian regimes already do much of what the most widely used democratization projects encourage: They hold regular multiparty elections, allow parliaments to function, and recognize, within limits, the rights of citizens to form associations and of an independent press to operate. Indeed, many countries with semi-authoritarian regimes are beehives of civil-society activity, with hundreds of nongovernmental organizations, or NGO's, operating with foreign support. Many have a very outspoken, even outrageously libelous, independent press. Nevertheless, incumbent governments and parties are in no danger of losing their hold on power, not because they are popular but because they know how to play the democracy game and still retain control. Imposing sanctions on these regimes is usually ineffective, and the political and economic costs it entails, both for those who impose the measures and for the citizens of the targeted country, do not appear justified under the circumstances.

If sticks are in short supply for donors seeking to address the problem of semi-authoritarian regimes, carrots are even scarcer: There is little the international community can offer to a stable regime to entice it to risk losing power. The deepening of democracy is in the long-run interest of these countries, but it is definitely not in the short-term interest of the leaders who stand to lose power if their country becomes more democratic. Going down in history as an enlightened leader appears to be less attractive to most politicians than maintaining their power intact.

Such regimes challenge the assumption, dominant since the end of the cold war, that the failure of the socialist regimes means the triumph of democracy. This "end of history" argument, encapsulated in a book by Francis Fukuyama, of the Johns Hopkins University, puts too much emphasis on the importance of ideologies. It accurately notes that socialism, viewed for the best part of the 20th century as the ideological alternative to democracy, lost its appeal with the collapse of the Communist regimes of the Soviet Union anti Eastern Europe. As a result, the particular type of naked, institutionalized authoritarianism associated with socialism, with its massive single party and complex ideological apparatus, has become exceedingly rare. But relatively few governments, propelled by the genuine pluralism of their society and by an economic system capable of supporting such pluralism, have embraced democracy. Many have devised less heavy-handed, more nimble, and in a sense more imaginative systems that combine authoritarian and liberal traits.

The deliberate character of semi-authoritarian regimes also forces a reconsideration of the visually appealing image of countries that fail to democratize because they are caught in a "reverse wave." This idea, set forth and popularized by Samuel Huntington, of Harvard University, is that in a particular period many countries embrace democracy—figuratively, a wave propels them forward. Some of these countries safely ride the wave to dry land and prosper as democracies. Others are sucked back into the nondemocratic sea as the wave recedes, hopefully to be pushed back toward land by the next wave some decades in the future. It is an enticing idea, but it is not entirely accurate. It assumes that the leaders of all the countries supposedly being caught in a reverse wave intended to reach the shore, but in many cases they did not, and probably neither did many of these countries' citizens. Most countries that fail to reach the shore are not failed democracies caught in the wave's reflux; on the contrary, many are successful semi-authoritarian states that rode the wave as far as they wanted and managed to stop.

Another widespread idea challenged by the proliferation of semi-authoritarian regimes is that liberalization is a step toward democracy because it unleashes the democratic forces of a country. Liberalization undoubtedly allows all types of previously repressed ideas and political forces to bubble up. What actually surfaces depends on what was there. If a strong substratum of democratic ideas and, above all, of democratic organizations existed in the country, then liberalization indeed leads to greater democracy. But it can also lead to an outburst of ethnic nationalism, as in Yugoslavia, or of religious fundamentalism, as in Egypt.

How should such regimes be dealt with? Should the United States try to force democratization programs on Egypt, an important U.S. ally in the Middle East, although the Egyptian government would resist and the programs might even prove destabilizing? How should the international community react to Heydar Aliyev's plan to anoint his son as his successor as president of Azerbaijan, as if the country were a monarchy rather than a republic? What action is warranted when Venezuela starts slipping back from democracy to a semi-authoritarian populism? How can donors facilitate Croatia's second transition, the one from semi-authoritarianism?

But there is another layer of issues raised by semi-authoritarian regimes, which may appear abstract when first formulated but are actually very important to the outcome of democracy-promotion policies. Generally, these issues can be organized under the question, Why do semi-authoritarian regimes come into existence? Is it because of bad leaders (support efforts to vote them out of office), weak institutions (set up a capacity-building program), or a disorganized civil society incapable of holding the government accountable (finance and train nongovernmental organizations)? Or is it because there are underlying conditions that seriously undermine the prospects for democracy (and what can be done about underlying conditions)? Even more fundamentally, does the proliferation of semi-authoritarian regimes indicate that the assumptions about democratic transitions that undergird assistance programs need rethinking?

Democracy-assistance programs are based a lot on theory and relatively little on concrete evidence. That's not strange. Democratization is a complicated and little-understood process. In part, that is because the number of well-established democracies is relatively small, making it difficult to detect regular patterns. In part, it is because studies of democratization vary widely in their approaches and methodologies, yielding non-comparable conclusions. As a result, we understand much better how democratic systems function than why and how they emerged in the first place.

In the course of more than a decade of democracy-promotion efforts, policy makers in the United States and other countries have developed their own model of democratic transitions. That model is based in part on a highly selective reading of the literature on democratization and in part on the operational requirements of agencies that need to show results within a fairly short time frame—in the world of democracy promotion, 10 years already qualifies as long-term, although many studies of democratization highlight processes unfolding over many decades and even centuries. Inevitably, historical studies of democratization that point to the long process of socioeconomic transformation underlying the emergence of democracy have been ignored. There is little policy guidance to be derived from learning that the social capital that made democratic development possible in Northern Italy after World War II started to be built up in the 15th century, or that the rise of the gentry in the 17th century contributed to the democratic evolution of Britain. As a result, the studies with the greatest impact on democracy promotion have been those that looked narrowly at the final phase of democratic transitions, without asking too many questions about what had happened earlier or what kind of conditions had made the democratic outcome possible.

Furthermore, sophisticated studies are often given simplistic interpretations when they become a tool to justify policy choices. For example, among the most influential works often cited by democracy promoters are the studies of transitions from authoritarian rule in Latin America and Southern Europe carried out in the 1980s by a team of investigators, with Philippe Schmitter, now an emeritus professor at Stanford, and Guillermo O'Donnell, of the University of Notre Dame, drawing the overall conclusions. These conclusions were highly preliminary, as Schmitter and O'Donnell made clear with the final volume's subtitle: *Tentative Conclusions about Uncertain Democracies.* As is often the case with successful works, these highly qualified conclusions took on a life of their own, losing their nuances and turning into outright policy prescriptions. In the midst of the transition from apartheid in South Africa in the early 1990s, I heard many political commentators invoke O'Donnell and Schmitter in support of their favorite policies, ignoring the two authors' careful qualifications of their conclusions. A similar fate has befallen Robert Putnam, of Harvard, whose concept of social capital has been transformed to denote not a culture of trust and cooperation developed over centuries, but something that could be quickly created by financing NGO's and training them in the techniques of lobbying the government, administering funds, and reporting to donors.

Through this process of distilling the complex lessons of history into policy prescriptions capable of implementation, donors have developed a simple model of democratization as a three-phase process: liberalization, lasting at most a few years, but preferably much less; the transition proper, accomplished through the holding of a multiparty election; and consolidation, a protracted process of strengthening institutions and deepening a democratic culture. The tools used to facilitate this project are also fairly simple: in the liberalization phase, support for civil society and the independent press; during the transition, support for elections, including voter education, training of NGO's for observing elections, and, more rarely, training of all political parties in the techniques of organizing and campaigning; and in the consolidation phase, new programs to build democratic institutions and the rule of law, as well as the continuation of activities to further strengthen civil society and the media, educate citizens, or train parties.

Semi-authoritarian regimes call into question the model's validity. First, these regimes show that liberalization and transitional elections can constitute the end of the process rather than its initial phases, creating governments determined to prevent further change rattier than imperfect but still-evolving democracies. Furthermore, this outcome is not necessarily a failure of democratization, but the result of a deliberate decision to prevent democratization on the part of the elites controlling the process.

Second, an analysis of the workings of semi-authoritarian regimes shows that all sorts of conditions—for example, stagnant economies or ethnic polarization—matter, and matter a great deal at that. The semi-authoritarian outcome is not always something imposed by autocratic leaders on a population that wanted something quite different, but is often accepted and even desired by the population. In many countries—Venezuela, for example—people willingly, even enthusiastically, reject democracy at least for a time. The problem cannot be explained away by arguing that what people reject in such cases was not true democracy to begin with. The reality is more complicated. Conditions affect citizens' priorities and the way they perceive democracy.

Third, semi-authoritarian regimes also challenge the view that democracy can be promoted by an elite of true believers.

Democracy promoters extol in theory the virtue and necessity of broad citizen participation beyond the vote, and innumerable projects target the strengthening of civil society. But civil society as defined by donors is much more part of the elite than of the society at large. Donors favor professional-advocacy NGO's, which speak the language of democracy and easily relate to the international community. For understandable reasons, donors are leery of mass movements, which can easily slip into radical postures and can get out of hand politically. But a problem strikingly common to all countries with semi-authoritarian regimes is that the political elite, whether in the government, opposition parties, or even civil-society organizations, has great difficulty reaching the rest of the society. In the end, that situation plays into the hands of semi-authoritarian regimes.

Dealing with semi-authoritarian regimes thus requires going beyond blaming leaders for nondemocratic outcomes of once-promising democratization processes, no matter how tempting that is. To be sure, leaders with authoritarian tendencies are a real obstacle to democratic transformation. It was pointless to hope for real democratization in Serbia as long as Slobodan Milosevic was in power, and Azerbaijan will likely never be a democratic country under the leadership of Heydar Aliyev. Hugo Chavez is not the man who will restore and revitalize Venezuela's now-shaky democracy. But the problem goes well beyond personalities. Countries do not necessarily deserve the leaders they get, but they do get the leaders whose rise conditions facilitate. If the leader is removed, the conditions remain. For democracy promoters that is an unpleasant thought, because it is easier to demonize individuals and even to oust them from power than to alter the conditions that propel those leaders to the fore.

MARINA OTTAWAY is senior associate in the Democracy and Rule of Law Project at the Carnegie Endowment for International Peace. This is an excerpt from her new book, *Democracy Challenged: The Rise of Semi-Authoritarianism* (Carnegie Endowment).

People Power

In Africa, Democracy Gains Amid Turmoil

SARAH CHILDRESS

In late March, Noel Kututwa's colleagues fanned out across Zimbabwe to monitor the country's presidential elections. The democracy advocates quickly published their tally, projecting President Robert Mugabe had lost his first election since taking power in 1980.

"We expected to be arrested immediately," he says in an interview, but "we wanted to make sure our election was legitimate."

Mr. Kututwa's work in Zimbabwe is part of a shift obscured by his country's bloody election season: Democracy is making gradual gains in sub-Saharan Africa. The trend is driven by a cadre of activists, armed with little more than determination and cheap cellphones, who are outmaneuvering Africa's ruling strongmen.

African democracy has faced jarring setbacks recently. In Kenya, tribal violence killed more than 1,000 people and threatened to tear the nation apart after contested elections earlier this year. In Nigeria, the ruling party blatantly stuffed ballot boxes in national polls last year, according to international observers.

In Zimbabwe today, the opposition party and human-rights groups report near-daily acts of intimidation carried out by Mugabe supporters. Since the election, the opposition Movement for Democratic Change says at least 60 members have been killed, including four who had their eyes and tongues cut out. The government denies participation in the violence. Morgan Tsvangirai, the opposition leader, has been detained by police five times.

Mr. Mugabe raised the stakes this week, promising "war" if Mr. Tsvangirai triumphs in the hotly contested run-off scheduled for June 27, and accused the opposition of fomenting the violence. On Monday, Mr. Mugabe vowed to hold on to power even if he loses. If he acts on that threat, Africa's democratic march will have suffered a significant blow.

But in many ways, the unrest stirring Zimbabwe and other nations is coming because democracy has chalked up modest advances. Mr. Mugabe's ruling party lost its stranglehold on Parliament in the March 29 vote. And the president, whom international observers and the opposition accuse of rigging previous elections, was forced into an embarrassing run-off.

Mr. Kututwa and the Zimbabwe Election Support Network—the nonpartisan coalition of local nonprofit groups he heads—played a crucial role in that defeat. Field workers at far-flung polling stations called in, faxed or text-messaged results to organizers in the capital of Harare.

Working out of a command center at the capital's Holiday Inn, the group crunched the numbers and came up with Mr. Tsvangirai as the projected winner. Faced with an independent count, most of the international community accepted those numbers, making manipulation harder.

These days, "it is very difficult for any dictator or any incumbent to falsify the results of an election and just get away with it," says Mo Ibrahim, a Sudanese telecom tycoon who has become a democracy advocate.

The democratic gains across sub-Saharan Africa come amid the fastest economic growth the region has seen in three decades. Foreign investment is flooding in on the back of soaring prices for the oil, metals and minerals that are plentiful across the continent. The boom, coupled with the region's democratic progress, offers some hope that after a period of post-colonial turmoil, sub-Saharan Africa may be slowly emerging into a more peaceful and prosperous era.

In many countries, democracy is already robust. Ghana, sub-Saharan Africa's first independent nation, is now a thriving democracy and one of Africa's most stable countries. Tanzania, Mauritius, Senegal and Mozambique also have burgeoning, multiparty systems.

Late last year, South Africa's two-term President Thabo Mbeki was voted out of the ruling party's top seat. In April, Botswana's president handed over power to an interim leader ahead of elections next year.

The number of "free" countries among the 48 nations of sub-Saharan Africa—those with multiparty governance, civil rights and a free press—has risen to 11 in 2008 from just three in 1977, according Freedom House, a U.S.-based group that tracks freedom around the world. The number of nations ranked as not free at all has fallen to 14 from 25.

Some of the recent democratic setbacks may come to look less like catastrophic defeats than stress tests. Challengers sued over the disputed results of the 2007 elections in Nigeria, and the courts eventually threw out the results for seven governors, the senate president and several other lawmakers. In Kenya, the incumbent president was forced to share power with his opponent after results were contested.

In a growing number of countries, including Zimbabwe, grass-roots democracy groups are working to keep their leaders in check. The Africa Progress Panel, an international assessment body chaired by former United Nations chief Kofi Annan, released a report this week crediting nongovernmental organizations and other civil-society groups with increasingly holding governments accountable.

"Democratic change is coming to the forefront faster than institutional change," said Tendai Biti, the Zimbabwe opposition party's secretary-general, at a recent panel on African governance in Cape Town, South Africa.

Last week, Mr. Biti was jailed upon his return to Zimbabwe and charged with treason. The opposition party says he is innocent. Tuesday night, the High Court rejected the opposition's bid to have him released. He remains in jail.

Despite the tense situation in Zimbabwe, Mr. Kututwa says his Zimbabwe Election Support Network plans to mobilize again in next week's run-off.

Government spokesman Bright Matonga says the network is biased toward the opposition. But "they were open and honest with the way they put the results together," he says, adding that the government plans to accredit them again. The network says it is nonpartisan.

Mr. Kututwa's network had long sent observers to monitor Zimbabwean voting, typically issuing reports documenting government interference. A long-time human-rights worker in Zimbabwe, Mr. Kututwa took over as ZESN's chairman in 2002. He watched from afar as democracy advocates used cellphones to transmit local results during elections in Sierra Leone in 2007. The results, which affirmed President Ernest Bai Koroma's narrow victory, calmed tensions in the post-war environment.

Mr. Kututwa resolved to do the same during Zimbabwe's 2008 presidential election. "We wanted to take our observation to the next level," he says.

In March 2007, Mr. Tsvangirai was arrested and beaten in police custody. The government said he had attacked police. Images of his gashed and swollen face brought international outrage, and neighboring nations demanded talks between the government and the opposition over how to ensure a fair vote. The talks fell apart, but they produced one key change in election rules: The government agreed that results from each polling station would be posted locally before they were sent to election headquarters to be tallied by the country's election commission.

It seemed a small concession at the time. Mr. Mugabe was confident of a win. His policies have turned the region's onetime bread basket into an economic basket case. The International Monetary Fund says Zimbabwe is in hyperinflation, and can't even make meaningful projections about the rate anymore.

But Mr. Mugabe is revered, at home and across Africa, as the father of an independent Zimbabwe, having liberated the country from white rule in 1980. His freedom-fighter credentials had long bolstered his popularity in the countryside, and he had cracked down hard on dissenters. He had never lost an election, although he had been accused by international observers and the opposition of rigging the 2002 presidential vote and 2005 parliamentary elections.

Posting the local results, Mr. Kututwa knew, would allow monitors to make their own count before any alleged rigging began in Harare.

The network team settled on a technique known as "parallel-vote tabulation." The idea: Volunteers record local results from a sample of polling stations, and send them to a central database. Organizers then calculate a statistical projection of the total vote.

The method is simple enough to work in places with poor infrastructure, and it avoids the pitfalls of exit polling in oppressive regimes. The method isn't meant to replace an official count, but rather to serve as a barometer of the official tally's accuracy.

The counting method bolstered allegations of fraud in the Philippines' 1986 election. The vote, which had reinstated President Ferdinand Marcos, was later nullified after demonstrations that sent Mr. Marcos into exile. The method was also used later in elections in Malawi and Zambia.

By election day this March in Zimbabwe, 8,900 network volunteers had received official accreditation by the government to observe the voting. They spread out through Zimbabwe's bush to observe at 435 polling stations—about 5% of the total in a country slightly larger than the state of Montana.

The stations selected came from all of Zimbabwe's 10 electoral provinces, and were based on population density. Voters had camped out at polling places as early as 1 A.M. on the eve of the vote. When they began casting ballots six hours later, ZESN's command center at the Holiday Inn started buzzing.

Organizers' cellphones lighted up with received text-messages, and fax machines creaked to life. The polls closed that evening. ZESN's teams reported final local vote counts to Harare by text message, satellite phones and fax. Some drove in their findings.

Shortly after the polls closed, Mr. Kututwa and his team had their projection. The group decided to wait for the official count. In the past, the country's electoral commission—whose members are appointed by Mr. Mugabe's government—announced official results around midnight. But that night the commission stayed silent.

The following day, Sunday, came and went with no word from the commission. The opposition, which had conducted its own polling, claimed victory. Riot police patrolled the capital streets.

By late Monday, March 31, Mr. Kututwa decided his group couldn't wait any longer and called a news conference for 8 that evening.

The group's projections showed Mr. Tsvangirai winning 49.8%, just shy of the majority he needed to avoid a run-off. Mr. Mugabe captured 41.3%. A third independent candidate won 8%. The group determined the margin of error at a little over 2%.

Journalists, human-rights groups and governments around the world seized on the numbers. Rumors swirled that Mr. Mugabe was considering stepping down.

But the regime slowly regrouped. Four weeks after the ZESN news conference, armed Zimbabwean police raided the group's Harare office. Carrying a warrant to search for "subversive material," they carted away documents. A member of ZESN was beaten and his home burned, the group says.

The police also detained another member, questioning him for six hours. When he heard police were looking for him, Mr. Kututwa fled the country, though he returned days later.

On May 2, five weeks after Mr. Kututwa's news conference, the electoral commission announced its own results. They jibed with ZESN's figures—up to a point. Mr. Mugabe received 43.2%, the highest number statistically consistent with ZESN's projection and margin of error, according to Mr. Kututwa. Mr. Tsvangirai received 47.9%, the lowest possible figure.

"Statistically, it's unusual," Mr. Kututwa says, but he felt validated anyway. "We still don't agree with the final results, but it's not [altered] as much as it could have been," he says.

The group hopes to conduct another projection for the June 27 run-off.

Mr. Kututwa's project has inspired others. Ghana is respected as a model of democracy in Africa. President John Kufuor, after serving two elected terms, will step aside this year as two new candidates vie for his seat. Most observers predict a fair contest.

But E. Gyimah-Boadi, executive director of the Ghana Center for Democratic Development, and other advocacy groups plan to compute their own statistical projection for the December elections. The vote could be close, and the winner will likely emerge with only a slight majority.

"There will be a lot of room for dispute," Mr. Gyimah-Boadi says. "Which means, we'd better get it right."

Bin Laden, the Arab "Street," and the Middle East's Democracy Deficit

"Bin Laden speaks in the vivid language of popular Islamic preachers, and builds on a deep and widespread resentment against the West and local ruling elites identified with it. The lack of formal outlets to express opinion on public concerns has created [a] democracy deficit in much of the Arab world, and this makes it easier for terrorists such as bin Laden, asserting that they act in the name of religion, to hijack the Arab street."

DALE F. EICKELMAN

In the years ahead, the role of public diplomacy and open communications will play an increasingly significant role in countering the image that the Al Qaeda terrorist network and Osama bin Laden assert for themselves as guardians of Islamic values. In the fight against terrorism for which bin Laden is the photogenic icon, the first step is to recognize that he is as thoroughly a part of the modern world as was Cambodia's French-educated Pol Pot. Bin Laden's videotaped presentation of self intends to convey a traditional Islamic warrior brought up-to-date, but this sense of the past is a completely invented one. The language and content of his videotaped appeals convey more of his participation in the modern world than his camouflage jacket, Kalashnikov, and Timex watch.

Take the two-hour Al Qaeda recruitment videotape in Arabic that has made its way to many Middle Eastern video shops and Western news media.[1] It is a skillful production, as fast paced and gripping as any Hindu fundamentalist video justifying the destruction in 1992 of the Ayodhya mosque in India, or the political attack videos so heavily used in American presidential campaigning. The 1988 "Willie Horton" campaign video of Republican presidential candidate George H. W. Bush—in which an off-screen announcer portrayed Democratic presidential candidate Michael Dukakis as "soft" on crime while showing a mug shot of a convicted African-American rapist who had committed a second rape during a weekend furlough from a Massachusetts prison—was a propaganda masterpiece that combined an explicit although conventional message with a menacing, underlying one intended to motivate undecided voters. The Al Qaeda video, directed at a different audience— presumably alienated Arab youth, unemployed and often living in desperate conditions—shows an equal mastery of modern propaganda.

The Al Qaeda producers could have graduated from one of the best film schools in the United States or Europe. The fast-moving recruitment video begins with the bombing of the USS *Cole* in Yemen, but then shows a montage implying a seemingly coordinated worldwide aggression against Muslims in Palestine, Jerusalem, Lebanon, Chechnya, Kashmir, and Indonesia (but not Muslim violence against Christians and Chinese in the last). It also shows United States generals received by Saudi princes, intimating the collusion of local regimes with the West and challenging the legitimacy of many regimes, including Saudi Arabia. The sufferings of the Iraqi people are attributed to American brutality against Muslims, but Saddam Hussein is assimilated to the category of infidel ruler.

Osama bin Laden . . . is thoroughly imbued with the values of the modern world, even if only to reject them.

Many of the images are taken from the daily staple of Western video news—the BBC and CNN logos add to the videos' authenticity, just as Qatar's al-Jazeera satellite television logo rebroadcast by CNN and the BBC has added authenticity to Western coverage of Osama bin Laden.

Alternating with these scenes of devastation and oppression of Muslims are images of Osama bin Laden: posing in front of bookshelves or seated on the ground like a religious scholar, holding the Koran in his hand. Bin Laden radiates charismatic authority and control as he narrates the Prophet Mohammed's flight from Mecca to Medina, when the early Islamic movement was threatened by the idolaters, but returning to conquer them. Bin Laden also stresses the need for jihad, or struggle for the cause of Islam, against the "crusaders" and "Zionists." Later images show military training in Afghanistan (including target practice at a poster of Bill Clinton), and a final sequence—the word "solution" flashes across the screen—captures an Israeli soldier in full riot gear retreating from a Palestinian boy throwing stones, and a reading of the Koran.

The Thoroughly Modern Islamist

Osama bin Laden, like many of his associates, is imbued with the values of the modern world, even if only to reject them. A 1971 photograph shows him on family holiday in Oxford at the age of 14, posing with two of his half-brothers and Spanish girls their own age. English was their common language of communication. Bin Laden studied English at a private school in Jidda, and English was also useful for his civil engineering courses at Jidda's King Abdul Aziz University. Unlike many of his estranged half-brothers, educated in Saudi Arabia, Europe, and the United States, Osama's education was only in Saudi Arabia, but he was also familiar with Arab and European society.

The organizational skills he learned in Saudi Arabia came in to play when he joined the mujahideen (guerrilla) struggle against the 1979 Soviet invasion of Afghanistan. He may not have directly met United States intelligence officers in the field, but they, like their Saudi and Pakistani counterparts, were delighted to have him participate in their fight against Soviet troops and recruit willing Arab fighters. Likewise, his many business enterprises flourished under highly adverse conditions. Bin Laden skillfully sustained a flexible multinational organization in the face of enemies, especially state authorities, moving cash, people, and supplies almost undetected across international frontiers.

The organizational skills of bin Laden and his associates were never underestimated. Neither should be their skills in conveying a message that appeals to some Muslims. Bin Laden lacks the credentials of an established Islamic scholar, but this does not diminish his appeal. As Sudan's Sorbonne-educated Hasan al-Turabi, the leader of his country's Muslim Brotherhood and its former attorney general and speaker of parliament, explained two decades ago, "Because all knowledge is divine and religious, a chemist, an engineer, an economist, or a jurist" are all men of learning.[2] Civil engineer bin Laden exemplifies Turabi's point. His audience judges him not by his ability to cite authoritative texts, but by his apparent skill in applying generally accepted religious tenets to current political and social issues.

The Message on the Arab "Street"

Bin Laden's lectures circulate in book form in the Arab world, but video is the main vehicle of communication. The use of CNN-like "zippers"—the ribbons of words that stream beneath the images in many newscasts and documentaries—shows that Al Qaeda takes the Arab world's rising levels of education for granted. Increasingly, this audience is also saturated with both conventional media and new media, such as the Internet.[3] The Middle East has entered an era of mass education and this also implies an Arabic lingua franca. In Morocco in the early 1970s, rural people sometimes asked me to "translate" newscasts from the standard transnational Arabic of the state radio into colloquial

Arabic. Today this is no longer required. Mass education and new communications technologies enable large numbers of Arabs to hear—and see—Al Qaeda's message directly.

Bin Laden's message does not depend on religious themes alone. Like the Ayatollah Ruhollah Khomeini, his message contains many secular elements. Khomeini often alluded to the "wretched of the earth." At least for a time, his language appealed equally to Iran's religiously minded and to the secular left. For bin Laden, the equivalent themes are the oppression and corruption of many Arab governments, and he lays the blame for the violence and oppression in Palestine, Kashmir, Chechnya, and elsewhere at the door of the West. One need not be religious to rally to some of these themes. A poll taken in Morocco in late September 2001 showed that a majority of Moroccans condemned the September 11 bombings, but 41 percent sympathized with bin Laden's message. A British poll taken at about the same time showed similar results.

Osama bin Laden and the Al Qaeda terrorist movement are thus reaching at least part of the Arab "street." Earlier this year, before the September terrorist attacks, United States policymakers considered this "street" a "new phenomenon of public accountability, which we have seldom had to factor into our projections of Arab behavior in the past. The information revolution, and particularly the daily dose of uncensored television coming out of local TV stations like al-Jazeera and international coverage by CNN and others, is shaping public opinion, which, in turn, is pushing Arab governments to respond. We don't know, and the leaders themselves don't know, how that pressure will impact on Arab policy in the future."[4]

Director of Central Intelligence George J. Tenet was even more cautionary on the nature of the "Arab street." In testimony before the Senate Select Committee on Intelligence in February 2001, he explained that the "right catalyst—such as the outbreak of Israeli-Palestinian violence—can move people to act. Through access to the Internet and other means of communication, a restive public is increasingly capable of taking action without any identifiable leadership or organizational structure."

Because many governments in the Middle East are deeply suspicious of an open press, nongovernmental organizations, and open expression, it is no surprise that the "restive" public, increasingly educated and influenced by hard-to-censor new media, can take action "without any identifiable leadership or organized structure." The Middle East in general has a democracy deficit, in which "unauthorized" leaders or critics, such as Egyptian academic Saad Eddin Ibrahim—founder and director of the Ibn Khaldun Center for Development Studies, a nongovernmental organization that promotes democracy in Egypt—suffer harassment or prison terms.

One consequence of this democracy deficit is to magnify the power of the street in the Arab world. Bin Laden speaks in the vivid language of popular Islamic preachers, and builds on a deep and widespread resentment against the West and local ruling elites identified with it. The lack of formal outlets to express opinion on public concerns has created the democracy deficit in much of the Arab world, and this makes it easier for terrorists such as bin Ladin, asserting that they act in the name of religion, to hijack the Arab street.

The immediate response is to learn to speak directly to this street. This task has already begun. Obscure to all except specialists until September 11, Qatar's al-Jazeera satellite television is a premier source in the Arab world for uncensored news and opinion. It is more, however, than the Arab equivalent of CNN. Uncensored news and opinions increasingly shape "public opinion"—a term without the pejorative overtones of "the street"—even in places like Damascus and Algiers. This public opinion in turn pushes Arab governments to be more responsive to their citizens, or at least to say that they are.

Rather than seek to censor al-Jazeera or limit Al Qaeda's access to the Western media—an unfortunate first response of the United States government after the September terror attacks—we should avoid censorship. Al Qaeda statements should be treated with the same caution as any other news source. Replacing Sinn Fein leader Gerry Adams' voice and image in the British media in the 1980s with an Irish-accented actor appearing in silhouette only highlighted what he had to say, and it is unlikely that the British public would tolerate the same restrictions on the media today.

Ironically, at almost the same time that national security adviser Condoleezza Rice asked the American television networks not to air Al Qaeda videos unedited, a former senior CIA officer, Graham Fuller, was explaining in Arabic on al-Jazeera how United States policymaking works. His appearance on al-Jazeera made a significant impact, as did Secretary of State Colin Powell's presence on a later al-Jazeera program and former United States Ambassador Christopher Ross, who speaks fluent Arabic. Likewise, the timing and content of British Prime Minister Tony Blair's response to an earlier bin Laden tape suggests how to take the emerging Arab public seriously. The day after al-Jazeera broadcast the bin Laden tape, Blair asked for and received an opportunity to respond. In his reply, Blair—in a first for a Western leader—directly addressed the Arab public through the Arab media, explaining coalition goals in attacking Al Qaeda and the Taliban and challenging bin Laden's claim to speak in the name of Islam.

Putting Public Diplomacy to Work

Such appearances enhance the West's ability to communicate a primary message: that the war against terrorism is not that of one civilization against another, but against terrorism and fanaticism in all societies. Western policies and actions are subject to public scrutiny and will often be misunderstood. Public diplomacy can significantly diminish this misapprehension. It may, however, involve some uncomfortable policy decisions. For instance, America may be forced to exert more diplomatic pressure on Israel to alter its methods of dealing with Palestinians.

Western public diplomacy in the Middle East also involves uncharted waters. As Oxford University social linguist Clive Holes has noted, the linguistic genius who thought up the first name for the campaign to oust the Taliban, "Operation Infinite Justice," did a major disservice to the Western goal. The expression was literally and accurately translated into Arabic as *adala ghayr mutanahiya,* implying that an earthly power arrogated to itself the task of divine retribution. Likewise, President George W. Bush's inadvertent and unscripted use of the word "crusade" gave Al Qaeda spokesmen an opportunity to attack Bush and Western intentions.

Mistakes will be made, but information and arguments that reach the Arab street, including on al-Jazeera, will eventually have an impact. Some Westerners might condemn al-Jazeera as biased, and it may well be in terms of making assumptions about its audience. However, it has broken a taboo by regularly inviting official Israeli spokespersons to comment live on current issues. Muslim religious scholars, both in the Middle East and in the West, have already spoken out against Al Qaeda's claim to act in the name of Islam. Other courageous voices, such as Egyptian playwright Ali Salem, have even employed humor for the same purpose.[5]

We must recognize that the best way to mitigate the continuing threat of terrorism is to encourage Middle Eastern states to be more responsive to participatory demands, and to aid local nongovernmental organizations working toward this goal. As with the case of Egypt's Saad Eddin Ibrahim, some countries may see such activities as subversive. Whether Arab states like it or not, increasing levels of education, greater ease of travel, and the rise of new communications media are turning the Arab street into a public sphere in which greater numbers of people, and not just a political and economic elite, will have a say in governance and public issues.

Notes

1. It is now available on-line with explanatory notes in English. See <http://www.ciaonet.org/cbr/cbr00/video/excerpts_index.html>.

2. Hasan al-Turabi, "The Islamic State," in *Voices of Resurgent Islam,* John L. Esposito, ed. (New York: Oxford University Press, 1983), p. 245.

3. On the importance of rising levels of education and the new media, see Dale F. Eickelman, "The Coming Transformation in the Muslim World," *Current History,* January 2000.

4. Edward S. Walker, "The New US Administration's Middle East Policy Speech," *Middle East Economic Survey,* vol. 44, no. 26 (June 25, 2001). Available at <http://www.mees.com/news/a44n26d01.htm>.

5. See his article in Arabic, "I Want to Start a Kindergarten for Extremism," *Al-Hayat* (London), November 5, 2001. This is translated into English by the Middle East Media Research Institute as Special Dispatch no. 298, Jihad and Terrorism Studies, November 8, 2001, at <http://www.memri.org>.

DALE F. EICKELMAN is Ralph and Richard Lazarus Professor of Anthropology and Human Relations at Dartmouth College. His most recent book is *The Middle East and Central Asia: An Anthropological Approach,* 4th ed. (Englewood Cliffs, N. J.: Prentice Hall, 2002). An earlier version of this article appeared as "The West Should Speak to the Arab in the Street," *Daily Telegraph* (London), October 27, 2001.

UNIT 2

Political Parties and Interest Groups: From Preferences to Policies

Unit Selections

Key Points to Consider

- Why would you join a group?

- When is an interest group considered successful?

- When is an interest group considered to have failed?

- What are the roles of interest groups and political parties in a political system?

- When are political parties considered successful?

- What characterizes political parties as failures?

- Describe how "minority" interest groups are able to achieve their goals.

- What are the ways to mobilize? Explain why these ways are particularly helpful in mobilizing youths in contemporary politics.

Student Website
www.mhhe.com/cls

Internet References

Human Rights Watch
   http://www.hrw.org
National Geographic Society
   http://www.nationalgeographic.com
Research and Reference (Library of Congress)
   http://www.loc.gov/rr
Sun SITE Singapore
   http://sunsite.nus.edu.sg/noframe.html
UN Interactive Database
   http://cyberschoolbus.un.org/infonation/index.asp

Unit 2 builds upon the discussion of citizen participation in Unit 1 to address systematically why and how citizen participation is organized, and what forms it takes. The unit begins with Robert Dahl's article, "What Political Institutions Does Large-Scale Democracy Require?", which points out two obvious advantages to organizing citizens. First, it improves efficiency and effectiveness of participation. In particular, aggregating the interests or preferences of citizens is invaluable as the size of the citizenry increases and as more people are dispersed over larger geographic areas. Second, organized citizen groups provide the counterbalance to coercive governments who may not be willing to tolerate or accommodate interests that depart from the government's goals. As the author points out, "the degree of coercion" required to suppress larger associations is generally considered objectionable. Consequently, groups are able to exist and express themselves where individual citizens may not be able. The article, "Interest Groups: Ex Uno, Plures," adds two additional considerations. One, interest groups keep political parties and the politicians affiliated therewith, honest and accountable for their actions in between elections. Two, interest groups provide expertise and advice; after all, they have to be well versed in the area of their interest in order to put forth their arguments.

How are interests organized? Mancur Olson's *Logic of Collective Action,* which is discussed in the article "Interest Groups: Ex Uno, Plures," argues that citizens are not persuaded to join groups easily. Instead, there is a temptation to "free-ride," that is, to not participate in groups but, nevertheless, enjoy the fruits of policies that interest groups pressure their governments to implement. However, other scholars find numerous reasons beyond personal gain that motivate individual citizens to join interests groups. They include altruism, personal values, shared values, and self-expression.

The article on youth movements in the three post-communist countries of Serbia, Georgia, and Ukraine certainly supports the latter view. In particular, it describes how fear of the authorities hinders organizing and mobilizing. Likewise, the article on democratic movements in Asia notes the considerable cost—including a "bloody conflict in Timor"—that protestors accept as they mobilize for democracy and independence. Notably, both articles describe the movements as developing and mobilizing against strong odds. And, clearly, the participants described in either article are not "free-riding" but actively contribute and play a part in efforts to improve political conditions and civil rights.

Importantly, participation or zeal alone does not change the status quo. Thus, the article on the youth movements in the post-communist countries describes rigorous training and organization of the youths to undercut the fear of the authorities and to present cogent, coherent challenges. In contrast, the article on democracies in Asia describes situations with a lack of deliberate process to achieve the goals of the interest groups. In fact, Asian countries have seen governments apparently engaging in efforts to curtail democratization or even reverse some democratic processes. Thus, while it is clear that mass protests and

© The McGraw-Hill Companies, Inc/John Flournoy, photographer

demonstrations are not without their use, the articles on Asian democratic and youth movements point out that sole reliance on such mass demonstrations do not generally achieve the desired objectives. Instead, the articles show that success is based on regularized or even institutionalized funding and organization to raise awareness and support and defuse challenges to their agenda.

Equally important, the articles on Asia and post-communist countries show that political parties are important complements to their success. Political parties are like interest groups; indeed, Dahl's article points out that political parties are often morphed from interest groups. The transformation occurs when the interest groups or factions in legislature find themselves thwarted in pursuing policy ideas, or find that merely checking the policies of the existing government does not lead to the policies they desire. Thus, political parties have more depth and broader scope than interest groups. In the past, political parties enjoyed more successes. These days, they are caught in a web of growing public dissatisfaction. Thus, membership in political parties is declining. Also, ideological differences between political parties, which in part explain party appeal and loyalties, have narrowed. In fact, it may make more sense to speak of the Center-Left and Center-Right, rather than the traditional left-right distinction, because of this political convergence.[1] Even the traditional job of parties—communicating with members—has been replaced by the media.

Yet, notwithstanding evidence of party decline, political parties remain vital: they still control nomination for office. In fact, independent candidates are rarely successful. Membership may be down but the parties continue to be able to organize and bring in funding. And, political parties can count on increasing alliances with groups. Also, as the articles on the interest group show, parties continue to be able to exercise power in office. This power and the persistence of political parties is relevant: without the support of political parties, the effect of the most effective interest groups on policymaking and implementation is far from certain.

It is safe to say that political parties and interest groups are not likely to disappear from the political landscape. While we may be concerned about their effects from time to time, they allow for voices to be heard and act as relief valves that release pressures within the political system. As a result, the way to control undue influence from political parties or interest groups may not be to restrict them but, rather, to pluralize them.

Note

1. **The Right** is usually far more ready to accept as "normal" or "inevitable" the existence of social or economic inequalities, and normally favors lower taxes and the promotion of market forces—with some very important exceptions intended to protect the nation as a whole (national defense and internal security) as well as certain favored values and interest groups (clienteles). In general, the Right sees the state as an instrument that should provide security, order, and protection for an established way of life. **The Left,** by contrast, traditionally emphasizes that government has an important task in opening greater opportunities or "life chances" for everyone, delivering affordable public services, and generally reducing social inequality.

What Political Institutions Does Large-Scale Democracy Require?

ROBERT A. DAHL

What does it mean to say that a country is governed democratically? Here, we will focus on the political institutions of *democracy on a large scale*, that is, the political institutions necessary for a *democratic country*. We are not concerned here, then, with what democracy in a very small group might require, as in a committee. We also need to keep in mind that every actual democracy has always fallen short of democratic criteria. Finally, we should be aware that in ordinary language, we use the word *democracy* to refer both to a goal or ideal and to an actuality that is only a partial attainment of the goal. For the time being, therefore, I'll count on the reader to make the necessary distinctions when I use the words *democracy, democratically, democratic government, democratic country*, and so on.[1]

How Can We Know?

How can we reasonably determine what political institutions are necessary for large-scale democracy? We might examine the history of countries that have changed their political institutions in response, at least in part, to demands for broader popular inclusion and effective participation in government and political life. Although in earlier times those who sought to gain inclusion and participation were not necessarily inspired by democratic ideas, from about the eighteenth century onward they tended to justify their demands by appealing to democratic and republican ideas. What political institutions did they seek, and what were actually adopted in these countries?

Alternatively, we could examine countries where the government is generally referred to as democratic by most of the people in that country, by many persons in other countries, and by scholars, journalists, and the like. In other words, in ordinary speech and scholarly discussion the country is called a democracy.

Third, we could reflect on a specific country or group of countries, or perhaps even a hypothetical country, in order to imagine, as realistically as possible, what political institutions would be required in order to achieve democratic goals to a substantial degree. We would undertake a mental experiment, so to speak, in which we would reflect carefully on human experiences, tendencies, possibilities, and limitations and design a set of political institutions that would be necessary for large-scale democracy to exist and yet feasible and attainable within the limits of human capacities.

Fortunately, all three methods converge on the same set of democratic political institutions. These, then, are minimal requirements for a democratic country (figure 1).

The Political Institutions of Modern Representative Democracy

Briefly, the political institutions of modern representative democratic government are

- *Elected officials.* Control over government decisions about policy is constitutionally vested in officials elected by citizens. Thus modern, large-scale democratic governments are *representative*.
- *Free, fair and frequent elections.* Elected officials are chosen in frequent and fairly conducted elections in which coercion is comparatively uncommon.

What Political Institutions Does Large-Scale Democracy Require?

Large-scale democracy requires:

1. Elected officials
2. Free, fair, and frequent elections
3. Freedom of expression
4. Alternative sources of information
5. Associational autonomy
6. Inclusive citizenship

Figure 1

- *Freedom of expression*. Citizens have a right to express themselves without danger of severe punishment on political matters broadly defined, including criticism of officials, the government, the regime, the socioeconomic order, and the prevailing ideology.
- *Access to alternative sources of information*. Citizens have a right to seek out alternative and independent sources of information from other citizens, experts, newspapers, magazines, books, telecommunications, and the like. Moreover, alternative sources of information actually exist that are not under the control of the government or any other single political group attempting to influence public political beliefs and attitudes, and these alternative sources are effectively protected by law.
- *Associational autonomy*. To achieve their various rights, including those required for the effective operation of democratic political institutions, citizens also have a right to form relatively independent associations or organizations, including independent political parties and interest groups.
- *Inclusive citizenship*. No adult permanently residing in the country and subject to its laws can be denied the rights that are available to others and are necessary to the five political institutions just listed. These include the right to vote in the election of officials in free and fair elections; to run for elective office; to free expression; to form and participate in independent political organizations; to have access to independent sources of information; and rights to other liberties and opportunities that may be necessary to the effective operation of the political institutions of large-scale democracy.

The Political Institutions in Perspective

Ordinarily these institutions do not arrive in a country all at once; the last two are distinctly latecomers. Until the twentieth century, universal suffrage was denied in both the theory and practice of democratic and republican government. More than any other single feature, universal suffrage distinguishes modern representative democracy from earlier forms of democracy.

The time of arrival and the sequence in which the institutions have been introduced have varied tremendously. In countries where the full set of democratic institutions arrived earliest and have endured to the present day, the "older" democracies, elements of a common pattern emerge. Elections to a legislature arrived early on—in Britain as early as the thirteenth century, in the United States during its colonial period in the seventeenth and eighteenth centuries. The practice of electing higher lawmaking officials was followed by a gradual expansion of the rights of citizens to express themselves on political matters and to seek out and exchange information. The right to form associations with explicit political goals tended to follow still later. Political "factions" and partisan organization were generally viewed as dangerous, divisive, subversive of political order and stability, and injurious to the public good. Yet because political associations could not be suppressed without a degree of coercion that an increasingly large and influential number of citizens regarded as intolerable, they were often able to exist as more or less clandestine associations until they emerged from the shadows into the full light of day. In the legislative bodies, what once were "factions" became political parties. The "ins" who served in the government of the day were opposed by the "outs," or what in Britain came to be officially styled His (or Her) Majesty's Loyal Opposition. In eighteenth-century Britain, the faction supporting the monarch and the opposing faction supported by much of the gentry in the "country" were gradually transformed into Tories and Whigs. During that same century in Sweden, partisan adversaries in Parliament somewhat facetiously called themselves the Hats and the Caps.[2]

During the final years of the eighteenth century in the newly formed republic of the United States, Thomas Jefferson, the vice president, and James Madison, leader of the House of Representatives, organized their followers in Congress to oppose the policies of the Federalist president, John Adams, and his secretary of the treasury, Alexander Hamilton. To succeed in their opposition, they soon realized that they would have to do more than oppose the Federalists in the Congress and the cabinet: they would need to remove their opponents from office. To do that, they had to win national elections, and to win national elections they had to organize their followers throughout the country. In less than a decade, Jefferson, Madison, and others sympathetic with their views created a political party that was organized all the way down to the smallest voting precincts, districts, and municipalities, an organization that would reinforce the loyalty of their followers between and during election campaigns and make sure they came to the polls. Their Republican Party (soon renamed Democratic Republican and, a generation later, Democratic) became the first popularly based *electoral* party in the world. As a result, one of the most fundamental and distinctive political institutions of modern democracy, the political party, had burst beyond its confines in parliaments and legislatures in order to organize the citizens themselves and mobilize party supporters in national elections.

By the time the young French aristocrat Alexis de Tocqueville visited the United States in the 1830s, the first five democratic political institutions described above had already arrived in America. The institutions seemed to him so deeply planted and pervasive that he had no hesitation in referring to the United States as a democracy. In that country, he said, the people were sovereign, "society governs itself for itself," and the power of the majority was unlimited.[3] He was astounded by the multiplicity of associations into which Americans organized themselves, for every purpose, it seemed. And towering among these associations were the two major political parties. In the United States, it appeared to Tocqueville, democracy was about as complete as one could imagine it ever becoming.

During the century that followed, all five of the basic democratic institutions Tocqueville observed during his visit to America were consolidated in more than a dozen other countries. Many observers in Europe and the United States concluded that any country that aspired to be civilized and progressive would necessarily have to adopt a democratic form of government.

Yet everywhere, the sixth fundamental institution—inclusive citizenship—was missing. Although Tocqueville affirmed that "the state of Maryland, which had been founded by men of rank, was the first to proclaim universal suffrage," like almost all other men (and many women) of his time he tacitly assumed that "universal" did not include women.[4] Nor, indeed, some men. Maryland's "universal suffrage," it so happened, also excluded most African Americans. Elsewhere, in countries that were otherwise more or less democratic, as in America, a full half of all adults were completely excluded from national political life simply because they were women; in addition, large numbers of men were denied suffrage because they could not meet literacy or property requirements, an exclusion supported by many people who considered themselves advocates of democratic or republican government. Although New Zealand extended suffrage to women in national elections in 1893 and Australia in 1902, in countries otherwise democratic, women did not gain suffrage in national elections until about 1920; in Belgium, France, and Switzerland, countries that most people would have called highly democratic, women could not vote until after World War II.

Because it is difficult for many today to grasp what "democracy" meant to our predecessors, let me reemphasize the difference: in all democracies and republics throughout twenty-five centuries, the rights to engage fully in political life were restricted to a minority of adults. "Democratic" government was government by males only—and not all of them. It was not until the twentieth century that in both theory and practice democracy came to require that the rights to engage fully in political life must be extended, with very few if any exceptions, to the entire population of adults permanently residing in a country.

Taken in their entirety, then, these six political institutions constitute not only a new type of political system but a new kind of popular government, a type of "democracy" that had never existed throughout the twenty-five centuries of experience since the inauguration of "democracy" in Athens and a "republic" in Rome. Because the institutions of modern representative democratic government, taken in their entirety, are historically unique, it is convenient to give them their own name. This modern type of large-scale democratic government is sometimes called *polyarchal* democracy.

Although other factors were often at work, the six political institutions of polyarchal democracy came about, in part at least, in response to demands for inclusion and participation in political life. In countries that are widely referred to as democracies today, all six exist. Yet you might well ask: Are some of these institutions no more than past products of historical struggles? Are they no longer necessary for democratic government? And if they are still necessary today, why?[5]

The Factor of Size

Before answering these questions, I need to call attention to an important qualification. We are considering institutions necessary for the government of a democratic country. Why "country"? *Because all the institutions necessary for a democratic country would not always be required for a unit much smaller than a country.*

Consider a democratically governed committee, or a club, or a very small town. Although equality in voting would seem to be necessary, small units like these might manage without many elected officials: perhaps a moderator to preside over meetings, a secretary-treasurer to keep minutes and accounts. The participants themselves could decide just about everything directly during their meetings, leaving details to the secretary-treasurer. Governments of small organizations would not have to be full-fledged *representative* governments in which citizens elect representatives charged with enacting laws and policies. Yet these governments could be democratic, perhaps highly democratic. So, too, even though they lacked political parties or other independent political associations, they might be highly democratic. In fact, we might concur with the classical democratic and republican view that in small associations, organized "factions" are not only unnecessary but downright harmful. Instead of conflicts exacerbated by factionalism, caucuses, political parties, and so on, we might prefer unity, consensus, agreement achieved by discussion and mutual respect.

The political institutions strictly required for democratic government depend, then, on the size of the unit. The six institutions listed above developed because they are necessary for governing *countries*, not smaller units. Polyarchal democracy is democratic government on the large scale of the nation-state or country.

To return to our questions: Are the political institutions of polyarchal democracy actually necessary for democracy on the large scale of a country? If so, why? To answer these twin questions, let us recall what a democratic process requires (figure 2).

Why (and When) Does Democracy Require Elected Representatives?

As the focus of democratic government shifted to large-scale units like nations or countries, the question arose: How can citizens *participate effectively* when the number of citizens becomes too numerous or too widely dispersed geographically (or both, as in the case of a country) for them to participate conveniently in making laws by assembling in one place? And how can they make sure that matters with which they are most concerned are adequately considered by officials—that is, how can citizens *control the agenda of* government decisions?

How best to meet these democratic requirements in a political unit as large as a country is, of course, enormously difficult, indeed to some extent unachievable. Yet just as with

Why the Institutions Are Necessary

In a unit as large as a country, these political institutions of polyarchal democracy. . . are necessary to satisfy the following democratic criteria:

In a unit as large as a country, these political institutions of polyarchal democracy. . .	are necessary to satisfy the following democratic criteria:
1. Elected representatives. . .	Effective participation Control of the agenda
2. Free, fair and frequent elections. . .	Voting equality Control of the agenda
3. Freedom of expression. . .	Effective participation Enlightened understanding Control of the agenda
4. Alternative information. . .	Effective participation Enlightened understanding Control of the agenda
5. Associational autonomy. . .	Effective participation Enlightened understanding Control of the agenda
6. Inclusive citizenship. . .	Full inclusion

Figure 2

the other highly demanding democratic criteria, this, too, can serve as a standard for evaluating alternative possibilities and solutions. Clearly the requirements could not be met if the top officials of the government could set the agenda and adopt policies independently of the wishes of citizens. The only feasible solution, though it is highly imperfect, is for citizens to elect their top officials and hold them more or less accountable through elections by dismissing them, so to speak, in subsequent elections.

To us that solution seems obvious. But what may appear self-evident to us was not at all obvious to our predecessors.

Until fairly recently the possibility that citizens could, by means of elections, choose and reject representatives with the authority to make laws remained largely foreign to both the theory and practice of democracy. The election of representatives mainly developed during the Middle Ages, when monarchs realized that in order to impose taxes, raise armies, and make laws, they needed to win the consent of the nobility, the higher clergy, and a few not-so-common commoners in the larger towns and cities.

Until the eighteenth century, then, the standard view was that democratic or republican government meant rule by the people, and if the people were to rule, they had to assemble in one place and vote on decrees, laws, or policies. Democracy would have to be town meeting democracy; representative democracy was a contradiction in terms. By implication, whether explicit or implicit, a republic or a democracy could actually exist only in a small unit, like a town or city. Writers who held this view, such as Montesquieu and Jean-Jacques Rousseau, were perfectly aware of the disadvantages of a small state, particularly when it confronted the military superiority of a much larger state, and were therefore extremely pessimistic about the future prospects for genuine democracy.

Yet the standard view was swiftly overpowered and swept aside by the onrushing force of the national state. Rousseau himself clearly understood that for a government of a country as large as Poland (for which he proposed a constitution), representation would be necessary. And shortly thereafter, the standard view was driven off the stage of history by the arrival of democracy in America.

As late as 1787, when the Constitutional Convention met in Philadelphia to design a constitution appropriate for a large country with an ever-increasing population, the delegates were acutely aware of the historical tradition. Could a republic possibly exist on the huge scale the United States had already attained, not to mention the even grander scale the delegates foresaw?[6] Yet no one questioned that if a republic were to exist in America, it would have to take the form of a *representative* republic. Because of the lengthy experience with representation in colonial and state legislatures and in the Continental Congress, the feasibility of representative government was practically beyond debate.

By the middle of the nineteenth century, the traditional view was ignored, forgotten, or, if remembered at all, treated as irrelevant. "It is evident," John Stuart Mill wrote in 1861

that the only government which can fully satisfy all the exigencies of the social state is one in which the whole people participate; that any participation, even in the smallest public function, is useful; that the participation should everywhere be as great as the general degree of improvement of the community will allow; and that nothing less can be ultimately desirable than the admission of all to share in the sovereign power of the state. But since all cannot, in a community exceeding a single small town, participate personally in any but some very minor portions of the public business, it follows that the ideal type of a perfect government must be representative.[7]

Why Does Democracy Require Free, Fair, and Frequent Elections?

As we have seen, if we accept the desirability of political equality, then every citizen must have an *equal and effective opportunity to vote, and all votes must be counted as equal.* If equality in voting is to be implemented, then clearly, elections must be free and fair. To be free means that citizens can go to the polls without fear of reprisal; and if they are to be fair, then all votes must be counted as equal. Yet free and fair elections are not enough. Imagine electing representatives for a term of, say, twenty years! If citizens are to retain *final control over the agenda*, then elections must also be frequent.

How best to implement free and fair elections is not obvious. In the late nineteenth century, the secret ballot began to replace a public show of hands. Although open voting still has a few defenders, secrecy has become the general standard; a country in which it is widely violated would be judged as lacking free and fair elections. But debate continues as to the kind of voting system that best meets standards of fairness. Is a system of proportional representation (PR), like that employed in most democratic countries, fairer than the first-past-the-post system used in Great Britain and the United States? Reasonable arguments can be made for both. In discussions about different voting systems, however, the need for a fair system is assumed; how best to achieve fairness and other reasonable objectives is simply a technical question.

How frequent should elections be? Judging from twentieth-century practices in democratic countries, a rough answer might be that annual elections for legislative representatives would be a bit too frequent and anything more than five years would be too long. Obviously, however, democrats can reasonably disagree about the specific interval and how it might vary with different offices and different traditional practices. The point is that without frequent elections, citizens would lose a substantial degree of control over their elected officials.

Why Does Democracy Require Free Expression?

To begin with, freedom of expression is required in order for citizens to *participate* effectively in political life. How can citizens make their views known and persuade their fellow citizens and representatives to adopt them unless they can express themselves freely about all matters bearing on the conduct of the government? And if they are to take the views of others into account, they must be able to hear what others have to say. Free expression means not just that you have a right to be heard. It also means that you have a right to hear what others have to say.

To acquire an *enlightened understanding* of possible government actions and policies also requires freedom of expression. To acquire civic competence, citizens need opportunities to express their own views; learn from one another; engage in discussion and deliberation; read, hear, and question experts, political candidates, and persons whose judgments they trust; and learn in other ways that depend on freedom of expression.

Finally, without freedom of expression, citizens would soon lose their capacity to influence *the agenda* of government decisions. Silent citizens may be perfect subjects for an authoritarian ruler; they would be a disaster for a democracy.

Why Does Democracy Require the Availability of Alternative and Independent Sources of Information?

Like freedom of expression, the availability of alternative and relatively independent sources of information is required by several of the basic democratic criteria. Consider the need for *enlightened understanding*. How can citizens acquire the information they need in order to understand the issue if the government controls all the important sources of information? Or, for that matter, if any single group enjoys a monopoly in providing information? Citizens must have access, then, to alternative sources of information that are not under the control of the government or dominated by any other group or point of view.

Or think about *effective participation* and influencing the *public agenda*. How could citizens participate effectively in political life if all the information they could acquire were provided by a single source, say the government, or, for that matter, a single party, faction, or interest?

Why Does Democracy Require Independent Associations?

It took a radical turnabout in ways of thinking to accept the need for political associations—interest groups, lobbying organizations, political parties. Yet if a large republic requires that representatives be elected, then how are elections to be contested? Forming an organization, such as a political party, gives a group an obvious electoral advantage. And if one group seeks to gain that advantage, will not others who disagree with their policies? And why should political activity cease between elections? Legislators can be influenced; causes can be advanced, policies promoted, appointments sought. So, unlike a small city or town, the large scale of democracy in a country makes political associations both necessary and desirable. In any case, how can they be prevented without impairing the fundamental right of citizens to participate effectively in governing? In a large republic, then, they are not only necessary and desirable but inevitable. Independent associations are also a source of *civic education and enlightenment.* They provide citizens not only with information but also with opportunities for discussion, deliberation, and the acquisition of political skills.

Why Does Democracy Require Inclusive Citizenship?

We can view the political institutions summarized in figure 1 in several ways. For a country that lacks one or more of the institutions, and is to that extent not yet sufficiently democratized, knowledge of the basic political institutions can help us to design a strategy for making a full *transition* to modern representative democracy. For a country that has only recently made the transition, that knowledge can help inform us about the crucial institutions that need to be *strengthened, deepened, and consolidated.* Because they are all necessary for modern representative democracy (polyarchal democracy), we can also view them as establishing a *minimum level for democratization.*

Those of us who live in the older democracies, where the transition to democracy occurred some generations ago and the political institutions listed in Figure 1 are by now solidly established, face a different and equally difficult challenge. For even if the institutions are necessary to democratization, they are definitely not *sufficient* for achieving fully the democratic criteria listed in Figure 1. Are we not then at liberty, and indeed obligated, to appraise our democratic institutions against these criteria? It seems obvious to me, as to many others, that judged against democratic criteria, our existing political institutions display many shortcomings.

Consequently, just as we need strategies for bringing about a transition to democracy in nondemocratic countries and for consolidating democratic institutions in newly democratized countries, so in the older democratic countries, we need to consider whether and how to move beyond our existing level of democracy.

Let me put it this way. In many countries, the task is to achieve democratization up to the level of polyarchal democracy. But the challenge to citizens in the older democracies is to discover how they might achieve a level of democratization *beyond* polyarchal democracy.

Notes

1. Political *arrangements* sound as if they might be rather provisional, which they could well be in a country that has just moved away from nondemocratic rule. We tend to think of *practices* as more habitual and therefore more durable. We usually think of *institutions* as having settled in for the long haul, passed on from one generation to the next. As a country moves from a nondemocratic to a democratic government, the early democratic *arrangements* gradually become *practices*, which in due time turn into settled *institutions.* Helpful though these distinction may be, however, for our purposes it will be more convenient if we put them aside and settle for *institutions.*

2. "The Hats assumed their name for being like the dashing fellows in the tricorne of the day. . . . The Caps were nicknamed because of the charge that they were like timid old ladies in nightcaps." Franklin D. Scott, *Sweden: The Nation's History* (Minneapolis: University of Minnesota Press, 1977), 243.

3. Alexis de Tocqueville, *Democracy in America*, vol. 1 (New York: Schocken Books, 1961), 51.

4. Tocqueville, *Democracy in America*, 50.

5. Polyarchy is derived from Greek words meaning "many" and "rule," thus "rule by the many," as distinguished from rule by the one, or monarchy, and rule by the few, oligarchy or aristocracy. Although the term had been rarely used, a colleague and I introduced it in 1953 as a handy way of referring to a modern representative democracy with universal suffrage. Hereafter I shall use it in that sense. More precisely, a polyarchal democracy is a political system with the six democratic institutions listed above. Polyarchal democracy, then, is different from representative democracy with restricted suffrage, as in the nineteenth century. It is also different from older democracies and republics that not only had a restricted suffrage but lacked many of the other crucial characteristics of polyarchal democracy, such as political parties, rights to form political organizations to influence or oppose the existing government, organized interest groups, and so on. It is different, too, from the democratic practices in units so small that members can assemble directly and make (or recommend) policies or laws.

6. A few delegates daringly forecast that the United States might ultimately have as many as one hundred million inhabitants. This number was reached in 1915.

7. John Stuart Mill, *Considerations on Representative Government* [1861] (New York: Liberal Arts Press, 1958), 55.

ROBERT A. DAHL is Sterling Professor Emeritus of Political Science, Yale University. He has published many books on democratic theory and practice, including *A Preface to Democratic Theory* (1956) and *Democracy and Its Critics* (1989). This article was adapted from his recent book, *On Democracy,* Yale University Press.

Interest Groups: Ex Uno, Plures

The last article in our series on the mature democracies asks whether they are in danger of being strangled by lobbyists and single-issue pressure groups.

Previous briefs in this series have looked at the imperfections in democracy as it is currently practised in the rich countries, and at some of the efforts that different countries are making to overcome them. Evidence that all is not well includes declining public confidence in politicians, falling membership of political parties and smaller turnouts for elections. Ideas for improvement range from making greater use of referendums and other forms of direct democracy, to giving more power to courts to check the power of politicians. This article asks a different question: far from being too powerful, are elected politicians in modern democracies too weak?

When Alexis de Tocqueville visited the United States in the 19th century, he was impressed by the enthusiasm of Americans for joining associations. This, he felt, spread power away from the centre and fostered the emergence of democratic habits and a civil society. Until quite recently, most political scientists shared De Tocqueville's view. Lately, however, and especially in America, doubts have set in. At a certain point, say the doubters, the cumulative power of pressure groups, each promoting its own special interests, can grow so strong that it prevents elected politicians from adopting policies that are in the interest of the electorate as a whole.

A Hitchhiker's Guide

A key text for such critics was a short book published in 1965 by Mancur Olson, an American economist. Called "The Logic of Collective Action", this took issue with the traditional idea that the health of democracy was served by vigorous competition between pressure groups, with governments acting as a sort of referee, able to choose the best policy once the debate between the contending groups was over. The traditional view, Olson argued, wrongly assumed that pressure groups were more or less equal. In fact, for a reason known to economists as the free-rider problem, they weren't.

Why? Take the example of five car firms, which form a lobbying group in the hope of raising the price of cars. If they succeed, each stands to reap a fifth of the gains. This makes forming the group and working for its success well worth each firm's investment of time and money. If the car makers succeed, of course, motorists will suffer. But organising millions of individual motorists to fight their corner is a great deal harder

because it involves co-ordinating millions of people and because the potential gain for each motorist will be relatively small. Individual motorists will be tempted to reason that, with millions of other people involved, they do not need to do anything themselves, but can instead hitch a "free ride" on the efforts of everyone else.

This simple insight has powerful implications. Indeed, in a later book Olson went on to argue that his theory helped to explain why some nations flourish and others decline. As pressure groups multiply over time, they tend to choke a nation's vitality by impairing the government's ability to act in the wider interest. That, he argued, is why countries such as Germany and Japan—whose interest groups had been cleared away by a traumatic defeat—had fared better after the second world war than Britain, whose institutions had survived intact. With its long record of stability, said Olson, "British society has acquired so many strong organisations and collusions that it suffers from an institutional sclerosis that slows its adaptation to changing circumstances and changing technologies."

Olson's ideas have not gone unchallenged. But they have had a big impact on contemporary thinking about what ails American democracy. In "Demosclerosis" (Times Books, 1994), Jonathan Rauch, a populariser of Olson's work, says that America is afflicted by "hyperpluralism". With at least seven out of ten Americans belonging to at least one such association, the whole society, not just "special" parts of it, is now involved in influence peddling.

The result is that elected politicians find it almost impossible to act solely in the wider public interest. Bill Clinton wants to reform the health system? The health-insurance industry blocks him. China's membership in the World Trade Organisation would benefit America's consumers? America's producers of textiles and steel stand in the way. Jimmy Carter complained when he left the presidency that Americans were increasingly drawn to single-issue groups to ensure that, whatever else happened, their own private interest would be protected. The trouble is, "the national interest is not always the sum of all our single or special interests".

Pressure groups are especially visible in the United States. As Oxford University's Jeremy Richardson puts it ("Pressure Groups", Oxford University Press, 1993), "pressure groups take account of (and exploit) the multiplicity of access points which is so characteristic of the American system of government—the presidency, the bureaucracy, both houses of Congress, the powerful congressional committees, the judiciary and state and local government."

Nevertheless pressure groups often wield just as much influence in other countries. In those where parliaments exercise tighter control of the executive—Canada, Britain or Germany, say—the government controls the parliamentary timetable and the powers of committees are much weaker. This means that pressure groups adopt different tactics. They have more chance of influencing policy behind closed doors, by bargaining with the executive branch and its civil servants before legislation comes before parliament. In this way pressure groups can sometimes exert more influence than their counterparts in America.

Political Tribes

Many European countries have also buttressed the influence of pressure groups by giving them a semi-official status. In Germany, for example, the executive branch is obliged by law to consult the various big "interest organisations" before drafting legislation. In some German states, leading interest groups (along with political parties) have seats on the supervisory boards of broadcasting firms.

French pressure groups are also powerful, despite the conventional image of a strong French state dominating a relatively weak civil society. It is true that a lot of France's interest groups depend on the state for both money and membership of a network of formal consultative bodies. But a tradition of direct protest compensates for some of this institutional weakness. In France, mass demonstrations, strikes, the blocking of roads and the disruption of public services are seen as a part of normal democratic politics.

In Japan, powerful pressure groups such as the Zenchu (Central Union of Agricultural Co-operatives) have turned large areas of public policy into virtual no-go areas. With more than 9m members (and an electoral system that gives farming communities up to three times the voting weight of urban voters), farmers can usually obstruct any policy that damages their interests. The teachers' union has similarly blocked all attempts at education reform. And almost every sector of Japanese society has its *zoku giin* (political tribes), consisting of Diet members who have made themselves knowledgeable about one industry or another, which pays for their secretaries and provides campaign funds. A Diet member belonging to the transport tribe will work hand-in-glove with senior bureaucrats in the transport ministry and the trucking industry to form what the Japanese call an "iron triangle" consisting of politicians, bureaucrats and big business.

Pressure groups are also increasingly active at a transnational level. Like any bureaucracy, the European Union has spawned a rich network of interest groups. In 1992 the European Commission reckoned that at least 3,000 special-interest groups in Brussels employing some 10,000 people acted as lobbyists. These range from big operations, such as the EU committee of the American Chamber of Commerce, to small firms and individual lobbyists-for-hire. Businesses were the first to spot the advantages of influencing the EU's law making. But trade unions swiftly followed, often achieving in Brussels breakthroughs (such as regulations on working conditions) that they could not achieve at home.

The Case for the Defense

So pressure groups are ubiquitous. But are they so bad? Although it has been influential, the Olson thesis has not swept all before it. Many political scientists argue that the traditional view that pressure groups create a healthy democratic pluralism is nearer the mark than Olson's thesis.

The case in favour of pressure groups begins with some of the flaws of representative democracy. Elections are infrequent and, as a previous brief in this series noted, political parties can be vague about their governing intentions. Pressure groups help people to take part in politics between elections, and to influence a government's policy in areas that they care and know about. Pressure groups also check excessive central power and give governments expert advice. Although some groups may flourish at the expense of the common weal, this danger can be guarded against if there are many groups and if all have the same freedom to organise and to put their case to government.

Critics of Olson's ideas also point out that, contrary to his prediction, many broad-based groups have in fact managed to flourish in circumstances where individual members stand to make little personal gain and should therefore fall foul of his "free-rider" problem. Clearly, some people join pressure groups for apparently altruistic reasons—perhaps simply to express their values or to be part of an organisation in which they meet like-minded people. Some consumer and environmental movements have flourished in rich countries, even though Olson's theory suggests that firms and polluters should have a strong organisational advantage over consumers and inhalers of dirty air.

Moreover, despite "demosclerosis", well-organised pressure groups can sometimes ease the task of government, not just throw sand into its wheels. The common European practice of giving pressure groups a formal status, and often a legal right to be consulted, minimises conflict by ensuring that powerful groups put their case to governments before laws are introduced. Mr Richardson argues in a forthcoming book ("Developments in the European Union", Macmillan, 1999) that even the pressure groups clustering around the institutions of the EU perform a valuable function. The European Commission, concerned with the detail of regulation, is an eager consumer of their specialist knowledge. As the powers of the European Parliament have grown, it too has attracted a growing band of lobbyists. The parliament has created scores of "intergroups" whose members gain expertise in specific sectors, such as pharmaceuticals, from industry and consumer lobbies.

Governments can learn from pressure groups, and can work through them to gain consent for their policies. At some point, however, the relationship becomes excessively cosy. If pressure groups grow too strong, they can deter governments from pursuing policies which are in the wider public interest. The temptation of governments to support protectionist trade policies at the behest of producer lobbies and at the expense of consumers is a classic example supporting Olson's theories. But problems also arise when it is governments that are relatively strong, and so able to confer special status on some pressure groups and withhold it from others. This puts less-favoured groups at a disadvantage, which they often seek to redress by finding new and sometimes less democratic ways of making their voices heard.

In Germany, for example, disenchantment with what had come to be seen as an excessively cosy system of bargaining between elite groups helped to spark an explosion of protest movements in the 1980s. In many other countries, too, there is a sense that politics has mutated since the 1960s from an activity organised largely around parties to one organised around specialised interest groups on the one hand (such as America's gun lobby) and broader protest and social movements on the other (such as the women's movement, environmentalism and consumerism). One reason for the change is clearly the growth in the size and scope of government. Now that it touches virtually every aspect of people's lives, a bewildering array of groups has sprung up around it.

Many of Olson's disciples blame pressure groups for making government grow. As each special group wins new favours from the state, it makes the state bigger and clumsier, undermining the authority of elected parties, loading excessive demands on government in general, and preventing any particular government from acting in the interest of the relatively disorganised majority of people. By encouraging governments to do too much, say critics on the right, pressure groups prevent governments from doing anything well. Their solution is for governments to do less. Critics on the left are more inclined to complain that pressure groups exaggerate inequalities by giving those better-organised (ie, the rich and powerful) an influence out of all proportion to their actual numbers.

So what is to be done? A lot could be, but little is likely to be. There is precious little evidence from recent elections to suggest that the citizens of the rich countries want to see a radical cut in the size or scope of the state. As for political inequality, even this has its defenders. John Mueller, of America's University of Rochester, argues that democracy has had a good, if imperfect, record of dealing with minority issues, particularly when compared with other forms of government. But he claims that this is less because democratic majorities are tolerant of minorities and more because democracy gives minorities the opportunity

to increase their effective political weight—to become more equal, more important, than their arithmetical size would imply—on issues that concern them. This holds even for groups held in contempt by the majority, like homosexuals. Moreover, the fact that most people most of the time pay little attention to politics—the phenomenon of political apathy—helps interested minorities to protect their rights and to assert their interests.

Adaptability

This series of briefs has highlighted some of the defects in the practice of democracy, and some of the changes that the mature democracies are making in order to improve matters. But the defects need to be kept in perspective.

One famous critic of democracy claimed that for most people it did nothing more than allow them "once every few years, to decide which particular representatives of the oppressing class should be in parliament to represent and oppress them". When Marx wrote those words in the 19th century, they contained an element of truth. Tragically, Lenin treated this view as an eternal verity, with calamitous results for millions of people. What they both ignored was democracy's ability to evolve, which is perhaps its key virtue. Every mature democracy continues to evolve today. As a result, violent revolution in those countries where democracy has taken deepest root looks less attractive, and more remote, than ever.

Political Parties: Empty Vessels?

Alexis de Tocqueville called political parties an evil inherent in free governments. The second of our briefs on the mature democracies in transition asks whether parties are in decline.

What would democracy look like if there were no political parties? It is almost impossible to imagine. In every democracy worth the name, the contest to win the allegiance of the electorate and form a government takes place through political parties. Without them, voters would be hard put to work out what individual candidates stood for or intended to do once elected. If parties did not "aggregate" people's interests, politics might degenerate into a fight between tiny factions, each promoting its narrow self-interest. But for the past 30 years, political scientists have been asking whether parties are "in decline". Are they? And if so, does it matter?

Generalising about political parties is difficult. Their shape depends on a country's history, constitution and much else. For example, America's federal structure and separation of powers make Republicans and Democrats amorphous groupings whose main purpose is to put their man in the White House. British parties behave quite differently because members of Parliament must toe the party line to keep their man in Downing Street. An American president is safe once elected, so congressmen behave like local representatives rather than members of a national organisation bearing collective responsibility for government. Countries which, unlike Britain and America, hold elections under proportional representation are different again: they tend to produce multi-party systems and coalition governments.

Despite these differences, some trends common to almost all advanced democracies appear to be changing the nature of parties and, on one view, making them less influential. Those who buy this thesis of decline point to the following changes:

People's behaviour is becoming more **private**. Why join a political party when you can go fly fishing or surf the web? Back in the 1950s, clubs affiliated to the Labour Party were places for Britain's working people to meet, play and study. The Conservative Party was, among other things, a marriage bureau for the better-off. Today, belonging to a British political party is more like being a supporter of some charity: you may pay a membership fee, but will not necessarily attend meetings or help to turn out the vote at election time.

Running out of Ideas

Politics is becoming more **secular**. Before the 1960s, political struggles had an almost religious intensity: in much of Western Europe this took the form of communists versus Catholics, or workers versus bosses. But ideological differences were narrowing by the 1960s and became smaller still after the collapse of Soviet communism. Nowadays, politics seems to be more often about policies than values, about the competence of leaders rather than the beliefs of the led. As education grows and class distinctions blur, voters discard old loyalties. In America in 1960, two out of five voters saw themselves as "strong" Democrats or "strong" Republicans. By 1996 less than one in three saw themselves that way. The proportion of British voters expressing a "very strong" affinity with one party slumped from 44% to 16% between 1964 and 1997. This process of **"partisan de-alignment"** has been witnessed in most mature democracies.

The erosion of loyalty is said to have pushed parties towards the **ideological centre**. The political extremes have not gone away. But mainstream parties which used to offer a straight choice between socialists and conservatives are no longer so easy to label. In the late 1950s Germany's Social Democrats (SPD) snipped off their Marxist roots in order to recast themselves is a *Volkspartei* appealing to all the people. "New" Labour no longer portrays itself as the political arm of the British working class or trade-union movement. Bill Clinton, before he became president, helped to shift the Democratic Party towards an appreciation of business and free trade. Neat ideological labels have become harder to pin on parties since they have had to contend with the emergence of what some commentators call **post-material issues** (such as the environment, personal morality and consumer rights) which do not slot elegantly into the old left-right framework.

The **mass media** have taken over many of the information functions that parties once performed for themselves. "Just as radio and television have largely killed off the door-to-door salesman," says Anthony King, of Britain's Essex University, "so they have largely killed off the old-fashioned party worker." In 1878 the German SPD had nearly 50 of its own newspapers. Today the mass media enable politicians to communicate directly with voters without owning printing presses or needing party workers to knock on doors. In many other ways, the business of winning elections has become more capital-intensive and less labour-intensive, making political donors matter more and political activists less.

Another apparent threat to the parties is the growth of **interest and pressure groups**. Why should voters care about the broad sweep of policy promoted during elections by a party when other organisations will lobby all year round for their special interest, whether this is protection of the environment, opposition to abortion, or the defence of some subsidy? Some academics also claim that parties are playing a smaller role, and **think tanks** a bigger one, in making policy. Although parties continue to draw up election manifestos, they are wary of being too specific. Some hate leaving policymaking to party activists, who may be more extreme than voters at large and so put them off. Better to keep the message vague. Or why not let the tough choices be taken by **referendums**, as so often in Switzerland?

Academics have found these trends easier to describe than to evaluate. Most agree that the age of the "mass party" has passed and that its place is being taken by the "electoral-professional" or "catch-all" party. Although still staffed by politicians holding genuine beliefs and values, these modern parties are inclined to see their main objective as winning elections rather than forming large membership organisations or social movements, as was once the case.

Is this a bad thing? Perhaps, if it reduces participation in politics. One of the traditional roles of political parties has been to get out the vote, and in 18 out of 20 rich countries, recent turnout figures have been lower than they were in the 1950s. Although it is hard to pin down the reasons, Martin Wattenberg, of the University of California at Irvine, points out that turnout has fallen most sharply in countries where parties are weak: Switzerland (thanks to

those referendums), America and France (where presidential elections have become increasingly candidate- rather than party-centred), and Japan (where political loyalties revolve around ties to internal factions rather than the party itself). In Scandinavia, by contrast, where class-based parties are still relatively strong, turnout has held up much better since the 1950s.

Running out of Members

It is not only voters who are turned off. Party membership is falling too, and even the most strenuous attempts to reverse the decline have faltered. Germany is a case in point. The Social Democrats there increased membership rapidly in the 1960s and 1970s, and the Christian Democrats responded by doubling their own membership numbers. But since the end of the 1980s membership has been falling, especially among the young. In 1964 Britain's Labour Party had about 830,000 members and the Conservatives about 2m. By 1997 they had 420,000 and 400,000 respectively. The fall is sharper in some countries than others, but research by Susan Scarrow of the University of Houston suggests that the trend is common to most democracies (see figure 1). With their membership falling, ideological differences blurring, and fewer people turning out to vote, the decline thesis looks hard to refute.

Or does it? The case for party decline has some big holes in it. For a start, some academics question whether political parties ever really enjoyed the golden age which other academics hark back to. Essex University's Mr King points out that a lot of the evidence for decline is drawn from a handful of parties—Britain's two main ones, the German SPD, the French and Italian Communists—which did indeed once promote clear ideologies, enjoy mass memberships, and organise local branches and social activities. But neither of America's parties, nor Canada's, nor many of the bourgeois parties of Western Europe, were ever mass parties of that sort. Moreover, in spite of their supposed decline, parties continue to keep an iron grip on many aspects of politics.

In most places, for example, parties still control **nomination for public office**. In almost all of the mature democracies, it is rare for independent candidates to be elected to federal or state legislatures, and even in local government the proportion of independents has declined sharply since the early 1970s. When state and local parties select candidates, they usually favour people who have worked hard within the party. German parties, for example, are often conduits to jobs in the public sector, with a say over appointments to top jobs in the civil service and to the boards of publicly owned utilities or media organisations. Even in America, where independent candidates are more common in local elections, the parties still run city, county and state "machines" in which most politicians start their careers.

Naturally, there are some exceptions. In 1994 Silvio Berlusconi, a media tycoon, was able to make himself prime minister at the head of Forza Italia, a right-wing movement drawing heavily on his personal fortune and the resources of his television empire. Ross Perot, a wealthy third-party candidate, won a respectable 19% vote in his 1992 bid for the American presidency. The party declinists claim these examples as evidence for their case. But it is notable that in the end Mr Perot could not compete against the two formidable campaigning and money-raising machines ranged against him.

This suggests that a decline in the membership of parties need not make them weaker in **money and organisation**. In fact, many have enriched themselves simply by passing laws that give them public money. In Germany, campaign subsidies to the federal parties more than trebled between 1970 and 1990, and parties now receive between 20% and 40% of their income from public funds. In America, the paid professionals who have taken over from party activists tend to do their job more efficiently. Moreover, other kinds of political activity—such as donating money to a party or interest group, or attending meetings and rallies—have become more common in America. Groups campaigning for particular causes or candidates (the pro-Republican Christian Coalition, say, or the pro-Democrat National Education Association) may not be formally affiliated with the major party organisations, but are frequently allied with them.

The role of the mass media deserves a closer look as well. It is true that they have weakened the parties' traditional methods of communicating with members. But parties have invested heavily in managing relations with journalists, and making use of new media to reach both members and wider audiences. In Britain, the dwindling of local activists has gone hand-in-hand with a more professional approach to communications. Margaret Thatcher caused a stir by using an advertising firm, Saatchi & Saatchi, to push the Tory cause in the 1979 election. By the

time of Britain's 1997 election, the New Labour media operation run from Millbank Tower in London was even slicker.

Another way to gauge the influence of parties is by their **reach**—that is, their power, once in office, to take control of the governmental apparatus. This is a power they have retained. Most governments tend to be unambiguously under the control of people who represent a party, and who would not be in government if they did not belong to such organisations. The French presidential system may appear ideal for independent candidates, but except—arguably—for Charles de Gaulle, who claimed to rise above party, none has ever been elected without party support.

The Fire Next Time

Given the cautions that must be applied to other parts of the case for party decline, what can be said about one of the declinists' key exhibits, the erosion of ideological differences? At first sight, this is borne out by the recent movement to the centre of left-leaning parties such as America's Democrats, New Labour in Britain, and the SPD under Gerhard Schröder. In America, Newt Gingrich stoked up some fire amongst Republicans in 1994, but it has flickered out. The most popular Republican presidential hopefuls, and especially George W. Bush, the front-runner, are once again stressing the gentler side of their conservatism.

Still, the claim of ideological convergence can be exaggerated. It is not much more than a decade since Ronald Reagan and Mrs Thatcher ran successful parties with strong ideologies. And the anecdotal assumption that parties are growing less distinct is challenged by longer-term academic studies. A look at the experience of ten western democracies since 1945 ("Parties, Policies and Democracy", Westview Press, 1994) concluded that the leading left and right parties continued to keep their distance and maintain their identity, rather than clustering around the median voter in the centre. Paul Webb of Britain's Brunel University concludes in a forthcoming book ("Political Parties in Advanced Industrial Democracies", Oxford University Press) that although partisan sentiment is weaker than it was, and voters more cynical, parties have in general adapted well to changing circumstances.

Besides, even if party differences are narrowing at present, why expect that trend to continue? In Western Europe, the ending of the cold war has snuffed out one source of ideological conflict, but new sparks might catch fire. Battered right-wing parties may try to revive their fortunes by pushing the nationalist cause against the encroachments of the European Union. In some places where ideas are dividing parties less, geography is dividing them more.

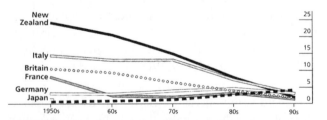

Figure 1   The Few Not the Many. Party members as % of electorate.

Source: Susan E. Scarrow, Centre for German and European Studies Working Paper 2.59, University of California, Berkeley.

Politics in Germany and Britain has acquired an increasingly regional flavour: Labour and the Social Democrats respectively dominate the north, Conservatives and Christian Democrats the south. Disaffected *Ossis* are flocking to the Party of Democratic Socialism in eastern Germany. Britain, Italy, Canada and Spain have strong separatist parties.

So there is life in the party system yet. But the declinists are on to something. The Germans have a word for it. One reason given for the rise of Germany's Greens in the 1980s and America's Mr Perot in 1992 was *Parteienverdrossenheit*—disillusionment with mainstream parties that seemed to have abandoned their core beliefs and no longer offered meaningful choices. A "new politics" of citizens' protests appeared to be displacing conventional politics.

In the end, far from undermining the domination of the parties, the German Greens ended up by turning themselves into one and joining the government in an uneasy coalition with the SPD. The balance of evidence from around the world is that despite all the things that are changing them, parties continue to dominate democratic politics.

Indeed, there are grounds for wondering whether their continuing survival is more of a worry than their supposed decline. Is it so very comforting that parties can lose members, worry less about ideas, become detached from broader social movements, attract fewer voters and still retain an iron grip on politics? If they are so unanchored, will they not fall prey to special-interest groups? If they rely on state funding instead of member contributions, will they not turn into creatures of the state? The role of money in politics will be the subject of another brief.

Asia's Democracy Backlash

Leaders of nations like Cambodia, Laos, and Vietnam have begun to debate how they can apply a Chinese model to their own nations.

Joshua Kurlantzick

So intense is the chaos in the Bangladeshi capital of Dhaka that to an outsider it often seems miraculous that the city actually functions. At intersections, mobs of rickshaws, motorcycles, and luxury cars vie for space with vendors and homeless people wandering in all directions. Sidewalks are crowded with so many people—the megacity is one of the largest in the world—that you must push through the pack just to move.

Normally, the city's politics mirrors its daily life. For years, university students allied with either of the two major parties have led boisterous rallies and street protests at election time, demonstrations often so fevered that they descend into violence. Vendors sell huge numbers of vernacular and English-language newspapers, which offer tens of thousands of words of political coverage.

But over the past two years, Dhaka—or at least its politics—has quieted considerably. In January 2007, a caretaker government preparing for a new Bangladeshi election stepped down, probably because of pressure from the military, and the army soon asserted itself even more. Working only barely behind the scenes, it organized a new government, declared a state of emergency, and soon detained thousands of political activists, putatively as part of a campaign to eliminate graft from politics. After promises to hold a new election, the military and its caretaker regime scheduled voting for the late date of December 2008.

Bangladesh is hardly unique in experiencing undemocratic developments. Asia once was regarded as the vanguard of a global wave of democratization that, over the past three decades, has swept through southern Europe, Latin America, and Africa as well. In recent years, however, Asia has witnessed a democracy backlash. Across the region, armed forces once believed confined to their barracks have begun to reassert their power. Quasi-authoritarian rulers in Sri Lanka, Cambodia, the Philippines, and other nations have drastically strengthened the power of the state, unleashing security forces on political opponents, using emergency decrees to consolidate power, and cracking down on civil society. And in the region's most repressive states, such as Myanmar (formerly Burma), progress toward greater freedom appears to have stalled entirely.

The Freedom Façade

South and Southeast Asia in the late 1990s and early in this decade rode the crest of a wave of democratization that encompassed much of the developing world. During the Asian financial crisis in the late 1990s, protesters in Indonesia toppled the long-ruling dictator Suharto and established a new, multiparty political system. In Malaysia at roughly the same time, protesters lashed out at the authoritarian rule of Mahathir Mohamad. Liberalization spread to East Timor, then a part of Indonesia, and after a bloody conflict Timor won its independence and established a nascent democracy. Cambodia emerged from years of civil war to hold a series of elections in the 1990s.

Across the region, armed forces once believed confined to their barracks have begun to reassert their power.

Even long-suffering Myanmar, ruled since 1962 by the military, seemed ready to change, as the junta released pro-democracy opposition leader Daw Aung San Suu Kyi from house arrest in 2002 and allowed her to tour the country. She drew massive crowds hopeful for political change and proclaimed "a new dawn for the country."

As economies grew rapidly and publics became more politically active, nations such as Thailand and Bangladesh drew up liberal constitutions supposedly designed to strengthen civil society, protect minority rights, and check the power of entrenched actors like the military and powerful business interests. In vibrant Asian cities like Bangkok and Kuala Lumpur, where rapid growth had produced towering skylines, sleek new roads, and flashy shopping districts, the idea of military coups now seemed obsolete.

But recent years have revealed that some of this democratization was a façade. (To be sure, Asia's longest-established democracies, Japan and India, suffer few of these weaknesses; and South Korea and Taiwan, though unruly, do not seem at risk of backsliding.) In some cases, the apparent vibrancy reflected merely economic liberalization, and democracy had not sunk deep roots.

Quasi-authoritarian states like Singapore and Malaysia did understand the need for financial transparency, since that was critical to attracting the foreign investment that has powered their economic miracles. Yet Singapore and Malaysia—like China and, to some extent, Vietnam—have managed to build walls around their political processes, promoting financial and economic transparency while using subtle means to undermine political liberalization. They have held highly controlled elections while allowing few other facets of democracy, such as union organizing, independent media, or trade associations. Foreign investors, who care mostly about financial probity, offer little protest about these dual policies, and have said nothing when countries like Malaysia jail activists.

Even countries in South and Southeast Asia that seem more democratic than Malaysia still have papered over major flaws. Few have established effective methods of probing state corruption or electoral fraud. Despite holding elections and writing constitutions, many Asian nations have never assimilated a central premise of democracy—the idea that once a party loses it must respect the system by serving as a loyal opposition, working within the established political framework and honoring constitutional rules.

Instead, from the Philippines to Bangladesh to Thailand—where large popular movements in the past have overthrown dictators—individuals and organized groups dissatisfied with the results of free elections have continually taken their cases to the streets. Because these nations constantly rely on "people power" to change governments, they have invested little in building democratic institutions or in promoting equitable development.

In Manila, street protests nicknamed People Power 2 toppled President Joseph Estrada in 2001 and brought to power his vice president, Gloria Macapagal Arroyo. Although Estrada had been far from flawless in office—he packed his administration with unqualified cronies and became enmeshed in vast corruption scandals—he had been popularly elected. Three years later, similar demonstrations almost brought Arroyo down.

In Bangladesh, political parties run by two women who reportedly detest each other, Sheikh Hasina Wazed and Begum Khaleda Zia, have taken this unwillingness to capitulate to rules to a perverse extreme. When one party wins an election, the opposition often responds with waves of paralyzing strikes and protests, attempting to make the country ungovernable. These strikes only foster political violence. Numerous assaults on party gatherings have occurred, including a 2004 grenade attack against Sheikh Hasina's entourage in which 21 people were killed.

Asians, meanwhile, have not entirely banished the men in green. Although militaries rarely intervened in domestic politics in the late 1990s and early in this decade, few Asian countries have established complete civilian control over their armed forces. (In several nations, like Pakistan and Myanmar, the military never truly left politics.) In many South Pacific nations such as Fiji, military officers have constantly threatened coups, sometimes successfully toppling governments. In the Philippines and Bangladesh (as in Kazakhstan and Uzbekistan, among other countries), security forces have continued to operate unencumbered by laws, killing suspected opponents of whichever government is in power, running off-the-books businesses, and trafficking in weapons and drugs.

The Fading Beacon

At the same time, over the past decade the balance of power among external actors in Southeast and South Asia has shifted dramatically. For decades, the United States was the major external power in Asia, and in the late 1990s and early in this decade Washington rhetorically committed itself to pushing for democratization and better governance in the region.

In the past five years, however, this commitment has weakened. The war on terror has consumed the White House's attention and undermined America's moral standing. Demanding counterterrorism cooperation in Asia, the United States often has ignored efforts by countries such as Cambodia and Malaysia to use the war on terror to crack down on critics—for example, through Malaysia's Internal Security Act, a colonial-era relic that allows for detention without trial.

Focused on Iraq, the United States also has had little time to confront problems like the ongoing human rights crisis in Myanmar, where the army's scorched-earth tactics—which include widespread rape—have displaced nearly 1 million people in the eastern part of the country, and where the junta this year held, just days after a catastrophic cyclone hit, a sham national "referendum" designed to strengthen its control.

Washington did help to push Myanmar onto the agenda of the United Nations Security Council after the junta's crackdown on the so-called Saffron Revolution in 2007. But when the Security Council refused to take tough action, the administration of George W. Bush declined to invest more time and resources in the issue. Some U.S. officials suggested that China should lead the effort to bring reform to Myanmar, a task for which Beijing has shown little appetite; it was China, in fact, that blocked UN action against Myanmar. The United States, meanwhile, does not even have an ambassador in the country.

More generally, scandals at Abu Ghraib in Iraq, Guantanamo Bay in Cuba, and other prisons have damaged the United States' image as a guarantor of freedom. Authoritarian nations like China and Russia, both of which are flexing their muscles in Asia, now have a ready response to American criticism of their human rights records—the United States, they argue, is no better. (For years, China has responded to the State Department's annual report on human rights in China with its own paper on human rights in America; Beijing now has considerable evidence it can marshal in its report.)

In the late 1990s, many reformers and activists in Asia wanted to be associated with the United States and its blossoming democracy promotion outfits, like the National Endowment for Democracy, the National Democratic Institute, and the International Republican Institute. By the mid-2000s, America's image in Asia had plummeted so far that many activists took pains not to be linked to U.S. funding. And President Bush's linking of democracy promotion to the war in Iraq led citizens of many nations to associate democratization with images of turmoil televised from Baghdad.

Model Competitors

As America's standing has weakened, China and Russia have made impressive gains in the region. Indeed, they are advertising their undemocratic systems—according to which they have moderately liberalized their economies while avoiding concurrent political reform—as development models that Asian countries should emulate. China and Russia also emphasize a doctrine of noninterference, arguing that countries should not intervene in other nations' internal affairs—interference that could include sanctioning human rights violators or supporting pro-democracy movements.

Beijing in particular, employing more effective diplomacy than the United States—and with a growing aid program that now outstrips American assistance in countries like the Philippines, Myanmar, and Cambodia—has transformed its image in Asia from that of an economic and political threat to a more benign neighbor, and even a model. China promotes its style of development through a rising number of training programs for top leaders and mid-level technocrats in countries like Vietnam, Laos, and Pakistan. It also provides sufficient aid and investment to authoritarian nations to render meaningless Western efforts to influence the regime in Myanmar, for example, or to pressure the Cambodian government into improving its human rights climate.

Russia, for its part, has begun to wield greater influence in Central Asia, where many top leaders still have Soviet backgrounds. With the growing cash hoard it is accumulating because of the high price of oil, Russia has funded the creation of new NGO-like organizations that *fight* democracy promotion efforts in Central Asia, while providing assistance to Central Asian autocrats and training to some of their security forces.

Some Asian countries appear to be listening to Beijing and Moscow. Leaders of nations such as Cambodia, Laos, and Vietnam have begun to debate how they can apply a Chinese model to their own nations. At the same time that Beijing promotes a nondemocratic model, China's growing power also ties the United States' hands in Asia. When faced with antidemocratic behavior across the region, Washington must be increasingly careful how it responds, for fear of pushing these countries more firmly into Beijing's orbit.

Quasi-authoritarian rulers in Sri Lanka, Cambodia, the Philippines, and other nations have drastically strengthened the power of the state.

Revenge of the Autocrats

Over the past five years, all these trends have coalesced, creating Asia's democracy backlash. The dangerous mix of years of venal and corrupt rule in countries like Bangladesh and the Philippines, combined with the failure to build institutions for funneling protest into peaceful channels, has finally exploded.

In East Timor, disgruntled young men descended last year on the streets of Dili, the low-rise capital, to fight it out with knives and slingshots. Until foreign troops intervened, rioters burned block after city block, leaving Dili a morass of charred and gutted buildings. In Bangladesh in 2007, thousands of protesters charged through Dhaka's alleys and tin-roofed slum dwellings. They attacked stores and clashed with riot police and thousands of soldiers, battling with stones and sticks until demonstrators fled the scene, their faces bleeding and clothes ripped apart.

Militaries have asserted themselves in Asian nations beyond Bangladesh. In Thailand, another supposedly consolidated democracy, the army seized power in a September 2006 coup. The coup followed months of street demonstrations against the government of then–Prime Minister Thaksin Shinawatra, a popularly elected leader who had used his power to neuter the courts, civil society, and the Thai bureaucracy, and to launch a war against drugs that killed thousands of innocent citizens. The Thai military soon shredded the country's reformist constitution, written in 1997.

In Fiji, the military seized power in December 2006 and amassed emergency powers, announcing that it did so to battle corruption and that it would hold elections in far-off 2010. The Fijian armed forces then censored the press and arrested at least two dozen prominent activists.

At first, many liberals embraced these military interventions. In Bangladesh, crowds initially cheered the takeover as a balm against the corruption and political violence that had created chaos in the run-up to the January 2007 election, in which at least 45 people were killed. In a poll taken in October 2006 by the Bangladeshi newspaper *Daily Star,* most respondents had expressed anger at "inter-party bickering, unbridled corruption [and] total lack of governance."

Likewise, many middle class Bangkok residents hailed the coup-makers. Thai girls celebrated the takeover by placing flowers in army tanks in the capital. Reform-minded Thai liberals (and some Western commentators), from newspaper editors to academics, praised the military for stepping in.

The generals, however, proved incapable of ruling. Asian military rulers who take power today must deal with far more complex and globalized economies than was the case in the 1960s and 1970s. They also must deal with publics that have become accustomed to democracy, and are less willing to abide by martial law and bans on political activity.

In Fiji, the government reserve bank admitted that the coup had depressed economic development. In Thailand, the army vacillated between reassuring investors and implementing measures such as currency interventions and new protectionist laws that terrified many foreign businesses. The military also demonstrated it did not understand how to interact with the modern media: The army cracked down on the press in 2007 and even banned CNN when it aired an interview with Thaksin, even as activists in Bangkok became more openly critical of the military regime.

Reforms under Siege

At the same time that these outright coups against democracies have been occurring, many of the region's other governments have used subtler means of undermining political freedoms. In quasi-authoritarian Cambodia, Prime Minister Hun Sen has consolidated near-total power over the past five years, using the legal system, which he dominates, to arrest opponents and silence prominent critics for defaming the government. He also has co-opted nearly the entire political opposition, so that his party is left with virtually no one arrayed against it in the legislature. A possible new gusher of oil to be exploited off Cambodia's shores will only add to Hun Sen's power, since it will further decrease the influence of foreign donors over his regime. In Vietnam, the government has arrested pro-democracy lawyers and other activists trying to build a political opposition.

Sri Lanka also has become a major offender. In December 2006, after a peace process with separatist Tamil Tigers collapsed, the government issued new emergency laws giving it greater power to control the media and civil society. Since then, the conservative Sri Lankan government, which is allied with Sinhalese hard-line nationalist parties, has become more and more repressive, using the civil war against the Tamil Tigers to crack down more broadly on legitimate dissent.

Over the past two years, according to Amnesty International, at least 10 journalists in Sri Lanka have been killed, while several others have disappeared or have been jailed under the emergency laws and tortured. The disappearances have extended beyond writers: Last year, the UN's working group on disappearances documented more such vanishings in Sri Lanka than in any other country in the world. Meanwhile, the Sri Lankan government has been expelling Tamils from the capital, Colombo, for no reason other than their ethnic background. The situation is unlikely to improve soon, as the government has recently stepped up its war against the Tamil Tigers, attacking them across the north of the country with heavy troop deployments.

The Philippines, a longstanding bastion of democracy, also has backslid badly. This year Freedom House downgraded its rating for the Philippines from "free" to "partly free." Indeed, it warned, "Asia's oldest democracy has become increasingly dysfunctional." Citing vast corruption and potential rigging of voting machinery, Freedom House also alleges that the Philippine military has had a hand in the killings of hundreds of activists, particularly left-leaning activists, in recent years. Journalists have been targets, with a rising number of reporters murdered as well. Two years ago, too, President Arroyo invoked emergency rule and then used that legislation to arrest many anti-government activists.

In Myanmar, of course, the regime responded to the 2007 Saffron Revolution with a brutal and bloody crackdown, after which thousands of monks and other activists were killed or tossed in prison. Then the junta exploited the devastating May 2008 cyclone to consolidate its hold on power, resisting all international efforts to use the disaster to push for political reform.

The Jakarta Model

Still, the trend is not all negative. In Thailand in 2007, a year after the coup, voters did elect a new government. The period spent under military rule left the country in such turmoil, however, that it now faces a near future of unstable governments and, possibly, frequent elections. In recent months, street protests have continued to dominate Bangkok, leading to clashes with security forces and even a protester takeover of the prime minister's offices. The elected prime minister, Samak Sundarvej, was forced out of office in September 2008, though his party still controlled the government.

In Malaysia, elections early this year, in which opposition parties won a far larger share of the vote than normal, suggested a possible opening of the political system. The kingdom of Bhutan held its first democratic elections in March 2008. And in Nepal, autocratic rule by the monarchy has given way to a democratic process, although recent elections brought into the government former Maoist insurgents, already known for their harsh repression of dissent.

But one young Asian democracy stands out. A decade ago, Indonesian protesters carrying firebombs and machetes rampaged through downtown Jakarta, furious over years of political repression and the country's impending economic collapse. Many took out their anger on Indonesia's Chinese minority, which controlled a high percentage of the nation's wealth. Mobs focused on ethnic Chinese-owned businesses such as shopping malls and gold stores, and men on motorcycles led some of the rioters to selected Chinese-owned shops, where they locked the proprietors inside and burned the buildings to the ground. Perhaps as many as 70,000 Chinese Indonesians fled the country, and many more escaped Jakarta for quieter parts of the archipelago, like Bali.

Other types of inter-ethnic and inter-religious violence raged through remote regions such as Aceh and the Maluku Islands, where warring bands of men chopped off their enemies' heads and posted them on spikes alongside roads.

Only a decade later, Indonesia has made astonishing strides, and can claim to have become the most stable democracy in Southeast Asia. Leaders have been pushing to enshrine minority rights, opening the political field to ethnic Chinese politicians: At least 30 Indonesian Chinese ran for parliament in 2004 elections.

And the acceptance of minority rights, in a nation where 10 years ago mobs burned ethnic Chinese alive, is but one sign of Indonesia's transformation. The government of President Susilio Bambang Yudhyono has tried to inculcate a stronger democratic culture. Yudhyono, himself a former general, was elected in 2004 in the first direct presidential poll in Indonesian history, and since then he has led a truly progressive government.

Rather than focusing on the elite, capital-centered politics of the kind found in Manila or Bangkok, the administration has built democratic culture from the grassroots, aggressively decentralizing power and bringing more control over local politics to local politicians, while also offering greater autonomy to regions of the country like Aceh, which suffered a 30-year-long separatist war. Thus far, though the region's erst-while rebels have engaged in sporadic firefights, the peace process in Aceh has mostly held, with rebels laying down arms, the Indonesian military withdrawing troops from the region, and Aceh holding local elections.

The decentralization has strengthened and stabilized rural democracy. A report by *Asia Times* found that in recent years voters have removed nearly 40 percent of local-level incumbents, fostering a healthy climate of accountability. Local-level democracy, *Asia Times* noted, is also healing religious differences and reducing the threat of political Islam, since Muslims and Christians are teaming up to form local tickets. And, combined with economic decentralization, the political decentralization has provided provincial and local governments with more resources, which they can use to improve social welfare.

Under Yudhyono, the state has strengthened Indonesian institutions designed to hold powerful politicians accountable. The president, for example, has backed court decisions that overturned Internal Security Act–like laws that protected Indonesian leaders from criticism and had been used in the past to jail political opponents. Increased accountability in turn has strengthened average Indonesians' belief in the democratic system.

Democratic Inroads

Almost alone among Southeast Asian leaders, Yudhyono also has realized that Asian nations must push for democracy among their neighbors if political liberalization is to entrench itself in the region. He has recognized that the most antidemocratic countries, like Myanmar, breed the type of instability that spreads transnational problems like drugs and illegal migration to the rest of Asia.

While most Southeast Asian leaders avoid even talking about Myanmar, Yudhyono has openly warned Myanmar officials that their country must move faster on its constitution-drafting process and work toward implementing democracy. In Thailand and even India, by contrast, leaders said little after the Saffron Revolution crackdown. India's petroleum minister even visited Myanmar to sign new contracts while the Saffron protests were still going on.

The recent changes within Indonesia have proved popular with the public. Opinion polls not only give Yudhyono high marks; they also strongly and repeatedly endorse democracy. In one comprehensive poll conducted by the Indonesia Survey Institute, 82 percent of respondents said that they supported democracy—even as Thais in Bangkok welcomed military rule. Indonesian opposition parties also have proved willing to resolve electoral losses within the political system, rather than demanding the overthrow of the government.

Economic transparency in Southeast Asia has not necessarily signified political liberalization.

Clearly Indonesia still faces high hurdles, including military officers reluctant to give up powers they gained during the 30-year Suharto era, and judges too often unwilling to punish military abuses. Before Yudhyono stands, as expected, for reelection in 2009, he will have to build a more consolidated and organized party around his progressive values to ensure that his ideas live on.

Yet Indonesia's transformation offers examples to other Asian states of how to consolidate a vibrant democracy. Indeed, before the region's democracy backlash gains more strength, progressive leaders from Cambodia to Bangladesh would be wise to pay attention to Jakarta. The United States, too, must pay more attention to a region that is economically dynamic and once seemed on the edge of total democratization. If Washington backs antidemocrats, it abandons its image as a guarantor of freedoms, and opens the door wider for other actors, like China, to make greater gains in the region.

JOSHUA KURLANTZICK, a *Current History* contributing editor, is a visiting scholar at the Carnegie Endowment for International Peace. He is the author of *Charm Offensive: How China's Soft Power Is Transforming the World* (Yale University Press, 2007).

From *Current History*, November 2008, pp. 375–380. Copyright © 2008 by Current History, Inc. Reprinted by permission.

Civil Society, Youth and Societal Mobilization in Democratic Revolutions

Taras Kuzio

In the pre-revolutionary era, young people had dominated the civil societies of many post-communist states, including countries which experienced democratic revolutions in Serbia (2000), Georgia (2003), Ukraine (2004) and Kyrgyzstan (2005). Most members of post-communist civil society NGOs were under 35 and it was they who provided huge numbers of activists and volunteers. One Orange Revolution activist recalled how: "this was a real extreme, underground, creative youth movement. People sat in offices all day not for money or because they were forced to, but because simply this was the place to be cool" (Ukrayinska Pravda, January 26, 2006). Similarly, in Serbia a "sophisticated market campaign" of posters, badges and tee shirts led to a "political youth cult". Identifying with *Otpor* (Resistance) became "cool" and "*Otpor* made it fashionable to be against Milosevic", one *Otpor* activist said (Collin, 2001, p. 208).

Young people have played a central role in all democratic revolutions going back to the Philippines people's power protests in the mid-1980s to Nepal in 2006. Democratic revolutions in Serbia (2000), Georgia (2003), and Ukraine (2004), the three countries under investigation in this article, would not have taken place without the energy of young people. Youth NGOs in Serbia, Georgia and Ukraine were crucial in three inter-related areas. First, they assisted in the mobilization of protestors. Second, they provided logistical support to the protests. Third, they were often the first wave of protestors (McFaul, 2005, p. 13; *Pora, 2005;* Demes and Forbrig, 2006; Kaskiv, 2005a,b; Kuzio, 2005a,b; Way, 2005).

In Ukraine, those in the age group up to 30 years old were three times more likely to join the Orange Revolution than other age categories (Stepanenko, 2005, p. 21). The two key social groups that made the Orange Revolution a success were youth and private businessmen (Reznik, 2005). Young people participate in revolutions because they have less to lose. Few have mortgages, families or careers to be concerned about losing if they joined the opposition, youth NGOs or the revolution. As their supporters grew, young people became less afraid of attending meetings and rallies as higher educational institutions could not expel all of them.

Young women played an important role in breaking down distrust between law enforcement and the revolutionaries. *Otpor* organized young women to march ahead of men as the police would be far less likely to attack them and, if they did, the ensuing footage of blood-stained girls would work to the advantage of the opposition. In Kyiv, teenage girls led the way in giving flowers to *spetsnaz* (police task forces) *Berkut* policemen posted in the cold weather outside the presidential administration. Their fraternization with the *Berkut* reduced chances of the non-violent protests becoming violent, which they had three years earlier in March 2001.

For many young people the theft of their vote in a crucial election was not simply election fraud but the theft of their future, which still lay ahead. Dmytro Potekhin, head of Ukraine's *Znayu* (I Know)! youth NGO, said, "this was a case in which something very personal was being stolen from us—our right to vote" (Slivka, 2004). In Serbia and Ukraine this sense of anger was made more urgent because Milosevic and Kuchma were both seen as criminals. Annual opinion polls by the Ukrainian Academy of Sciences from 1994 to 2005 found that "organized crime, mafia" was perceived by Ukrainians as the most influential group in Ukrainian society (Panina, 2005). The imposition of a successor who had a criminal past therefore came as a double affront. A young volunteer who ferried protestors to Kyiv for free asked, "How could they dare try to impose such a bandit on us? We will never accept it" (Daily Telegraph, November 28, 2004). Young Ukrainians especially refused to accept election fraud that led to the imposition of a "criminal" candidate as the successor to Kuchma.

The strategies deployed by Serbia's *Otpor,* Georgia's *Kmara* (Enough) and Ukraine's *Pora* (It's Time) were strikingly similar. They targeted urban youth who traditionally had been politically apathetic. Politics had to be made to be "cool". Young people were targeted because they made good volunteers and came into contact with a greater number of people each day than the older generation. The majority of the volunteers in *Otpor, Kmara* and *Pora* were students. *Otpor* was established by 15 Belgrade University students in 1998 who were, "Sick of the endless compromises, defeats and endemic apathy . . ." (Collin, 2001, p. 175). Students made up over 95 percent of members of *Pora* established in *Pora* cells in 20 universities throughout Ukraine. In Serbia, *Otpor* grew out of the Student Union of Serbia (SUS) and became a mass movement during the 2000 elections.

The article provides a five-point framework to understand the different aspects of the revolutionary process that took place in the three case studies covered in this article (Serbia, Georgia, Ukraine). Competitive authoritarian regimes are most vulnerable during a specific time, like election cycles, and regime change in Serbia, Georgia and Ukraine took place during *electoral revolutions*. *Organization* of young people in *Otpor*, *Kmara* and *Pora* was an important second condition in preparing to confront election fraud. Youth NGOs were able to overcome divisions and quarrels that plagued older generations and assisted in the creation of unified democratic opposition blocs. The third section deals with the importance of pre-revolutionary *training*. In the three countries discussed, the democratic revolutions were preceded by acute socio-economic and political crises when the opposition had failed in their attempts at removing the incumbents from power. The fourth section surveys the *strategies* employed by youth NGOs during the elections and democratic revolutions. This includes such strategies as an adroit use of humour and the provision of carnival-music festival atmospheres. The fifth section covers the *authorities' response* that targeted youth NGOs with repression and counter-propaganda.

Electoral Revolutions

Serbia differed from Georgia and Ukraine in that Milosevic could not, after being indicted for war crimes in Kosovo and Bosnia, convince the West that he would hold free and fair elections. In Georgia and Ukraine both leaders still sought to keep channels open to the West, particularly to the US. Both countries multi-vector foreign policies sought to balance relations with a hegemonic Russia by good relations with the US and NATO, with whom both countries participated in the Partnership for Peace program. Shevardnadze was also concerned at maintaining his reputation and integrity as the Soviet Foreign Minister under Mikhail Gorbachev who had refused to sanction military interventions in central Europe. In 2003, Kuchma sent the third largest military contingent to support US-led coalition forces in Iraq (the largest non-NATO member contingent) during the low ebb in Ukraine's relations with the West. Only a year earlier the US had accused Kuchma of authorizing the sale of "Kolchuga" military radars to Iraq in summer 2000.

Ukraine has a long-standing and respected election monitoring NGO staffed by young people, the Committee of Voters of Ukraine (http://cvu.org.ua). The assistance of the Committee of Voters (KVU) is invaluable for OSCE long-term observers who spend two months in Ukraine's regions prior to election day. The KVU has played an important role in organizing election monitoring and liaison with local OSCE observers and with the OSCE and Council of Europe headquarters in Kyiv. In Serbia, the Center for Free Elections and Democracy NGO played a similar role to the KVU.

The KVU have also assisted in coordinating election monitoring with the European Network of Election Monitoring Organizations (ENEMO). In the 2004 elections ENEMO sent 700–1000 monitors in rounds two and three (http://enemo.org.ua). ENEMO attends many election in post-communist states from which their monitors are drawn. In this sense they are able to

counter the views of the CIS Election Observation Mission (CIS EOM) established to give an alternative viewpoint to that of the OSCE.

Ukraine's youth election-monitoring groups organized two coalitions. The New Choice coalition brought together many well-known youth and election monitoring NGOs and was supported by the Europe XXI Foundation (http://europexxi.org.ua). New Choice grew out of the Civic Monitoring Committee that was active in the 2002 elections, and was one of the first examples of re-energized young activism. The Freedom of Choice coalition brought together 300 NGOs active in civil society and election monitoring (http://coalition.org.ua) and published a news web site (http:// hotline.net.ua). The Freedom of Choice coalition included the "yellow" wing of *Pora*.

Youth election-monitoring groups were involved in a wide range of activities in an attempt to counter violations and get out the youth vote. Youth groups launched legal cases against the common practice of state officials campaigning on the job for Yanukovych. Kherson oblast governor, Serhiy Dovhan, was forced to defend his agitation to vote for Yanukovych but was soon removed after the case became widely publicized.

In both Serbia and Ukraine, youth divided their tactics in two ways. "Get out the vote" campaigns were organized by one set of NGOs, following a pattern set in the 1998 Slovak elections. This type of NGO activity is not unusual in mature democracies and often targets those sectors of society most disinclined to vote, such as young people and uneducated voters.

A second tactic, closely related to the get out the vote campaigns, was to undertake "black operations" against corrupt officials who were suspected of being organizers of fraud in the upcoming elections. Both wings of this youth NGO strategy ("white" and "black operations") prepared to defend voters democratic choice through post-election protests. This made Serbia, Georgia and Ukraine different to Slovakia. In Slovakia the "get out the vote" campaign dominated NGOs' activity as the authorities were not expected to resort to election fraud and would accept the election result.

In Ukraine, "white operations" were led by the youth election-monitoring group *Znayu!* (I know) that provided positive information on the elections, educated election monitors, and attempted to block election fraud (http://znayu.org.ua). *Chysta Ukrayina* (Clean Ukraine) and student groups also took part in the "get out the vote" campaign (http://chysto.com and http:// studenty.org.ua). "Get out the vote" and information strategies complimented "black operations" by *Pora* to publicize corruption by election officials who were suspected of attempting to take bribes in return for falsifying the election results.

Organization

Serbia and Georgia produced united *Otpor* and *Kmara* NGOs whereas *Pora* in Ukraine was comprised of a "yellow" and "black" wing, named after the colour of their symbols. Both wings of *Pora* were established in spring 2004, although only "black" *Pora* had laid the groundwork in 2002–2003. *Otpor* was led by people born in the 1970s but the bulk of its rank and file members were born in the 1980s. *Otpor*, therefore, incorporated both the 1970s and 1980s generations or what constituted in Ukraine two wings of *Pora*. The former, the 1970s generation, remembered the Josip Broz Tito era while the latter only remembered war and economic collapse during the Slobodan Milosevic regime. In Georgia, veterans of earlier protests based at the Liberty Institute NGO functioned as *Kmara's* mother organization. As in Serbia, younger activists were brought into civil society activity by veterans involved in earlier civil society campaigns that had failed to meet their objectives.

Kmara and "black" *Pora* both had symbols similar to *Otpor's*; and *Kmara's* clenched fist was an exact replica of *Otpor's*. In Ukraine, *Pora* decided against using a clenched fist as this was believed to be too provocative. Instead, a clock was used showing how it was time for Kuchma to leave the office. Indeed, "black" *Pora* focused on the need to remove "Kuchmizm" from Ukraine.

Otpor, *Kmara* and "black" *Pora* had horizontal, leaderless structures working autonomously in decentralized networks with no leaders. "yellow" *Pora* was different. Vladyslav Kaskiv was the leader of "yellow" *Pora* and the Freedom of Choice coalition. Both wings of *Pora* and *Otpor* stressed underground, guerrilla style organization, a strategy that harped back to World War II Serbian partisans and Ukrainian nationalist guerrillas. In Georgia, such tactics could not be used as Georgia did not have a historical tradition of nationalist partisans. *Kmara* succeeded in exaggerating the size of their NGO's members by astute use of propaganda and street actions (Kandelaki, 2005).

Kmara and "black" *Pora* copied *Otpor's* tactics which were, in turn, taken from Western theories of non-violent resistance. The Belgrade-based Center for Non-violent Resistance provided non-violent training to Belarus's *Zubr* (Bison), *Kmara* and "black" *Pora*. "Yellow" *Pora* trained and operated independently of these three NGOs. Serbia's *Otpor* circulated Serbian-language versions of Gene Sharp's classic text on non-violent resistance, which has since been translated into Georgian, Belarusian and Ukrainian (Sharp, 1973; Ackerman and Duval, 2000; Karatnycky and Ackerman, 2005, http://aeinstein.org, http://nonviolent-conflict.org).

Robert Helvey, a retired US Army colonel worked closely with Sharp and assisted in training *Otpor* through the help of the US-based International Republican Institute. Advice centered on analyzing the sources of power within Serbian society, winning support within the government, the psychological effect of fear and methods of overcoming it, psychological methods to improve public views of *Otpor*, crisis management and how to avoid unnecessary risks. Sharp's work proved so influential that *Otpor* praised it as, "an astoundingly effective blueprint for confronting a brutal regime" (Whither the Bulldozer, August 2001).

In Ukraine two wings of Pora were a product of generational differences and different tactics. "Black" *Pora* incorporated Western traditions of non-violent resistance diffused through *Otpor*, *Zubr* and *Kmara*. "Yellow" *Pora* sought to find more specifically Ukrainian approaches to creating a youth NGO. At the same time, both *Poras* understood the need for non-violent strategies following the violent March 2001 riots in Kyiv. Mykhailo Svystovych, a founder of "black" *Pora* and the http://maidan.org.ua web site, was present during the 2001 riots and learnt lessons from them:

> And, only after two weeks did it become clear that a portion of people were frightened by potential repression and another part by hooligan actions. That was when we recalled *Otpor* and its successful non-violent movement. And in April 2001 the first *Otpor* members arrived in Ukraine (Ukrayinska Pravda, March 9, 2006).

The riots were provoked by extreme right nationalist provocateurs, working together with the Security Service of Ukraine (SBU). The public fall out led to the collapse of public support for the anti-Kuchma protests (Lutsenko, 2005). The authorities sentenced twenty members of UNA (Ukrainian National Assembly) providing them with ammunition to attack the opposition as "extremists". Throughout the 2004 elections the authorities staged numerous provocations in an attempt at inciting a violent counter-attack in what Russian political technologists working for the Yanukovych campaign described as "directed chaos" (Kuzio, 2005c). The opposition refused to rise to the bait and the Orange Revolution ended without violence (Kuzio, in press).

"Yellow" *Pora* was led by "professional radicals" of earlier campaigns going back to Ukraine's drive for independence and student hunger strike in 1990–1991 (Zerkalo Nedeli, December 11–17, 2004). Based in Kyiv, it was also closer to the Yushchenko election camp and his Our Ukraine bloc. The Freedom of Choice coalition had planned to establish Wave of Freedom as a "get out the vote" NGO, drawing inspiration from Slovakia's Campaign Ok 98. Pavol Demes, German Marshal Fund director in Slovakia and an activist from the 1998 Slovak elections, had close ties to "yellow" *Pora*. The planned Wave of Freedom NGO was renamed as *Pora*, copying the already launched "black" *Pora* and thereby creating confusion with the existence of two *Pora* organizations (http://kuchmizm.info, http://pora.org.ua). The "get out the vote" message was taken over by the *Znayu* NGO.

"Black" *Pora* was led by western Ukrainian students who had played a role in the anti-Kuchma protests of 2000–2001. They were younger, more active and better organized in Ukraine's regions. In 2001 the youth NGO *Za Pravdu* (For Truth) united different youth groups under the umbrella of the opposition Committee of National Salvation, the political body that had grown out of the Ukraine Without Kuchma! protests. Two smaller NGOs, *Opir Molodi* (Youth Resistance) and *Sprotyv* (Resistance) were spin offs of the *Za Pravdu* (For Truth) NGO.

Pora was organized in 2002–2003 from these hard-core activists spread over different youth NGOs. They also participated in supporting the democratic opposition in the 2002 parliamentary elections and the 2002–2003 Arise Ukraine! protests. In 2001–2002 they established links with Serbia's *Otpor* that then trained the "black" wing of *Pora*. Mykhailo Svistovych, editor of the http://maidan.org.ua website that had also grown out of the Ukraine Without Kuchma movement, provided key links to *Otpor* and became one of "black" *Pora's* founders.

Both *Otpor* and "black" *Pora* worked independently of the Vojislav Kostunica and Yushchenko campaigns. "Yellow" *Pora* was again different, working closely with the Yushchenko campaign in the 2004 elections and never attempted to prove its impartiality to the extent that *Otpor* and "black" *Pora* undertook to. "Yellow" *Pora* established an election bloc with the pro-Yushchenko Reform and Orders Party to contest the 2006 parliamentary elections. "Black" *Pora* refused to re-form as a political party. Both *Otpor's* and "yellow" *Pora's* attempts at entering the Serbian and Ukrainian parliaments failed.

In 2002–2003, Dutch, British and Polish foundations provided assistance for training seminars in 23 oblasts organized and coordinated by http://maidan.org.ua. *Otpor, Kmara* and *Zubr* (Bison) activists assisted the training seminars. "Black" *Pora's* main financial support came from domestic sources and West European foundations. This made "black" *Pora* very different to *Otpor* which could not rely on domestic sources for funding as the Serbian middle classes had been decimated by war, economic mismanagement and international economic blockade (Gordy, 1999; Krnjevic-Miskovic, 2001, p. 103; Thompson and Kuntz, 2004). *Otpor* received a large injection of US funds after Milosevic was indicted at the Hague for Kosovo crimes in 1999 and NATO's bombing campaign. The US did not provide funds for *Otpor's* partner in Ukraine, "black" *Pora,* while *Kmara* obtained its funds from the Soros Foundation, rather than from the US government (Fairbanks, 2004, p. 115).

"Yellow" *Pora* had greater access to domestic and international funds. Vladyslav Kaskiv, leader of "yellow" *Pora,* denied receiving funding from abroad (2000, January 21, 2005). However, they were able to tap into Western funds sent to the Freedom of Choice Coalition, a bloc of NGOs created to combat election fraud. Freedom House helped train the Coalition's election monitors at a Crimean camp in August 2004. Freedom of Choice volunteers often doubled as "yellow" *Pora* activists.

"Black" *Pora's* first activity was in March 2004 when it posted leaflets throughout Ukraine calling upon Ukrainians to remove "Kuchmizm" from Ukraine. One month later a second group, "yellow" *Pora,* emerged as a component of the Freedom of Choice Coalition. "Yellow" *Pora* underwent baptism by fire in the April 2004 mayoral election in the Trans-Carpathian town of Mukachevo. Although Yushchenko's candidate won the election the authorities declared their candidate victorious. They then dispatched organized crime enforcers ("skinheads") to intimidate and beat up officials and destroy evidence of election fraud.

Both wings of *Pora* played a crucial role in providing a dedicated, hard-core group of young activists who erected a tent city in Kyiv immediately after round two of the election on November 21, 2004. These hard-core *Pora* activists, together with other youth NGOs, helped mobilize millions of Ukrainians in Kyiv and the provinces to participate in the Orange Revolution. The same was true of *Otpor* in Serbia.

Training

During preceding political crises the opposition's attempts in Serbia, Georgia and Ukraine at removing incumbents from power invariably had failed leading to introspection within opposition movements as to the need to change tactics. After

numerous failed attempts by the Serbian opposition in the 1990s, the Serbs were beginning to lose faith in their ability to change the country's leadership. *Otpor* played a central role in revitalizing this apathy and feeling of lack of efficacy by, "shaking people out of their slumber" (Ilić, 2001). In Georgia, *Kmara* also faced the task of combating widespread political apathy among Georgians living in the provinces and among young people (Kandelaki, 2005).

Learning from past failures is taken on board in a greater way by the more impatient younger generation. *Otpor, Kmara* and *Pora* set examples to the older generation by uniting a broad range of political views within youth NGOs. Their elders continued to fail to unite into opposition blocs during parliamentary elections and failed to field a single candidate in presidential elections. The authorities divide and rule the opposition, eroding some parties while co-opting others with lucrative government or diplomatic positions.

Youth NGOs are usually the first to clamor for opposition parties to unite in the face of a common threat, either of Milosevic winning another election after being indicted for crimes in Kosovo and Bosnia or of Kuchma installing his successor, Yanukovch. In Georgia and Kyrgyzstan democratic revolutions took place during parliamentary elections where voter's protests were initially brought on by election fraud that then spiraled into demands for Eduard Shevardnadze and Askar Akayev to leave office. Opposition parties and *Kmara* had initially intended to use the example of 2003 parliamentary elections to mobilize in preparation for the 2005 presidential elections when Shevardnadze was to step down after two terms in office. The use of blatant election fraud, especially in Ajaria, Shevardnadze's refusal to compromise and public anger all combined to lead to the earlier than expected Rose Revolution. In all four cases there was a widespread feeling that the incumbent and the regime he had put in place needed to be changed.

Serbian democratic opposition leaders had failed to mount a serious challenge to Milosevic throughout the 1990s. Various democratic coalitions had been formed during elections and protests but none of them could match the breadth of the Democratic Opposition of Serbia (DOS) 18-party coalition established in the 2000 election, the successor to the Alliance for Change and Together coalitions. The only democratic party outside DOS was Vuk Draskovich's Serbian Renewal Movement. The failure of the 1996–1997 protests in Serbia galvanized Belgrade's students to create *Otpor* in 1998 (Collin, 2001, p. 175).

In Ukraine the opposition united in the second round around Yushchenko's candidacy with the Communists the only party refusing to join. *Otpor* played a greater role than *Pora* in pressurising the opposition to unite in crucial elections. Until spring 2000, Serbia's political opposition had proven itself unable to offer a serious alternative and a threat to the Milosevic regime (Ilić, 2001). Youth NGOs aligned with united opposition alliances proved unstoppable in Serbia, Georgia and Ukraine.

The creation of a united opposition was not the only required factor for a successful democratic revolution. There was also a need for a deep preceding crisis during which youth NGOs and parties could train, receive outside support and learn from their mistakes. Serbia experienced thirteen years of rule by Milosevic during which he had destroyed the most liberal of communist regimes, Yugoslavia, where standards of living had been relatively high for a communist state. By the 2000 elections many Serbs had reached the conclusion that they had enough of Milosevic, who had destroyed their own country and lost nationalistic wars in Slovenia, Croatia, Bosnia and Kosovo.

Georgia was similar to Serbia in being a post-war country. Shevardnadze had come to power in a *coup d'état* after President Zviad Gamsakhurdia had launched disastrous wars to withdraw autonomous status from Abkhazia and South Ossetia that he had then lost to Russian-backed separatists. Shevardnadze had presided over a stagnating and corrupt failed state and proved unable to re-take two territories beyond central control. In a third—Ajariad—the local elites were permitted, like Donetsk in Ukraine, to act as though it was their personal fiefdom provided they did not threaten to secede (King, 2001; Miller, 2004; Fairbanks, 2004).

There would have not been an Orange Revolution in Ukraine without the preceding Kuchmagate crisis, when a tape was released in parliament allegedly showing President Kuchma having authorized violence against opposition journalist Heorhiy Gongadze. The Kuchmagate crisis and subsequent protests did not lead to Kuchma's downfall. Nevertheless, they severely undermined the legitimacy of the ruling elites, discredited Kuchma, and created a hard core group of activists ready to participate in the 2002 and 2004 elections. Most importantly, they awakened the traditionally apathetic young people from their political lethargy.

"Black" *Pora* activists defined the anti-Kuchma protests as Ukraine's "1905", because they failed to unseat Kuchma, while Ukraine's "1917" (Orange Revolution) successfully prevented Kuchma's chosen successor, Yanukovych, from coming to power. The 2000 movement "Ukraine without Kuchma", during which young people created their own NGOs that evolved into *Pora*, was the "first rehearsal". The follow up Arise Ukraine! protests, "showed leadership ability to magnetize and guide large numbers of people". These two rehearsals, Interior Minister Yuriy Lutsenko believes, "made the Maidan possible" (Zerkalo Nedeli, December 11–17, 2004).

Protests in Ukraine after November 2000 elections had a profound effect on young people who, like the generation before them, dreamt and worked towards living in a "normal" European country. During the anti-Kuchma protests a revolution did not take place, but a profound change did take place in people's hearts and minds, a young activist, Volodymyr Chemerys, argued. This was especially among young people. Accusations against Kuchma meant he could no longer "stand above the political process" and claim to be the nation's leader. Ukrainians withdrew their support from Kuchma whose ratings plummeted and trust in state institutions reached an all-time low. "Internally Ukraine is already without Kuchma", Chemerys concluded. A revolutionary situation failed to materialize in 2002 during the Arise Ukraine! protests and only arose in 2004 during the Orange Revolution (Ukrayinska Pravda, December 13, 2002).

Since the 1980s a new post-communist generation has grown up in Serbia, Georgia and Ukraine which is less affected by, and tolerant of, communist and Soviet political culture. In Serbia the left was destroyed under Milosevic when he transformed the Socialist Party into an extreme nationalist party. In Serbia, Georgia and Ukraine the young post-communist generation emerged as a civil society force first in Serbia after the 1996 protests and then in Georgia and Ukraine during the 2000–2004 elections.

"Generation Orange" was a new phenomenon for Ukraine. "Kuchma never feared my generation. However, he forgot that we would have children and these children never knew the KGB", Andre Kurkov said (Gruda, 2004). "Generation Orange" has traveled abroad to work, for holidays or on scholarships, and has access to a globalized world through satellite television and the internet. "Generation Orange" knew there were alternatives to a Ukraine ruled by Kuchma's anointed successor, Yanukovych.

Strategies
Globalization and Modern Communication

Young people use modern communications to a greater extent than other generations and modern communications are often introduced into households by its younger members. These "e-revolutionaries" drew on the latest technology and communications to circumvent the authorities. The "info-age revolution" meant that a *"coup d'état* without violence" was possible (Durden-Smith, 2005).

In Serbia the internet took off during the 1999 NATO bombardment. But, by the 2000 elections and revolution the internet was still a low-used medium. The bombing of Kosovo did lead to a massive surge in cell phones as parents bought them for their children. Cell phones were useful in ensuring rapid communication between different areas of the country and NGOs. They were used for mass messages. During the elections the texts would be mass mailed and the recipients would be asked to send them on further.

Cell phones also played a useful role as camera phones. Evidence of fraud was collected by students in Ukraine who filmed professors illegally ordering them how to vote. This film was made available to download from the internet and used as evidence in court prosecutions during which the authorities were accused of rigging the election results.

Georgia and Ukraine proved to be different to Serbia where the internet played a less important role (Prytula, 2006). The internet had sufficiently developed in Georgia and Ukraine to ensure that this medium played an important role in their revolutions. Ukraine has been described as the world's first "internet revolution". The internet opened up possibilities for private chat rooms to discuss tactics and strategy, e-mail, bloggers, and hosting NGO web sites.

Modern technology was also used in promoting reports by independent television stations, such as Rustavi-2 in Georgia and Channel 5 and Era in Ukraine (http://rustavi2.com.ge, http://5tv.com.ua, http://eratv.com.ua). Large television screens provided 24-hour news and commentary by Channel 5 during the Orange Revolution. US scholars and policy makers could be interviewed in the Voice of America office in Washington and then be broadcast live on Channel 5 and on the Maidan.

Humor and Ridicule

Fear of instability, civil war and extremism were potent weapons in damping political activism and atomizing the Serbian and Ukrainian populations (Collin, 2001, pp. 191–192). Humor and ridicule were crucial in undermining fear of the authorities with young people playing a central role in promoting them. Ridicule and humor broke down fear of the authorities which had played an important role in de-mobilizing the middle aged and older generations and creating widespread apathy. Older Serbs, Georgians and Ukrainians felt they could do nothing to change their situations.

Fear had also been ingrained from the Soviet era in Ukraine because of a past history of periodic cycles of repression, a factor especially prevalent in Ukraine leading to the common refrain "*Moya khata z krayu*" (literally "My house is on the outskirts" but meaning "I'm staying out"). *Otpor* activists, "hoped to resuscitate Serbia with demonstrations of individual courage. The idea was to deprive the regime of the fear that had become its greatest weapon and thereby withdraw the consent of Serbia's governed" (Whither the Bulldozer, August 2001).

Otpor was one of the first to ridicule the Serbian authorities. Such ridicule could draw on the most unlikeliest of influences, such as the British 1970s comedy series, Monty Python's Flying Circus. Monty Python was useful in providing "silly, provocative humor" (Markovic, 2005). Monty Python provided, "allegorical, absurdist performance art", one *Otpor* activist recalled (Collin, 2001, p. 177).

In Georgia, the humorous message propagated by *Kmara* also poked fun of the regime. In one street action, similar to those by *Otpor* and *Pora* in Serbia and Ukraine, *Kmara* displayed large banners on streets where passers by could take photos of themselves flushing Shevardnadze and his government down the toilet. Other street actions included mock funerals when the government presented its new economic program. Such actions, "produced a group of young people with an extremely high degree of motivation, courage and 'quality activism'", capable of mobilizing broad swathes of Georgian society 5(Kandelaki, 2005).

The most elaborate campaign that drew upon humor was in Ukraine and the choice of official candidate—Yanukovych—made the use of humor easy and enjoyable (Chornuhuza, 2005; Yanuykdotyi. Politicheskiye anekdotyi). With young NGOs and the opposition dominating the internet, this forum became a major location for a wide range of humor and ridicule against the authorities. Internet web sites, "savaged Yanukovych with high road criticism and low road ridicule, inflicting a political death of a thousand cuts" (Kyj, 2006, p. 79).

That Yanukovych was intellectually challenged could be readily seen by his inability to speak either literary Russian or Ukrainian. His official CV submitted to the Central Election Commission was signed by "Proffessor" at a fictitious Western scholarly institution. "Proffessor Yanukovych" became the butt of jokes throughout the 2004 elections and Orange Revolution.

Yanukovych's intellectual challenge led to the emergence of an entire sub-culture within youth NGOs and web sites directed against him.

Yanukovch's intellectual challenge was also ridiculed because of his frequent use of criminal slang and his illiteracy. A 13-series internet film ('Operation ProFFessor') was produced consisting of excerpts of popular Soviet comedies with voices performed by impersonators of well known politicians dubbed over the characters. The series was a massive hit.

Yanukovych collapsed after being hit by an egg on a visit to Ivano-Frankivsk after the attempted poisoning of Yushchenko. The incident, filmed by independent Channel 5 Television, became a smash hit, downloadable from numerous web sites and re-played ridiculing the "tough man Yanukovych". Yanukovych had been primed before traveling to Ivano-Frankivsk that he was to be hit by a blank bullet in an attempt at portraying Yushchenko's supporters as "terrorists", a precursor to similar accusations against youth NGOs the following month. Immediately after Yanukovych was struck by an egg the authorities' political machine went into high gear blaming the "terrorist" attack on Yushchenko's "nationalist" supporters.

Dmytro Romaniuk, the student who threw the egg before the blank could be fired, was a typical product of the gradual politicization of young people during the 2004 elections. Romaniuk was disinterested in politics until he threw the egg that made him an instant celebrity. At the last minute he had decided to purchase two eggs because he was angry at how the local authorities were pretending that Yanukovych had great support in his home town in Western Ukraine. After the egg incident he was arrested and accused of "terrorism", steps that made him an instant local and national celebrity. He joined the Student Brotherhood who elected him to be its deputy head. "With many friends I took part in the Orange Revolution in the Khreshchatyk", Romaniuk recalled (Ukrayina Moloda, December 23, 2004).

A traveling "Political Theatre" mocked Yanukovych over his presumed fear of eggs using a traveling artificial egg. *Pora* released chickens outside the Cabinet of Ministers building in Kyiv where Yanukovych had his offices. Web sites appeared that included a rapidly growing number of egg jokes. There were many series of egg cartoons "Merry Eggs" (*Veseli Yaytsa*) in which two funny eggs sang songs and joked. "Boorish Egg" and "Jolly Eggs" games and cartoons were developed on-line (http://eggs.net.ua, http://ham.com.ua).

Yanukovych's criminal past also provided a great deal of ammunition for humor. On weekends *Pora* members dressed in prison uniform and campaigned for Yanukovych on Kyiv's main thoroughfare. Passers by were told that "prisoners" had been let out for the weekend to campaign for one of their own (Yanukovych). If there was a Yanukovych election stand the *Pora* members would stand next to it and chant "Yanukovych!, Yanukovych!". Yanukovych was depicted in numerous cartoons as a former "*zek*" (prisoner) or "bandit", accusations made easier by his origins in Donetsk, a region with the highest rate of criminality in Ukraine. A play on his name, "Yanucharii" (Janissaries), was made popular through posters and cartoons.

A cartoon printed in the mass circulation Silski Visti (December 23, 2004), a newspaper sympathetic to the Socialist Party, included two prison guards talking to each other outside an empty prison cell. One asked the other, "Where are the brothers (reference to criminal brotherhoods)?" His fellow officer replied, "Don't worry. They will soon return as they have just gone to campaign for their own . . ." (that is Yanukovych).

Music and Carnivals

Traditional music, concerts and carnivals have been used by nationalist and regional groups throughout Europe to raise national consciousness and politically mobilize voters. Regions in the Celtic fringe—Wales, Ireland, Scotland, Cornwall and Brittany—have revived traditional music festivals to raise national awareness. Such festivals have played an important role in re-connecting to young people, traditionally the most integrated generation in the globalized English-speaking world (Gemie, 2005).

Democratic revolutions in Serbia, Georgia and Ukraine took place in late autumn or winter. Young people are more hardy to cold weather and more capable of living in tent camps or roughing it on sofas or floors. Assisting them in staying for long periods of time and roughing the accommodation was an adroit use of music and carnival atmosphere. The most well known youth bands played for free for weeks to large crowds.

In Serbia the music scene was confused as the nationalist authorities had attempted to influence young people through their promotion of turbo-folk, a mix of patriotic folk and modern rave music (Gordy, 1999). *Otpor* had to be more adroit in its use of patriotic motives in music as nationalism had been monopolized and discredited by the Milosevic regime. Nevertheless, "healthy" nationalism, as one *Otpor* activist described it, did play a role inside the NGO (Collin, 2001, p. 200). Instead, they mocked the post-Tito Socialist-nationalist regime with dark humor and playing on totalitarian motifs. The inspiration for this Serbian opposition music was New Slovenian Art and bands such as Labiach, a play on the German name for Ljubljana. Yugoslav rock from the 1980s touched on nostalgia for an era which was peaceful, prosperous and the state took care of its citizens.

Politics and music were deliberately mixed together. The Millennium concert was preceded by a four minute film on recent Serbian and Yugoslav history. After the film the 10,000 strong crowds were advised to go home as there was nothing to celebrate with a concert (Collin, 2001, p. 177). The *"Vremie je"* (Its Time) rock concert tour with the independent B2-92 radio station featured the best Yugoslav bands in 25 cities throughout Serbia and reaching 150,000 young people (Collin, 2001, p. 208).

In Georgia, young artists, poets and musicians toured the country supporting change and calling on students in regional universities to join the Rose Revolution. In Ukraine the opposition could draw on patriotic music as the authorities could be readily portrayed as disinterested in national interests and the rights of citizens. Ukraine's Orange Revolution was a symbiosis of "political meeting and rock festival" (Klid, 2006, p. 2). Ukraine's best known and modern bands played for Yushchenko while traditional bands and singers from Russia played for Yanukovych.

The hymn of the Orange Revolution was written by the hitherto unknown Ivano-Frankivsk hip hop band *Grandzioly*. Their song "We are many, we cannot be defeated" became a rallying cry in the Orange Revolution and was downloaded 1.5 million times from the internet. The elite Kyiv Mohyla Academy, the location of Yushchenko's press center, coined the slogan. The "spirit of the opposition lives in the yards" of the Academy and "its students make up *Pora's* avant guard", one "yellow" *Pora* activist recalled (Polyukhovych, 2004). *Otpor's* slogans were typically more forthright: *Gotov Je* (He's Finished), "Kill Yourself Slobodan and Save Serbia" and "To The Hague, to the Hague, get Slobodan to the Hague".

Another *Pora* activist remembered, "From 2000 we studied the experience of non-violent revolution in different countries—and one of these factors contributing to these changes was carnival" (Ukrayinska Pravda, November 22, 2005). Young people creatively thought up ways to distribute information. Vendors selling music CDs would provide free copies of other CDs with windows media player files showing "How the authorities are undertaking free elections".

Okean Yelzy, one of Ukraine's most popular bands, was typical of the apolitical Ukrainians who became politicized during the elections and Orange Revolution. *Okean Yelzy* singer Sviatoslav Vakarchuk was made an adviser to President Yushchenko. *Okean Yelzy* played on the Maidan throughout the Orange revolution and one of their new songs gave hope to the protestors that "spring" was very close at hand. "Spring" was a euphemism for the victory of Yushchenko. As in Serbia, Ukrainian well known sports personalities, such as Vitali and Vladimir Klichko brother boxers, who were icons for young people, often appeared on the Maidan. During the 2006 elections the Klichkos headed the *Pora*-Reforms and Order election bloc.

Orange Revolution music, which was continually played on the Maidan either by live bands or through music CDs, also touched upon Ukraine's national identity and the choice they were making at that moment in history. As with the name of Yushchenko's bloc, Our Ukraine, many songs mobilized Ukrainians to demand the return of what was understood as their stolen country. This is "Our Ukraine" which had been taken over by a small group of usurpers; it was time for the country to be returned to its rightful owners, Ukraine's citizens. These usurpers were depicted as a de *facto* foreign occupation army supported by Russia.

Orange Revolution songs also demanded that Ukrainians did not contemplate passivity as the stakes were too high. Some songs, such as *Okean Yelzy's* song *"Vstavay!"* (Arise!) openly called for an uprising. Although written before the elections, became popular during the Orange Revolution. Songs such as *"Ukrayina"* by the well known band *Mandry* called upon Ukrainians to look at their ancestors who were looking down upon them at this critical time. The option of staying passive was morally wrong as too many Ukrainian intellectuals had already suffered and died in the former USSR. The insinuation was that with the election of Yanukovych their Ukraine, from a nationally conscious point of view, would be irrevocably lost. Other Orange Revolution music called upon Ukrainians to rush to Kyiv to defend this "sacred" city from a Yanukovych victory.

Everybody should travel to Kyiv as soon as they could by any means possible.

Music also played a role in humor. During the separatist congress held on December 2, 2004 after round two, Ludmilla Yanukovych, the wife of a presidential hopeful, accused the organizers of the Yushchenko tent city of distributing oranges injected with narcotics to force protestors to stay there. She also claimed that *valenki* (fur knee length boots) had been sent free of charge by the US, a hint that the CIA was behind the Orange Revolution. Satirical songs immediately appeared that poured ridicule on these claims by inter-lacing her comments with other words. The tent city began to hang up *valenki* with "MADE IN USA" scrawled on them.

Authorities' Response

During the 2003 Georgian and 2004 Ukrainian elections the authorities came to increasingly fear *Otpor, Kmara* and *Pora,* even though their numbers and influence were often exaggerated. Ukrainian authorities feared the diffusion of Serbian and Georgian revolutionary know-how. During the 2004 elections, Aleksandar Marich, a founder of *Otpor,* was detained at Kyiv's Borispol airport and deported. Marich had a multi-entry visa and had spent most of the previous two months in Ukraine, but official fear of *Otpor* bringing the "Serbian-Georgian scenario" into Ukraine led to his deportation from Ukraine.

Democratic diffusion through Western assistance was understood by the Serbian, Georgian and Ukrainian authorities as "subversion". One week before the October 2004 crackdown on Ukrainian youth NGOs, the pro-presidential camp had called upon the National Security and Defense Council to take tougher action against opposition plans to undertake mass civil disobedience (Ukrayinska Pravda, October 7, 2004). Valeriy Pustovoitenko, head of the coordinating council of political parties supporting Yanukovych, warned that, "certain forces are preparing for disturbances on election night in all of Ukraine's regions" (Ukrayinska Pravda, October 13, 2004).

The reason for the rising tension was that the Ukrainian authorities' repeated claim that they were organizing free and fair elections was at odds with reality. Ukrainian youth NGOs were alerted to the authorities' plans for election fraud after the April 2004 mayoral elections in Mukachevo. These elections were the first occasion when one wing of *Pora* had taken an active role. The presidential election campaign was not conducted in a free and fair manner.

After Yushchenko was poisoned in September 2004, the opposition camp reached the conclusion that the authorities would never let them win. As in Mukachevo, the opposition could win the election but the authorities would declare their own candidate to be elected. It was therefore rational for the opposition and civil society to prepare to defend their vote and counter election fraud in a non-violent manner. Youth NGOs played a central role in these preparations, as did training assistance from Otpor and *Kmara.*

Opposition and civic groups attempted to ensure as few violations as possible on election day, given the proclivity of law enforcement bodies and election officials to support the authorities. Yushchenko's campaign also issued a statement that the authorities were losing control of the situation and were not confident of Yanukovych's victory, making them nervous and thereby rely to an even greater extent on election fraud. Presidential adviser Mikhail Pogrebynsky admitted, "We have a situation whereby the bigger part of the authorities' team does not believe in their success". He added that there was a widespread, "feeling that the authorities will lose" (glavred.info, October 6, 2004).

During Ukraine's 2004 presidential election the authorities became increasingly nervous about the increased activity of youth NGOs monitoring the election. This culminated in an onslaught against youth NGOs in October 2004 that included a large number of intimidation tactics and targeted violence. As in Serbia, these tactics failed and backfired, only serving to attract larger numbers of members.

Different youth NGOs had complained that the SBU (*Sluzhba Bezpeky Ukrainy* or Security Service of Ukraine) had questioned their members regarding opposition's preparation for an alleged coup. President Kuchma had repeatedly warned throughout the 2004 elections that the authorities would not tolerate a "Georgian-style" revolution. Both wings of *Pora* were especially targeted because the authorities labeled them "extremists" and "terrorists", as *Otpor* had been in Serbia. Both *Pora* and *Otpor* were denounced as "fascist" and "terrorist" structures beholden to American paymasters. The Serb authorities introduced new anti-terrorist legislation to counter *Otpor* which they described as "hooligans, terrorists and paramilitaries" (Collin, 2001, p. 179). Such charges failed to find fertile ground in Serbia but had considerable resonance in russophone Eastern Ukraine. This was a component of the anti-Yushchenko campaign that depicted him as an American stooge and "nationalist extremist".

Otpor and *Pora* were perceived as radical by the Serbian and Ukrainian authorities because their young members were not cowed by fear. Ukrainian authorities remained fixated on the possibility that the 2004 election would trigger a repeat of the Serbian and Georgian revolutions in Ukraine, which they believed were instigated by the US. To counter *Pora's* success, the authorities created an anti-*Pora* organization, *Dosyt'* (Enough) which proved to be a flop (http://maidan.org.ua, November 10, 2004, Ukrayinska Pravda, November 12, 2004).

During a search of *Pora's* Kyiv office, witnessed by opposition parliamentary deputies, the police found nothing incriminating except anti-Yanukovych leaflets. But during a second search, with only the police present, a bomb was allegedly found. The Prosecutor General then launched a criminal case accusing *Pora* leaders of "terrorism" and "destabilization of the situation in the country". *Pora* was accused of being an illegal "military formation—a terrorist group" (Ukrayinska Pravda, October 16, 2004). The Prosecutor General's office attempted to link the alleged bomb to the August 2004 terrorist act in a Kyiv market which it had originally blamed on political parties allied to Our Ukraine.

A widespread media campaign linked *Pora* to Our Ukraine, and thus its presidential candidate Yushchenko, whom the authorities were desperate to portray as an "extremist" in media outlets that specialized in blackening the opposition (http://temnik.com.ua, October 18 and 19, 2004).

Such tactics were part of an overall strategy advised by Russian political technologists on how to destabilize Ukraine and pit the "pro-Russian" Yanukovych against the "nationalist" Yushchenko. It was more difficult for the Serbian authorities to describe Kostunica as an "extremist" as he held moderate nationalist views and had eschewed politics until the 2000 elections. In Georgia the authorities never resorted to the same extreme measures as in Ukraine in trying to discredit opposition parties. The Georgian elections were dominated by competition between two Georgian and Ajarian parties of power, on the one hand, and the opposition.

"Yellow" *Pora* issued a rebuttal to charges of "terrorism" in which they described themselves as the "vanguard of peaceful opposition". They called upon all of their activists and Ukrainian citizens to "legally, peacefully, and in a non-violent manner defend constitutional rights and freedoms in Ukraine" (http://pora.org.ua, October 18, 2004). This statement reflected a desire, as in Serbia and Georgia, to use non-violent tactics.

What most perturbed the authorities was that Yushchenko had overwhelming support among the educated younger generation, those most likely to be mobilized and active in civil society. In Serbia and Ukraine the authorities usually paid people, including students, to attend rallies on behalf of their candidates, a step that often backfired. On September 29, 2004 Ukrainian students paid to join a Kyiv rally responded "Yes!" to a call from Yanukovych's campaign activists when asked if they desired "Free and Fair Elections". But when asked "And you will vote for Yanukovych?" they replied "No!" on live television. The organizers abruptly ended the rally.

Student Wave organized a mass student rally on October 16, 2004 in Kyiv that brought 30,000 students from across Ukraine in support of Yushchenko. The rally began with a free concert in central Kyiv featuring Ukraine's two best known rock bands. As with all student rallies, it was intended to mobilize students behind demands for a free and fair election and provide concrete advice to students on how to resist pressure and intimidation from the authorities. According to the organizers, "The authorities are not happy of the level of support of the people's candidate, Viktor Yushchenko, among students" (http://yuschenko.com.ua, October 12, 2004).

The training and functions of Ukrainian police *spetsnaz* units were televised with the intention of instilling fear against undertaking election protests. Kuchma had warned against revolution and street protests during a deliberately timed visit to a Crimean BARS *spetsnaz* unit in August 2004. The unit had belonged to one of the best National Guard units until it was dismantled and transferred to the Interior Ministry in 2000. During the Orange Revolution the Crimean BARS unit guarded the presidential administration, leading to rumors that Russian *spetsnaz* units were in Kyiv. Oleksandr Milenin, Deputy Minister of Interior and head of Kyiv's police, leaked the existence of a new "ninja" police unit "trained in special measures" (Financial Times, October 19, 2004). Milenin also claimed that "new means" had "been approved by the health ministry" and were available to suppress protests, making him confident that "There won't be any revolution here" in Ukraine.

Ultimately, these threats to use force failed as Kuchma could not rely on the military, SBU or parts of the Interior Ministry who defected in the Orange Revolution to Yushchenko (Kuzio, in press). The use of non-violent tactics by both wings of Ukrainian *Pora, Otpor* in Serbia and *Kmara* in Georgia proved better at undermining the security forces than the violent tactics used by some elements of the opposition in Kyiv in March 2001.

Another related aspect of the authorities' response in both Serbia and Ukraine was an unprecedented rise in anti-Americanism (UKRAINE, 2004; Kuzio, 2004a). This aspect of the authorities' response proved to be less pronounced in Georgia, although Shevardnadze and other senior Georgian officials did denounce George Soros's funding of the Liberty Institute NGO. The Georgian Young Lawyers Association, Open Society-Georgia Foundation and International Society for Fair Elections and Democracy were also important NGOs. But, the main target of official attacks was on alleged links between *Kmara* and the Russian intelligence services. Shevardnadze had narrowly missed two assassination attempts that were assumed to have been organized by Russia and two separatist regions were under *de facto* Russian control. This made the Georgian authorities more nervous of Russia than the USA.

In Serbia the inflaming of anti-Americanism was not surprising as NATO had bombed Serbia in 1999 to force it to halt its ethnic cleansing of Kosovo. Anti-Americanism was a staple of Milosevic's xenophobic view of the outside world, pitting "little Serbia" against the US, NATO and the West. *Otpor* was routinely denounced as an "agent of American imperialism" (Ilić, 2001).

In Ukraine, anti-Americanism was a new and contradictory phenomenon associated with Kuchma's second term in office after he re-oriented Ukraine to Russia in the wake of the Kuchmagate crisis. Anti-Americanism was promoted at the same time as Ukraine outlined a desire for NATO membership (2002), had sent a large military contingent to Iraq (2003) and changed its military doctrine to include a desire for NATO and EU membership (2004). This was during the same period when anti-Americanism was used as part of an election strategy to blacken Yushchenko (Kuzio, 2004b).

The aspect of the anti-American campaign that concerns this study is the attempts to link domestic NGOs to Western (especially the US) governments. This alleged link reflected the deeply ingrained Soviet political culture evident in the pro-Kuchma centrist camp and Communists. In the former USSR, Soviet propaganda regularly denounced domestic dissidents as allegedly possessing links to Western intelligence. Such links were brought out in Russia in December 2005 when it linked Russian NGOs to British intelligence. The new Russian law on NGOs is imbued with this Soviet era culture that attempts to portray NGOs as imported, unnatural, un-Russian implants. Similar legislation and regime propaganda is evident in Belarus.

In Georgia and Ukraine the alleged American connection was made through direct US and Western support to civil society and NGOs, as well as through training assistance provided by Serbian *Otpor* activists. *Otpor* had been instrumental in assisting in the establishment of the Belarusian youth *Zubr* NGO in February 2001 with the aim of it taking a leading role in that year's September presidential elections. In Ukraine, *Otpor* activists had begun to train Ukrainian young NGO activists in 2002–2003. Following the Rose Revolution of November 2003, Georgian *Kmara* activists also became active in training Ukrainians. During the Orange Revolution, Georgian and Belarusian flags were conspicuously the largest of all foreign flags.

Conclusion

This article has shown how in Serbia, Georgia and Ukraine there were striking similarities in how young people played a decisive role in their democratic revolutions. The five factors that this article focused on to provide a cross-country comparative study are electoral revolutions, organization, training, strategies and the authorities response. All three revolutions in Serbia, Georgia and Ukraine followed similar paths of eschewing violence and upholding non-violent tactics, the ideas for which drew upon earlier successful examples of people power and Western theories. These three case studies in turn, drew upon the diffusion of ideas and strategies employed earlier in other post-communist states (Bunce and Wolchik, in this issue). Non-violent tactics adopted by youth NGOs, together with the presence of large numbers of people on the streets, proved to be crucial in undermining the competitive regimes in Serbia, Georgia and Ukraine. These strategies also dissuaded the regimes from using violence to suppress protests.

Hale and D'Anieri in this issue devoted to democratic revolutions focus upon elites and, particularly, splits in ruling elites as leading to regime fragmentation. There is little doubt that in Serbia, Georgia and Ukraine, divisions within the ruling elites worked towards a democratic revolution. Elites brought with them resources (finances, media outlets, institutions, international ties) that were crucial to the success of the opposition. Oligarchs are typically untrustworthy allies of the executive in elections and crises.

A focus on elites should not lead to an ignoring of the election and revolutionary process from the bottom up where young people play a central role. In Serbia, Georgia and Ukraine the new post-communist young generation and civil society NGOs played a disproportionate role in overcoming widespread fear and apathy and in mobilizing millions of people to participate in the democratic revolutions. Their selfless actions provided an example to older generations that empowered them with the view that "We have the power to change things". Young people also proved instrumental in setting aside their personal differences and successfully pushing political parties to unite into opposition coalitions.

Since these three democratic revolutions have taken place, followed by Kyrgyzstan in 2005, authoritarian elites in the CIS have understood the importance of youth and civil society to democratic change (Herd, 2005). In Russia and Belarus the introduction of legislation to control NGOs has been introduced since the success of these four democratic revolutions. Anti-Western youth NGOs in Russia and Belarus have also been launched by the regimes to counter local manifestations of *Otpor, Khmara* and *Pora*.

Websites

http://www.5tv.com.ua
http://www.aeinstein.org
http://www.dif.org.ua
http://www.eggs.net.ua
http://www.eratv.com.ua
http://www.glavred.info
http://www.ham.com.ua
http://www.helsinki.org.yu
http://www.kuchmizm.info.org
http://www.maidan.org.ua
http://www.nonviolent-conflict.org
http://www.pora.org.ua
http://www.pravda.com.ua
http://www.rustavi2.com.ge
http://www.temnik.com.ua
http://www.yuschenko.com.ua
http://www.zn.kiev.ua

References

Ackerman, P., Duval, J., 2000. *A Force More Powerful. A Century of Nonviolent Conflict.* Palgrave, New York.

Chornuhuza, O. (Ed.), 2005. *Tak! Ukrayintsi Peremahayut Smiyuchys.* VUS, Kyiv.

Collin, M., 2001. *This is Serbia. Rock 'N' Roll Radio and Belgrade's Underground Resistance.* Serpents Tail, London.

Demes, P., Forbrig, J., 2006. Pora— "Its Time" for Democracy in Ukraine. In: Aslund, A., McFaul, M. (Eds.), *Revolution in Orange.* Carnegie Endowment, Washington, DC, pp. 85–102.

Durden-Smith, J., October 3, 2005. *No more people power.* The New Statesman.

Fairbanks, C.H., 2004. Georgia's rose revolution. *Journal of Democracy* 15 (2), 110–124.

Gemie, S., 2005. Roots, rock, Breizh: music and the politics of nationhood in contemporary Brittany. *Nations and Nationalism* 11 (1), 103–120.

Gordy, E.D., 1999. *The Cult of Power in Serbia. Nationalism and the Destruction of Alternatives.* Penn State University, University Park.

Gruda, A., December 5, 2004. *Generation orange.* La Presse.

Herd, G.P., 2005. Colorful revolutions and the CIS. "Manufactured" versus "managed" democracy? *Problems of Post Communism* 52 (2), 3–18.

Ilić, V., 2001. *Otpor—in or beyond Politics,* Helsinki Committee for Human Rights in Serbia. http:// www.helsinki.org.yu/files_contents.php?lang=en&;idpub=54.

Kandelaki, G., 2005. *Rose Revolution: A Participants Story.* US Institute of Peace.

Karatnycky, A., Ackerman, P., 2005. *How Freedom is Won. From Civic Resistance to Durable Democracy.* Freedom House, New York.

Kaskiv, V., January 21, 2005a. *Interview.* 2000 Newspaper.

Kaskiv, V., 2005b. *A case study of the civic campaign PORA and the Orange Revolution in Ukraine.* Kyiv, Pora. http://pora.org.ua/eng/content/view/2985/325/.

King, C., 2001. Potemkin democracy. Four myths about post-Soviet Georgia. *The National Interest,* 93–104.

Klid, B., March 23–26, 2006. Rock, pop and politics in the 2004 Ukrainian presidential elections and Orange Revolution. Association for the Study of Nationalities. convention paper.

Krnjevic-Miskovic, D. de, 2001. Serbia's prudent revolution. *Journal of Democracy* 12 (3), 96–110.

Kuzio, T., October 8, 2004a. Large scale anti-American campaign planned in Ukraine. Jamestown Foundation, *Eurasian Daily Monitor* 1 (102).

Kuzio, T., September 30, 2004b. Ukrainian officials increasingly denounce opposition as "extremists" and "terrorists". Jamestown Foundation, *Eurasian Daily Monitor* 1 (96).

Kuzio, T., 2005a. Ukraine's Orange Revolution. The opposition's road to success. *Journal of Democracy* 16 (2), 117–130.

Kuzio, T., 2005b. Kuchma to Yushchenko: Ukraine's 2004 elections and "Orange Revolution". *Problems of Post-Communism* 52 (2), 29–44.

Kuzio, T., 2005c. Russian policy to Ukraine during elections. *Demokratizatsiya* 13 (4), 491–517.

Kuzio, T. *"Directed chaos" and non-violence in Ukraine's Orange Revolution.* Swedish National Defense College, Stockholm, in press.

Kyj, M.J., 2006. Internet use in Ukraine's Orange Revolution. *Business Horizons* 49 (1), 71–80.

Lutsenko, Y., February 10, 2005. Minister of Interior, Interview, Washington, DC.

Markovic, I., March 5, 2005. Otpor activist, Interview, Washington, DC.

McFaul, M., 2005. Transitions from postcommunism. *Journal of Democracy* 16 (3), 5–19.

Miller, E.A., 2004. Smelling the roses. Eduard Shevardnadze's end and Georgia's future. *Problems of Post-Communism* 51 (2), 12–21.

Panina, N., 2005. *Ukrainian Society 1994–2005: Sociological Monitoring.* Institute of Sociology, National Academy of Sciences. Available at http://www.dif.org.ua/publics/doc.php?action=11/us5.

Polyukhovych, Y., November 11, 2004. Interview with Kyiv Coordinator of Pora. Kyiv Post.

Pora, February 2005. Ukraine's Orange Revolution. A Chronicle in PORA Newsletters. Pora, Kyiv.

Prytula, O., 2006. The Ukrainian media rebellion. In: Aslund, A., McFaul, M. (Eds.), *Revolution in Orange.* Carnegie Endowment, Washington, DC, pp. 103–124.

Reznik, O., 2005. Sotsialno-Politychni peredumovy Fenomenon Pomaranchevoii Revolutsii. *Politychnyi Portret* 33, 5–14.

Sharp, G., 1973. *The Politics of Nonviolent Action.* Porter Sargent Publishers, Boston.

Slivka, A., January 1, 2004. *Orange alert.* The New York Times Magazine.

Stepanenko, V., 2005. Chy povernetsia dzyn u pliashku? Osoblyvosti natsionalnoii hromadianskoii aktyvnosti. *Politychnyi Portret* 33, 15–27.

Thompson, M.R., Kuntz, P., 2004. Stolen elections: the case of the Serbian October. *Journal of Democracy* 15 (4), 159–172.

UKRAINE: *Anti-Americanism an election tool for Kuchma,* January 8, 2004. Oxford Analytica.

Way, L., 2005. Kuchma's failed authoritarianism. *Journal of Democracy* 16 (2), 131–145.

Whither the Bulldozer? Nonviolent Revolution and the Transition to Democracy in Serbia, United States Institute of Peace Special Report, August 6, 2001.

UNIT 3

The Executive: Instituting Accountability and Responsiveness

Unit Selections

Key Points to Consider

- What are the roles of the executive?

- What are the constraints on the executive?

- How do we measure executive success?

- How and why do executives who are not popularly elected demonstrate accountability or responsiveness?

- Can strong executives act without restraint? Explain why or why not.

- What factors are necessary for successful executive leadership?

Student Website
www.mhhe.com/cls

Internet References

Asian Development Bank
   http://www.adb.org/Countries
BBC World News
   http://news.bbc.co.uk/2/hi/middle_east/default.stm
Germany Chancellor's website
   http://www.bundesregierung.de/Webs/Breg/EN/Homepage/home.html
Latin American Network Information Center, University of Texas at Austin
   http://lanic.utexas.edu/la/region/government
Russian and East European Network Information Center, University of Texas at Austin
   http://reenic.utexas.edu
U.S. White House and Cabinet
   http://www.whitehouse.gov/government/cabinet.html

The previous units focused on citizens and groups and their impact on government and policy-making. The next three units address the questions: How do governments govern? and How is the performance evaluated? That is, we consider the institutions of governments and their roles in policy-making, specifically, the executive, the legislature, and the bureaucracy and judiciary. Unit 3 addresses the systematic questions (why, what, and how) regarding executives and their roles.

Why executives? The explanation may be found in political theories of government, articulated by venerated theorists such as John Locke, John Stuart Mill, Jean-Jacques Rousseau, and the framers of the U.S. Constitution: to achieve efficient and efficacious policy-making. Even if a community is small enough to allow everyone to partake in policy-making and implementation, it is inefficient to do so. Think about a community the size of a country and it becomes clear that it is prohibitive to have everyone partake in policy-making. Thus, citizens choose a representative government to make those policies on their behalf.

The paradox is that the more diverse the society, the larger and more diverse the representative government becomes. That, in turn, progressively works against efficient policy-making. This is why we need executives in political systems: Executives remove that potential spiral into inefficiency by bringing the "power," "tyranny," and "arbitrariness" of a single decisionmaker into policy-making without the objectionable aspects of those qualities.[1] Or, to put it kindly, they rise above the fray of legislative bickering or indecision to ensure that policies are formulated, approved, and implemented.

What are the roles of the executive? As the articles in this unit point out, there are many, from the lofty to the petty, including originating policies; executing policies; acting as the point person for the day-to-day operations of government; meeting and negotiating with foreign governments; meeting and negotiating with local governments; meeting and negotiating with corporations, interest groups and other key groups; presenting agreements for public support, brokering, budgeting, and so on. Thus, the article on Angela Merkel, the Chancellor of Germany, describes her accomplishments in terms of the success of day-to-day government operations, which relies on her ability to navigate policies through a coalition-government that comprises a major party that is ideologically opposed to her own. The duties of Mexico's President Calderon and Iran's President Ahmadinejad include defusing tensions from bitterly contested presidential elections. Then, there are the articles on Vladimir Putin, the former president and current premier of Russia, and the political executives in Thailand that describe their efforts as developing populist appeals to broaden their constituency base.

All these duties may be condensed to providing leadership.[2] That is, the executive's performance is ultimately based on his or her ability to lead. How does the executive achieve such leadership? Institutionally, the executive is structured in one of three ways: as president in a presidential system; as prime minister and cabinet in a parliamentary system; as president and prime minister in a presidential-parliamentary hybrid system. In a presidential system, the executive—the president—is independently

© Getty Images/fStop

elected to office from the legislature. In a parliamentary system, the executive—generally a reference to the Prime Minster, but more accurately applied to the entire cabinet—is chosen by the elected legislature or parliament. In parliamentary systems, there is no independent election for the executive. In a presidential-parliamentary hybrid system, also known as the semi-presidential system or mixed system, the President is elected independently, while the Prime Minister and cabinet are chosen by the legislature. The mixed system is becoming the political system of choice in emerging democracies: At last count in 2002, there were 25 nations with mixed systems, up from only three in 1946.[3] Why is that? Michael Sodaro suggests that it is because the mixed systems maximize efficiency in policy-making while maintaining stability in the executive authority. In short, it ensures the executive's performance.

This leads us to the question of how to assess executive performance. Some of the readings in this unit suggest that it is captured through policy success. Thus, Angela Merkel's performance on foreign policy is considered excellent. Some of the readings suggest that it is popularity. By this measure, Putin in Russia and also Thaksin of Thailand may be considered successful executives. In the case of Thaksin, his popularity was such that it ensured the electoral success for members of his party even when he was unable to contest elections.

Yet, there is a higher bar of executive performance: the executive's responsiveness and accountability. This responsiveness and accountability bring us full-circle to why executives are needed: to bring the power and tyranny of a single decisionmaker into policy-making without his or her objectionable aspects. The hope is that, notwithstanding the efficient policymaking and implementation, the executive embraces and promotes "social diversity" rather than chokes it.[4]

This is where some executives fail. Some executives—such as Putin and Ahmadinejad—substitute popularity for responsiveness and accountability. Thus, the article on Putin points out that Putin's popularity rests heavily on what Russian sociologist Emil Pain calls a "revival of the imperialist syndrome," which the global economic downturn will undoubtedly dampen. In Iran, Ahmadinejad's political fortunes appeared secure; he appeared successful in riling up the Iranians by adopting anti-Western rhetoric. Yet, the political disarray following the June 12, 2009, elections make clear that it is not enough: He needed to maintain the support of all the conservatives among the political elites and the Ayatollah. At this task, he has not succeeded, as the article points out. There are also executives such as Thaksin in Thailand, who use populist appeals that appear responsive. The American Politics site, an ongoing collaborative project between the Department of Government and Liberal Arts Instructional Technology Services at The University of Texas at Austin, defines populism as

> A political ideology that emphasizes government's role as an agent of the common man, the worker, and the farmer, in struggles against concentrated wealth and power. Historically in the United States, "populist" describes any political movement having popular backing which is also perceived to be acting in the interests of ordinary people rather than elites.[5]

Yet, even this appeal to populism could not save Thaksin's premiership; his failure to sell his political ideas broadly, to include the "guardians" of Thai politics—the "holy trinity" comprising bureaucrats, military, and the monarchy—led to a conflicted state that continues to challenge government rule. Clearly, executive responsiveness and accountability does not mean "buying" off the people.

Instead, to achieve governability and tenure, executives need to pursue real policy objectives with measurable successes and move beyond cronyism, corruption, moral manipulation, and divisive policies. Thus, Angela Merkel's leadership is judged less by her foreign policy success than by her ability to implement the difficult, but necessary reforms favored by the Germans. Even though there were protests against Calderon's presidency, his ability to respond and demonstrate accountability since the 2006 elections is more important for assessing his performance than the conditions under which he took office. We need to look no further than Manuel Zelaya and Thaksin to see what happens to executives who fail to deliver on this higher bar. This explains why many analysts expect Ahmadinejad's second term in office to be short-lived.

Notes

1. See Jeffrey Sedgwick, "James Madison and the Problem of Executive Character," *Polity* vol 21 no 1 (1988): pp. 5–23.

2. See Michael Sodaro, *Comparative Politics: A Global Introduction* (3rd edition). New York: McGraw-Hill (2007)

3. See José Antonio Cheibub and Svitlana Chernykh. 2008. "Constitutions and Democratic Performance in Semi-Presidential Democracy." *Japanese Journal of Political Science* vol. 9 no 3: 269–303.

4. Sedgwick 1988, p. 5

5. http://www.laits.utexas.edu/gov310/IPOM/glossary.html <last accessed August 12, 2009>

Angela Merkel's Germany

"In part because of deadlock within the government on domestic policy, the chancellor has turned to foreign policy as her main stage."

JACKSON JANES AND STEPHEN SZABO

Angela Merkel, whom *The Economist* has called a "world star," is the most prominent of a new generation of leaders emerging in Europe. She is in charge of Europe's pivotal country at a time of great challenges to the EU as it seeks to come out of its constitutional and enlargement crises. Germany has the presidency of the EU and of the Group of Eight industrial nations in 2007, but Merkel and her country will be central to Europe's evolution long beyond this spring.

With Tony Blair in Britain and Jacques Chirac in France serving as lame ducks, and with many other European countries locked in political stalemates, much of Europe today is experiencing a vacuum of leadership. Thus, both George W. Bush and his successor as US president will look to the German chancellor as America's most important partner in Europe for years to come. Understanding Merkel and the political and economic context in which she operates is, consequently, important for anticipating what to expect from her chancellorship—in its impact both on Germany and on the future direction of the continent.

The Pragmatist

A number of Merkel's personal characteristics influence her approach to leadership and policy making. First, as a natural scientist, having studied and practiced physics, she is a highly rational person, without a strong ideological bent or approach. A problem solver and an incrementalist, Merkel favors a trial-and-error approach to policy and is able to make quick adjustments when they are needed. As she put it, "Many will say, 'This government takes a lot of small steps but not one decisive one.' And I reply, 'Yes. That is precisely what we are doing. Because this is the modern way to do things.'" Merkel lacks a big, unifying vision, and in this respect resembles her predecessor as chancellor, Gerhard Schröder. Unlike Schröder, however, she avoids personalizing political relationships and prefers a businesslike and interest-based approach in policy making.

Second, Merkel is a political latecomer and an outsider to German politics. An East German, she did not become active in politics until after the fall of the Berlin Wall, when she was well into her 30s. She is, consequently, not anchored in her party,

the Christian Democratic Union (CDU), and has not been able to take advantage of an extensive political network—a problem aggravated by her gender in a male-dominated party. She has begun to change this by creating her own network, both within and outside the party, but she still faces many rivals and lacks a deep regional base, something that is normally essential in German politics.

Third, her East German upbringing has made her a very private person who reveals very little about herself or what she is thinking. She is not a social animal or backslapper and is always in control of her emotions.

Finally, Merkel is not among the so-called '68ers, the generation of Schröder and his Green foreign minister, Joschka Fischer, who cut their political teeth in the late 1960s partly in resistance to the American role in the world. Merkel, born in 1954 and raised in East Germany, is the first of a new generation of leaders who were never among the 1960s rebels nor among the Atlanticist generation of her mentor, Helmut Kohl. Although she came of age during the end of the cold war, her political career was shaped in the post–Berlin Wall era of a unified Germany.

Merkel will be joined in power soon by others of her generation in France and the United Kingdom—people like Ségolène Royal or Nicolas Sarkozy in France, and David Cameron or Gordon Brown in Britain—as well as José Manuel Barroso in the EU. This group is pragmatic regarding both Europe, which is no longer seen as the great peace project of the Kohl-Mitterrand era, and the United States, which is neither the model it was for the postwar leaders who shaped Europe nor the anti-model it was for many of the '68ers.

Squabbling in the Ranks

Merkel was sworn in as chancellor on November 22, 2005. The first year of her tenure was marked by uncertainty over whether her political coalition (the "grand coalition"), which includes both Merkel's CDU and the Social Democratic Party (SPD), would have the stamina to hold together for another three years. The SPD holds almost as many seats in the Bundestag (parliament) as does Merkel's own CDU—making the coalition far more challenging to manage than was Schröder's coalition, which consisted of the SPD and the smaller, ideologically kindred Green party.

The German people's skepticism regarding domestic reforms is compounded by a policy making system that discourages strong leadership.

Despite current tensions between the parties in Merkel's coalition, however, there is at present no real alternative to this political equation in Germany. Speculation about the need for new elections remains exactly that, primarily because the voters would lose even more confidence in the political leadership if it declared bankruptcy so soon after taking over. Neither the Greens nor the Free Democrats can offer a viable alternative by themselves. And the idea of creating a red, green, and yellow mixture (SPD, Greens, and Free Democrats) or a black, green, and yellow coalition (CDU, Greens, and Free Democrats) is not in the cards. There is still a great deal of political baggage left over from the September 2005 elections that will prevent any such reconfiguring from happening very soon.

Merkel enjoys a solid level of personal popularity among Germans, but confidence in the two large political partners, the CDU and SPD—which between them have close to three-quarters of the Bundestag under their control—has waned. After all, voters ask, if there is no viable opposition to stop them, why can they not get more done in the way of reforms instead of making so much noise about why they cannot agree on such reforms? Even the CDU and its conservative Bavarian partner, the Christian Social Union, are increasingly bickering over the issue of health care reform.

All this wrangling comes during a continuing slide in membership in the SPD and the CDU. The Social Democrats have lost over 40 percent of their members from a high of more than 1 million in 1980, while the Christian Democrats in the same period have lost 14 percent of their members. Currently, the two parties are virtually tied in membership, at around 600,000 each. The smaller parties have lost ground in the past eight years as well, and the number of citizens choosing not to vote has been increasing steadily.

This frustration is causing a backlash that has allowed a right-wing party, the National Party of Germany (NPD), to squeeze into two state parliaments in eastern Germany. Many of the NPD votes have come from Germans under 30 years old who are beleaguered by high unemployment rates and see dim prospects for their future.

Still, the general loss of confidence among voters and the cross-party bickering that has contributed to it should come as no surprise. Domestic political battles were destined to throw sand into the machine of the CDU-SPD coalition. After all, the domestic policy realm is where the full forces of particular interests meet in battle. Health care reform legislation is the best, or worst,

example, and not only in Germany. It remains a dangerous area for the coalition's future. Indeed, one can also see the wreckage of health care reform efforts in the United States going back many years, not to speak of social security reform efforts more recently. These are the deadly third rails for all politicians.

Pressures for Reform

Merkel has been able to push through important reforms that have toughened up policies dealing with pensions. And corporate tax rates are set to come down significantly. As Germany's export machine continues to hum along at record levels, the economy in 2007 looks to be as strong as it was last year.

In general, though, reform efforts so far have produced a mix of some change but also continued stalemate. Germans are struggling to finance the social systems they have built up over the past five decades, and are trying to redistribute the load. This is not unique to Germany—Sweden, Denmark, and the Netherlands have been struggling with these problems as well. Yet Germany seems to be uncertain about the scope and pace of change. A question being newly framed amid today's global competition is how much of the acclaimed "social market economy" that was developed after World War II should be accounted for by "market" and how much by "social."

The very fact that the 2005 elections resulted in a so-called grand coalition of the two major political blocs was a reflection of the voters' uncertainty in the face of rising pressures to reform social and labor protections. The challenge any government faces is proposing realistic goals and then maintaining support for reaching them, even when changes pinch people where it hurts. It is precisely then when a government must be persuasive in explaining to the public why the goal is worth the pain and the adjustments needed to reach the goal.

On EU enlargement, Germany has moved from being the great promoter to being a skeptic.

This has proved difficult in Germany. For example, the government's decision in November 2006 to raise the statutory retirement age from 65 to 67 was vital to maintaining the viability of the social security system, but it requires a major adjustment in the national psyche. Likewise, reducing unemployment insurance is crucial in encouraging people to search for new jobs, but it violates long-entrenched expectations of the unemployed.

The German people's skepticism regarding domestic reforms is compounded by a policy-making system that is designed for consensus politics and discourages strong leadership. Suspicion of strong leaders is a legacy of Hitler's Third Reich, with its concentration of power at the top. In contrast to Japan, for example, contemporary Germany has a weak state and a strong civil society. This makes unpopular reforms very difficult to achieve.

On top of this, Germany's parliament is one of the largest in the world, with 614 representatives. And Germany has a federal system with powerful state governments. Wrestling with serious problems that involve so many actors, in a 24-7 media environment no less, is not a formula for smooth decision-making.

Berlin's coalition partners are stuck with each other for the moment, whether they like it or not. But they should not be stuck in political mud when it comes to implementing their agenda. Bringing down the national debt and encouraging job growth by deregulating the labor market can generate some confidence in the future. Yet Germany also faces formidable structural problems in the business and banking sectors, and it continues to pay a high cost for the reintegration of (less affluent) eastern Germany. The coalition partners need to look like they are focused on confronting the country's problems, rather than themselves, if they are to bring the voters along with them. This seems to work better with foreign policy than it does at home.

Balancing with Bush

In part because of deadlock within the government on domestic policy, the chancellor has turned to foreign policy as her main stage. Schröder had centralized policy making in the chancellery and marginalized the role of the foreign office and the parliament—since his Social Democrats were in a coalition with the small Green party, this was relatively easy to accomplish. Merkel, on the other hand, is in a much more challenging coalition. In contrast to Fischer, who was Schröder's foreign minister, Merkel must contend with a Social Democrat, Frank Walter Steinmeier, as foreign minister. This means there are far greater checks on Merkel's power than on any chancellor over the past three decades.

This has not stopped her from forming an effective foreign policy team. Merkel generally values analytical thinkers over party politicians in the chancellery. As her chief of staff, Thomas De Mazière, told the German weekly *Die Zeit,* "A clear head can learn about compromises and contacts better than a political tactician can learn clear thinking." Thus, Merkel has tended to hire technocrats or specialists in foreign policy positions. A good example is her key foreign policy adviser, Christoph Heusgen, a thorough Europeanist who served six years in Brussels working for the EU foreign policy chief, Javier Solana.

Merkel entered office believing that the Schröder foreign policy had lost the traditional German balance between France and the United States. She has made the US relationship her primary responsibility and priority, with the goal of reestablishing a constructive and balanced relationship with Washington after the *Sturm und Drang* of the Schröder years. Her East German experience left her with a very positive image of America, which she associates not only with freedom but also with innovation and flexibility.

Nevertheless, Merkel is a politician who understands the deep suspicion toward George W. Bush among the German public and media. This reflects in part the new sense of sovereignty and status of a unified Germany that is no longer as dependent on the United States as it was during the cold war. Merkel understands that she needs to be regarded as a reliable partner in Washington while not being seen as Bush's dachshund back home.

Ever the realist, the German chancellor understands that it is in the national interest to have a good working relationship with the world's dominant power, and that trying to use Europe as a counterweight to America only ends up splitting Europe and isolating Germany. On the other hand, drawing too close to Bush and to America carries its own dangers, as the case of Britain's Blair demonstrates. Thus, the Merkel approach toward the United States combines a close personal relationship between Merkel and Bush with a continuing, critical distance from unilateral aspects of Bush's foreign policy. In many ways she is rebuilding some bridges while waiting for the next American administration, which she hopes will be more user-friendly for Europe.

This approach is apparent in a number of policy areas. On NATO, the Merkel government has emphasized a NATO-first approach, giving the alliance priority in the security realm over the European Union's Security and Defense Policy. The new German Defense White Book, issued in November 2006, underlines a shift in German defense strategy away from the old territorial-defense focus of the cold war to a crisis-intervention rationale with light, mobile forces. Merkel intends to maintain the important German contribution to NATO peacekeeping forces in Afghanistan, without widening its mandate or increasing that commitment. She has also deployed German peacekeepers to Congo and Lebanon, and a German commander now heads the EU force in Bosnia. Along with France and Britain, Germany is working closely with the us administration to forge a unified approach toward thwarting Iran's nuclear ambitions.

In foreign economic policy, the chancellor is interested in maintaining some momentum in trade liberalization despite the likely failure of the Doha round of global trade negotiations. In particular, she has put forward new proposals for a transatlantic free trade area. Merkel has also moved to reduce the German fiscal deficit by raising the value-added tax, thus restoring Germany's reputation for fiscal responsibility in hopes of serving as an example to other EU deficit states. The German leadership remains concerned about the impact that US trade and fiscal deficits will have on the international financial system. As the world's largest exporter, German business worries about the impact of a falling dollar on its foreign markets.

Enlargement Fatigue

Merkel is now on center stage in Europe. Germany will hold the EU presidency during the first half of 2007. In this capacity, Merkel will have a chance to help restore some momentum to the European project, which has been staggering since the rejection of the EU constitutional treaty by French and Dutch voters in 2006. Because of the current leadership vacuum in Europe and the impending French presidential election this spring, the German role is likely to be limited to finding some ground for action in the future regarding the constitutional treaty. So no dramatic breakthroughs should be expected during the German term.

On the other important dimension of the European project, EU enlargement, Germany has moved from being the great promoter to being a skeptic. Past German governments supported the "big bang" enlargement of 2004, which brought in 10 member states, mostly from East-Central Europe. The Merkel government reluctantly went along with the entry of Bulgaria and Romania on January 1, 2007, but seems to have reached its limit regarding future enlargement. The Schröder government supported the entry of Turkey, but the Christian Democrats are opposed, and the governing coalition remains deeply divided on this key issue.

Germany's enlargement fatigue results in part from a fear of immigration and the cheap labor that it brings. Although immigration into Germany has been curtailed by legislation, the foreign population of the country stands at 7.3 million, or about 9 percent of the population. This is a larger proportion of the population than is the case in the United States. Of this group, 1.8 million have Turkish origins, with about one-third having been born in Germany. Another half-million of Turkish origin have been naturalized and are now German citizens. Germans are struggling to deal with the issue of how to define citizenship, which has traditionally been based on German heritage. Although citizenship laws have been liberalized somewhat, Germany is still a long way from becoming a multicultural society, and demands for German language competence for new immigrants have been increasing.

Germany's growing skepticism about enlargement is also the result of strained federal budgets, themselves a consequence of years of slow economic growth and high unemployment. Berlin in the past financed the union's enlargement through its contributions to the EU budget. But Germany is no longer willing or able to serve as Europe's pay-master. This marks an important shift in German foreign policy and implies that the EU is probably approaching its final borders.

Realism on Russia

The German-Russian relationship is once again a central issue in the European political equation. During the cold war, when Germany was divided, it depended on American security guarantees for its territorial integrity. This situation, and the Soviet occupation of East Germany and East-Central Europe, limited Germany's options and flexibility in dealing with the Soviet Union, although the German policy of détente (known as *Ostpolitik*) did develop an independent German approach toward the East.

She needs to be regarded as a reliable partner in Washington while not being seen as Bush's dachshund back home.

After the cold war, the German-Russian relationship regained dynamism. Chancellor Kohl ensured that Russian interests were taken into account during NATO's enlargement to the east. But Schröder took the relationship to a new level by siding with Russia and France against the Bush administration during the lead-up to the Iraq War. He forged an unusually close personal relationship with Russian President Vladimir Putin. He signed the important Baltic Sea gas pipeline agreement with Russia just before leaving office and then, after leaving office, joined the board of Russia's state-controlled energy giant Gazprom.

Merkel came into office resolved to change the tenor of this relationship. She has depersonalized the relationship with Putin, and in her first visit to Moscow as chancellor openly showed her support for human rights groups. Her suspicion of Russian power has been deepened by Russia's use of its energy resources as a foreign policy tool in its relations with Ukraine, Belarus, and Georgia. She is also aware of the suspicions that the close Schröder-Putin relationship raised in the Baltic states and Central Europe, especially in Poland, and wants to repair Germany's relationships with these states.

Merkel has made a priority of improving the Polish-German relationship, but has met resistance from the Polish government, led by the Kaczynski brothers. The German government's decision to establish a Center for Refugees and Expellees, possibly in Berlin, has raised concerns in Poland about potential German property claims for land taken from Germans who lived in Poland before the end of World War II. More generally, the Law and Justice Party of the twins is suspicious of Europe and of Germany in particular. A deeply parochial and nationalist grouping, it has questioned attempts by Poles to reconcile with Germany and is deeply suspicious of Germany's close relationship with Russia.

Yet Merkel the realist has continued to talk about a "strategic partnership" with Russia. Whatever this might mean, it implies that energy dependence and the close economic ties between the two countries remain paramount in German policy. Russia is Germany's largest natural-gas provider, currently providing 40 percent of Germany's natural gas, and this dependence is due to rise above 60 percent once the Baltic pipeline is completed. While Merkel would like to find alternative sources of energy, and is looking at a combination of liquefied natural gas, Central Asian gas, and nuclear power, her options are severely limited. She and her successors are faced with no real alternatives to substantial dependence on Russian natural gas during the coming decades. Moreover, although Russia has used energy as a lever against its former republics, it has never done so with Germany. For its part, Russia has no real alternatives to the EU market for its gas in the medium term. Half of Russia's energy trade is with the EU.

Germany is likely to remain Russia's most important advocate in the EU. The Merkel government continues to resist a common EU energy policy, and thus has made it easier for Russia to play off one EU state against another. In addition, Merkel's foreign minister was a key architect of the close German-Russian relationship when he was Schröder's chief of staff. His presence in the Merkel government is seen as a guarantee of continuity in this policy area.

A New Role in the World

A key change in German foreign policy since the end of the cold war is its increasingly global perspective. While the transatlantic and European relationships remain central to Berlin's view of the world, the Middle East and Asia have increased in importance. This reflects the end of a Western-centric world order and the need for Germany to adapt to the rise of new economic and military powers as well as to its vulnerabilities in the Middle East.

China and India have emerged both as important economic partners and as competitors for scarce sources of energy and raw materials. Germany's role in negotiations with Iran over its nuclear program, its participation in a peacekeeping force in Lebanon, and its efforts to engage Syria in a constructive relationship with the West are further indications of an expanding sense of German interests and responsibilities. As Germany's role in the world expands, it sees itself as deserving more international recognition. This includes a desire to have a seat as a permanent member of the UN Security Council. While Merkel has been less vocal in her pursuit of this goal than was her predecessor, it remains a key objective.

The agenda for the European Union is going to be a difficult one for Merkel to steer. Apart from the uncertain outcome of leadership changes in Great Britain and France, achieving consensus on anything among the union's now-27 members is a challenge at any time and on any issue one picks. Merkel has sent a clear signal that she intends to exercise leadership this year in shaping the still-fragile framework of the EU foreign policy agenda. But merely pushing forward the next phase of the EU constitutional process will give her a full plate, and keeping her fellow member states in line on everything from the Balkans to the Middle East will be a tall order.

The longer-term issues of further EU expansion, particularly with regard to Turkey, will consume Merkel's energies well after this leadership year for Berlin. Here there is a clear division between the views of the chancellor and her party and those of her coalition partners, the Social Democrats. The CDU is opposed to Turkish membership in the EU, favoring a "privileged partnership" instead, while the SPD continues to strongly advocate Turkish membership.

Since becoming chancellor, Merkel has felt confident in the international arena. As with many politicians facing domestic troubles—her coalition with the SPD continues to be a noisy and uncomfortable one—the opportunity to shine as a world leader offers advantages. Despite low poll numbers on domestic issues during the past year, both Merkel and her foreign minister, Steinmeier, top the popularity scales among the German public. The year ahead therefore offers unique opportunities to make progress on the foreign policy front.

Of course, the opportunities will be shadowed by risks. Keeping political squabbles from affecting the foreign policy agenda will not be easy, either at home or within the EU. Still, Merkel has the baton now in Berlin and in Brussels. We will have to wait to see how well the orchestras can perform.

JACKSON JANES is executive director of the American Institute for Contemporary German Studies at Johns Hopkins University. **STEPHEN SZABO** is research director at the institute and a professor of European Studies at Johns Hopkins's School of Advanced International Studies.

Russia's Transition to Autocracy

PIERRE HASSNER

It was with great trepidation that I accepted the invitation to deliver this distinguished lecture, together with the suggestion that my remarks should focus on Russia. Although my lifelong preoccupation with international politics—and in particular with the struggle between freedom and tyranny—has led me to follow closely developments in Russia (and, of course, the Soviet Union), I must confess at the outset that I am not an "old Russia hand." I do not speak Russian, and I have never spent more than two consecutive weeks in Russia.

Why, then, did I agree to speak on this subject? In the first place, as an analyst of international relations I have a strong interest in the political role of human passions, and I think that understanding wounded pride, repressed guilt, resentment, and the manipulation of fear is central for interpreting Russia today. But I was also attracted by the idea of paying tribute to the memory of Seymour Martin Lipset. I met him and his wife Sydnee only once, toward the end of his life, at a celebration of the fiftieth anniversary of the Congress for Cultural Freedom. To my knowledge, Lipset did not write much on Russia or on communism, but he did write extensively on the connection between economic development, the rise of a middle class, and democracy, as well as on the impact of political culture and traditions. As I expected, in preparing this lecture, I found a good deal of inspiration in Lipset's intellectual approach.

Today, analysts of Russia are threatened by three temptations: economic determinism, cultural determinism, and political determinism. For instance, the excellent Russian author Dmitri Trenin is optimistic about Russia's future because, although not democratic, it is capitalist; hence he argues that it will give birth to a middle class that will want the rule of law.[1] Other authors believe that Russia will never become democratic, because its culture is basically authoritarian. A third group, composed largely of Americans, believes in politics as a *deus ex machina:* Because all people want democracy and the market, no matter what their culture or their state of economic development is, these can be installed virtually overnight. For avoiding these simplifications and for grasping the complicated interrelationship between politics, economics, and culture, I think there is no better guide than the work of Seymour Martin Lipset.

For my part, I shall concentrate on the role of politics and especially of a single person—Vladimir Putin. Although he is neither the beginning nor the end of the story of democracy and capitalism in Russia, he does play a crucial role.

The Seymour Martin Lipset Lecture on Democracy in the World

Pierre Hassner delivered the fourth annual Seymour Martin Lipset Lecture on Democracy in the World on 15 November 2007 at the Canadian Embassy in Washington, D.C., and on November 22 at the Munk Centre for International Studies at the University of Toronto. The Lipset Lecture is cosponsored by the National Endowment for Democracy and the Munk Centre, with financial support this year from the Canadian Donner Foundation, the Canadian Embassy in Washington, the American Federation of Teachers, the Albert Shanker Institute, William Schneider, and other donors.

Seymour Martin Lipset, who passed away at the end of 2006, was one of the most influential social scientists and scholars of democracy of the past half-century. A frequent contributor to the *Journal of Democracy* and a founding member of its Editorial Board, Lipset taught at Columbia, the University of California at Berkeley, Harvard, Stanford, and George Mason University. He was the author of numerous important books including *Political Man, The First New Nation, The Politics of Unreason,* and *American Exceptionalism: A Double-Edged Sword.* He was the only person ever to have served as president of both the American Political Science Association (1979–80) and the American Sociological Association (1992–93).

Lipset's work covered a wide range of topics: the social conditions of democracy, including economic development and political culture; the origins of socialism, fascism, revolution, protest, prejudice, and extremism; class conflict, structure, and mobility; social cleavages, party systems, and voter alignments; and public opinion and public confidence in institutions. Lipset was a pioneer in the study of comparative politics, and no comparison featured as prominently in his work as that between the two great democracies of North America. Thanks to his insightful analysis of Canada in comparison with the United States, most fully elaborated in *Continental Divide,* he has been dubbed the "Tocqueville of Canada."

I came here, however, neither to praise Putin nor to bury him. I did not come to praise him because I agree with Sergei Kovalev that "Putin is the most sinister figure in contemporary Russia history."[2] He has led Russia into a harsh brand of authoritarianism with some fascist features, and he remains under strong suspicion of having inspired a number of criminal acts, including the fires that served as a pretext for launching the second war in Chechnya, and the assassination of political opponents such as Anna Politovskaya.

On the other hand, I did not come to bury him. His rule is full of contradictions and, while it has some extremely ominous aspects, he cannot be said to have burned all his bridges or to have made it impossible for Russia to evolve in a more positive direction once circumstances change. Whatever our final judgment, we must not close our minds to the case made by his defenders, who stress his popular support among the Russian people, the improvements that he has achieved in certain areas (as compared to the catastrophic situation he found when coming to power), and the fact that his undoubtedly authoritarian rule has stopped well short of totalitarian terror.

Many Russians and some Westerners assert that, no matter how dubious public opinion polls or how rigged elections are in Russia, a majority of the people still support Putin. In their eyes, that is sufficient to make the regime a democracy of sorts, and one more in line with Russian traditions than is the pluralistic Western model. According to Putin's defenders, he is not hostile to pluralism as such but merely claims the right to choose a different model, equally imperfect but more suitable to Russia's present circumstances. For precedents, they cite not only Peter the Great and Alexander Nevsky but also Franklin Roosevelt, who also fought the oligarchs of his time and, in addition, ran for a third (and fourth) term.

Another comparison, implicit in some sympathetic French commentaries, invokes the precedent of Charles de Gaulle. One of the most shocking features of Putin's policies is his attempt to claim continuity with both the Czarist and the Soviet pasts. In a way, de Gaulle followed a similar approach in a France that traditionally had been divided between the heirs of the French Revolution and those of the *ancien régime*. De Gaulle belonged to the Bonapartist tradition, which wanted to unify French history and to promote a nationalism that embraced *all* of France's past. Moreover, although France was no longer a great power, de Gaulle's great game was to pretend that she still was and to get her to punch above her military or economic weight in the Great Powers League. As we shall see, Putin has been trying to do something similar with Russia.

Unfortunately, however, there is also much else in Putin's dossier, and the overall verdict has to be much harsher. True, the case made by defenders of Putin's foreign policy, largely backed even by many liberal Russians who are critical of Putin's authoritarianism, should not be dismissed out of hand: After all the shocks that Russia has suffered—the loss of Eastern Europe, the dissolution of the Soviet Union, the great economic crisis of 1998, the huge increase in economic inequality through the enrichment of some and the impoverishment of most, the

enlargement of NATO, the presence of U.S troops in Central Asia, and the talk of Ukraine and Georgia joining NATO—it is only normal that there should be a reaction of resentment and a wish for reassertion now that conditions permit. But, his liberal defenders add, with time a more balanced attitude will emerge. The problem with this argument is that the evolution of Putin's policies is heading in the wrong direction. Rather than being a preparation for democracy or for a more realistic and constructive role in world affairs, it looks much more like a tendency toward greater authoritarianism at home and troublemaking abroad.

The first question I would like to consider concerns the link between the evolution of the Russian regime and changes in its attitude toward the outside world. Recent years have witnessed a spectacular hardening against the domestic opposition, the freedom of the press, and any democratic life inside Russia, as well as against Russia's former satellites and the West. There has also been an encouragement of nationalism, which initially took on a primarily ethnic character (directed particularly against people from the Caucasus), but has increasingly targeted the West. The most dangerous aspect of all this is the growing hostility toward Russia's neighbors—Estonia, Georgia, and other former members of the Soviet Union and even of the Warsaw Pact (such as Poland). This is especially worrying because, paradoxically, it is in dealing with its neighbors that Moscow's policy has been the least successful and has met the greatest resistance—much more than from either the Russian population or the West.

From Anarchy to Autocracy?

Russia's progress toward democracy began going off the rails even before Putin came to power. Lilia Shevtsova dates the trouble from 1993, when Yeltsin ordered troops to fire on a rebellious parliament.[3] The crisis of democracy under Yeltsin culminated with his reelection in 1996 , which was manipulated by the oligarchs to give him a victory in spite of his disastrous standing in the opinion polls. This was an essential first step for Putin's subsequent ascension to power. Under Yeltsin, of course, some important elements of democracy existed that have vanished under Putin—above all, freedom of the media and wide-ranging public debate. But there was no equality and no real rule of law; privatization amounted to a seizure of public wealth by the oligarchs; the power and corruption of the Yeltsin family turned the pretense of democracy into a farce; and Moscow (though it had the power to start a war in Chechnya) was unable to collect taxes from many regions.

Early in Putin's presidency, there emerged some open signs of a further slide toward autocracy in the name of restoring the authority of the state (indicated by such slogans as "the dictatorship of the law"). But the predominant strategy sought to maintain the appearance of democracy while progressively emptying democratic institutions of their content. This kind of deception is an old art in Russia, whose most famous example is the Potemkin villages of the eighteenth century; various contemporary authors have coined new terms for the phenomenon more appropriate to the Putin era, speaking of "virtual" or "imitation" democracy. While under Gorbachev and Yeltsin a real attempt had been made to emulate Western democracy and to follow Western models and advice, under Putin the attempt at deception became ever more apparent.

A residual desire for respectability in the eyes of the West and the world is evident, however, in Putin's decision not to modify the constitution in order to run for a third term. Instead he has chosen to designate a virtual president for a virtual democracy, while keeping real power himself. Throughout his second term, one could observe an increasingly self-assured and provocative claim that Russia had come up with its own brand of "sovereign democracy," which was probably superior to Western-style liberal democracy and certainly more appropriate for Russian conditions. One can debate whether this term merely implies a rejection of Western interference and lecturing, or whether "sovereign" also means that this kind of democracy is based on the authority of the leader and the unity of the nation, to the exclusion of any real pluralism.

What is certain, however, is that key aspects of the new dispensation are strongly reminiscent of fascism. These include not only the elimination of any rival centers of power (whether economic, political, legal, or cultural), but also phenomena such as the "personality cult" of Putin, the appeals to proclaim him "leader of the nation," and the creation of youth organizations devoted to bullying the opposition and ethnic minorities and to helping the police. These trends seem increasingly to be influencing the Russian population at large. Two indications of this are the rise in xenophobia to a level comparable to that found among Germans in the years preceding Nazism,[4] and the growing public admiration for Stalin, whose ranking as a leader is second only to that of Putin himself and contrasts sharply with the popular contempt toward Gorbachev and Yeltsin. Yet, according to the polls, while an increasing proportion of Russians (2 percent) believe that Russia should follow its own path in terms of government, a plurality (42 percent) are still in favor of liberal democracy.

From Joining the West to Blasting It

Since Putin came to power, Russia has continually been moving away from democracy, and of late at an accelerating pace. By contrast, Moscow's foreign policies and Russian attitudes toward the outside world, in particular toward the West, have made a number of spectacular U-turns. After the collapse of the Soviet Union, attraction to the West, the urge to imitate it, and the hope of being welcomed and helped by it were predominant, as reflected in the stance of Yeltsin's foreign minister, Andrei Kozyrev. Toward the end of the Yeltsin period, however, Russian dissatisfaction with the West started to show, and Kozyrev was replaced by Yevgeny Primakov, who favored a policy oriented toward "multi-polarity" and a greater emphasis on Asia. Another sign of the shift was Yeltsin's unhappiness with the NATO intervention in Kosovo. This led him into an intemperate outburst mentioning Russia's nuclear might, but ultimately did not prevent him from contributing to peace by pressuring Serbian dictator Slobodan Milošević to give in.

During the early years of Putin's presidency, Russian policies toward the United States were remarkably conciliatory. Putin's passive reaction to U.S. abandonment of the Anti–Ballistic-Missile Treaty, his immediate offer of support for the United States after 9/11, his cooperation against terrorism, and his acceptance (apparently against the objections of the Russian elite) of a U.S. military presence in Central Asia all contributed to what seemed to be a very positive relationship. This was the period when President George W. Bush looked into Putin's soul and famously declared that he could trust him.

After 2003, however, the relationship changed radically. Putin started to hurl the wildest accusations and insults against the West, charging that the Beslan atrocity had been engineered by those who always wanted to isolate Russia and to put it down, calling Western powers neocolonialists, and comparing the United States to Nazi Germany. Putin began to take the most intransigent diplomatic positions against U.S. initiatives on almost every subject (ranging from Kosovo to anti-missile systems in Eastern Europe), threatening escalation and retaliation.

What caused this shift? First of all, there was a change in what the Soviets used to call "the correlation of forces." This is best summed up by a formulation often used nowadays by Russian interlocutors: "Russia up, America down, and Europe out." Russia is up because of the price of oil, America down due to the consequences of its Iraq adventure, and Europe out because of the defeat of the EU Constitution, the failure to get its act together on energy matters, and the influence of new member states (like Poland and the Baltic republics) that Russia considers both hostile and contemptible.

Second, by warning against external dangers and enemies, Putin helps to inspire a "fortress" mentality in Russia, and gives himself a pretext for branding any domestic opposition as treason and for calling upon everyone to rally behind the leader. But while the first reason explains what made the change possible and the second what makes it useful for the transition to autocracy, Russia's foreign policy cannot be fully understood without taking into account the postimperial humiliation and resentment of the Russian people and the neoimperial ambition of its leaders.

Imperialism, Nationalism, and Autocracy

Two quotations seem to me to sum up the role of these sentiments. The first was stated by Andrei Kozyrev, Russia's most pro-Western foreign minister, in 1995: "Two things will kill the democratic experiment here—a major economic catastrophe and NATO enlargement."[5] Both, of course, came to pass. So it was very easy to convince the Russian public that *both* were engineered by the West, that the advice of Western economic experts, like the admission of former Soviet allies into NATO, was part of a great conspiracy against Russia.

The second statement was made by Vladimir Putin himself a number of times, most conspicuously, if in condensed form, in May 2005 in Germany. The complete text, as quoted by the British historian Geoffrey Hosking, is as follows: "He who does not regret the break-up of the Soviet Union has no heart; he who wants to revive it in its previous form has no head."[6]

Together these two statements point to the twin problems of resentment and revanchism on the part of postimperial powers, and to the effects of these passions upon the prospects for democracy. Zbigniew Brzezinski has suggested that it was in Russia's interest to lose Ukraine, because Russia can either be an empire or a democracy, but it cannot be both.[7] With Ukraine, Russia is an empire; without Ukraine it is not an empire and thus can become a democracy. This may well be true in the long run, but in the short term losing an empire is not the most promising prelude to the task of building democracy. The Weimar syndrome inevitably comes to mind.

If you have lost an empire and not found a role, as Dean Acheson once said about Britain, what can you do? One solution, adopted in various ways by Germany, France, Britain, Austria, and Turkey, is to try to adapt to the new situation. You may do this by abandoning imperial ambitions, or by trying to transfer them to a larger whole like Europe, or by becoming the junior partner of a bigger power, as Britain has done with the United States. On the other hand, one can try to recover one's past imperial position, a process that members of the permanent Russian elite such as Sergei Karaganov think is well under way. Dmitri Rogozin, a well-known nationalist leader and Russia's new ambassador to NATO, calls upon his fellow radical nationalists to join the government in helping Russia to "recover its status as a great power."[8]

> **Virtual democracy and virtual empire go together. Just as Russia's leaders pretend that they are ruling over a democracy, they also pretend that they are ruling over an empire.**

A third possibility is simply to *pretend* that you still are (or again have become) a superpower. Here, virtual democracy and virtual empire go together. Just as Russia's leaders pretend that they are ruling over a democracy, they also pretend that they are ruling over an empire.

Gorbachev, Yeltsin, and the whole Russian elite had been entertaining a somewhat analogous hope ever since the collapse of the Soviet Union. They thought that Russia's conversion to democracy would automatically earn it a kind of duopoly—the co-leadership of the West with the United States, and the co-leadership of Europe with the European Union (with a special sphere of influence over the former Soviet satellites). As Dmitri Trenin puts it, "What Russia craves is respect. It does not want to be a junior partner—it wants to be an equal."[9]

To some extent, Western leaders understood this craving and tried to satisfy it by such steps as inviting Russia to join the G-7 and creating the NATO-Russia Council. But Russians soon concluded that the West, instead of giving them the "instant accession to co-leadership" to which they felt entitled, was "trading symbolism for substance."[10] This gave rise to feelings of disappointment, suspicion, and resentment, which were exacerbated by the Russians' view that the United States and Europe, adding insult to injury, were adopting former Russian satellites and penetrating former Russian territory.

Today, thanks to his country's improved economic and strategic bargaining position, Putin has found a rather skillful way to make Russia's virtual empire seem more credible. It is to demonstrate that Russia (to borrow Madeleine Albright's expression about the United States) is "the indispensable nation," that it is a great power at least in a negative sense, inasmuch as it can block any Western strategy or diplomatic initiative with which it does not agree or on which it was not consulted. Sometimes opposing the West—or at least not following its lead—may be based on strategic considerations, such as competition for clients. But obstructionism seems to be a priority even when Moscow shares Western goals, such as avoiding an Iranian nuclear capacity. Indeed, in some cases thwarting the West appears to become a goal in itself, as recent Russian policy toward Kosovo illustrates.

The same mindset is applied even more strongly to the weaker states surrounding Russia. Putin may not be able to reintegrate them into the Russian empire, but, as a second-best alternative, he can punish them for wanting to be independent. Above all, he seeks to prevent them from becoming models of democracy and prosperity that might be compared favorably to Russia. Ivan Krastev may exaggerate in stating that the 2004 Orange Revolution in Ukraine had the same effect on Russia as 9/11 had on the United States,[11] but it does seem that it really was a shock. Putin's highest priority is to oppose "color revolutions"—to keep them from succeeding where they have occurred, and to prevent one from coming to Russia.

The Russians and the World

Two questions crucial to our subject remain to be answered: What has been the reaction of Russian society to Putin's policies, and what has been their global or international impact?

As regards the first question, the evidence seems to show that, while most Russians are aware of and condemn the regime's human rights violations, and in principle favor liberal democracy, they are also grateful to Putin for restoring Russia's international power and authority. As a researcher at the Levada Analytical Center, Russia's leading institute for the study of public opinion, writes: "Today, all categories of the population care about Russia recovering its power. As soon as a young man becomes conscious of his citizenship, the following idea emerges: The country is in bad shape, its authority in the world needs to be enhanced."[12] Indeed, in 2006, among those who regret the collapse of the USSR, 55 percent (as opposed to only 29 percent in 1990) cite as their main reason: "People no longer feel they belong to a great power." And those who regret the passing of the Soviet Union are not a small minority. In answer to the question, "Would you like the Soviet Union and the socialist system to be reestablished," 12 percent answer, "Yes, and I think it quite realistic"; 48 percent say, "Yes, but I think now it is unrealistic"; and only 31 percent say, "No, I would not."[13]

Russian sociologist Emil Pain speaks of a "revival of the imperialist syndrome." While, in principle, imperial sentiment should be an antidote to ethnic nationalism directed against non-Russian peoples from the former Soviet Union, Pain points out that the two are currently blended in a generalized xenophobia.[14] Gorbachev, in trying to save the Soviet system, opened the way to forces that overwhelmed it; is it possible that Putin, by encouraging radical nationalists, may similarly unleash forces that will go well beyond his intention and his capacity to control them? There are signs, albeit disputed ones, that he may already be more and more isolated, that he has to arbitrate a severe fight between competing "clans," and that he may experience "the impotence of omnipotence"[15] and be sidelined by his own appointees. While we cannot exclude the hypothesis that Russia (or China) will become a stable authoritarian or illiberal capitalist regime, it does seem more likely that in the long run both these countries will have to evolve either toward new forms of nationalistic fascism or toward some form of democracy.

Internationally, Putin is playing a skillful and (for the time being) successful game. He has effected a turn toward Asia in Russian foreign policy (not out of any Eurasian ideology, although he does play upon this strand of Russian public opinion). His motive is, first, to play the China card as a way of balancing the United States (as Nixon and Kissinger did to balance the Soviet Union). Putin knows full well that in the long run China constitutes a bigger danger to Russia than does the United States, but this approach offers him a way to invoke the virtual multipolar world to which China also pays lip service and to buttress Russia's credentials as a virtual Asian power. More important, Russia and China jointly are able to use their indifference to human rights to block Western attempts to sanction rogue states, from Uzbekistan and Burma to Sudan and Zimbabwe, and instead to deal with these countries in purely economic and strategic terms.

In this, Russia and China are at one with almost all the countries of the global South, including India, for whom national sovereignty and noninterference in internal affairs trump democracy promotion and the defense of human rights. Russia and China thus put themselves in the position of balancers, mediators, or arbiters in a potential conflict between the North and the South, or between the United States and countries like Iran or North Korea.

One should not see this new situation as a universal confrontation between the democratic West and a coalition of totalitarians that includes everyone from Putin to Ahmadinejad and Bin Laden. It comes closer to the triangular configuration that prevailed between the two World Wars, though it is even more complicated. But one result is clear and obvious: The

international struggle for democracy and human rights is made much more difficult by the existence of countries that are, at the same time, indispensable partners for the West (as Russia is for nuclear and energy matters), but also competitors and adversaries. If one adds to this the non-Western world's quasi-universal distrust of the West, it is hard not to be pessimistic about the international prospects for democracy, at least in the near term.

But lack of optimism for the short run should not mean lack of commitment and faith. The French philosopher Henri Bergson put forward a thesis that seems to me as true as it is shocking: Liberal democracy is the least natural regime on earth.[16] What is natural is the rule of the strongest. Democracy can come into being only through an uphill struggle that requires courage and perseverance and that aims at a profound change in attitudes and institutions. That is why I would like to dedicate this lecture to those who, in the most difficult situations, fight against the tide—in the first place, to the late Anna Politovskaya, but also to all those who, in Russia and countries with similar regimes, continue to write freely and truthfully about democracy and about autocracy.

Notes

1. Dmitri V. Trenin, *Getting Russia Right* (Washington, D.C.: Carnegie Endowment for International Peace, 2007), 101–15.

2. Sergei Kovalev, "Why Putin Wins," *New York Review of Books,* 22 November 2007.

3. Lilia Shevtsova, *Russia—Lost in Transition* (Washington, D.C.: Carnegie Endowment for International Peace, 2007), ch. 2.

4. Paul Goble, citing Sergei Arutyunov, head of the Caucasus section of the Institute of Ethnology at the Russian Academy of Sciences, in "Window on Eurasia: Russia Ever More Like Pre-Nazi Germany, Moscow Scholar Says," 12 October 2007, http://windowoneurasia.blogspot.com.

5. Quoted by Zoltan Barany, *Democratic Breakdown and the Decline of the Russian Military* (Princeton: Princeton University Press, 2007), 184.

6. Quoted by Geoffrey Hosking, *Rulers and Victims: The Russian in the Soviet Union* (Cambridge: Belknap Press of Harvard University Press, 200), 409.

7. See Zbigniew Brzezinski, *The Grand Chessboard* (New York: Basic Books, 1997), 92, 104, 122; and Zbigniew Brzezinski, "The Premature Partnership," *Foreign Affairs* 73 (March–April 1994): 80.

8. Paul Goble, "Window on Eurasia: Putin's New Man at NATO Urges Russian Nationalists to Infiltrate Moscow Regime," 13 January 2007, http://windowoneurasia .blogspot.com.

9. "Last Tango in Tehran," *Economist,* 20 October 2007.

10. A. Horelick and T. Graham, *U.S.-Russian Relations at the Turn of the Century* (Washington, D.C.: Carnegie Endowment for International Peace, 2000).

11. Ivan Krastev, "Russia vs. Europe: The Sovereignty Wars" *Open Democracy,* 5 December 2007. See also his "Ukraine

and Europe: A Fatal Attraction," *Open Democracy,*
16 December 2004.

12. Alexei Levinson cited by Leonid Sedov, "Les Russes
    et les valeurs démocratiques," *Futuribles* (September 2006),
    n322.

13. Levada Analytical Center, *Russian Public Opinion 2006*
    (Moscow, 2007), 183.

14. Emil Pain, "On the Revival of the Imperialist Syndrome," in
    After Empire (Moscow: Liberal Mission Foundation Press,
    2007), 115.

15. Shevtsova, *Russia—Lost in Transition,* 324.

16. Henri Bergson, *Les deux sources de la morale et de la religion,*
    Remarques finales, Société naturelle et démocratie (Paris: Presses
    Universitaires de France, 1932), 299, in Quadrige Series, 1990.

PIERRE HASSNER, research director emeritus at the Centre d'Etudes et de Recherches Internationales (CERI) in Paris, delivered the 2007 Seymour Martin Lipset Lecture on Democracy in the World. For many years he was a professor of international relations at the Institut d'Etudes Politiques in Paris and a senior visiting lecturer at the European Center of Johns Hopkins University in Bologna. He is the author of *La terreur et l'empire* (2003) and *La violence et la paix: De la bombe atomique au nettoyage ethnique* (1995, with an English translation in 1997).

How Did We Get Here?

Mexican Democracy after the 2006 Elections

CHAPPELL LAWSON

1. Introduction

On July 2, 2006, Mexican voters elected National Action Party (PAN) candidate Felipe Calderón as the next president of Mexico. Calderón's victory was extremely narrow; he won under 36% of the total vote and less that 0.6% more than his leftist rival, Andrés Manuel López Obrador. This potentially problematic situation was aggravated by López Obrador's decision to challenge Calderón's victory, both in the courts and in the streets. López Obrador's protest campaign culminated on September 16, when tens of thousands of his followers gathered in downtown Mexico City to acclaim him "legitimate president" of Mexico. Meanwhile, in the legislature, leaders of López Obrador's Party of the Democratic Revolution (PRD) oscillated between hints that they would collaborate with Calderón's administration and signs that they would adopt a posture of untrammeled hostility.

Post-electoral controversies raised the specter of a Left that had abandoned parliamentary tactics and returned to mass mobilization as its principal political strategy. At worst, they presaged the sort of political upheaval that could threaten Mexico's young democratic institutions. There was certainly no missing the symbolism involved in López Obrador's choice of the date on which he would take the oath of office—November 20, the anniversary of the Mexican Revolution—nor could students of Mexican history fail to recall that a contested election had sparked that decade-long conflagration.

How did Mexico find itself in the middle of such a crisis? Why had the country's vaunted electoral regime, generally regarded as a model for other democracies, failed to produce an outcome that all parties considered legitimate? Were Mexican political institutions so shaky that the actions of a single man could threaten their collapse? And, given the answers to these questions, what does the future hold for Mexico's political system?

Over the last decade, research on Mexican politics has focused on (1) institutional reform, especially in the electoral sphere, and (2) mass behavior, especially voting. Both areas of research are, of course, essential to understanding Mexico's transition from a one-party-dominant regime to a multiparty democracy.

However, scholarly attention to them has tended to understate the importance of political leadership and informal arrangements among elites, topics which were so central to earlier work on democratization (see O'Donnell and Schmitter 1986).

This article argues that the way these elites interact plays a pivotal role in the current situation. It first summarizes Mexico's transition to democracy over the last 15 years. It then addresses the simmering tensions between the PRD and the PAN during the administration of Vicente Fox that boiled over in the 2006 elections. The third section suggests that Mexico's current climate of polarization is a function of elite attitudes and interactions, rather than those of the mass public. The fourth section shows how these same interactions exercise a far greater influence on Mexican politics than do those institutions most often implicated in poor governance. The route out of Mexico's political impasse thus runs through pacting and compromise among members of Mexico's current political class, rather than further institutional tinkering.

2. Incomplete Transition

For close to seven decades, a single party (known today as the Institutional Revolutionary Party, or PRI) won all elections for significant posts. Over time, however, modernization weakened the corporatist and clientelist apparatuses through which the "official" party and the state had ensured social control. The collapse of Mexico's economy in the 1980s further undermined autocratic institutions and provoked mass disaffection with the old regime.

In the face of mounting social unrest, representatives of Mexico's political establishment negotiated a series of reforms with the leaders of the main opposition parties during the 1990s. These elite pacts, most notably the 1996 "Reform of the State," ultimately leveled the electoral playing field. In 1997, the PRI lost control of the Chamber of Deputies, and in 2000 PAN candidate Vicente Fox captured the presidency.

Data from standard measures of democracy nicely capture both the scope and the limitations of Mexico's political transition during the 1990s. In 1991, Mexico scored a zero on the combined Polity IV index; by 2001, it scored an eight.[1] Freedom House scores show a similar trend, with Mexico's score falling from eight in 1991 to four 10 years later.[2] By either measure, this transition left Mexico in the same league as many other new democracies at the beginning of the twenty-first century, such as Argentina, Brazil, Mongolia, South Korea, Taiwan, or Romania. In the prevailing scholarly discourse, Mexico had undergone a gradual transition from a moderately authoritarian regime to an "electoral democracy," but it had not yet become a "liberal democracy" (Diamond 1999).

A closer view of Mexico's political transition reveals the unevenness of democratization across different institutions and spheres of governance. For instance, Mexico's electoral regime and party system were quite well developed (see Todd Eisenstadt's essay in this symposium). As in the old regime, the military and the security services remained small and firmly under civilian control. Finally, despite the domination of broadcast television by two relentlessly commercial networks, Mexico's mass media had become quite open by the time of Fox's election in 2000 (Lawson 2003). By contrast, progress toward reforming the police, the judiciary, the prosecutorial apparatus, and other parts of the bureaucracy remained painfully slow. The PRI remained the country's largest party (until 2006); businessmen with longstanding ties to conservative factions of the regime continued to monopolize most sectors of the economy; and corrupt bosses affiliated with the PRI controlled most labor unions.

As president, Fox presided over modest democratic deepening. Civic groups and opposition parties successfully challenged the PRI's remaining strongholds at the state and local level; independent newspapers sprouted throughout the country; state-level electoral authorities became more independent and professional; prominent PRI figures and organizations began to defect to the opposition; and the passage of a federal Transparency Law exposed government operations to public scrutiny. Although corruption remained a serious problem, especially in the criminal justice system, the administration itself managed to avoid major scandals.

For most Mexicans, the PRI's defeat in 2000 represented the culmination of a long process of democratic transition and the beginning of an equally arduous process of democratic deepening. For the Left, however, alternation in power between the old ruling party and the conservative PAN constituted only partial or cosmetic change. Three episodes during Fox's tenure seemed to confirm their fears.

In 2003, the PAN and the PRI joined forces to name the new leaders of the Federal Electoral Institute (IFE) over the objections of the PRD. In contrast to the previous set of "Citizen Councilors," who included a number of distinguished academics and activists, the new cohort included a number of political unknowns and party hacks. Their selection signaled the breakdown of the partisan consensus that had characterized the political accords of 1996–1997.

Two years later, PAN and PRI legislators voted to impeach López Obrador, then mayor of Mexico City, on the grounds that he had violated a court injunction in a zoning dispute. Had the legal proceedings continued, they would have prevented López

Obrador from seeking the presidency. The Fox administration backed down in the face of widespread public opposition, international pressure, and massive demonstrations in Mexico City organized by López Obrador. Most Mexicans saw the affair as an attempt to trump up charges against a popular rival.

A third insult came in the midst of the 2006 presidential race, with the passage of the new broadcasting law (the "Ley Televisa") that was notoriously favorable to Mexico's two main television networks. During the second half of the race, television coverage of Calderón became more favorable, while reporting on López Obrador turned rather sour. In the leftist narrative, all of these events signaled a conspiracy between the government, the PAN, the old ruling party, leading businessmen, and a now-perverted electoral authority to deprive their candidate of victory.

Panistas (PAN partisans), of course, saw matters in an entirely different light. Their party stood for the same Christian Democratic principles that it had represented steadfastly since the late 1930s; by contrast, the PRD represented both the radicalism of the Marxist left and the corruption of the old PRI (from which many of the PRD's founders had come). It was the PRD that had rejected Fox's offer to form something like a government of national unity in 2000, and it was PRD obstructionism that had prevented partisan consensus in the selection of a new set of IFE Councilors.

Despite López Obrador's moderate position on many policy issues, his administration as mayor of Mexico City struck opponents as eerily reminiscent of PRI rule. For instance, López Obrador incorporated whole hog into the PRD apparatus almost two dozen PRI organizations, several with decidedly unsavory reputations. Episodes of corruption among his top aides, some captured on videotape, raised serious questions about financial probity, as did López Obrador's refusal to endorse a local transparency law modeled after the federal statute.

For his opponents, post-electoral controversies only confirmed their instincts: López Obrador was simply unwilling to accept the results of an election that the IFE, the Federal Electoral Court, and most international observers considered free and fair (see Eisenstadt's article). His ad-libbed responses to critics in speeches after the elections—e.g., "to hell with your institutions"—betrayed a casual attitude toward the rule of law that would have imperiled democracy had he won. This perspective contrasted starkly with Calderón's pledges to respect the autonomy of regulatory institutions, insulate the office of the public prosecutor from direct control by the executive, reform the judicial system, and further devolve authority to state and local governments—precisely the steps Mexico needed to overcome its autocratic legacy.

Since 2003, the tactics adopted by Mexican political elites in their partisan disputes have proven more tendentious and incendiary than analysts predicted. For instance, few political observers in 2001 would have anticipated PRI and PAN attempts to prevent López Obrador from contesting the 2006 elections through an act of legal legerdemain. Even fewer would have guessed how far López Obrador was willing to escalate his tactics after July 2, 2006.

3. Elites or Masses?

Do trends at the elite level reflect increasing polarization among ordinary Mexicans? Over the last five decades, support for the PRI in the mass public has declined at a rate of about 3% per election cycle. The weakness of the PRI's presidential candidate in 2006, Roberto Madrazo, only accelerated this process by hastening defections from the old ruling party (see Langston's contribution to this symposium). Because the PRI was ideologically and socially amorphous, its unraveling should theoretically have divided Mexico along lines of class and ideology. Left-Right differences should also become more salient as the issue of democratization faded from the agenda, forcing people to choose between very different political alternatives rather than simply selecting the one that was most likely to defeat the regime.

Nevertheless, the way in which voters have attached themselves to the PRD and the PAN has not seem to followed such a clear logic. Most Mexicans do not base their electoral choices on the policy positions adopted by parties and candidates (see Moreno's and Bruhn and Greene's articles in this collection). Still less do Mexicans vote along class lines (see Moreno). Although indicators of social status—such as living standards, education, skin color, and occupation—influence voting behavior at the margin, for ordinary Mexicans, region is a far more important predictor.[3] Consider, for instance, the "classic" PRD voter in May 2006: a brown-skinned, low-income man with a modest education who never attends church. A person with this demographic profile living in the north of the country had a 20% chance of favoring López Obrador—far lower than his probability of favoring Calderón. If his home was in the center of the country, however, his probability of supporting López Obrador rose to 34%. If he lived in the south, it was 44%, and if he resided in the Mexico City metropolitan area, it was 72%. Even this regional cleavage is muddled by the continued strength of the PRI in many areas of the country (see Klesner's essay in this symposium). In other words, divisions between the PRD and the PAN at the mass level are not simply less pronounced than those at the elite level, the fundamental axis of cleavage is different.

The episodes so central to polarization at the elite level have played out very differently in the electorate. For instance, polling data indicate that there is little support for continued protests by López Obrador; even many of those who voted for him express ambivalence about his tactics.[4] This situation echoes public sentiment during the impeachment of López Obrador: not only did an overwhelming majority of Mexicans oppose attempts to prevent him from running in the 2006 election, so did a majority of *panistas*.[5] These facts lend credence to arguments advanced by Bermeo (2003) and others that political crises are typically the product of elite machinations, rather than of mass preferences.

Acknowledging the truth of this argument, however, tells us little about why elite conflict has become so pronounced. The principal answer to this question lies in the patterns of party-building in Mexico. During the period of one-party rule, the PRI's eclectic nature gave rise to a fragmented opposition. Because opposition politics promised few tangible rewards, it tended to draw more extreme or ideologically purist members of society, on both the Right and the Left (Greene, forthcoming). Today, PAN and PRD activists come from strikingly different backgrounds. PAN candidates to Congress in 2006 were generally introduced to politics through their ties to the private sector and the Church; PRD candidates came up through labor unions and popular social movements (see the Mexico 2006 Candidate and Party Leader Survey, described in Bruhn and Greene's contribution to this collection). Although many leaders in both parties have attended public school, PAN politicians are far more likely to have attended private or parochial institutions. As a result of these patterns of political recruitment, party elites share relatively few cultural reference points.

Despite steps toward internal democracy in both parties, old guard elements still exercise substantial influence. The PAN remains a "club" party, in the sense that membership is not automatically open to anyone. Rather, those who wish to join must first be accepted as junior members (*miembros adherentes*); after a minimum trial period of six months and participation in various party activities, they may then apply to become full, dues-paying members (*miembros activos*). Both types of members could vote in the 2006 presidential primary, but only full members can vote for candidates for other offices or for party leaders. Not surprisingly, the party's current leadership remains far more conservative than party voters, not to mention ordinary citizens. In the case of the PRD, presidents have exercised rather wide discretion in whom they appoint to the National Executive Committee. Many of the current members were placed there by López Obrador. This fact may help to explain why, despite the steady influx of pragmatic PRI defectors into the PRD, its leadership supported López Obrador's post-electoral protest movement. These party elites are, in turn, the principal source of political polarization in Mexico.

4. Elites or Institutions?

For those political scientists who emphasize the role of institutions, the roots of Mexico's current political predicament lie in a cluster of familiar constitutional rules. First, Mexico's electoral system contains a large component of proportional representation, which in turn encourages multipartism. A multiparty system is not inherently problematic, but it becomes so when paired with a second institution: presidentialism. The combination of these two institutions virtually guarantees divided government. The adverse effects of these arrangements are compounded by the lack of run-off elections for president, which permits the election of non-Condorcet winners, and by the length of the presidential term (six years). Finally, to make matters worse, the prohibition on consecutive reelection renders politicians less accountable.

Dysfunctional institutions, however, cannot account for the most salient features of Mexico's current political topography. Most obviously, they cannot explain why one of the best-designed electoral systems in the world failed to produce a result that party leaders on the losing side would accept. If institutions are the main issue, governance problems should be the product of gridlock, rather than political polarization. Today, the reverse is true: as a result of likely collaboration between the PAN and elements of the PRI, legislative gridlock is now relatively unlikely; on the other hand, alleged electoral irregularities provoked a crisis.

Choice and leadership have more to do with today's situation than do formal institutions. In the case of post-electoral protests, for instance, other men in the same situation would have made different decisions than did López Obrador. In 1988, PRD candidate Cuauhtémoc Cárdenas proved less vigorous in protesting the official results of the election than López Obrador is today, even though the Left had much stronger grounds to do so then. Likewise, had Calderón lost the election, there is no doubt that he would have accepted the result or challenged it through strictly constitutional channels. The problem, then, lies less in how Mexico's president was elected than in how elites reacted to his election.

The simple fact that institutions have played a role in permitting the overrepresentation of extremists at the top of Mexico's main parties does not consign Mexico to crisis. Even fairly doctrinaire politicians can compromise, as the 1996–1997 inter-party negotiations showed. Nothing in the current context compels the PRD's leadership in Congress to adopt a relentlessly obstructionist stance, and the electoral benefits of doing so are at best unclear. Nor do present circumstances prevent Mexico's president-elect from reaching out to the Left.

There is not necessarily anything wrong with further institutional reform in Mexico, of course. But such reform is important as a symptom of agreement among the main political parties, not as its cause. In the end, it is the way particular leaders interact that will propel events toward compromise, or toward crisis.

References

Bermeo, Nancy. 2003. *Ordinary People in Extraordinary Times: The Citizenry and the Breakdown of Democracy.* Princeton: Princeton University Press.

Bruhn, Kathleen, and Kenneth F. Greene. 2007. "Elite Polarization Meets Mass Moderation in Mexico's 2006 Elections." *PS: Political Science and Politics* 40 (January): 33–38.

Diamond, Larry. 1999. *Developing Democracy: Toward Consolidation.* Baltimore: Johns Hopkins University Press.

Eisenstadt, Todd A. 2007. "The Origins and Rationality of the 'Legal versus Legitimate' False Dichotomy Invoked in Mexico's 2006 Post-Electoral Conflict." *PS: Political Science and Politics* 40 (January): 39–43.

Greene, Kenneth F. Forthcoming. *Defeating Dominance: Party Politics and Mexico's Democratization in Comparative Perspective.* Cambridge: Cambridge University Press.

Klesner, Joseph. 2007. "The 2006 Mexican Elections: Manifestation of a Divided Society?" *PS: Political Science and Politics* 40 (January): 27–32.

Langston, Joy. 2007. "The PRI's 2006 Electoral Debacle." *PS: Political Science and Politics* 40 (January): 21–25.

Lawson, Chappell. 2003. *Building the Fourth Estate: Democratization and the Rise of a Free Press in Mexico.* Berkeley: University of California Press.

———. 2006. "Preliminary Findings from the Mexico 2006 Panel Study: Blue States and Yellow States." Unpublished manuscript available at http://web.mit.edu/polisci/research/mexico06/Pres.htm.

Mainwaring, Scott. 1993. "Presidentialism, Multipartism, and Democracy: The Difficult Combination." *Comparative Political Studies* 26 (2): 198–228.

Moreno, Alejandro. 2007. "The 2006 Mexican Presidential Election: The Economy, Oil Revenues, and Ideology." *PS: Political Science and Politics* 40 (January): 15–19.

O'Donnell, Guillermo, and Philippe C. Schmitter. 1986. *Transitions from Authoritarian Rule: Tentative Conclusions about Uncertain Democracies.* Baltimore: Johns Hopkins University Press.

Notes

1. The combined Polity IV score ranges from –10 (utter autocracy) to 10 (full democracy). A score of zero indicates that autocratic features of the regime evenly balance.

2. Freedom House scores range from 2–14; higher scores indicate *less* freedom.

3. Results are based on simulations from a multinomial logit model of vote choice, in which the dependent variable took on one of four values (Calderón, López Obrador, Madrazo, or none/undecided). Independent variables included: age, gender, living standards (as measured by an index of material possessions, education, church attendance, region, political engagement, skin color, and urban or rural residence). Data are taken from the Mexico 2006 Panel Study, Wave 2. For full results, see Lawson 2006, available at: http://web.mit.edu/polisci/research/mexico06/Pres.htm.

4. Mexico 2006 Panel Study, Wave 3 and accompanying cross-section; Consulta Mitovsky, National Household Survey, August 2006.

5. Parametría, "El desafuero de López Obrador," National Household Survey, August 2004; Consulta Mitovsky, Household Survey in the Federal District, September 2004; Consulta Mitovsky, National Household Survey, January 2005; Consulta Mitovsky, National Telephone Survey and National Household Survey, April 2005; Consulta Mitovsky, Household Survey in the Federal District, February 2005.

Behind the Honduran Mutiny

JOSE DE CORDOBA

During Honduras' Independence Day celebrations last September 15, then-President Manuel Zelaya turned up for a time-honored ritual meant to promote national unity. But rather than merely making the traditional presidential cry "Long Live the Republic!" Mr. Zelaya treated political, civic and business leaders to a 15-minute diatribe against capitalism.

"The businessmen and corrupt oligarchy are responsible for our country's two centuries of poverty because they support an unjust neoliberal economic model that exploits humans and our natural resources," said Mr. Zelaya, wearing his trademark white Stetson hat, as members of the crowd began to shout "*Fuera! Fuera! Fuera!*" ("Out! Out! Out!").

Forced out of the country last month by the military, Mr. Zelaya returned Friday—at least temporarily. Trailed by reporters and talking on a cell phone, Mr. Zelaya crossed the border into Honduras from his Nicaraguan exile. He walked to the rusty chain that marks the border, lifted it and walked a few feet onto his native soil.

"We are unarmed. I come in peace," Mr. Zelaya said, shaking hands with a Honduran army officer, before retreating back into Nicaragua under threat of arrest by the provisional Honduran government. U.S. Secretary of State Hillary Clinton called the stunt "reckless."

It's the latest turn in a growing regional crisis that's far more complicated than it appears. The episode may seem like a flashback to a tragicomic era of Latin American history when presidents were regularly overthrown in coups. That's how the Obama administration has responded so far, voting with the Organization of American States to suspend Honduras and calling for Mr. Zelaya's reinstatement.

But in fact, a close look at Mr. Zelaya's time in office reveals a strongly antidemocratic streak. He placed himself in a growing cadre of elected Latin presidents who have tried to stay in power past their designated time to carry out a populist-leftist agenda. These leaders, led by Venezuela's Hugo Chavez, have used the region's historic poverty and inequality to gain support from the poor, but created deep divisions in their societies by concentrating power in their own hands and increasing government control over the economy, media and other sectors.

Mr. Zelaya, a 56-year-old former rancher and logger with a handlebar moustache, joined this group, which includes Mr. Chavez, Rafael Correa in Ecuador, Evo Morales in Bolivia, and Daniel Ortega in Nicaragua. This past week, Mr. Ortega laid out plans for a referendum to rewrite Nicaragua's Constitution and allow him to be re-elected indefinitely, something Mr. Chavez has already achieved in oil-rich Venezuela.

It was such a move that led to trouble in neighboring Honduras. For the past year, Mr. Zelaya led a drive to rewrite the constitution to abolish term limits. On the day of his ouster, he was planning a referendum to call a constitutional assembly, even though the vote had been declared illegal by the country's Supreme Court.

The crisis has put the Obama administration in a difficult spot. Mindful of past U.S. support of coups in Latin America, it condemned the ouster and has led efforts to find a negotiated solution. But its insistence on Mr. Zelaya's return to power has angered many middle-class Hondurans, who feel the ouster defended the country's institutions from a Chavez-style power grab.

"This is a showdown which will determine if the *Chavista* model triumphs or not," says Moises Starkman, who advised Mr. Zelaya on special projects and now works for the interim government in the same capacity.

Little in Mr. Zelaya's background suggested he would become an international symbol of a democratically elected leader forced from office. Mr. Zelaya is a product of Olancho, a violent, macho state in central Honduras that is dominated by pistol-packing landowners who run huge estates. His family, involved in logging and ranching, has been one of the dominant forces in Olancho for decades.

One of four children, Mr. Zelaya grew up the son of rural privilege, distinguished by little but a love for the guitar, Harley Davidsons and horses. In 1975, when Mr. Zelaya was 23 years old, his father, also named Jose Manuel, was put on trial for helping army officers torture and murder 14 rural activists, including two priests. Convicted and sentenced to 20 years in prison, Mr. Zelaya's father served little more than a year before being freed in a general amnesty.

The elder Zelaya's incarceration deeply affected his son, friends say. Mr. Zelaya dropped out of college after a spotty period studying industrial engineering and went home to Olancho to take care of the family businesses. Mr. Zelaya visited his incarcerated father often, at times even sleeping in the prison, says Victor Meza, who served as Mr. Zelaya's last interior minister. "That shaped him," says Mr. Meza.

As a young man, Mr. Zelaya didn't have strong ideological leanings. He ran his family's logging operations and eventually became a director of Honduras' top business organization. He also worked his way up the ranks of the Liberal Party, the country's oldest and most important political party, serving first as a deputy then as head of Honduras' social investment fund.

Colleagues say Mr. Zelaya is disorganized and lacks formal education but has animal-like political instincts. "His background is milking cows, and all of a sudden he's speaking before the United Nations," says Mr. Meza. Despite his lack of formal education, Mr. Zelaya is a quick study.

Soon, he was a rising star in the Liberal Party, making an unsuccessful run for the presidency in 2001. In 2005, he ran again, this time winning the presidency by a sliver. At his inaugural, Mr. Zelaya threw away his prepared speech and improvised, making numerous gaffes. "It would be a sign of the way he would run his government," says Honduran political scientist Miguel Calix.

In his first year, Mr. Zelaya didn't seem very ideological and spent a lot of time traveling. He was a big spender. On one notable trip to Washington, he took along a large group, including family members. He handed off his infant granddaughter to a startled President George W. Bush at a White House ceremony.

Two years into his term, Mr. Zelaya reshuffled his government, bringing into his cabinet a hard-line cadre of ministers dominated by Patricia Rodas, his foreign minister. The daughter of a famous right-wing Liberal party leader, Ms. Rodas has a reputation as a doctrinaire, hard-line Marxist from her university days.

Even as leftist associates increased their influence on Mr. Zelaya, the world economy also pushed him leftwards. In 2007, Honduras was hit hard by record high oil prices. The country imports all its fuel needs, and also has no refining capacity. That means four companies—Chevron, Exxon Mobil, Royal Dutch Shell and the local Dipsa—control the market, importing the fuel directly and distributing it through their own service stations. As oil prices climbed, Honduras, whose power plants run on fuel, was forced to hike electricity prices, and ration power.

At first, Mr. Zelaya, desperate for relief, tried to lower the cost of imports by buying oil products in bulk, but the plan failed because the government didn't have its own oil-storage facilities. So, in 2007, Mr. Zelaya decreed a cut in fuel prices. But this move led to fuel shortages as importers complained that the price cuts undermined revenues. By mid 2008, the oil companies threatened to halt all new investment in Honduras.

Neighboring Nicaragua, which had been getting cut-rate fuel from Caracas since 2005 under a program called *Petrocaribe,* had no such problems. A brainchild of Mr. Chavez, *Petrocaribe* sells Venezuelan oil at market prices but allows its 18 member countries to finance a part of the oil at very low interest rates. As of 2007, *Petrocaribe* had provided $1.2 billion in financing— similar to the Washington-based Inter-American Development Bank's soft loans in that period.

As Mr. Zelaya fought with foreign oil companies, Mr. Chavez offered cheap oil. Few here opposed the country's entry into the Venezuelan oil pact when the Congress approved it in March of 2007. "I pushed hard for *Petrocaribe,*" says Adolfo Facusse, the

head of Honduras' industrialists' chamber and now an opponent of Mr. Zelaya. Since then, *Petrocaribe* has provided Mr. Zelaya's government some $126 million in savings, officials say.

Mr. Zelaya, who at first had kept his distance from Mr. Chavez, was quickly ensconced in the Venezuelan's tight embrace. "They get along very well, and trade jokes," says Mr. Meza. "On one trip to Caracas, Chavez joked with Zelaya, 'Mel, where did you tie up your horse?'"

Mr. Zelaya soon copied the Venezuelan's inflammatory rhetoric. In August, Mr. Zelaya joined the ALBA—a nine-nation trade and political pact that Mr. Chavez designed to counter U.S. influence in the region. Its other members include Bolivia, Cuba, Ecuador, and Nicaragua.

On Aug. 26, Mr. Zelaya joined Mr. Chavez and Nicaragua's Mr. Ortega before an audience of some 30,000 Hondurans, most of whom the government had paid a few dollars to attend. "Today we are taking a step towards becoming a government of the center-left, and if anyone dislikes this, we'll just remove the word 'center' and keep the left," he said.

Mr. Chavez didn't go down well in deeply conservative Honduras. "Any Honduran who is against joining ALBA is either an idiot or a traitor," the Venezuelan shouted to the crowds at the ALBA event, where he gave Mr. Zelaya a new nickname: *"Comandante Cowboy."*

Like Mr. Chavez, Mr. Zelaya was soon battling most of Honduras' institutions. Obliged by the constitution to send a budget to Congress by September 15, Mr. Zelaya refused, alleging various reasons, including that the world's financial crisis made it impossible for him to draw up numbers.

No one was more disappointed with Mr. Zelaya than his former mentor, Honduras' Cardinal Oscar Rodriguez, a top candidate to replace the late Pope John Paul II at the time of the pontiff's death. Cardinal Rodriguez blames Mr. Zelaya for using public money to promote his referendum instead of spending it on the poor. Earlier this year, cameras at Honduras' Central Bank caught government officials withdrawing about $2 million from its vaults in a suitcase, presumably to fund Mr. Zelaya's referendum drive. Three of Mr. Zelaya's former top officials, and Mr. Zelaya himself, have been charged with misappropriating public funds in that case. The officials deny the charges and say they are politically motivated.

"We were good friends. But he changed drastically," the Cardinal concludes. "It was Chavez. It was Chavez."

Some saw other Chavez-like traits emerging in Mr. Zelaya, including megalomania. Like his Venezuelan mentor, Mr. Zelaya took often to the airwaves commandeering all of the country's television channels for long speeches. Mirroring Mr. Chavez's fascination with Venezuelan independence hero Simon Bolivar, who tried to unite much of Latin America, Mr. Zelaya asked El Salvador's president if he could borrow the remains of Central America's 19th century hero, Gen. Francisco Morazan, who is buried in El Salvador, so he could tour Central America with the bones to push regional integration.

Mr. Zelaya took much of his cabinet when he went scuba diving in a tourist development, wearing his cowboy hat until the last moment before hitting the water. Earlier this year, he skipped a meeting with donor countries to attend a private concert of Mexico's Los Tigres del Norte, who serenaded Mr. Zelaya at the presidential palace with one of their hits "Jefe de Jefes," or "Boss of Bosses."

What really set Mr. Zelaya and most of the establishment on a collision course was what many Hondurans saw as his bold drive to perpetuate himself in power by rewriting the constitution to permit re-election—which is forbidden by Honduras' charter.

In the weeks before the referendum, the Supreme Court had ruled the vote illegal for two reasons: First, only Honduras' election agency, not the president, can call a referendum. Second, the article in Honduras' constitution that bars re-election is unchangeable—so much so that even attempting to change it leads to automatic dismissal from public office.

When the military, following court rulings, refused to help distribute the ballots days before the referendum, the president fired the military's chief of staff, Gen. Romeo Vasquez, and accepted the resignations of the heads of the army, navy and air force and the defense minister.

"I told the president we could not act against a court order. If we did so, we would be committing a crime," says former defense minister Edmundo Orellana, a close friend of Mr. Zelaya, who refused to go along with the president and resigned over the issue.

Tensions spiked two days later when Mr. Zelaya, defying the courts, led a mob to seize the disputed ballots at an Air Force base. "That was traumatic for the armed forces," says Mr. Orellana, referring to the mob's forced entry. "At that moment everyone said 'the man is crazy. We have to get him out."

The Supreme Court responded by ordering Mr. Zelaya stripped of his office and arrested. The military carried out the order, but feared his arrest would spark violence. So the army sent Mr. Zelaya packing, breaking another constitutional article that states a citizen can't be forcibly exiled and leading to an image— a president in his pajamas forced into exile at gunpoint—that led nearly everyone around the world to conclude the ouster qualified as a coup.

Mr. Orellana, who had resigned days earlier because he believed Mr. Zelaya was breaking the law, also believes the soldiers' action in exiling Mr. Zelaya constituted a coup. "It's the worse thing that could have happened," he says.

Thailand in 2008
Crises Continued

KITTI PRASIRTSUK

Thailand is currently facing a political crisis without precedent, with the country increasingly divided by political disagreements and social polarization. Anti-Thaksin and pro-Thaksin groups are engaged in a stand-off and are prepared for violence. The causes of the crisis are many, but at the heart of the problem lies the urban-rural divide. Although the judicial branch has stepped up its efforts to discharge the conflict through legal means, the populace has apparently found it impossible to wait or accept the rulings.

The political crisis began in 2005 with demonstrations against then-Prime Minister Thaksin Shinawatra and seemed to end with the coup d'état that deposed him in September 2006.[1] The coup leaders promised a quick return to democracy through the drafting of a new constitution and the convening of a general election for the House of Representatives in late 2007. As it turned out, the former Thai Rak Thai (Thai Love Thai) Party, reborn as the Palang Prachachon Party (People's Power Party, PPP), gained the majority thanks to Thaksin's continued popularity in rural areas. In brief, the coup succeeded neither in dismantling Thaksin's power base nor in solving the political crisis.

The Nominee Government

After the 2007 election, the PPP formed a coalition government with another five parties, namely Chart Thai (Thai Nation), Pue Paendin (For the Motherland), Matchimathippatai (Neutral Democratic Party), Ruamjai-thai Chartpattana (Thais United National Development Party), and Pracharaj (State's Citizens), leaving the Democrat Party alone in the opposition. Samak Suntaravej, a sharp-tongued veteran politician with a firm commitment to Thaksin, assumed the premiership.

The Cabinet, filled with detested ministers, was unpopular—particularly among the urban populace. As Thai Rak Thai boards of directors were banned from

politics for five years following the dissolution of the party because of election fraud, their spouses and relatives stepped in to take charge. For example, Newin Chidchob, a northeastern boss, landed his relative, Songsak Tongsri, in the lucrative Transportation Ministry. Some officials sent their wives to replace them, whether or not they were experienced in politics. These include Ranongrak Suwanchawee (a professional nurse) as deputy finance minister; Poonpirom Liptapallop (an army general) as energy minister; and Anongwan Thepsutin (a grade-school teacher by training) as minister of natural resources and environment. Thaksin's brother-in-law, Somchai Wongsawat, took the posts of deputy prime minister and minister of education. Most of these were running for election for the first time. Another notorious appointment was the distasteful Chalerm Yoobamrung to the powerful Ministry of Interior.[2] The Cabinet was thus dubbed a "nominee government," paving the way for anti-government sentiment to grow.

A New Round of Crises

Against the background of this unpopular government, two additional factors contributed to the new round of political crises in 2008. First, in spite of the problems facing Thailand, including an insurgency in the south and economic problems resulting from the hike in oil prices, the Samak government focused on proposing a constitutional amendment to protect officials' political interests.[3] Existing Articles 237 and 309 were key. Article 237 stipulates that election fraud by a party's board of directors will result in the compulsory dissolution of the party and the banning of all board members from election for five years. Because the Election Commission has found Yongyuth Tiyapairat, a PPP director, guilty of election fraud, a revision of this article could save the PPP. And an amendment of Article 309 would annul all organs and personnel set up by the coup, including the Asset Scrutiny Commission (ASC), which found Thaksin guilty on several corruption charges.

When the amendment efforts were intensified in the Parliament in March, the People's Alliance for Democracy (PAD), which had vocally staged an anti-Thaksin campaign since 2005, returned to the streets to pressure the PPP to back off. This time the PAD gathered at Makavan Bridge on Rajdamnoen Avenue, where many government agencies are located. The PAD's renewed efforts were also stirred by Thaksin's return to Thailand in February after 17 months in exile.[4]

Second, with a majority in the Parliament, the Samak administration claimed legitimacy, agitating the PAD crowds. Apart from Samak's volubly confrontational stance, at least three of his ministers committed political blunders. The first was Public Health Minister Chaiya Sasomsab, a local boss from Nakhon Pathom Province, who immediately after taking office vowed to undo Compulsory Licensing (CL), a policy enacted by the coup government that provided access to expensive medicines for the poor. The next blunder occurred with Jakrapob Penkhae, a minister in charge of mass media. Jakrapob made statements considered disrespectful to the monarchy. Because the PAD rides on a nationalist agenda of "rescuing the nation" and "revering the monarchy," the anti-government campaign intensified. Jakrapob came under political fire for lèse majesté and was later forced to step down in disgrace.

The Crisis Escalates

In May, the crisis escalated further when the government mishandled the Preah Vihear Temple case, leading to a territorial conflict with Cambodia. The dispute began when Thai Foreign Minister Noppadol Pattama signed a joint communiqué supporting a Cambodian proposal to have the ancient Angkorean temple listed as a world heritage site. Thailand and Cambodia had bitterly disputed rights to the temple in the 1950s, until the International Court of Justice ruled in favor of Cambodia. Although the mountain on which the temple is sited is considered Thai territory, Cambodia came to own the building itself. Thailand had no choice but to grudgingly accept the court's decision at that time. The problem became more acute when the United Nations Educational, Scientific, and Cultural Organization (UNESCO) in 2008 approved the Cambodian proposal to list the Preah Vihear Temple as a world heritage site.

With such world heritage status, Cambodia would allegedly be able to expand conservation areas around the site, encroaching on Thai territory. Rumor had it that Noppadol endorsed the Cambodian proposal in exchange for Thaksin's receiving a lucrative concession to set up casino and petroleum projects in Koh Kong Island, Cambodia. This case dealt a serious blow to the government and stirred nationalism among PAD demonstrators in particular. The PAD drew more demonstrators and stepped up its pressure on the government. Noppadol was compelled to resign soon thereafter. Although its initial plan was to fight against the government's attempt to amend the Constitution to protect officials, the PAD escalated its agenda, demanding Samak's resignation and later, the dissolution of Parliament. Since then, the PAD has continued to gain momentum.

The People vs. The People

Meanwhile, the pro-Thaksin crowds were reassembling under a new banner, the United Front of Democracy against Dictatorship (UDD). They took Sanamluang, the public ground in front of the Grand Palace, as their stage.[5] Many key Thai Rak Thai/PPP politicians have been heavily involved in UDD activities. Although PAD demonstrators wear yellow, the color showing respect for the king, UDD crowds wear red, in the past, the color signifying communists. Initially, UDD demonstrators (popularly called Reds) were despised as paid crowds who gathered for money. The crowds expanded remarkably, however, revealing a deep-seated division among the Thai people.

According to Dr. Prinya Thaewanarumitkul, this political crisis differs from past crises in a profound way. Whereas previous uprisings (in 1973, 1976, and 1992) entailed a struggle between people and government, this current conflict is a clash *among* citizens with different political orientations.[6] Notions of democracy differ starkly among Thais. As Anek Laothamatas pointed out long ago, Thailand has two contrasting visions of democracy, one rooted in the rural areas and one in the urban. The urban middle class, having higher levels of education and greater exposure to information, tends to vote for parties with high-profile politicians and sound policy platforms. Rural dwellers, meanwhile, tend to cast their votes based on the personal patronage networks of individual politicians, regardless of personal profiles or policy platforms. Vote buying, in fact, is the norm in most rural areas.

Things have become more complicated since Thaksin first came to power, however. Rural people became fond of Thai Rak Thai's populist policy platform. Political alignments also became divided by region. People in Bangkok and the southern provinces have opposed Thaksin and the PPP-based governments, while those in the northeast and the north support them. Southerners, who enjoy a strong economic base compared to other regions, share the political orientation of Bangkokians. Yet, even in the north and northeast, urban dwellers are aligned with the PAD.[7] Urban dwellers with lower incomes tend to favor Thaksin and the PPP. There is also a split within the middle class, as a large segment of urban dwellers and many intellectuals have come to favor Thaksin's policies and bold initiatives. The pro-Thaksin middle class takes performance and efficiency as a priority, while the anti-Thaksin group favors morality and good governance. As Thitinan Pongsudhirak cogently puts it, the political crisis should be characterized as the confrontation between the traditional establishment and the challengers. The former is represented by the "holy trinity" of monarchy, military, and bureaucracy; the latter is led by the Thaksin camp, which weds new business groups to provincial politicians in support of populist currents.[8] Thailand is thus becoming further divided, signified by the Yellows (PAD) versus the Reds (UDD).

Violence

Nationalist sentiment around the Preah Vihear case increased the momentum of the PAD, bringing the crisis to another level by mid-2008. When Interior Minister Chalerm visited the southern province of Krabi, he was faced with fierce booing and picketing by PAD demonstrators and had to return to Bangkok. The regional divide was becoming increasingly clear.

The first violence around the demonstrations broke out in the northeastern province of Udornthani, where a pro-government mob attacked PAD demonstrators. The police remained on the sidelines, watching as the violence happened before their eyes. PAD members, in turn, armed themselves by recruiting their own volunteer guards, who used wooden sticks, golf clubs, and helmets. The PAD's rhetoric became more militant, including anti-police sentiment. In response, Prime Minister Samak called for PAD demonstrators to be dispersed by force and the Makavan Bridge taken back. Samak backed off later that day, however, as PAD demonstrators gathered, showing no fear of the government's threat. Notably, many of these demonstrators were women, making it more difficult for the government to use force while maintaining its assertion of legitimacy.

The PAD declared August 26 "Whistle Day," a D-Day to mount pressure for dislodging the Samak government through a siege of Government House, the Prime Minister's Office compound, National Broadcasting Television (NBT), and some other government agencies.[9] The timing was important, with the PAD acting before the retirement of their allied military top brass at the end of September (these officers were supposed to protect the PAD; they were key players in the 2006 coup that toppled Thaksin). PAD members successfully occupied Government House and made it their main stage. Without access to his office, Samak had to use the Office of the Supreme Commander in Chief instead. Hardcore PAD demonstrators in the southern provinces also besieged airports at Phuket and Krabi in an attempt to pressure the government to resign. Railway workers stopped southbound train service as well. Interestingly, PAD leaders resisted arrest warrants for invading the government offices. At any rate, the PAD was inconsistent, disobeying laws while insisting on punishing Thaksin through the legal process. In addition, the PAD has proposed a "new politics" of 70% appointed and 30% elected representatives. Accordingly, the PAD has alienated many of its supporters who disagreed with the increasingly aggressive nature of PAD strategy and the proposed system of representative appointment. At the same time, these bold moves have significantly agitated the Samak government and pro-government groups.

The second major instance of violence erupted on the night of September 1, 2008, when a UDD mob clashed with PAD demonstrators on Rajdamnoen Avenue, near Government House. One person was killed and several were injured. The police again failed to take action to stop the violence. Amid high tension and mounting pressures for Samak to step down, the Constitutional Court ruled him disqualified for the premiership in early September, citing the payment he received to host a weekly TV cooking show. To avoid conflicts of interest, the current Constitution prohibits any political appointee from working outside their political post for compensation. The Samak administration came to an end on this point. By that time, the PPP was experiencing internal fighting for Cabinet posts.

With its dominant majority in the Parliament, the PPP successfully held the coalition parties together and installed Somchai Wongsawat, Thaksin's brother-in-law, as the new prime minister in mid-September. With his quiet personality and a reputation as a professional judge and long-serving permanent secretary of Justice, there was a flicker of hope for compromise with the PAD. This might have occurred if Somchai had appointed a significant number of acceptable figures to his Cabinet and opened a dialogue with the PAD. However, he broke his promise to do so, instead filling most ministerial posts with unpopular politicians based on a quota system. As a result, the PAD has viewed the Somchai government as a proxy for Thaksin and has stepped up its efforts to topple the government once again.

The third major incidence of violence took place on October 7, when PAD demonstrators surrounded the Parliament to protest the newly established Somchai government during its first policy address. The demonstrators were this time faced with fierce opposition by anti-riot police. Without warning, the police fired tear gas grenades into the crowds, rather than discharging them in a manner meant to safely deter people. The Chinese-made tear gas grenades proved fatal, as they contained strong explosive elements. Gunshots and a car bomb aggravated the situation further. As a result, two people were killed and more than 400 injured, many critically. After this incident, the PAD regained significant public support while increasing its opposition to the Somchai government. PAD morale was significantly boosted when Queen Sirikit presided over the funeral of a dead PAD victim at a small local temple in an unprecedented expression of sympathy.

The tense political climate, poised to give way to violence, has continued. The PAD had been firmly entrenched at Government House, while the UDD gathered often at Sanamluang to support the PPP-led government that emerged from the election claiming to defend democracy. Each side is conducting a campaign of hatred against the other. In late October, grenades were thrown at the residences of a Constitutional Court judge and an Administrative Court judge, threatening the judicial branch that had repeatedly handed down decisions opposing Thaksin and PPP. On the other side, grenades were thrown at PAD guards, leading to one death and several injuries. Although many intellectuals have proposed negotiation, these calls have fallen on deaf ears, with each side remaining staunchly opposed to the other.

It has been hard for all involved to remain neutral in this deep-seated conflict. Claims by both the anti- and pro-Thaksin groups have been extreme and have tended to push people to one side or the other. Street quarrels between people of different political views have been widespread. The PAD's position became so extreme that anyone who disagreed or failed to give them support could be heavily condemned.[10]

Unexpectedly, the PAD escalated their pressures by seizing both major airports in Bangkok (Suvanaphumi and Donmuang) on November 26 in a blackmail strategy to paralyze the Somchai government. These occupations in effect shut down the nation and halted most international flights and air cargo, thus further alienating PAD supporters and stirring anti-PAD sentiments. The police failed to act and the military remained on the sidelines. In response, the Reds [i.e., Thaksin supporters] threatened to use force themselves to free the airports. Amid the heightened tensions, the Constitutional Court tendered rulings on December 2 to dissolve three major government parties—PPP, Chart Thai, and Matchimathippatai—on charges of vote buying during the 2007 election. The PAD thus found a reason to withdraw from both the airports and the Government House because the party dissolutions, in effect, terminated the Somchai government.

The Opposition Turnaround

Apart from those party board directors who are now banned from politics for five years following the party dissolutions, most remaining politicians moved to join recently registered replacement parties, namely Pue Thai

(For Thais) for the PPP, Chart Thai Pattana (Thai National Development) for Chart Thai, Bhumjaithai (Thai Pride) for Matchimathippatai. The Pue Thai Party tried hard to hold the coalition parties together but failed. It was the breakaway by the Newin faction (about 25 representatives) of the PPP that paved the way for the Democratic Party to form a new government as the former coalition parties also switched side to join the Democrats. These small and medium parties, namely Chart Thai Pattana, Bhumjai-thai, Pue Pandin, and Ruamjaithai Chartpattana, held strong bargaining power on ministerial posts. Ranongrak returned as minister of information and communication technology (ICT), while Porntiwa Nakasai (a former air hostess) now became commerce minister. The Newin faction was the most highly rewarded group, receiving several key ministerial posts, including interior, transportation, industry, and energy.

In mid-December, Abhisit Vejjajiva, at 44, a young Oxford-graduate politician with a sound image, was eventually elected Thailand's 27th prime minister. Only the Pue Thai and Pracharaj parties are now in the opposition. Yet, the Abhisit government is likely to be far from stable, for several reasons. First, many ministers were unpopular and possibly may be implicated in corruption scandals later on. Second, with quite a few problematic cabinet members, coalition management will probably prove to be tough for the Democrats: dismissing anyone could knock down the coalition.

Importantly, the pro-Thaksin groups remain entrenched and ready to use any tactics employed by PAD or even beyond to bring down the Democrat-led government.[11] Predictably, the Reds shut down the Parliament to stall the government's first policy address. Abhisit had to silently switch the venue to the Ministry of Foreign Affairs instead, the next day. Apart from agitating Democrat politicians by picketing and egg throwing, the Reds now promise to obstruct the ASEAN (Association of Southeast Asian Nations) Summit scheduled for February 2009.[12] The survival of the Abhisit government will largely hinge on how well officials manage to patch the divisiveness among Thai people and tackle economic problems resulting from the global economic crisis, while keeping the coalition parties intact. Such tasks are far from easy.

The Fate of Thaksin

Although Thaksin and his family were able to return temporarily to Thailand after the PPP took office, they faced severe difficulties. The corruption charges against Thaksin have proceeded to the Supreme Court's Division of Crimes by Political Office Holders. Thaksin is being charged over a land purchase deal as well as for the disbursement of government loans to Myanmar, which benefited Shin Corp., a conglomerate owned by the former premier's family.

The PPP's attempts to annul the procedural legality of Thaksin's corruption cases through constitutional amendment were effectively blocked by PAD demonstrations and social pressures: thus, nothing interrupted the ongoing judicial process. In August, Thaksin and his family fled to Britain, considering it unlikely that the tables would turn in their favor. As predicted, in October the court declared Thaksin guilty and sentenced him to two years of imprisonment; his assets in Thailand were subsequently confiscated. Although this new round of exile has weakened Thaksin's status somewhat, his power remains formidable, thanks to his financial resources and support among the rural voting base.

Territorial Disputes with Cambodia

As mentioned above, the dispute over the Preah Vihear Temple has re-emerged, this time very much linked to domestic politics in both Thailand and Cambodia. In Thailand, the PAD invoked nationalist sentiments around this issue, cornering the Samak government and forcing the resignation of Foreign Minister Noppadol. The Hun Sen government in Cambodia, meanwhile, gained timely popularity before the general election in June. It was expected that once the election was over, Cambodia would show a friendlier face on this issue, helping to alleviate the conflict. Yet, territorial disputes have instead expanded to areas including the Angkorean sites of Ta Muantom and Ta Kwai, on the two countries' border. Moreover, at a time of Thai political instability, Hun Sen issued an uncompromising demand for Thai troops to withdraw from the Preah Vihear area.

Eventually, Cambodian troops clashed with their Thai counterparts on October 15 after a long stand-off, resulting in one dead on each side and quite a few casualties. Somchai and Hun Sen managed to negotiate a peaceful settlement at the Asia-Europe Meeting (ASEM) summit in Beijing in late October, yet tensions remain high and the situation is uncertain.

Crisis in the South

The conflict in Thailand's south continues but has been eclipsed by the political crisis. The southern insurgency rarely made headlines in 2008. Yet, one incident did: in mid-July, alleged leaders of separatist groups announced a ceasefire on television. General Chetta Thanajaro, the leader of Ruamjaithai Chartpattana and a former army chief, was instrumental in organizing the secret press conference. This event was soon revealed as a farce, however, as killing and terrorism continued on a daily basis.

The government has remained blind, unable to clearly identify the enemy it is fighting. Casualties in 2008 have been considerable. Both the Samak and the Somchai administrations deferred to the military to take charge, as both administrations lacked the capacity and the political will to resolve the conflict. It would not be an exaggeration to say that the PPP-based governments have given up on the southern problem.

Conclusion

The post-2006 coup settlement, which culminated in the 2007 Constitution and subsequent general election, has failed to solve the political crisis that has plagued Thailand for more than three years. The divisiveness that now exists among Thai people is unprecedented and can be traced along the rural-urban fissure, among regions (North/Northeast-South), between preference for the values of efficiency or integrity, and along information divides. The situation is deadlocked without any clear light at the end of the tunnel. Worse, 2009 promises to be another tough year for Thailand, as economic difficulties resulting from the global financial crisis loom large on the horizon. Crises will most likely continue to bombard Thailand in the years to come.

Notes

1. See details in Kasian Tejapira, "Topping Thaksin," *New Left Review* 39 (May–June 2006), pp. 5–37; and Kitti Prasirtsuk, "From Political Reform and Economic Crisis to Coup d'État in Thailand," *Asian Survey* 47:6 (November/December 2007), pp. 872–93.
2. Chalerm, a blunt veteran politician, has long been branded as old-style and corrupt. He was most infamous for defending his misbehaving sons in several pub brawls, one of which involved murder of a police officer.
3. Interior Minister Chalerm refused to visit the three southern provinces where insurgency is rampant, arguing that he knew the situations well enough and his visit would disrupt the regular operation of peace officers there. The general public, however, perceived Chalerm as a coward, not daring to go to the South.
4. Thaksin cleverly returned to Thailand on Valentine's Day with dramatic live media coverage featuring himself kneeling on the ground upon arrival at the airport.
5. UDD initially used the name "Democratic Alliance against Dictatorship" (DAAD) during the coup government period.
6. TV 9, *Nightly News,* May 17, 2008.
7. In fact, numerous PAD demonstrators from provincial areas came to assemble in Bangkok, proudly presenting their hometown banners.
8. Thitinan Pongsudhirak, "Thailand since the Coup," *Journal of Democracy* 19:4 (October 2008), pp. 140, 144.
9. NBT was targeted because the government launched a nightly TV program called *Today Truth* to retaliate against the PAD.

10. This has even been true for some military top brass who supposedly sympathized with the PAD. Dr. Prinya has been heavily criticized by the PAD for launching the "White Ribbon Campaign" to oppose violence and political agitation that might lead to violence. Many scholars have become mute, fearing that their statements would draw criticism from one side or the other.

11. The Democrat Party cannot really detach itself from PAD, as at least two Democrats were heavily involved in PAD campaigns. One of them is Kasit Piromya, now foreign minister, dubbed as a "lightning rod" in the government political context.

12. With the ASEAN Summit, Thailand will also host ASEAN + 3 and East Asia Summits, featuring China, Japan, Korea, India, Australia, and New Zealand. The government decided to move the venue from Bangkok to Hua Hin, a seaside town southwest of Bangkok where the king resides.

KITTI PRASIRTSUK is Assistant Professor of Political Science at Thammasat University, Bangkok, Thailand. Email: <kitt@tu.ac.th>.

From *Asian Survey,* January/February 2009, pp. 174–184. Copyright © 2009 by University of California Press, Journals Division. Reprinted by permission.

Iranian Infighting Leaves Mahmoud Ahmadinejad Isolated

Iran's President Mahmoud Ahmadinejad was left dangerously isolated yesterday as factional infighting further divided the country's regime.

DAMIEN MCELROY AND AHMED VAHDAT

He came under attack from the inner circle of Ayatollah Ali Khamenei, the Supreme Leader, who had given him their support after he won Iran's disputed presidential election six weeks ago.

Officials announced that the ayatollah had ordered the closure of Kahrizak detention center where, they said, hundreds of people had been detained outside the scope of the judiciary and in violation of their basic rights.

The officials also said that Ayatollah Khamenei had ordered the release of 140 people from Evin prison, Tehran's main jail. The decisions were seen as a direct rebuke to Ahmadinejad allies who orchestrated the recent action against opposition protesters. The ayatollah had been under pressure to overrule Mr. Ahmadinejad and curtail the continued detention of almost 2,000 people.

The beleaguered president suffered a second blow yesterday when members of Iran's parliament supported a resolution praising Gholam Hossein Mohseni Ejeie, the intelligence minister sacked by Mr. Ahmadinejad at the weekend. The minister lost his job after backing Ayatollah Khamenei's demands for Esfandiar Rahim Mashaie, a controversial Ahmadinejad aide, to be removed as vice-president. The resolution said: "In the past few days we saw (Eejie) passing a great test in which he defended the Supreme Leader and showed he would not hesitate when it comes to defending him." Meanwhile, another presidential ally—Ali Akbar Mehrabian, the industry minister—was found guilty of fraud.

Candidates defeated by Mr. Ahmadinejad in the election have not given up their campaign of defiance against the result.

Mir-Hossein Mousavi, the most prominent challenger, called on his supporters to gather tomorrow to publicly commemorate the 40th day since demonstrators were killed by the security forces. The interior ministry said yesterday it had denied permission for a ceremony at a mosque in central Tehran.

Mr. Ahmadinejad is due to be inaugurated for a second term next week, but his political survival remains in question. Observers in Iranian politics say Ayatollah Khamenei's lieutenants were signalling a willingness to drop the controversial politician. Such a move could ease Iran's international isolation. Mr. Ahmadinejad has attracted international condemnation for his declarations that Israel should be "wiped out" as well as domestic criticism for his erratic approach to government.

Baqer Moin, a London-based Iran analyst, said: "It boils down to Ahmadinejad's single-minded and volatile behavior. If they can't control him, they will get rid of him, but not now. There would be too great an upheaval." But the president remains popular with Iran's poor and socially deprived, who see him as a man close to interests of ordinary people. If he were to be deposed by a coup within the elite, there could be a backlash from groups that have loyally supported the Islamic regime since its foundation in 1979.

Ayatollah Khamenei also faced dissent yesterday as two grand ayatollahs left the country in an attempt to undermine his position. The pair, who are more theologically distinguished than the Supreme Leader, took the step to show their anger at attempts to rein in Hashemi Rafsanjani, a former president, who has dissented from the official line on the election dispute.

UNIT 4

The Legislature: Representation and the Effects of Electoral Systems

Unit Selections

Key Points to Consider

- What does *accountability* mean?

- In what ways are legislators accountable?

- How has modern technology affected the ways by which legislators are accountable?

- Why is it important to elect minority groups to the legislature?

- What are the impediments to successful election of minority groups in the legislature?

- What are the different types of electoral systems?

- How does a single-member plurality election work?

- How does proportional representation work?

- What are the ways to realize minority representation?

Student Website
www.mhhe.com/cls

Internet References

Asian Development Bank
http://www.adb.org/Countries
Inter-Parliamentary Union
http://www.ipu.org/wmn-e/world.htm
Latin American Network Information Center, University of Texas at Austin
http://lanic.utexas.edu/la/region/government

U.S. Information Agency
http://www.america.gov
World Bank
http://www.worldbank.org

Unit 4 focuses on the legislature's role in government, its significance, and how its performance is evaluated; in short, the systematic questions of "why, what, and how" regarding the legislature. The question "Why do we need legislatures?" coincides with the previous unit regarding the executive: Legislatures demonstrate and capture representation of their constituents in government. Whereas the executive imposes the "discipline" of a single policymaker in lawmaking, the legislature aims at representing the range of citizens' responses and needs in policy and legislation making. Indeed, the ideal legislature may be a small replica of the citizenry in all its diversity.

This speaks to one of the most important tasks of the legislature—to represent. This essential role is described in all the articles in this unit. It is important to note that this is the role embraced by legislators, even though there are some costs to doing so. Thus, the article on legislatures in Latin America points out that the costs to legislators in Latin American countries may include re-election: Legislators who do not toe the party-line are often labeled "trouble makers" and "would-be rebels" and "demoted" down election lists to "hopeless" positions. Similarly, the article on Zimbabwe point out that legislators who stick to their opposition role against Mugabe forgo the patronage—which includes a Mercedes Benz—that he doles out to win the allegiance of the parliamentary cabinet.

How does the legislator represent his or her constituency? Usually, the legislator does this through policy-making. That is, the legislator's support or opposition to policies should reflect a considered representation of the range of citizens' wishes. It is important to note that legislators do not have to initiate policies in order to support or oppose them. What legislatures must do to demonstrate representation in policy-making is to pass or decline legislation, which entails the essential tasks of discussing, examining, and debating the policies introduced. At the various points of discussing, examining, and debating the proposed legislation, the individual legislator gets to perform her or his role of representing his or her constituency's responses and needs. Thus, in principle, the aggregation of all legislators' input ensures that proposed legislation captures or is amended in the end product to contain the diversity of citizens' responses and needs, or it is rejected.

In this role of approving legislation, the tension between representing constituency interests versus party interests become acute. Some studies suggest that policy-making tension exists when the legislature finds itself pitted against the executive. Some of the articles in this unit suggest that this often occurs with divided government, a situation where competing political parties control different branches of government. For instance, the article on the possibility of a U.S. parliament and Zimbabwe point out that opposition dominance of the legislative branches of government reifies such challenges against the executive. However, the article on Latin America and India point out that the tension does not necessarily derive from opposing parties in control of different branches of government. Rather, it derives from the different constituencies that support or elect each member into the different branches of government.

Given the significance of the legislature as a representative institution, how is this representativeness ensured? The article on Latin American legislatures notes that this representation is ensured through single-member districts, where candidates who are able or promise to deliver on policies to their constituencies

© Royalty-Free/CORBIS

are the ones who will most likely be chosen as the legislative representative. According to the article on the Latin American legislatures, this enables candidates to overcome party pressure and represent their constituencies faithfully.

However, in practice, single-member district electoral systems also potentially skew, rather than ensure, representativeness. Two readings on women and minority representation describe how this occurs: single-member district electoral systems may not achieve representation because of several factors, including the high costs of campaigning that deters new candidates, the benefits of incumbency that penalizes new candidates, the advantage of political families that daunts minorities and newcomers, and electoral rules that favor candidates with the largest popular appeal, generally the majority group. Electoral systems such as the single-member district leads to overrepresentation of the majority and underrepresentation of minorities. In these cases, a change from an electoral system of first-past-the-post, or single-member districts, to proportional or at-large systems may remove any financial or majority advantage to balance representation.

Unfortunately, however, such systems lead to candidates that remain beholden to the party, which, as the articles on Latin America and Rwanda note, is not always a good thing for representation. What is clear is that electoral systems, including quota systems that mandate minority representation, must be considered as the first of a series of processes to facilitate representation.

To end on a positive note, many of the potential barriers to representation from electoral systems are easily remedied. For instance, transparent campaign finance laws have helped address the disadvantages faced by minority or women candidates. Electronic voting has undermined the strength of party discipline and emphasized individual representation in legislators. Is ensuring representation important? The readings suggest so: Thus, in Zimbabwe, the opposition representation in government has enabled basic government services—such as teaching and healthcare—to be restored. The articles on India and Rwanda show that representation in legislatures reduces political alienation and, consequently, the tensions and conflicts from such alienation. Thus, increasing the representativeness of legislature is not merely a political principle but a means to ensuring political stability.

Discipline, Accountability, and Legislative Voting in Latin America

JOHN M. CAREY

This article examines the internal dynamics of parties across a number of Latin American legislatures, assessing the responsiveness of legislators to competing pressures from party leaders and other actors. Latin America illustrates the frequent tension between partisan and individual accountability among legislators, but this tension is manifest to varying degrees within legislatures generally. By accountability, I mean that representatives communicate to voters what they will do if elected, that information about actions once in office is available to constituents, that representatives are responsive to the preferences and demands of constituents, and that they are punished for lack of responsiveness.

In a recent landmark study, Stokes articulates a related notion of accountability of executives and parties as the embodiments of national government but focuses mainly on the first and last elements of my definition, campaign promises and electoral punishment.[1] My conception of accountability encompasses transparency and responsiveness as well, in order to direct attention to the perspective of legislators, who are often subject to competing demands from national parties and more narrow electoral constituencies and whose individual roles in the policymaking process are often obscured from public scrutiny. Changes on both these fronts, in representatives' ties to constituencies and in the information about legislators' actions, increase the premium on individual accountability among representatives.

Recent institutional reforms in many Latin American countries have altered the balance of resources that induce party discipline. Drawing on interview data with party leaders, legislators, and staff, surveys of legislators, and records of debates and votes, I illustrate how political elites regard these reforms, outline the strain they perceive between loyalty to party and responsiveness to constituents, and discuss the connection between these matters and the normative concept of democratic accountability. I argue that legislators are subject to increasing pressures from sources other than party leaders. . . .

Parties and Individuals in Comparative Legislatures

Legislative representation is almost always and almost everywhere partisan, and legislative accountability is complicated by a basic tension between party discipline and individual responsiveness. In a nutshell, unified collective action by its legislators is necessary for a party to pursue its collective goals, but the discipline required for effective collective action can undermine individual legislators' responsiveness to their constituents, whether representation is based on geography, as in single member district electoral systems, or on ideology, sectors, or patron-client relations, as in many multimember systems.

The tension between collective and individual accountability is central to scholarship on legislative representation, both formal and empirical, and in all regions.[2] Common to many empirical studies of legislatures is a normative preference for party unity in legislative voting as a necessary condition for accountability. A recent study of discipline throughout Europe opens with the following premise:

> The maintenance of a cohesive voting bloc inside a legislative body is a crucially important feature of parliamentary life. Without the existence of a readily identifiable bloc of governing politicians, the accountability of the executive to both legislature and voters falls flat. It can be seen, then, as a necessary condition for the existence of responsible party government.[3]

The case studies in the book, however, demonstrate that breaches of discipline are more common in legislative voting than the conventional wisdom on parliamentary systems would hold and that such breaches result from demands for direct responsiveness of representatives to their electoral constituencies, even when such responsiveness contradicts collective partisan objectives.[4]

Two recent studies suggest a cross-national trend, broader in scope than legislative voting alone, to resolve the tension between partisan representation and direct responsiveness to citizens by moving toward the latter. Scarrow documents a rise in provisions for direct election of executives and local officials, as well as in initiatives and referenda, among OECD countries over the past three decades. She attributes them to citizens' increasing distrust of parties and a preference for leaders who are "more likely to challenge party policies and to forge cross-party alliances."[5] In a parallel manner, but based on an entirely different set of cases, Barczak documents a sharp increase in provisions for and the use of direct democracy throughout Latin

America. Similarly, she attributes this pattern to reformers' response to widespread popular dissatisfaction with political parties and promises to strengthen responsiveness of policy to public demand.[6]

Studies of comparative institutions, then, widely acknowledge the tension between partisan and individualized accountability and in a few cases have noted trends toward increased accountability. For the most part, however, studies of legislatures in presidential systems and in Latin America in particular have been critical of individualized representation and have demonstrated a normative bent toward strong parties capable of coordinating legislative actions.[7] Mainwaring and Scully, for example, provide a series of indicators by which party systems might be evaluated; they argue that highly institutionalized party systems are essential to democratic performance.[8] A central idea here, as in the studies of accountability in parliamentary systems, is that strong parties are necessary in order to offer citizens coherent choices over policy and, in turn, be judged by citizens in elections on the basis of past performance and the credibility and appeal of their promises for the future.

Many recent studies of Latin American democracy have occupied themselves with identifying the conditions under which parties lack these properties. Ames argues that open list legislative elections in Brazil induce legislators to undervalue public goods and thereby undermine the coherence of partisan platforms and accountability between citizens and their representatives.[9] Coppedge, in contrast, argues that closed list legislative elections in Venezuela and national party organizations that dominated political resources and career opportunities precluded the development of meaningful links between legislators and constituents and undermined accountability.[10]

Other authors have similarly pointed toward characteristics of Latin American parties to explain accountability deficits. Gibson argues that the heterogeneity of interests among voters encouraged party leaders in Argentina and Mexico to abandon long-standing policy positions.[11] Cameron points to the internal weakness of Peruvian parties as facilitating the legislature's dominance by President Fujimori in the 1990s.[12] Weyland attributes regressive economic policy in Brazil to the failure of collective action by parties.[13] There are, in short, meticulous accounts of the historical contingencies, economic conditions, and national and subnational political factors to explain failures of specific parties to act consistently and coherently in delivering on policy promises. The heterogeneity of explanations of these deficiencies, however, suggests the lack of a general theory of accountability and of the factors that encourage various forms of it.

Stokes addresses the issue of accountability more generally by asking whether and how voters attribute responsibility when policy promises are broken. She finds that older, more established parties are less prone than new ones to policy betrayal. Stokes focuses, however, on presidents and their relationship with their parties, rather than on the way parties function in legislatures. A substantial gap is left in her account of the mechanism by which parties do or do not deliver on promises. Indeed, Stokes concludes that a central challenge facing the application of her theory to Latin America is an explanation of how parties work.[14]

Political Reforms and Individual Accountability

Political reformers appear little concerned with the normative emphasis in the academy on strong parties. Some reform measures in recent years have aimed to disconnect legislators from national party leaders when they conflict with responsiveness to local constituencies. Is there a common motivation behind reforms of this sort? In the strong party systems of Latin America, reform adherents describe popular disenchantment with disciplined parties directed by leaders who are insulated from punishment by voters. In many cases, moreover, both the strong discipline and the insulation of the top dogs are causally connected to a common source: closed list proportional representation with centralized control over candidate nominations.

The basic problem can be described as follows. As politicians advance within the party leadership, their access to power and perks increases dramatically, but their electoral vulnerability decreases in a corresponding manner because leaders occupy the top positions on party electoral lists. The leadership's susceptibility to electoral punishment is mitigated, even if the party as a whole loses electoral ground. Therefore, the leaders who stand to gain the most from violating public trust and pillaging state resources stand to suffer the least electorally if their party is punished. Rank-and-file politicians, whose heads are the first to roll in any partisan electoral setback, might object to being relegated to the marginal list positions that buffer their leaders, but would-be rebels face a serious collective action problem in revolting against party leaders, because troublemakers are simply removed from the lists or demoted to perilous or even hopeless list positions by the leadership.

This key component of party discipline appears in all five of the countries in which field research was conducted for this article, as well in other closed list systems. As the importance of electoral rules suggests, some dissatisfaction with strong party systems has been channeled toward electoral reform, but others seek to enhance legislative transparency by dragging legislators' actions into the public spot-light. All the reforms discussed in this section share the potential to shift the trade-off between partisan discipline and individual legislator flexibility toward the latter. Considered, in turn, are the adoption of mixed electoral systems, constitutional changes in Venezuela, and public voting in legislatures.

Mixed electoral systems. Since the 1980s mixed electoral systems, combining single member districts with proportional representation (PR) in overarching districts, have been adopted in Bolivia, Guatemala, Panama, Venezuela, and Mexico. The explicit goal of such reforms is most often to tighten the local constituent-legislator bond, even at the expense of discipline among national parties.[15] As part of an effort to resuscitate support for a discredited party system in the early 1990s, for example, the President's Commission on State Reform (COPRE) in Venezuela advocated the shift from closed list PR to SMD/PR on the grounds that the previous system strengthened the party line, which is defined by the top party leaders and the tribunals of discipline responsible for its application. As a result, the legislators vote as the party dictates without attending to the demands and interests of voters in their regions . . . [whereas legislators elected under the proposed single member districts] ought to act in the interests of their electors, ought to attend to their demands, ought to respond to their mail, and will have to explain to their electors why they vote as they do in the deliberative body.[16]

The same motivation spurred the shift from pure closed list PR to SMD/PR in Bolivia in 1994, where the plummeting stature of political parties, evident in street protests as well as opinion polls, was understood as a demand from voters "that deputies should be known and acknowledged representatives of their constituencies and not anonymous representatives of party leaders."[17] Precisely the same arguments are made by advocates of a pending proposal for SMD/PR in Costa Rica. In Venezuela, of course, electoral reform proved insufficient to salvage public support for the traditional parties, yet the COPRE's recommended SMD/PR format survived even President Chavez's institutional overhaul, as has the rationale of strengthening ties to local constituencies. Finally, it is worth noting that the arguments made in that region resonate as well among SMD/PR advocates in Europe.[18]

Venezuela's constitution of 1999. Venezuela's 1999 constitution also includes a number of new measures designed specifically to foster personal responsibility of legislators to their district constituencies. There is a four year residency requirement for eligibility to run for the legislature, designed to ensure that representatives know firsthand the needs and preferences of district voters (Article 188). Legislators are obliged to "render accounts" of their activities each year in public forums (*rendiciones de cuentas*) in their districts to explain and defend their behavior and their votes (Articles 197, 199). All legislative votes are explicitly deemed matters of individual conscience for representatives, rather than matters of partisan obligation (Article 201). Finally, all elected officials are subject to recall elections, which can be initiated by petition of 10 percent of the voters in their districts (Articles 72, 197).

The requirement that legislators report to constituents in their districts about their actions is connected straightforwardly to the idea of accountability. More broadly, game theoretical analysis suggests that requiring individual representatives to explain votes increases the efficiency of electoral punishment for legislators otherwise inclined to ignore constituents' wishes and in doing so enhances individual responsiveness.[19] All these anticipated effects were articulated-albeit, without the game theory-by Venezuelan legislators in interviews. Ricardo Combellas, a constituent assembly delegate and opponent of President Chavez, described the motivation behind the reforms as follows.

We wanted to eliminate partyarchy—not to eliminate it constitutionally, but in terms of norms, for the representative to respond more directly to the wants and needs of his constituents. His responsibility in parliament is personal—the constitution says so—not to respond to a party but to his constituents. We established a rendering of accounts that didn't exist before . . . [and] a vote of

conscience that wasn't there either. . . . [In the past] the parties overwhelmed their representatives. They imposed the line, imposed the vote, imposed attitudes. We have tried to relax this and create a more fluid relationship between legislators and their constituents.

Referring to the same set of provisions, *chavista* constitutional delegate, now deputy, Tarek William Saab's enthusiasm was even more unrestrained. "A big space is opened where the parties used to have complete control, and power is completely realigned. I think that we have put organized society above the parties—that the organized people, the organized popular movement will have a chance now because these constitutional measures give them a chance." It is too early to determine how these provisions will be applied or what their effects will be, but Chavez's supporters and skeptics alike argue that their intent is to increase the personal accountability of politicians, even if they loosen the bonds of party.

Recorded legislative votes. A third reform with the potential to affect the visibility of individual legislators' actions and thus to alter the balance between the pressures placed on them by local constituencies and national parties is public voting within legislatures themselves. All Latin American legislatures have provisions in their rules of order allowing roll call votes (*nominales* or *nominativas*) under certain conditions, generally at the request of the chamber leadership (*mesa directiva* or *directorio*), by consensus of the leadership of the various parties (*bancadas, fracciones, grupos*), or by petition of some qualified quorum (one-fifth, one-fourth, one-third, or one-half of the membership or of those present). Literally calling the roll in order to take votes, however, is always an impracticably time-consuming process. In short, logistics alone are sufficient to rule out the traditional nominal as a means of legislative voting throughout Latin America under all but exceptional circumstances.

The procedures for taking standard votes (often referred to as *económicos*) vary. In chambers with smaller memberships, such as the Central American assemblies and senates in bicameral legislatures, individuals generally cast votes either by standing or raising hands, with a head/hand count conducted from the *mesa directiva*. This procedure is impractical when membership rises much above a hundred, however, and larger chambers, such as Mexico's and Venezuela's, have conventionally expedited matters by allowing party leaders to cast votes for their entire blocs. Legislators who are present and do not explicitly state their opposition are counted as having voted as the leadership declares.

The rare existence of individual records precludes public scrutiny of individual legislators' votes. In the smaller chambers those present, including journalists, interest group leaders, and activists, can conduct unofficial head/hand counts and report the results. In Costa Rica and El Salvador, at least, deputies' votes occasionally find their way into newspapers by this route, but it is a costly and imperfect means of gathering and disseminating information. The adoption of electronic voting technology in many legislatures in recent years, however, threatens the anonymity of legislative voting.

Electronic voting systems were adopted in the lower legislative chambers more or less concurrently with the return to democracy in the mid 1980s in Argentina and Brazil and in the 1990s in Chile. They have been used in Mexico and Peru since 1998 and in Nicaragua since 2000.[20] A system has been in place in Venezuela since 1997 but has not yet been used. The same is true for Costa Rica's first generation system, installed in the mid 1970s. . . .

There are purely pragmatic reasons to adopt electronic voting. It yields a faster, more accurate count than handraising. It is a concrete manifestation of modernization, an ideal widely embraced in the abstract by governments and legislative leaders. The impact of electronic voting, however, is potentially more substantial than the logistics alone imply. Electronic voting generates records of individual legislators' votes. If the records are available to the public, it effectively transforms all votes into *nominales,* matters of record that individual legislators could be called upon to defend. There is no guarantee that journalists, interest group leaders, and activists will register how legislators vote or that constituents will pay attention. Without a record, however, the prospect is moot, and until recently there was no record most of the time. With the adoption of electronic voting records are being created in many places, and the existence of records opens the possibility that the information will enter into political discourse.

This prospect was explicitly on the minds of Peruvian legislators in 1998 as they considered the implications of switching from the traditional handraising method of voting to the electronic system that had recently been installed as part of a broader government modernization plan. On September 24, in an effort to embarrass the pro-Fujimori majority on a motion related to a corruption investigation, the opposition demanded that the electronic voting machines be incorporated into standard legislative procedure.

> The whole reason for electronic voting is so citizens know how their representatives voted, so [votes] can be publicly justified. It's an instrument of democracy and transparency. . . . What the country is going to notice is that the parliamentary majority is afraid that, through the Internet and other mechanisms, its votes on some matters will be made visible.[21]

The opposition threatened procedural maneuvers designed to grind progress on all matters to a halt if the electronic system were not employed. The majority eventually broke ranks, with one of its members concurring on the matter of transparency and accountability. "One reason for this system is that it leaves a record of votes for current political analysts and for history, so that how each one of us voted is known; and those congresspersons that run for reelection, when they face the voters, they'll have to explain how it is that on each of the issues they voted as they did."[22]

Soon after the old system was breached, the Peruvian congress began posting records of all electronic votes on its website. Two parallels with the Venezuelan electoral reform discussed above merit comment. Any increase in transparency this reform produced was insufficient to prop up a system poised to collapse

under the weight of its own corruption. However, like the mixed electoral system in Venezuela, public voting in Peru survived the collapse of the old regime.

The reforms discussed here were developed independently in different legislative environments, but a common thread running through them was the stated intention to strengthen the accountability of individual legislators to voters. At least in their rhetoric, Latin American political reformers in the 1990s were critical of the principle of legislative party discipline on the grounds that it conflicted with the individual accountability they endorsed.

Institutional Pressures on Legislative Behavior Parties and Discipline

Most legislatures are organized along party lines. Party units are accorded rights over legislative resources, including representation on the organ that controls the legislative agenda, as well as whatever offices and staff are available. The norm among legislative party groups in Latin America is to meet at least weekly when the legislature is in session to discuss the upcoming agenda and to establish a group position (if any) on each issue. Party groups are subordinate to national party organizations and generally can be instructed by them as to how to vote on specific issues.[23] National party congresses invariably occur less frequently than legislative party group meetings, but national party executive committees generally have authority to establish the party line. Many parties also retain disciplinary bodies, composed of national party leaders, that are authorized to impose sanctions on legislators who break discipline on votes for which a party line has been established.

The sixteen partisan groups I interviewed in Mexico, El Salvador, Nicaragua, Costa Rica, and Venezuela show remarkable consistency on how decisions are made. Unless consultation is sought from or imposed by the national party organization, decisions are made in party group meetings by majority rule. This procedure applies to both decisions to require discipline (or to leave matters open to conscience) and the content of the party line.

Across all parties in these countries there was consensus that most votes are matters of discipline. In explaining the sources of intrapartisan divisions, interviews with de la Cruz, Hernandez, and Hurtado concurred that cohesiveness tends to be greater in smaller groups, where opinions are more homogeneous, but that this advantage is offset by economies of scale that larger groups enjoy in providing benefits that induce loyalty among legislators. Benefits range from physical resources, like offices and staff, to committee assignments, favorable treatment for private member bills, and budgetary funds for individual legislators' chosen projects.

Legislators from all parties could cite cases of indiscipline, and they offered various accounts of how and how effectively parties respond. Consistent with academic accounts, pre-Chavez Venezuela appears to have produced nearly airtight discipline across the party spectrum.[24] Combellas affirmed that breaches of party discipline in legislative voting were rare in all parties and that every instance, in state assemblies as well as nationally, triggered expulsion by the national party organization. He noted, however, that the "conscience" provision in the 1999 constitution (Article 201) may provide judicial protection for undisciplined politicians. Legislators in Costa Rica, Nicaragua, and El Salvador all acknowledged the existence of procedures to provide for expulsion on grounds of indiscipline but emphasized that less public and dramatic measures are generally preferred by party leaders. In the latter two countries, electoral party lists assign both a primary legislator (*propietario*) and a substitute (*suplente*) to each legislative seat. When the *propietario* is unwilling to support the party line but willing to recuse himself from a vote, parties summon the corresponding *suplente,* according to interviews with Alvarenga and Samper. Only in Mexico, where I interviewed only the president of the lower (Paoli) house and his staff, was there any reluctance to discuss mechanisms by which party discipline is enforced.

The most common theme running through accounts of party discipline by legislators across parties and systems was control over career prospects. It is the bottom line resource of parties, as legislators are acutely aware across the board. Alexis Sibaja, Costa Rica's minority party leader, sums it up.

> There is party discipline because political careers in Costa Rica are partisan. My future is in *Liberación Nacional* (PLN), not outside it. I am disciplined every day because I'm always interested in advancing within the PLN. . . . Desertions on important matters are judged harshly by party militants and supporters. Those who have deserted the party line in the past have effectively been retired from politics because the party is very strict.

Academic accounts, as well as those of other interview subjects (Vargas and Vargas Pagan), suggest that Sibaja overstates the inviolability of party discipline in Costa Rica, but he is unambiguous about the source of discipline. To the extent that legislators are politically ambitious and that parties can control access to political careers, parties can induce legislative discipline. In August 2000 Mònica Baltodano described hardball politics within Nicaragua's *Frente Sandinista* (FSLN) over her breach of discipline two months earlier on an electoral reform bill on which the FSLN had agreed to a compromise with the governing Liberals.

> Party rules say that on issues of national importance, the party organs decide and the *bancada* is subordinate to these decisions. . . . The Sandinista national assembly decided to go ahead with this reform. . . . We broke discipline. Then, according to the statutes, we could have been sanctioned with expulsion or other measures. This wasn't convenient to them, politically. So they ruled that whoever did not accept party decisions could not aspire to electoral posts. Everyone knew I wanted to run for mayor of Managua, and this way I couldn't be nominated. It's almost certain that they won't permit me to run for reelection as a deputy either. And they took other measures. I was Vice President of the Assembly's executive committee, and they took that away, and they won't let me chair any committees.

Baltodano correctly anticipated continued conflicts with party leaders over her aspirations. In December 2000 the party's executive committee formally barred her from nomination for reelection as deputy, citing her vote in the assembly against the electoral reform law.[25]

These examples illustrate the most consistent theme in the interviewees' responses regarding sources of party discipline: that parties have sanctioning mechanisms on the books but except in exceptional circumstances less formal measures serve to induce discipline by appealing to legislators' career ambitions.

Individualistic voting and indiscipline. What about breakdowns, however, such as the case of Baltodano? Legislators sometimes risk the wrath of party leaders by staking out independent positions on legislative votes. What motivates such behavior? Principle, or less piously a legislator's preference on the policy at stake, is one possible explanation. When asked about their own motivations for breaches of voting discipline, legislators invariably refer to their beliefs about what was right or about what their constituents demanded they do. Legislators' proclivity to engage in such behavior might well be driven by whether the electoral system in which they operate allows voters to cast preference votes among candidates within parties. Moreover, voting independence might be tolerated by parties in personal vote systems to the extent that such flexibility helps maximize the total votes won by their candidates. Where candidates must distinguish themselves from their copartisans in order to win office, there should be less party unity in legislative voting.[26] Legislators' personal preferences and those induced by electoral pressures can both explain voting indiscipline.

Whatever the motivation, making votes public increases the value to legislators of staking out independent positions. Recorded votes can serve as means for maverick legislators to go public over the heads of party leaders and in so doing to establish reputations either among a target audience of supporters or perhaps nationally. The rare decisions to hold *nominales* in systems where anonymous legislative voting is the norm can illustrate this point. According to Costa Rican minority leader Sibaja:

> One sign that there's going to be a nominal isn't that the opposition is divided—that's no problem. The problem is when the governing party is divided. There was a famous case here in the early 1970s, having to do with student protests over an agreement that permitted a transnational company to mine [in a wilderness area]. It was called the Alcoa Agreement. At that time, the PLN controlled the presidency and had a big parliamentary majority. One government deputy started the fight. That deputy himself later became president, but not as a member of the PLN. . . . He led a group of PLN deputies to break the party line. I think that was the last time they used a nominal on an important issue, precisely because the government's *fracción* divided at that moment. That was thirty years ago. It's not common.

Sibaja's account raises a couple of points. First, it suggests that public voting on the Alcoa Agreement was a mechanism for a deputy with national ambitions to draw a line in the sand between himself and his party's leadership. The nominal signals a showdown, in which those who control the legislative agenda are determined to proceed to a vote even on matters sufficiently controversial that legislators are determined to go on record in opposition. These circumstances are rare in Costa Rica, where *nominales* must be requested by a majority vote (*Reglamento*, Article 101), but rules of procedure present lower thresholds elsewhere and no obstacle at all where votes are recorded as a matter of standard procedure. Electronic voting, therefore, should encourage independence in legislative voting, at least where the records are made public, both insofar as it provides party mavericks with a forum to take positions and insofar as it opens legislators to demands of accountability for their votes from actors outside the chamber.[27] The second important point of Sibaja's story is that governing and opposition parties differ on their proclivities to divide in legislative votes. This point was made by deputies in parties across countries and warrants further development.

Executives as legislative coalition brokers. It is useful to distinguish sources of unity that operate at the systemic level from those that can vary across parties within legislatures. Among the former are constitutional rules and characteristics of electoral systems. It is widely held, for example, that party discipline is encouraged by parliamentary more than by presidential constitutions and by closed list elections more than by other systems.[28] These sorts of institutional constraints operate on all parties in a legislature. Other factors affecting discipline, however, can vary across parties within legislatures. Parties on the outside of the ideological spectrum, for example, may be more disciplined than centrist parties.[29] Parties that are part of the governing coalition may be more disciplined than those in opposition.[30] This last proposition echoes throughout the interviews with Latin American legislators.

I asked legislators in various systems: "On what are voting coalitions based common ideology, party, electoral interests, control of the legislative agenda, support for the executive, etc.?" Apart from party, responses most commonly pointed to the executive. For example, Nicaraguan deputy Luis Urbina of the president's Liberal Party explained:

> The executive normally works better when it has an assembly majority. The majority party tries to support projects from the executive, of which it is part. . . . So when the executive wants to submit a law, it calls on the majority *bancada*, explains the benefits of approving the law, and generally we vote in line with the directives we are given.

Urbina's account relies on an inherent compatibility between the executive's interests and those of his legislative copartisans'. More frequently, legislators pointed to concrete resources executives use to elicit support. Critics of Urbina's Liberal Party in Nicaragua, such as Baltodano and Hurtado, invariably point to patronage as the source of support for the executive. According to Jorge Samper of the Sandinista Renewal Movement (MRS):

> The Liberal bancada has been very obedient, through presidential discipline more than party discipline. They take almost no decisions autonomous from the president. . . . One or another deputy has voted against the president's wishes, and then along comes some bit of patronage that makes him change his vote, and we vote again the way the president orders. [Interviewer: What are examples of patronage?] Public jobs, for deputies and relatives. The deputy might be made ambassador to some country, and maybe they send his family or relatives. . . . The rest of the deputies, that are not from the Sandinista or Liberal *bancadas,* many of them have formed alliances with the government. . . . [but] these aren't real political alliances, but rather alliances based on patronage.

Accounts of presidential influence do not necessarily hinge on improper exchanges, but they share a focus on the resources executives control that appeal to legislators' ambitions. Combellas cites President Chavez's control over party nominations to all electoral posts as the main source of his influence within the MVR party in Venezuela. Vargas Pagan cites the Costa Rican president's ability to expedite or hold up disbursement of funds budgeted for projects in deputies' districts as a source of influence. Hernandez laments: When a party wins, the *fracción* generally forms a stronger connection to the executive. The strongest relationship is legislative *fracción*-executive, president of the republic, ministers and all the apparatus of public administration. The losing *fracción* does not maintain much of a strong connection with its party either.

There is a consensus in the interview responses that presidents in these systems control resources that are highly valued by legislators and that can be exchanged for legislative votes. The interviews suggest that these transactions are easiest within parties; legislators from the president's party enjoy privileged but not exclusive access to the market for executive resources. Two points follow. First, legislative voting discipline should be higher in presidents' parties than in others. Second, all the accounts of presidential influence offered in the interviews rely on executive-legislative exchanges that would attract criticism if exposed to public scrutiny. The presidential advantage might therefore be reduced by public voting. . . .

The Changing Nature of Legislative Accountability

There is a basic trade-off between party discipline and local or sectoral particularism in legislative representation. Over the past decade several factors have increased the sensitivity of legislators in Latin America to pressures other than the demands of national party leaders. It is important to acknowledge that even party leaders should not necessarily demand blind responsiveness. Total failure by legislators to attend to local, sectoral, and even individual constituent demands can leave national leaders sitting atop organizations with no electoral support.[31] This calculus by national leaders was responsible for the adoption of mixed member electoral systems in Venezuela and Bolivia.[32] National party leaders pursuing such a strategy may parcel out reforms providing a modicum of individual flexibility while retaining other powers and resources that ensure discipline. Thus, for example, leaders of most Bolivian, Mexican, and Venezuelan parties have maintained centralized control over candidate nominations, seriously limiting the extent to which district pressures induce even legislators from single member districts to buck party discipline.[33] Similarly, leaders have been slow to make legislative voting records public in Argentina, Mexico, and Nicaragua and even to use electronic voting machines where they are installed in Costa Rica, Peru, and Venezuela.

Despite these constraints, however, the overall trend is toward the exposure of legislators to increasing pressures from sources besides their parties. In the mixed member systems, single member districts induce individual legislative entrepreneurship and constituency service. Moreover, other electoral reforms aimed at increasing voter discretion among candidates within parties, such as preference voting within lists and primary elections for candidate nominations, are being seriously considered at least in Colombia, Costa Rica, Mexico, and Venezuela. These reforms are expected to increase the willingness of legislators to break party discipline in legislative voting.[34]

Outside of electoral reforms, the spread of public legislative voting, particularly through the technology of electronic voting, tips the balance between party and individual accountability toward the latter. In addition to the cases reviewed here, the establishment of public voting is central to reform proposals pending before the Colombian congress. Indeed, public voting is singled out as the most important reform available to increase the transparency of the legislative process in that country.[35] The argument rests on the widely held idea that political elites and ordinary citizens differ in their claims to anonymity in political action. Whereas voter anonymity, through the secret ballot, is necessary for democratic elections, anonymity in legislative voting undermines democratic accountability.[36]

The balance between party discipline and individual responsiveness among legislators in many Latin American countries has been and continues to be subject to pressures favoring individual responsiveness in recent years. Key institutional factors driving this trend are electoral reforms that increase voter discretion over individual candidates within parties and procedural reforms that make legislative votes public.

Other new measures included in the new Venezuelan constitution were adopted in the same spirit. Indeed, across countries, and with respect to different reform proposals, there is a distinct flavor against party discipline in the rhetoric of reform. The rhetoric must be evaluated with a good deal of salt, given the inclination of politicians to pay lip service to responsiveness to the grass roots. Nevertheless, the substance of reforms has pushed in the same direction in important ways.

Finally, it is worth noting that these trends may extend far beyond the handful of Latin American cases documented in some detail here. The primary institutional mechanisms that facilitate constituent demands for individual accountability, mixed electoral systems, and electronic voting in legislatures have been adopted in a broad array of countries over the past decade. Outside Latin America, Italy, Japan, New Zealand, the Philippines, Russia, Ukraine, and of course Germany (since 1949) use mixed SMD/PR electoral systems, while electronic voting systems are in place in the Czech Republic, Israel, Italy, Poland, and Russia. As technological barriers to electronic voting in particular shrink, it should become increasingly ubiquitous. Students of comparative democratic performance, therefore, should pay serious attention to evaluating the effects of this pattern of reforms for individual accountability on legislative behavior.

Notes

1. Susan C. Stokes, *Mandates, Markets, and Democracy: Neoliberalism by Surprise in Latin America* (New York: Cambridge University Press, 2001).

2. Bruce Cain, John Ferejohn, and Morris Fiorina, *The Personal Vote: Constituency Service and Electoral Independence* (New York: Cambridge University Press, 1987); Gary W. Cox, *The Efficient Secret: The Cabinet and the Development of Political Parties in Victorian England* (New York: Cambridge University Press, 1987); Daniel Diermeier and Timothy J. Feddersen, "Cohesion in Legislatures and the Vote of Confidence Procedure," *American Political Science Review, 92* (1998), 611–22.

3. Shaun Bowler, David M. Farrell, and Richard S. Katz, "Party Cohesion, Party Discipline, and Parliaments," in Shaun Bowler, David M. Farrell, and Richard S. Katz, eds., *Party Discipline and Parliamentary Government* (Columbus: Ohio State University Press, 1999), p. 3.

4. Paul F. Whiteley and Patrick Seyd, "Discipline in the British Conservative Party: The Attitudes of Party Activists toward the Role of Their Members of Parliament," in Bowler, Farrell, and Katz, eds., pp. 53–71; Prisca Lanfranchi and Ruth Luthi, "Cohesion of Party Groups and Interparty Conflict in the Swiss Parliament: Roll Call Voting in the National Council," in ibid., pp. 99–120.

5. Susan E. Scarrow, "Direct Democracy and Institutional Change: a Comparative Investigation," *Comparative Political Studies, 34* (August, 2001), 661.

6. Monica Barczak, "Representation by Consultation? The Rise of Direct Democracy in Latin America," *Latin American Politics and Society, 43* (Fall 2001), 39.

7. Juan J. Linz, "Presidentialism or Parliamentarism: Does It Make a Difference?," in Juan J. Linz and Arturo Valenzuela, eds., *The Failure of Presidential Democracy: The Case of Latin America,* vol. 2 (Baltimore: The Johns Hopkins University Press, 1994), pp. 3–90; Arturo Valenzuela, "Party Politics and the Crisis of Presidentialism in Chile: A Proposal for a Parliamentary Form of Government," in ibid., pp. 91–150.

8. Scott P. Mainwaring and Timothy Scully, eds., *Building Democratic Institutions: Party Systems in Latin America* (Stanford: Stanford University Press, 1993).

9. Barry Ames, "Electoral Strategy under Open List Proportional Representation," *American Journal of Political Science, 39* (May 1994), 406–33.

10. Michael J. Coppedge, *Strong Parties and Lame Ducks: Presidential Partyarchy and Factionalism in Venezuela* (Stanford: Stanford University Press, 1994).

11. Edward Gibson, "The Populist Road to Market Reform: Policy and Electoral Coalitions in Mexico and Argentina," *World Politics, 49* (1997), 339–70.

12. Maxwell A. Cameron, "Political and Economic Origins of Regime Change in Peru: The 18th Brumaire of Alberto Fujimori," in Maxwell A. Cameron and Philip Mauceri, eds., *The Peruvian Labrynth: Polity, Society, Economy* (University Park: Penn State University Press, 1997), pp. 37–69.

13. Kurt Weyland, *Democracy without Equity: Failures of Reform in Brazil* (Pittsburgh: University of Pittsburgh Press, 1996); Kurt Weyland, "'Growth with Equity' in Chile's New Democracy?," *Latin American Research Review, 32* (1997), 37–67.

14. Stokes, p. 121.

15. Mexico used a straight SMD plurality until the 1970s, approaching the mixed system from the opposite direction by adding PR seats gradually from the late 1970s to the early 1990s.

16. Manuel Rachadell, "El sistema electoral y la reforma de los partidos," in *Venezuela, democracia y futuro: Los partidos politicos en la decada de los 90* (Caracas: Comision Presidencial para la Reforma del Estado, 1991), pp. 207–8.

17. René Antonio Mayorga, "Electoral Reform in Bolivia: Origins of the Mixed-Member Proportional System," in Mathew Soberg Shugart and Martin P. Wattenberg, eds., *Mixed- Member Electoral Systems: The Best of Both Worlds?* (Oxford: Oxford University Press, 2001), pp. 194–208.

18. Interviews with Sibaja, Combellas, Saab, and Fernandez; Richard S. Katz, "Reforming the Italian Electoral Law, 1993," in Shugart and Wattenberg, eds., p. 103; Susan E. Scarrow, "Germany: The Mixed- Member System as a Political Compromise," in ibid., p. 63.

19. David Austen-Smith, "Explaining the Vote: Constituency Constraints on Sophisticated Voting," in Ken Binmore, Alan Kirman, and Piero Tani, eds., *Frontiers of Game Theory* (Cambridge, MA: MIT Press, 1993), pp. 49–70.

20. Nicaraguan deputies have registered some votes electronically since 1994, but the system was served by an IBM 386 microprocessor that occasionally crashed, thus failing to produce records. There was also no screen to display outcomes, so the votes were not public.

21. Congreso de Peru, Diario de los Debates, Primera Legislatura Ordinaria de 1998, 1 la Sesi6n (Lima, 24 September).

22. Ibid.

23. Venezuela's 1999 constitutional provision (Article 201) prohibiting such constraints is unusual in this respect.

24. Coppedge.

25. Latin America Data Base, "Nicaragua: Governing Party and Sandinistas Nominate Presidential Candidates," in *NotiCen: Central American and Caribbean Political and Economic Affairs, 6* (2001).

26. John M. Carey and Matthew S. Shugart, "Incentives to Cultivate a Personal Vote: A Rank Ordering of Electoral Systems," *Electoral Studies, 14* (1995), 417–39.

27. Testing this proposition empirically, for example, by comparing party unity levels in legislatures with electronic voting against levels on recorded votes in legislatures without electronic voting, is problematic because votes that are recorded in the latter may be biased toward disunity. In the Alcoa vote described by Alexis Sibaja, for example, both major parties split.

28. Diermeier and Feddersen, p. 618; interview with Nicaraguan deputy Monica Baltodano.

29. Scott P. Mainwaring, *Rethinking Party Systems in the Third Wave of Democratization: The Case of Brazil* (Stanford, CA: Stanford University Press, 1999).

30. Michael Laver and Norman Schofield, Multiparty Government: The Politics of Coalition in Europe (New York: Cambridge University Press, 1990).

31. John M. Carey, *Term Limits and Legislative Representation* (Cambridge, UK: Cambridge University Press, 1996).

32. Brian E. Crisp and Juan Carlos Rey, "The Sources of Electoral Reform in Venezuela," in Shugart and Wattenberg, eds., pp. 173–93.

33. René Antonio Mayorga, "The Mixed-Member Proportional System and Its Consequences in Bolivia," in Shugart and Wattenberg, eds., pp. 432–46 (p. 436); Jeffrey A. Weldon, "The Consequences of Mexico's Mixed-Member Electoral System: 1988–1997," in Shugart and Wattenberg, eds., pp. 447–76.

34. Kulisheck and Crisp, p. 422; Mayorga, "The Mixed Member," p. 440; Weldon, p. 453; interview with Costa Rican deputy Eliseo Vargas.

35. Gerard Roland and Juan Gonzalo Zapata, "Colombia's Electoral and Party System: Proposals for Reform" (Bogota: Fedesarollo Working Paper Series No. 16, August 2000); Maurice Kugler and Howard Rosenthal, "Checks and Balances: An Assessment of the Institutional Separation of Powers in Colombia" (Bogota: Fedesarollo Working Paper Series No. 17, August 2000).

36. The basic principle is layed out in the U.S. Supreme Court majority decision in *NAACP v. Alabama ex rel. Patterson, Attorney General,* No. 91 Supreme Court of the United States 357 U.S. 449; 78 S. Ct. 1163, 1958. I thank Anabelle Lever for pointing this decision out.

From *Journal of Comparative Politics,* January 2003, Vol. 35, No. 2, pp. 191–211. Copyright © 2003 by Journal of Comparative Politics. Reprinted by permission.

The Case for a Multi-Party U.S. Parliament?
American Politics in Comparative Perspective

This article supports the inclusion of American political institutions within the study of comparative politics. This is a brief on behalf of a multi-party parliamentary system for the United States that can be read as a "what if" experiment in institutional transplantation. It underscores the basic insight that institutions are not neutral but have consequences for the political process itself and encourages American students to think more broadly about the possibilities of reforming the American political system.

CHRISTOPHER S. ALLEN

Introduction

Americans revere the constitution but at the same time also sharply and frequently criticize the government. (Dionne 1991) Yet since the constitution is responsible for the current form of the American government, why not change the constitution to produce better government? After all, the founders of the United States did create the amendment process and we have seen 27 of them in 220 years.

Several recent events prompt a critical look at this reverence for the constitution: unusual developments regarding the institution of the Presidency, including the Clinton impeachment spectacle of 1998–1999; the historic and bizarre 2000 Presidential election that required a Supreme Court decision to resolve; the apparent mandate for fundamental change that President Bush inferred from this exceedingly narrow election; and the increasingly numerous constitutional questions concerning Presidential powers and the conduct of the "war on terror." In the early 21st century, American politics confronted at least three other seemingly intractable problems: significant erosion in political accountability; out of control costs of running for public office; and shamefully low voter turnout. More seriously, none of these four problems is of recent origin, as all four have eroded the functioning of the American government for a period of between 25 and 50 years! The core features of these four problems are:

- Confusion of the roles of head of state and head of government, of which the impeachment issue—from Watergate through Clinton's impeachment and beyond— is merely symptomatic of a much larger problem.
- Eroding political accountability, taking the form of either long periods of divided government, dating back to the "Do Nothing" 80th congress elected in 1946, to the recent "gerrymandering industry" producing a

dearth of competitive elections. The result is millions of "wasted votes" and an inability for voters to assign credit or blame for legislative action.

- Costly and perennial campaigns for all offices producing "the best politicians that money can buy." This problem had its origins with the breakdown of the party caucus system and the growth of primary elections in the 1960s; and
- The world's lowest voter turnout among all of the leading OECD countries, a phenomenon that began in the 1960s and has steadily intensified.

When various American scholars acknowledge these shortcomings, however, there is the occasional, offhand comparison to parliamentary systems which have avoided many of these pathologies. The unstated message is that we don't—or perhaps should never, ever want to—have that here.

Why not? What exactly is the problem with a parliamentary system? In the US, durable trust in government, sense of efficacy, and approval ratings for branches in government have all declined in recent decades. Such phenomena contribute to declining voter turnout and highlight what is arguably a more significant trend toward a crisis in confidence among Americans concerning their governing institutions. So why is institutional redesign off the table?

This article examines these four institutional blockages of the American majoritarian/Presidential system and suggests certain features of parliamentary or consensus systems might overcome these persistent shortcomings of American politics.

Less normatively, the article is framed by three concepts central to understanding and shaping public policy in advanced industrialized states with democratic constitutional structures.

First, is the issue of comparability and 'American Exceptionalism' (Lipset 1996). The article's goal is to initiate a long-delayed dialogue on comparative constitutional structures with scholars of American politics. Second, the article hopes to participate in the active discussion among comparativists on the respective strengths and weaknesses of majoritarian and consensus systems. (Birchfield and Crepaz 1998) Third, scandals surrounding money and politics in a number of democratic states (Barker 1994) should prompt a comparison of parties and party systems and the context within which they function.

This article does not underestimate the quite significant problems associated with "institutional transplantation" (Jacoby 2000) from one country to another. The more modest and realistic goal is to engage American and Comparative scholars in a fruitful debate about political institutions and constitutional design that (finally) includes American politics in a Comparative orbit.

This article is organized in 5 sections that address: 1) the cumbersome tool of impeachment; 2) eroding political accountability due to divided government and safe seats; 3) the costly, never-ending campaign process; 4) the continued deterioration of voter turnout; and 5) the quite formidable obstacles that initiating a parliamentary remedy to these problems would clearly face.

1. Impeachment: Head of State vs Head of Government

The tool of impeachment is merely a symptom of a larger problem. Its more fundamental flaw is that it highlights the constitutional confusion between the two functions of the US presidency: head of state and head of government.

Americanists have delved deeply into the minutiae of the impeachment process during the past thirty years but comparativists would ask a different question. How would other democracies handle similar crises affecting their political leaders? More than two years transpired from the Watergate break-in to Nixon's resignation (1972–74), the Iran-Contra scandal (1986–87) produced no impeachment hearings; and an entire year (1998–99) transpired from the onset of the Clinton-Lewinsky saga to the completion of the impeachment process. Finally, the revelations from 2005–2007 concerning the Bush Administration's clandestine spying on American citizens by the National Security Agency have once again caused some Democrats to mention preliminary impeachment inquiries. Comparativists and citizens of other democratic polities find this astounding, since in a parliamentary system a fundamental challenge to the executive would take the form of a vote of no confidence, (Lijphart 1994) and the issue would be politically resolved within weeks. The executive would either survive and continue or resign.

The portrayal of the Clinton impeachment and trial is characterized as historic. For only the second time in American politics, an American president has been impeached in the House and put on trial in the Senate. Yet, the idea of using impeachment has been much less rare, having been raised three times in the past thirty years; and has only a very slim possibility of being seriously considered in the early 21st century. Basically, impeachment is an extremely blunt tool that has not "worked" at all. It is either not brought to fruition (Watergate), not used when it should have been (Iran-Contra), or completely

trivialized (Clinton-Lewinsky) when another path was clearly needed. But impeachment itself isn't the real problem; a larger constitutional design flaw is.

The United States has a constitutional structure based on a separation of powers, while most parliamentary systems have a "fusion" of powers in that the Prime Minister is also the leader of the major party in parliament. However, within the American executive itself, there is a "fusion" of functions, which is the exact opposite of Parliamentary regimes.

The US is the only developed democracy where head of state and head of government are fused in one person. The President is the Head of State and, effectively, the Head of Government. In Parliamentary systems these two functions are performed by two different people. (Linz 1993) Thus impeachment of one person removes two functions in one and likely explained the dichotomy of popular desire for Clinton's retention on the one hand, but also for some form of political censure on the other.

Beyond the impeachment issue, when American presidents undertake some action as head of government for which they are criticized, they then become invariably more remote and inaccessible. For example, Presidents Johnson (Vietnam), Nixon (Watergate), Reagan (Iran/Contra), Clinton (the Lewinsky Affair) and G.W. Bush (Iraq) all reduced their appearances at press conferences as criticism of their policies mounted. In short, when criticized for actions taken in their head of government capacity, they all retreated to the Rose Garden or other "safe" locations and sometimes created the impression that criticizing the President—now wearing the head of state hat (or perhaps, crown)—was somehow unpatriotic. This was especially the case with George W. Bush, who in the post 9/11 and Iraq war periods, has tried to emphasize the commander in chief aspect of the presidency rather than his role as steward of the economy and domestic politics.

Toward a Politically Accountable Prime Minister and a Ceremonial President

A parliamentary system with a separate head of state and head of government would produce two "executive" offices instead of just one. It's odd that the US is so fearful of centralized power yet allows the executive to perform functions that no other leader of an OECD country (France excepted) performs alone. The US Vice President serves many of the functions of heads of state in other countries. But the United States has a comparatively odd way of dividing executive constitutional functions. One office, the Presidency, does everything while the other, the Vice Presidency, does virtually nothing and simply waits until the president can no longer serve (although Vice President Cheney sees this role differently). An American parliamentary system would redefine these 2 offices so that one person (the head of state) would serve as a national symbol and preside over ceremonial functions. The second person (the head of government) would function much like a prime minister does in a parliamentary system, namely as the head of government who could be criticized, censured and held accountable for specific political actions without creating a constitutional crisis.

Thus were it necessary to censure or otherwise take action against the head of government (i.e. prime minister), the solution would be a relatively quick vote of no confidence that would solve the problem and move on and let the country address its political business. (Huber 1996) And unlike impeachment which is the political equivalent of the death penalty, a vote of no confidence does not preclude a politician's making a comeback and returning to lead a party or coalition. Impeachment and removal from office, on the other hand, is much more final.

Prime Ministers, unlike US presidents, are seen much more as active politicians and not remote inaccessible figures. In a parliament, the prime minister as the head of government is required to engage—and be criticized—in the rough-and-tumble world of daily politics. In short, the head of government must be accountable. The British prime minister, for example, is required to participate in a weekly "question time" in which often blunt and direct interrogatories are pressed by the opposition. (Rundquist 1991) There is no equivalent forum for the American president to be formally questioned as a normal part of the political process.

But could such a power be used in a cavalier fashion, perhaps removing the head of government easily after a debilitating scandal? This is unlikely in a well-designed parliamentary system because such cynicism would likely produce a backlash that would constrain partisanship. In fact, the Germans have institutionalized such constraints in the "constructive vote of no confidence" requiring any removal of the head of government to be a simultaneous election of a new one. The context of such a parliamentary system lowers the incentives to engage in the politics of destruction. The political impact of destroying any particular individual in a collective body such as a cabinet or governing party or coalition is much less significant than removing a directly elected president.

A parliamentary head of state is above the kind of criticism generated from no confidence votes and simply serves as an apolitical symbol of national pride. In nation states that have disposed of their monarchies, ceremonial presidents perform many of the same roles as constitutional monarchs such as Queen Elizabeth do, but much less expensively. In fact, many of these ceremonial roles are performed by the American vice president (attending state dinners/funerals, cutting ribbons, presiding over the Senate, etc.) The problem is that the Vice President is often a political afterthought, chosen more for ticket-balancing functions and/or for inoffensive characteristics than for any expected major political contributions. On the other hand, the type of individual usually chosen as a ceremonial president in a parliamentary system is a retired politician from the moderate wing of one of the major parties who has a high degree of stature and can serve as a figure of national unity. In effect, the office of ceremonial president is often a reward or honor for decades of distinguished national service, hardly the characteristics of most American vice presidents.

In retrospect, one might say that President Clinton was impeached not for abusing head of government functions, but for undermining the decorum and respect associated with heads of state. The separation of head of state and head of government would have a salutary effect on this specific point. Scandals destroying heads of state would have little real political significance since the head of state would not wield real political power. Similarly, scandals destroying heads of government would have significantly less impact than in the current American system. The head of government role, once separated from the head of state role, would no longer attract monolithic press and public attention or be subject to extraordinarily unrealistic behavioral expectations.

2. Political Accountability: Divided Government & "Safe Seats"

From the "do nothing" 80th Congress elected in 1946 to the 110th elected in 2006, a total of thirty-one Congresses, the United States has experienced divided government for more than two-thirds of this period. In only ten of those thirty-one Congresses has the president's party enjoyed majorities in both houses of Congress. (Fiorina 1992; Center for Voting and Democracy 2007) Some might observe this divided government phenomenon and praise the bipartisan nature of the American system. (Mayhew 1991) But to justify such a conclusion, defenders of bipartisanship would have to demonstrate high public approval of governmental performance, particularly when government was divided. Based on over four decades of declining trust in government, such an argument is increasingly hard to justify.

One explanation for the American preference for divided government is the fear of concentrated political power. (Jacobson 1990) Yet in a search for passivity, the result often turns out to be simply inefficiency.

While the fear of concentrated government power is understandable for historical and ideological reasons, many of the same people who praise divided government also express concern regarding government efficiency. (Thurber 1991) Yet divided government quite likely contributes to the very inefficiencies that voters rightfully lament. Under divided government, when all is well, each of the two parties claims responsibility for the outcome; when economic or political policies turn sour, however, each party blames the other. This condition leads to a fundamental lack of political accountability and the self-fulfilling prophesy that government is inherently inefficient.

Rather than being an accidental occurrence, divided government is much more likely to result due to the American constitutional design. For it is constitutional provisions that are at the heart of divided government; 2 year terms for Congress, 4 year terms for the Presidency, and 6 year terms for the Senate invariably produce divided government.

Were it only for these "accidental" outcomes of divided government, political accountability might be less deleterious. Exacerbating the problem, however, is the decline of parties as institutions. This has caused individuals to have weaker partisan attachments—despite the increased partisan rhetoric of many elected officials since the 1980s—and has thereby intensified the fragmentation of government. (Franklin and Hirczy de Mino 1998) Clearly, divided government is more problematic when partisan conflict between the two parties is greater as the sharper ideological conflict and the increased party line congressional

Table 1 Trust in the Federal Government 1964–2004

Year	None of the Time	Some of the Time	Most of the Time	Just about Always	Don't Know
1964	0	22	62	14	1
1966	2	28	48	17	4
1968	0	36	54	7	2
1970	0	44	47	6	2
1972	1	44	48	5	2
1974	1	61	34	2	2
1976	1	62	30	13	3
1978	4	64	27	2	3
1980	4	69	23	2	2
1982	3	62	31	2	3
1984	1	53	40	4	2
1986	2	57	35	3	2
1988	2	56	36	4	1
1990	2	69	25	3	1
1992	2	68	26	3	1
1994	1	74	19	2	1
1996	1	66	30	3	0
1998	1	58	36	4	1
2000	1	55	40	4	1
2002	0	44	51	5	0
2004	1	52	43	4	0

Percentage within study year.

Source: The National Election Studies (http://www.electionstudies.org/nesguide/toptable/tab5a_1.htm)

Question Text:

"How much of the time do you think you can trust the government in Washington to do what is right—just about always, most of the time or only some of the time?"

Source: The National Election Studies, University of Michigan, 2005

Table 2 The Persistence of Divided Government

Year	President	House	Senate	Divided/ Unified Government
1946	D – Truman	Rep	Rep	D
1948	D – Truman	Dem	Rep	D
1950	D – Truman	Rep	Rep	D
1952	R – Eisenhower	Rep	Rep	U
1954	R – Eisenhower	Dem	Dem	D
1956	R – Eisenhower	Dem	Dem	D
1958	R – Eisenhower	Dem	Dem	D
1960	D – Kennedy	Dem	Dem	U
1962	D – Kennedy	Dem	Dem	U
1964	D – Johnson	Dem	Dem	U
1966	D – Johnson	Dem	Dem	U
1968	R – Nixon	Dem	Dem	D
1970	R – Nixon	Dem	Dem	D
1972	R – Nixon	Dem	Dem	D
1974	R – Ford	Dem	Dem	D
1976	D – Carter	Dem	Dem	U
1978	D – Carter	Dem	Dem	U
1980	R – Reagan	Dem	Rep	D
1982	R – Reagan	Dem	Rep	D
1984	R – Reagan	Dem	Rep	D
1986	R – Reagan	Dem	Dem	D
1988	R – Bush	Dem	Dem	D
1990	R – Bush	Dem	Dem	D
1992	D – Clinton	Dem	Dem	U
1994	D – Clinton	Rep	Rep	D
1996	D – Clinton	Rep	Rep	D
1998	D – Clinton	Rep	Rep	D
2000	R – Bush	Rep	Dem*	D
2002	R – Bush	Rep	Rep	U
2004	R – Bush	Rep	Rep	U
2006	R – Bush	Dem	Dem	D

*After a 50-50 split (with Vice President Cheney as the tiebreaker), Senator Jeffords (I-VT) switched from the Republican Party shortly after the 2000 Election, thereby swinging the Senate to the Democrats.

voting since the mid-1990s would suggest. Under these circumstances, divided government seems to be more problematic, since two highly partisan parties within the American political system seem potentially dangerous. Persistent divided government over time will likely produce a fundamental change in the relationship between Presidents and the Congress. Presidents are unable to bargain effectively with a hostile congress—witness the 1995 government shutdown—leading the former to make appeals over the heads of Congress directly and, hence undermine the legitimacy of the legislative branch. (Kernell 1997) This argument parallels the one made in recent comparative scholarship (Linz 1993) regarding the serious problem of dual legitimacy in presidential systems.

A second component of the political accountability problem is the increasing non-competitiveness of American elections. Accounts of the 2000 Presidential election stressed its historic closeness, settled by only 540,000 popular votes (notwithstanding the Electoral College anomaly). And the narrow Republican majorities in the House and Senate apparently indicated that every congressional or senate seat could be up for grabs each election. The reality is something different. (Center for Voting and Democracy 2007) Out of 435 House seats, only 60 (13.8%)

were competitive, the outcome of most Senate races is known well in advance, and the 2000 and 2004 Presidential races were only competitive in 15 of 50 states. In the remaining 35, the state winners (Bush or Gore; or Bush or Kerry, respectively) were confident enough of the outcome to forgo television advertising in many of them. In essence, voters for candidates who did not win these hundreds of "safe seats" were effectively disenfranchised and unable to hold their representatives politically accountable.

For those who lament the irresponsibility—or perhaps irrelevance—of the two major parties, an institutional design that would force responsibility should be praised. Quite simply, those who praise divided government because it "limits the damage" or see nothing amiss when there are hundreds of safe seats are faced with a dilemma. They can not simultaneously complain about the resulting governmental inefficiency and political cynicism that ultimately follows when accountability is regularly clouded.

Political Accountability and the Fusion of Government

A number of scholars have addressed the deficiencies of divided government, but they suggest that the problem is that the electoral cycle, with its "midterm" elections, intensifies the likelihood of divided government in non-presidential election years. Such advocates propose as a solution the alteration of the electoral cycle so that all congressional elections are on four year terms, concurrent with presidential terms, likely producing a clear majority. (Cutler 1989) Yet this contains a fatal flaw. Because there is no guarantee that this proposal would alleviate the residual tension between competing branches of government, it merely sidesteps the accountability factor strongly discouraging party unity across the executive and legislative branches of government.

This suggestion could also produce the opposite effect from divided government, namely exaggerated majorities common to parliamentary regimes with majoritarian electoral systems such as the UK. The "safe seats" phenomenon would be the culprit just as in the UK. The most familiar examples of this phenomenon were the "stop-go" policies of post-World War II British governments, as each succeeding government tried to overturn the previous election. While creating governing majorities is important for political accountability, the absence of proportional representation creates a different set of problems.

Under a fusion of power system, in which the current presidency would be redefined, the resulting parliamentary system would make the head of the legislative branch the executive, thus eliminating the current separation of powers. Yet if a government should lose its majority between scheduled elections due to defection of its party members or coalition partners, the head of state then would ask the opposition to form a new government and, failing that, call for new elections. This avoids the constitutional crises that the clamor for impeachment seems to engender in the American system.

But what if coalition members try to spread the blame for poor performance to their partners? In theory, the greater the flexibility available in shifting from one governing coalition to another (with a different composition), the greater is the potential for this kind of musical cabinet chairs. The potential for such an outcome is far less than in the American system, however. A century of experience in other parliamentary regimes (Laver and Shepsle 1996) shows that members of such a party

capriciously playing games with governing are usually brought to heel at the subsequent election.

In other words, the major advantage to such a parliamentary system is that it heightens the capacity for voters and citizens to evaluate government performance. Of course, many individuals might object to the resulting concentration of power. However, if voters are to judge the accomplishments of elected officials, the latter need time to succeed or fail, and then the voters can make a judgment on their tenure. The most likely outcome would be a governing party or coalition of parties that would have to stay together to accomplish anything, thereby increasing party salience. (Richter 2002) Phrased differently, such an arrangement would likely lead to an increase in responsible government.

Many Americans might react unfavorably at the mention of the word coalition due to its supposed instability. Here we need to make the distinction between transparent and opaque coalitions. Some argue that coalition governments in parliamentary systems have the reputation of increased instability. That, or course, depends on the substance of the coalition agreement and the willingness of parties to produce a stable majority. (Strom et al. 1994) But in most parliamentary systems, these party coalitions are formed transparently before an election so the voters can evaluate and then pass judgment on the possible coalition prior to Election Day. It's not as if there are no coalitions in the US Congress. There they take the opaque form of ad-hoc groups of individual members of Congress on an issue-by-issue basis. The high information costs to American voters in understanding the substance of such layered bargains hardly are an example of political transparency.

Finally, for those concerned that the "fusion" of the executive and legislative branches—on the British majoritarian model—would upset the concept of checks and balances, a multi-party consensus parliamentary system produces them slightly differently. (Lijphart 1984) Majoritarianism concentrates power and makes "checking" difficult, while consensus democracies institutionalize the process in a different and more accountable form. A multi-party parliamentary system would also provide greater minority representation, fewer safe seats, and protection by reducing majoritarianism's excessive concentration of power. A consensus parliamentary system would also address the "tyranny of the majority" problem and allow checking and balancing by the voters in the ballot box since the multiple parties would not likely allow a single party to dominate. Consensus systems thus represent a compromise between the current U.S. system and the sharp concentration of British Westminster systems. Americans who simultaneously favor checks and balances but decry inefficient government need to clarify what they actually want their government to do.

Table 3 Comparative Coalitions

American	Parliamentary
Opaque	Transparent
Issue-by-Issue	Programmatic
Back Room	Open Discussion
Unaccountable	Election Ratifies
Unstable	Generally Stable

3. Permanent and Expensive Campaigns

The cost to run for political office in the United States dwarfs that spent in any other advanced industrialized democracy. The twin problems are time and money; more specifically a never-ending campaign "season" and the structure of political advertising that depend so heavily on TV money. (Gans 1993) In listening to the debates about "reforming" the American campaign finance system, students of other democratic electoral systems find these discussions bizarre. More than $2 billion was raised and spent (Corrado 1997) by parties, candidates and interest groups in the 1996 campaign, and for 2000 it went up to $3 billion. Finally, the Center for Responsive Politics estimated the total cost for 2004 Presidential and Congressional elections was $3.9 billion (Weiss 2004) and the preliminary estimates for the 2006 midterm elections—in which there was no presidential race—were approximately $3 billion.

The two year congressional cycle forces members of the House of Representatives to literally campaign permanently. The amount of money required to run for a Congressional seat has quadrupled since 1990. Presidential campaigns are several orders of magnitude beyond the House of Representatives or the Senate. By themselves they are more than two years long, frequently longer. Unless a presidential candidate is independently wealthy or willing and able to raise upfront $30–$50 million it is simply impossible to run seriously for this office.

Many of the problems stem from the post-Watergate "reforms" that tried to limit the amount of spending on campaigns which then produced a backlash in the form of a 1976 Supreme Court decision (Buckley vs Valeo) that undermined this reform attempt. In essence, Buckley vs Valeo held that "paid speech" (i.e. campaign spending) has an equivalent legal status as "free speech". (Grant 1998) Consequently, since then all "reform" efforts have been tepid measures that have not been able to get at the root of the problem. As long as "paid speech" retains its protected status, any changes are dead in the water.

At its essence this issue is a fissure between "citizens" and "consumers". What Buckley vs Valeo has done is to equate the citizenship function (campaigning, voting, civic education) with a market-based consumer function (buying and selling consumer goods as commodities). (Brubaker 1998) Unlike the United States, most other OECD democracies consider citizenship a public good and provide funding for parties, candidates and the electoral process as a matter of course. The Buckley vs Valeo decision conflates the concepts of citizen and consumer, the logical extension of which is there are weak limits on campaign funding and no limits on the use of a candidate's own money. We are all equal citizens, yet we are not all equal consumers. Bringing consumer metaphors into the electoral process debases the very concept of citizenship and guarantees that the American political system produces the best politicians money can buy.

Free Television Time and the Return of Political Party Dues

Any broadcaster wishing to transmit to the public is required to obtain a broadcast license because the airways have the legal status of public property. To have access to such property, the government must license these networks, cable channels, and stations to serve the public interest. In return, broadcasters are able to sell airtime to sponsors of various programs. Unfortunately for those concerned with campaign costs, candidates for public office fall into the same category as consumer goods in the eyes of the broadcasters. (Weinberg 1993) What has always seemed odd to observers of other democratic states is that there is no Quid Pro Quo requiring the provision of free public airtime for candidates when running for election.

Any serious reform of campaign finance would require a concession from all broadcasters to provide free time for all representative candidates and parties as a cost of using the public airways. Since the largest share of campaign money is TV money, this reform would solve the problem at its source. Restricting the "window" when these free debates would take place to the last two months before a general election would thus address the time dimension as well. Such practices are standard procedure in all developed parliamentary systems. Very simply, as long as "reform" efforts try to regulate the supply of campaign finance, it will fail. A much more achievable target would be the regulation of demand.

The United States could solve another money problem by borrowing a page from parliamentary systems: changing the political party contribution structure from individual voluntary contributions (almost always from the upper middle class and the wealthy) to a more broad-based dues structure common to parties other developed democracies. This more egalitarian party dues structure would perform the additional salutary task of rebuilding parties as functioning institutions. (Allen 1999) Rather than continuing in their current status as empty shells for independently wealthy candidates, American political parties could become the kind of dynamic membership organizations they were at the turn of the 20th century when they did have a dues structure.

4. Low Voter Turnout?

The leading OECD countries have voter turnout ranging from 70% to 90% of their adult population while the US lags woefully behind.

Among the most commonly raised explanations for the US deficiency are: registration requirements, the role of television, voter discouragement, and voter contentment (although the latter two are clearly mutually exclusive). None are particularly convincing nor do they offer concrete suggestions as to how it might be overcome.

The two party system and the electoral method that produces it: the single member district, first past the post, or winner take all system with its attendant "safe seats" often escapes criticism. The rise of such new organizations as the Libertarian, and Green parties potentially could threaten the hegemony of the Democrats and Republicans. Yet the problem of a third (or fourth) party gaining a sufficient number of votes to actually win seats and challenge the two party system is formidable. The electoral arithmetic would require any third party to win some 25% of the vote on a nationwide basis—or develop a highly-concentrated regional presence—before it would actually gain more than a token number of seats. And failing to actually win seats produces a "wasted

Table 4   Voter Turnout and Type of Electoral System Major Developed Democracies–1945–2005

Country	% Voter Turnout	Type of Electoral System
Italy	91.9	PR
Belgium	84.9	PR
Netherlands	84.8	PR
Australia	84.4	Mixed Member
Denmark	83.6	PR
Sweden	83.3	PR
Germany	80.0	Mixed-PR
Israel	80.0	PR
Norway	79.2	PR
Finland	79.0	PR
Spain	76.4	PR
Ireland	74.9	SMD
UK	73.0	SMD
Japan	68.3	SMD/Mixed
France	67.3	SMD + runoff
Canada	66.9	SMD
USA – Presidential	55.1	SMD
USA – Congress (Midterm)	40.6	SMD

Source: Voter Turnout: A Global Survey (Stockholm: International IDEA, 2005)

Table 5   The Advantages of Proportional Representation

Higher Voter Turnout
No "Wasted" Votes
Few Safe, Uncontested Seats
More Parties
Greater Minority Representation
Greater Gender Diversity in Congress
Greater Ideological Clarity
Parties Rebuilt as Institutions
6% Threshold Assumed
No More Gerrymandered Redistricting

vote" syndrome among party supporters which is devastating for such a party. (Rosenstone et al. 1996) Most voters who become disillusioned with the electoral process refer to the "lesser of two evils" choices they face. In such a circumstance, declining voter turnout is not surprising.

The US is a diverse country with many regional, religious, racial, and class divisions. So why should we expect that two "catch all" parties will do a particularly good job in appealing to the interests of diverse constituencies? The solution to lower voter turnout is a greater number of choices for voters and a different electoral system.

Proportional Representation

Under electoral systems using proportional representation, the percentage of a party's vote is equivalent to the percentage of seats allocated to the party in parliament. Comparative analysis shows that those countries with proportional representation—and the multiple parties that PR systems produce—invariably have higher voter turnout. (Grofman and Lijphart 1986) In other words, PR voting systems provide a wider variety of political choices and a wider variety of political representation.

Eliminating majoritarian single member districts (SMDs) in favor of PR voting would have several immediate effects. First, it would increase the range of choices for voters, since parties would have to develop ideological and programmatic distinctions to make themselves attractive to voters. As examples in other countries have shown, it would lead to formation of several new parties representing long underserved interests.

Such a change would force rebuilding of parties as institutions, since candidates would have to run as members of parties and not as independent entrepreneurs. The so-called Progressive "reforms" at the turn of the 20th century and the 1960s introduction of primaries—plus TV advertising—plus the widespread use of referenda have all had powerful effects in undermining parties as coherent political organizations. (Dwyre et al. 1994) In trying to force market-based individual "consumer choice" in the form of high-priced candidates, the collective institutions that are political parties have been hollowed out and undermined.

There are, of course, a wide range of standard objections to PR voting systems by those favoring retention of majoritarian SMD systems.

The first of these, coalitional instability, was addressed briefly above, but it needs to be restated here. The US has unstable coalitions in the Congress right now, namely issue-by-issue ones, usually formed in the House cloakroom with the "assistance" of lobbyists. Few average voters know with certainty how "their" member of Congress will vote on a given issue. (Gibson 1995) With ideologically coherent parties, they would.

An American parliament with several parties could very effectively produce self-discipline. Clearly there would have to be a coalition government since it is unlikely that any one party would capture 50% of the seats. The practice in almost all other coalition governments in parliamentary systems is that voters prefer a predictable set of political outcomes. Such an arrangement forces parties to both define their programs clearly and transparently, once entering into a coalition, and to do everything possible to keep the coalition together during the course of the legislative term.

The second standard objection to PR is the "too many parties" issue. PR voting has been practiced in parliaments for almost 100 years in many different democratic regimes. There is a long history of practices that work well and practices that don't. (Norris 1997) Two countries are invariably chosen as bad examples of PR, namely Israel and Italy. There is an easy solution to this problem of an unwieldy number of parties, namely an electoral threshold requiring any party to receive a certain minimal percentage to gain seats in the parliament. The significant question is what should this minimal threshold be? The Swedes have a 4% threshold and have 7 parties in their parliament, the Germans have a 5% threshold and have 5 parties represented in the Bundestag.

The third standard objection to PR voting is "who's my representative?" In a society so attuned to individualism, most Americans want a representative from their district. This argument presumes that all Americans have a member of Congress that represents their views. However, a liberal democrat who lived in former House Speaker Tom Delay's district in Texas might genuinely wonder in what way he represented that liberal's interests. By the same token, conservative Republicans living in Vermont had for almost twenty years the independent socialist, Bernard Sanders as the state's lone member of Congress representing "their" interests.

Yet if Americans reformers are still insistent on having individual representatives (Guinier 1994) the phenomenon of "Instant Runoff Voting" (Hill 2003) where voters rank order their preferences could produce proportionality among parties yet retain individual single member districts. It also could be used in Presidential elections and avoid accusations of "spoiler" candidates such as Ralph Nader in 2000.

If there were PR voting in an American parliament, what would the threshold be? The US threshold probably should be at least 6%. The goal is to devise a figure that represents all significant interests yet does not produce instability. The "shake out" of parties would likely produce some strategic "mergers" of weak parties which, as single parties, might not attain the 6% threshold. For example, a separate Latino party and an African-American party might insure always attaining a 6% threshold by forming a so-called "rainbow" party. Similarly the Reform Party and the Libertarian Party might find it electorally safer to merge into one free market party.

There are four primary arguments in favor of PR.

The first is simplicity; the percentage of the votes equals the percentage of the seats. To accomplish this, the more individualistic US could borrow the German hybrid system of "personalized" proportional representation. This system requires citizens to cast two votes on each ballot: the first for an individual candidate; and the second for a list of national/regional candidates grouped by party affiliation. (Allen 2001) This system has the effect of personalizing list voting because voters have their own representative but also can choose among several parties. Yet allocation of seats by party in the Bundestag corresponds strongly with the party's percentage of the popular vote.

The second advantage to PR is diversity. The experience of PR voting in other countries is that it changes the makeup of the legislature by increasing both gender and racial diversity. Obviously, parties representing minority interests who find it difficult to win representation in 2 person races, will more easily be able to win seats under PR. (Rule and Zimmerman 1992) Since candidates would not have to run as individuals—or raise millions of dollars—the parties would be more easily able to include individuals on the party's list of candidates who more accurately represent the demographics of average Americans. What a multi-party list system would do would provide a greater range of interests being represented and broaden the concept of "representation" to go beyond narrow geography to include representation of such things as ideas and positions on

policy issues that would be understandable to voters. Moreover, as for geographic representation on a list system, it would be in the self interest of the parties to insure that there was not only gender balance—if this is what the party wanted—on their list, but also other forms of balance including geography, ideology, and ethnicity, among others.

The third advantage is government representativeness. Not only is a consensus-based parliamentary system based on proportional representation more representative of the voting public, it also produces more representative governments. (Birchfield and Crepaz 1998) This study finds that consensus-based, PR systems also produce a high degree of "popular cabinet support," namely the percentage of voters supporting the majority party or coalition.

The fourth advantage to a PR system in the US is that it would eliminate the redistricting circus. Until recently, the decennial census occasioned the excruciating task of micro-managing the drawing of congressional districts. Yet, since the 2002 elections, Republicans in Texas and Georgia have redistricted a second time, creating even "safer" seats by manipulating district lines to their advantage. (Veith et al. 2003) Under PR however, districts would be eliminated. Candidate lists would be organized statewide, in highly populated states, or regionally in the case of smaller states like those in New England. To insure geographical representation, all parties would find it in their own self-interest that the candidate list included geographical diversity starting at the top of the list.

Getting from Here to There: From Academic Debates to Constitutional Reform?

Clearly, none of these four structural reforms will take place soon. But if reformers wanted to start, what would be the initial steps? Of the four proposals, two of them could be accomplished by simple statute: campaign reform and the electoral system. The other two would require constitutional change: head of state/government and divided government. Given the above caveats, it would be easiest to effect campaign reform (the Supreme Court willing) and to alter the electoral system.

The largest obstacles to such a radical change in the American constitutional system are cultural and structural. Culturally, the ethos of American individualism would have difficulty giving up features such as a single all-powerful executive and one's own individual member of congress, no matter how powerful the arguments raised in support of alternatives. Ideology and cultural practice change very slowly. A more serious obstacle would be the existing interests privileged by the current system. All would fight tenaciously to oppose this suggested change.

Finally, specialists in American politics may dismiss this argument as the farfetched "poaching" of a comparativist on a terrain that only Americanists can write about with knowledge and expertise. However, the durability of all four of the above-mentioned problems, stretching back anywhere from 25 to 50 years, suggests that Americanists have no monopoly of wisdom on overcoming these pathologies. More seriously, what this comparativist perceives is a fundamental failure of imagination based largely on the "N of 1" problem that all comparativists struggle to avoid. If a single observed phenomenon—in this case, the American political system—is not examined comparatively, one never knows whether prevailing practice is optimal or suboptimal. In essence, those who do not look at these issues comparatively suffer a failure of imagination because they are unable to examine the full range of electoral and constitutional options.

References

Allen, Christopher S. 1999. *Transformation of the German Political Party System: Institutional Crisis or Democratic Renewal?* New York: Berghahn Books.

———. 2001. "Proportional Representation." In *Oxford Companion to Politics of the World,* ed. J. Krieger. Oxford: Oxford University Press.

Barker, A. 1994. "The Upturned Stone: Political Scandals and their Investigation Processes in 20 Democracies." *Crime Law and Social Change* 24 (1):337–73.

Birchfield, Vicki, and Markus M. L. Crepaz. 1998. "The Impact of Constitutional Structures and Collective and Competitive Veto Points on Income Inequality in Industrialized Democracies." *European Journal of Political Research* 34 (2):175–200.

Brubaker, Stanley C. 1998. "The Limits of U.S. Campaign Spending Limits." *Public Interest* 133:33–54.

Center for Voting and Democracy. *Dubious Democracy 2007,* September 3 2007 [cited. Available from http://www.fairvote .org/?page=1917.

Corrado, Anthony. 1997. *Campaign Finance Reform: A Sourcebook.* Washington, D.C.: Brookings Institution.

Cutler, Lloyd. 1989. "Some Reflections About Divided Government." *Presidential Studies Quarterly* 17:485–92.

Dionne, E. J., Jr. 1991. *Why Americans Hate Politics.* New York: Simon and Schuster.

Dwyre, D., M. O'Gorman, and J. Stonecash. 1994. "Disorganized Politics and the Have-Notes: Politics and Taxes in New York and California." *Polity* 27 (1):25–48.

Fiorina, Morris. 1992. *Divided Government.* New York: Macmillan.

Franklin, Mark N., and Wolfgang P. Hirczy de Mino. 1998. "Separated Powers, Divided Government, and Turnout in U.S. Presidential Elections." *American Journal of Political Science* 42 (1):316–26.

Gans, Curtis. 1993. "Television: Political Participation's Enemy #1." *Spectrum: the Journal of State Government* 66 (2):26–31.

Gibson, Martha L. 1995. "Issues, Coalitions, and Divided Government." *Congress & the Presidency* 22 (2):155–66.

Grant, Alan. 1998. "The Politics of American Campaign Finance." *Parliamentary Affairs* 51 (2):223–40.

Grofman, Bernard, and Arend Lijphart. 1986. *Electoral Laws and Their Consequences.* New York: Agathon Press.

Guinier, Lani. 1994. *The Tyranny of the Majority: Fundamental Fairness in Representative Democracy.* New York: The Free Press.

Hill, Steven. 2003. *Fixing Elections: The Failure of America's Winner Take All Politics.* New York: Routledge.

Huber, John D. 1996. "The Vote of Confidence in Parliamentary Democracies." *American Political Science Review* 90 (2): 269–82.

Jacobson, Gary C. 1990. *The Electoral Origins of Divided Government: Competition in U.S. House Elections, 1946–1988.* Boulder, CO: Westview.

Jacoby, Wade. 2000. *Imitation and Politics: Redesigning Germany.* Ithaca: Cornell University Press.

Kernell, Samuel. 1997. *Going Public: New Strategies of Presidential Leadership.* 3rd ed. Washington, D.C.: CQ Press.

Laver, Michael, and Kenneth A. Shepsle. 1996. *Making and Breaking Governments: Cabinets and Legislatures in Parliamentary Democracies.* New York: Cambridge University Press.

Lijphart, Arend. 1984. *Democracies: Patterns of Majoritarian and Consensus Government in Twenty-One Countries.* New Haven: Yale University Press.

———. 1994. "Democracies: Forms, Performance, and Constitutional Engineering." *European Journal of Political Research* 25 (1):1–17.

Linz, Juan. 1993. "The Perils of Presidentialism." In *The Global Resurgence of Democracy,* ed. L. Diamond and M. Plattner. Baltimore: Johns Hopkins University Press.

Lipset, Seymour Martin. 1996. *American Exceptionalism: A Double-Edged Sword.* New York: Norton.

Mayhew, David. 1991. *Divided We Govern: Party Control, Lawmaking, and Investigations, 1946–1990.* New Haven: Yale University Press.

Norris, Pippa. 1997. "Choosing Electoral Systems: Proportional, Majoritarian and Mixed Systems." *International Political Science Review* 18 (3):297–312.

Richter, Michaela. 2002. "Continuity or Politikwechsel? The First Federal Red-Green Coalition." *German Politics & Society* 20 (1):1–48.

Rosenstone, Steven J., Roy L. Behr, and Edward H. Lazarus. 1996. *Third Parties in America: Citizen Response to Major Party Failure.* Princeton: Princeton University Press.

Rule, Wilma, and Joseph F. Zimmerman, eds. 1992. *United States Electoral Systems: Their Impact on Women and Minorities.* New York: Praeger.

Rundquist, Paul S. 1991. *The House of Representatives and the House of Commons: A Brief Comparison of American and British Parliamentary Practice.* Washington, DC: Congressional Research Service, Library of Congress.

Strom, Kaare, Ian Budge, and Michael J. Laver. 1994. "Constraints on Cabinet formation in Parliamentary Democracies." *American Journal of Political Science* 38 (2):303–35.

Thurber, James A. 1991. "Representation, Accountability, and Efficiency in Divided Party Control of Government." *PS* 24:653–7.

Veith, Richard, Norma Jean Veith, and Susan Fuery. 2003. "Oral Argument." In *U.S. Supreme Court.* Washington, DC.

Weinberg, Jonathan. 1993. "Broadcasting and Speech." *California Law Review* 81 (5):1101–206.

Weiss, Stephen. 2004. "'04 Elections Expected to Cost Nearly $4 Billion." In *opensecrets.org—Center for Responsive Politics:* http://www.opensecrets.org/pressreleases/2004/04spending.asp.

An original essay written for this volume. Copyright © 2007 by Christopher S. Allen. Reprinted by permission of the author.

India's Election

Singh When You're Winning

The Congress party romps to victory by a surprisingly big margin. Its next government will be expected to do rather more than its current one.

Ever unpredictable, Indian voters delivered their pentennial surprise on May 16th, when over 417m ballots were totted up. Reversing decades of decline, the Congress party had won the country's month-long election, which ended on May 13th, by a bigger margin than its most enthusiastic cheer-leaders had dared dream of. Congress and its electoral allies won 261 of 543 available seats. With support from a few tiny regional parties and independents, they will have a majority in India's 15th parliament. On May 20th India's president, Pratibha Patil, therefore reappointed Manmohan Singh prime minister, making him the first prime minister to achieve this distinction at the end of a five-year term since India's first, Jawaharlal Nehru.

Congress itself won 206 seats. This was the best result by any party since 1991, when the murder of Congress's leader Rajiv Gandhi half way through the poll gave it a huge sympathy vote. The Hindu-nationalist Bharatiya Janata Party (BJP), Congress's main rival, won 116 seats, its lowest tally for two decades. In a double boon for Sonia Gandhi, Congress's leader and Rajiv's widow (shown above with Mr Singh), Sri Lanka's government on May 18th declared a final military victory against the Tamil Tiger rebels, her husband's assassins.

Even some who mourn the BJP's lesser thrashing are encouraged by Congress's victory. The outgoing government, formed after Congress surprisingly triumphed in the 2004 election, winning 145 seats, was hobbled by the many venal and incompetent regional and Communist allies that it needed to make up its majority. Unencumbered by this rabble, Congress's next government is expected to be more stable, less corrupt and, at a time of economic crisis, more efficient. Shorn of the Communists, who blocked a clutch of liberal measures before they abandoned the government last year, it could also pass some overdue economic reforms. On May 18th, in two dramatically curtailed sessions of trading, lasting a minute in total, the Bombay Stock Exchange jumped by over 17%. This was close to its biggest daily gain, and roughly the same proportion by which the markets plummeted on May 17th 2004 in response to the current government's formation.

Completing the symmetry, the Communists, who in 2004 won 62 seats, their best result ever, won 24 seats, their worst since 1952. Their decision to campaign against Congress on an arcane foreign-policy issue, a nuclear co-operation deal with America, which was sealed last year despite their efforts to kill it, backfired utterly. According to the National Election Study, a post-poll survey of 30,000 voters by the Delhi-based Centre for the Study of Developing Societies (CSDS), only 37% had even heard of the deal.

Voters in the Communist stronghold of West Bengal, where Congress made a formidable alliance with the Trinamul Congress party, were more concerned by the Communist state-government's thuggish efforts to acquire farmland for industrial development. Congress and its ally won 25 of West Bengal's 42 seats, and are now hoping to wrest control of a state the leftists have ruled for over three decades. In Nandigram, a picturesque rice-growing region, where West Bengal's rulers tried to acquire land for a petrochemical hub in 2007, sparking battles between peasants and party thugs, crowds gathered to cheer the left's defeat. Abdul Daiyan Khan, a peasant whose son was shot dead by the police during the land war, said he and his neighbours had voted against the Communists for the first time, because: "The party that gave us land now wants to take it away."

In Uttar Pradesh (UP), India's most populous state, for which 80 seats are reserved, another would-be kingmaker, the Bahujan Samaj Party (BSP), also collapsed. Dedicated to *dalits* (Hinduism's former "untouchables"), the BSP had hoped to win most of UP's seats, replicating its success in the 2007 state assembly election. With 50 seats, its autocratic leader, Mayawati, had planned to bargain with either the BJP or the Congress to become India's first *dalit* prime minister. But the BSP won only 21 seats, largely because its sometime non-*dalit* supporters forsook it. Many of these Muslims and higher-caste Hindus voted for Congress, which came away with 21 seats, more than double its previous tally.

As Miss Mayawati takes revenge for her humiliation—on May 18th she sacked 100 senior civil servants to whom she had given the task of delivering her victory—Congress's progress in UP has inspired some excited analysis. The rise of regional and caste-based parties, such as the BSP, has been the dominant theme in Indian politics for two decades. Some pundits see an end to this. They argue that Indian voters, showing unsuspected perspicacity, have recognised the need for stable central governments, which only national parties can provide. The survey by CSDS seems to agree with this. Only 20% of respondents did not consider coalition governments harmful, down from 31% in 2004.

Yet the results do not support this theory. The combined vote-share of India's two national parties has continued to fall, to 47.3%. And the increase in Congress's share, from 26.5% in 2004 to 28.5%, was quite modest considering that, with fewer allies than in 2004, it contested 23 more seats. Congress's relative leap in seats bespeaks an increasingly crowded field. This worked to its advantage in many places, including Mumbai, Tamil Nadu and, especially, Andhra Pradesh (AP), where it won 33 seats and retained control of the state government in a concurrent poll.

According to AP's chief minister, Y.S. Rajasekhara Reddy, who has now delivered Congress's biggest tranche of seats in consecutive elections: "The credibility of the government of India and of Andhra has been established in the minds of the people." But without the vote-splitting debut of a small party led by the state's most revered film-star, known as Chiranjeevi (the "immortal one"), Congress would have suffered.

In fact, many regional parties did fine, including two with well regarded governments in Bihar and Orissa. Perhaps the most that can be said is that Indians are growing impatient with parties that appeal to them only on the basis of caste, region or religion, neglecting their welfare. Congress may have prospered in UP, speculates Yogendra Yadav of CSDS, partly because it was the only main party not to have run a dreadful government there recently. Vinay Tiwari, a Brahmin landowner in the remote village of Harihar Patti, in a region of northern UP swept by Congress, is a speck of evidence for this. He had previously voted for the low-caste Samajwadi party and the BJP. But he was turned off by the record of the former party's candidate and by the Hinduist party's habit of inciting violence against Muslims. So Mr Tiwari plumped for Congress—"the party of my forefathers"—and instructed his 12 relatives and 50-odd *dalit* labourers to do likewise.

Yet he would not have done so if he, like millions of others, had not felt surprisingly sunny towards the Congress-led government. According to CSDS's survey, 57% of Indians wanted to give the government in Delhi another go, compared with 48% in 2004. Thus, Congress fulfilled, or surpassed, its most optimistic expectations in almost every state.

In Rajasthan, a sometime BJP stronghold, it picked weak candidates, ran a ragged campaign, and won 20 of 25 seats. In Madhya Pradesh, where the BJP retained power in a state election last December, and expected to clean up, Congress won 12 of 29. In Gujarat, India's most industrialised and Muslim-phobic state, where the BJP has won four successive state elections and has its most talismanic leader, Narendra Modi, Congress got 11 of 26 seats. Clearly, this election was more than the usual aggregate of state-level verdicts.

Two explanations suggest themselves, starting with the obvious one. In the past five years, India's economy has grown at an average annualised rate of 8.5% a year, including a relative slump to less than 7% in the financial year that

ended in March. Driven by services, which contribute over half of GDP but employ only a quarter of the workforce, this boom has benefited too few Indians—yet more than is often supposed. Blessed with four good monsoons and high food prices, agriculture, which contributes around 20% of India's GDP but supports over 60% of its 1.1 billion people, has grown at a relatively healthy 3.4% a year. Until late last year, most Indians' main economic worry was inflation, which soared to 13% last August, largely because of high oil prices. But in the slowdown, from which rural India is somewhat immune, inflation has fallen sharply.

A Thank-You to Congress

Under Mr Singh, who as finance minister in 1991 unleashed historic economic reforms, Congress can claim to have managed the economy quite well. Despite failing to bring much further reform, it has clearly allayed the market's dread. It is, CSDS suggests, the most popular party among the richest 20% of Indians, who traditionally vote BJP. This helped Congress get every seat in Mumbai and Delhi.

On the back of some lavish welfare schemes, Congress also strengthened its base among the rural poor. The National Rural Employment Guarantee Scheme, a huge public-works project from which the government says 44m families have benefited, was especially popular in Rajasthan and AP. A massive debt write-off for some 43m farmers last year, which cost 1.6% of GDP, was another vote-winner.

In north-eastern Maharashtra, a parched cotton-growing terrain where rates of indebtedness and suicide among farmers are high, Congress and its regional ally, the Nationalist Congress Party, gained four seats. In Keljhar, a village in Wardha district, where one farmer took poison last year and another hanged himself, everyone seems to have voted Congress. Asked why, they cite the loan-waiver scheme, the decent price for cotton set by Maharashtra's Congress government—and their fear for the future. "This is among the worst years ever. There has been little rain and the canals are dry," said Ganand Dada Narad, who had been forgiven almost half his 50,000-rupee debt ($1,100), which he had incurred when marrying off his daughters.

Wardha was also where Rahul Gandhi, who is Mrs Gandhi's 38-year-old son, Mr Singh's presumed successor and Congress's most energetic campaigner, opened his campaign. Mr Gandhi, who entered politics in 2004, can seem naive and awkward—and by extension, in India's filthy politics, sincere and uncorrupted. Credited with Congress's decision to fight alone in UP and Bihar, where it won a healthy 10% of the vote though only two seats, he suddenly appears more astute.

Reinforcing this impression, he is reported to have declined to join the new cabinet in order to spend time strengthening the party. As a faint echo of his mother's hugely respected renunciation of prime ministerial office in 2004, in favour of Mr Singh, this strikes some as further proof of Mr Gandhi's integrity.

Leader Wanted for the BJP

The Congress trinity—the two Gandhis and Mr Singh—does not set Indian hearts ablaze. Yet their quiet virtues look uncommonly good against their vagabond peers—including the 72 about to enter the Lok Sabha, India's parliament, charged with serious crimes.

This may be another reason for Congress's strong showing. Asked by CSDS who they wanted to be prime minister, 14% of respondents named the BJP's chosen man, L.K. Advani. Congress's three leaders got lower ratings, but together were selected by 38%. By contrast, the next-placed BJP man, Atal Behari Vajpayee, Mr Singh's now non-functioning predecessor, was named by 3%, and Mr Modi, Mr Advani's expected successor, by only 2%.

That leadership is a problem for the BJP has long been clear. Mr Vajpayee, a charismatic and conciliatory figure, had been able to appeal to the BJP's Hinduist ideologues—and also allay the concerns of his secular allies over their crackpot, Hinduised version of history and enthusiasm for inciting religious violence. Mr Advani, an octogenarian Hindu hardman, who led the campaign that propelled the BJP to power in the 1990s, demanding that a Hindu temple be built on the site of a 16th-century mosque in UP, is more divisive.

With Indians showing little appetite for Hindu chauvinism, he has downplayed it, but fitfully. His stuttering failure to take action against a BJP candidate, Varun Gandhi, who in a campaign speech issued vile threats against Muslims, suggested either weakness or approval. Unsurprisingly, Mr Advani has failed to woo back the several important allies who deserted the BJP after its 2004 defeat. He must also have unnerved the party's main remaining ally, Bihar's leader, Nitish Kumar, who has many Muslim supporters. Mr Kumar demanded that Varun Gandhi be prosecuted and, until the voting in Bihar was over, avoided appearing alongside Mr Modi.

Meanwhile the BJP failed to convince with its pet secular boasts: that it could manage India's economy and national security better than Congress. Against the sagacious Mr Singh, Mr Advani is an economic illiterate. Nor, given most Indians' aversion to liberal reform, can the BJP boast of its relatively pro-reform record. Twisting the dirk, Congress's manifesto includes a rejection of "the policy of blind privatisation followed by the BJP-led . . . government".

Congress's attack on the BJP's national-security credentials was more sophisticated. In particular, the government's response to the devastating attack in Mumbai by Pakistani terrorists last November was impressive. Mixing aggressive statements at home with resourceful diplomacy abroad, it managed to seem tough, but not reckless. By sacking its home minister and forcing out the Congress chief minister of Maharashtra, it assuaged public anger over its lousy first reaction to the crisis. The BJP, by castigating Mumbai's police and using blood-spattered images of the tragedy for its propaganda, presented itself as opportunistic, if not unpatriotic.

Even without these failures, the Hindu nationalists were always bound to struggle against a resurgent Congress. Given the usual anti-incumbency instincts of Indian voters, they were expected to lose ground in several of their northern strongholds, including Rajasthan where they fared well in 2004. The BJP and Congress were both relatively unbolstered by electoral allies—and Congress has more national appeal. The BJP ran 433 candidates in this election, almost as many as Congress, and 69 more than in 2004. But whereas Congress came in first or second in 350 seats, the BJP achieved this in only 225. Indeed, the difference between the two parties' reach has widened. In UP, where the BJP surged in the 1990s and had hoped to win 30 seats, it won ten. And more than 30 of its candidates allegedly lost their deposits.

The Hindu nationalists can recover. As Indians become rapidly more urban, consumerist and, perhaps, nationalistic, the BJP's target-audience is growing. But to take advantage of this, the party will have to ease its ideological strictures and expand geographically. Under Mr Modi, who is currently barred by America because of his alleged complicity in an anti-Muslim pogrom in Gujarat in 2002 in which 2,000 people died, it might find this impossible. He is clearly the party's most charismatic leader. Yet on current form the 182 seats won by the BJP in 1999, after a small war with Pakistan roused nationalist and Hinduist sentiment, look like its peak potential. If so, all it can hope for is to lead the sort of fractious coalition government that many now pray to have seen the back of.

The Challenge of Rising Expectations

It would be unwise to bank on Congress answering that prayer. With a history of arrogance and infighting, it could squander its advantage—a decade ago, after all, it had only 114 seats. But that was after several years without Gandhi leadership. And, remarkable as it would have seemed then, Mrs Gandhi, Italian-born and a reluctant politician, has proved sufficient to restore order to the party's disparate factions and regional parts. On the strength of this poll, Rahul Gandhi, for all his shortcomings, now has a fine opportunity to rebuild Congress. And if it could do even better in UP in India's next general election, as seems possible, its government in Delhi could prove awfully hard to dislodge.

Then again, Indian voters are not to be second-guessed. And Congress must now earn their support. In a country with 60m malnourished children, 40% of the world's total, and an abysmal record in providing its citizens with the basic education and medical care that is supposed to be theirs by right, there is much to be done. And freed of its most troublesome allies, Congress will have no excuse for failure.

Mr Singh, who says the party's victory "comes with a challenge of rising expectations", appears to welcome this. On May 19th he challenged his new government to provide "a social and political environment in which new investment can be made." If that promises some liberal reforms, of the country's statist financial sector, for example, or its ruinously politicised higher education, Congress's victory would be welcome indeed.

Few in Congress claim to want such changes, however, and Mr Singh, beholden to Mrs Gandhi, does not command his party. Sadly, not much reform may follow. But for many Indians, and all who wish the country well, this is still a pleasing moment. The divisive BJP and belligerent Communists have been forced to think again. The venal SP, whose manifesto included a pledge to curb the worrying spread of computers and English, is not in the government. And Miss Mayawati, who had hoped to be India's next prime minister, is stuck in UP, inspecting the many statues of herself that she is building there.

Fragile Signs of Hope Emerging in the Gloom of Mugabe's Rule

Celia W. Dugger

Harare, Zimbabwe—On his first day as education minister in a government so broke that most schools were closed and millions of children idle, David Coltart said he got a startling invitation.

"Come and get your brand-new white Mercedes," an official told Mr. Coltart, a veteran opposition politician, as President Robert Mugabe peered down from a portrait on the minister's office wall.

The offer of an E-Class Mercedes to every minister in the month-old power-sharing government was vintage Mugabe, an effort to seduce his political enemies with the lavish perks he has long bestowed on loyalists.

Mr. Coltart said no thanks.

Opposition members like Mr. Coltart who joined Mr. Mugabe in office last month have already achieved some successes, like getting teachers back to work and winning the release of some political prisoners.

But many of them warned in interviews that the progress would be short-lived if Western nations, meeting Friday in Washington to discuss expanding assistance, did not extend billions of dollars to rebuild Zimbabwe.

Zimbabwe's main donors of emergency medical and food aid—the United States, Britain and other European nations—face a painful question posed by those pleas for more help. How do the wealthiest nations pump money into Zimbabwe's crippled economy without propping up Mr. Mugabe, feeding his patronage machine and extending his disastrous three decades in power?

Before fully re-engaging with Zimbabwe's government, the donors have said they want to see the release of all political prisoners, the adoption of sensible economic policies, a halt to seizures of white-owned farms, and the restoration of a free press. But some diplomats here say hard-liners in Mr. Mugabe's old guard seem determined to sabotage the power-sharing deal and the infusion of Western aid that the public would credit to the newcomers, led by Prime Minister Morgan Tsvangirai of the Movement for Democratic Change.

The most critical test for Mr. Tsvangirai is whether he can deliver on his inaugural promise to pay the civil service in foreign currency—particularly the police officers and soldiers who have enforced the repressive rule of Mr. Mugabe and his party, ZANU-PF, but whose pay in local currency is now worthless.

Even some diplomats who were most skeptical about Mr. Tsvangirai's deal to govern with Mr. Mugabe, 85, now sense an opportunity to weaken "the old man," as he is called here.

"There's a creeping sense that we are in an endgame, that there is a new dynamic here," said one Western diplomat who spoke anonymously according to diplomatic protocol. "Never before has the government been this prostrate. Never before has ZANU-PF been so weak or the opposition in office."

The opposition politicians say that they, too, sense an opportunity to loosen Mr. Mugabe's grip on power.

Mr. Coltart's experience is a good example. He faces huge hurdles, not least the fact that his ministry's foul-smelling headquarters had no running water to flush toilets when he arrived. But he has coaxed most of the nation's teachers back to work with little more than a paltry $100 monthly allowance and the promise to try to give them more.

The sight of children in tattered uniforms walking to school has become another sign of encroaching normalcy—along with affordable loaves of bread and well-stocked grocery shelves—in a country ravaged by hunger, hyperinflation and cholera.

But the teachers' unions have warned Mr. Coltart that their members will soon stop working unless he can get them better salaries, akin to what the British, the United Nations and other donors are already paying to more than 20,000 doctors, nurses and other workers in Zimbabwe's collapsed public health system.

"If we don't get support for education in, literally, the next few weeks, there's a very real danger the teachers will leave in their thousands as they did last year," Mr. Coltart said.

Teachers at the Fungisai Primary School in Chitungwiza, a city south of Harare, the capital, say $100 a month does not come close to paying for the essentials: rent, clothing, food, school fees. Still, they seem hopeful.

"The government is broke, but it's better to have someone promising something better," said Mercy Manza, 38, a third-grade teacher and mother of two. "Before, it was as if we didn't exist. They just ignored us."

The hyperinflation became so bad last year that the teachers' pay in Zimbabwean dollars was worth almost nothing. Many teachers emigrated to South Africa to work as maids or grape pickers. Mrs. Manza and Kudzayi Chivasa, 44, a widowed teacher, said they sold their clothes, plates and silverware to raise cash to feed their families.

"I went for a week in January without food," Mrs. Chivasa said.

The teachers said their lives had gotten materially better this year. The Zimbabwean dollar has effectively died, and all goods are now priced in United States dollars and South African rand. With the lifting of price controls and some import restrictions, goods have flowed into the country and food staples cost less.

The Fungisai school, a complex of single-story red brick buildings, was empty for months last year. All its 52 teachers are back, along with 2,200 neatly dressed children in royal blue uniforms.

But the headmistress, Angela Katsuwa, doubts she can hold on to her staff unless they get a raise. "I'm afraid they may go away," she said. "They're grumbling because that $100 is not enough to take them to the end of the month."

The teachers are not the only ones challenged by poor pay. Every minister in the new government makes the same as a teacher—or a janitor, for that matter.

Sitting in his 14th-floor office, with a sweeping view of Harare's skyline, Mr. Coltart took his crumpled pay stub out of his wallet. His earnings were 4,224 worthless Zimbabwean dollars and the voucher for $100. Mr. Coltart is a prominent human rights lawyer from Bulawayo who describes himself as "completely self-funding at present."

Some new ministers, however, have devoted years to political activism in a country whose economy is crumbling. Diplomats here worry that Mr. Mugabe will exploit this vulnerability with his usual strategy of "bait the hook." Many new ministers have accepted the Mercedes-Benzes that Mr. Coltart refused.

"There's a very real danger our members and ministers could be sucked into the patronage system," said Deputy Prime Minister Arthur Mutambara, who is now driving an E280 Mercedes. "Our members have to be vigilant and principled."

Eric Matinenga, one of Zimbabwe's most respected trial lawyers and the new minister of constitutional and parliamentary affairs, said he talked to others in the Movement for Democratic Change about taking a unified stand on the cars. "I said, 'Look, how would we justify getting these luxury vehicles when there is a humanitarian crisis out there?' " he said. "To my disappointment, we were not able to come up with a single position."

Mr. Matinenga, who braved arrest and weeks in jail last year after representing victims of political violence, took a metallic green E-Class Mercedes. "I know it's not a good excuse," he said, "but will I make a difference if I turn this down?"

Diplomats and local analysts say that despite some missteps the Movement for Democratic Change ministers, led by Mr. Tsvangirai and Mr. Mutambara, are standing up to Mr. Mugabe and demanding a say in how the country is governed.

Finance Minister Tendai Biti is credited with taking control of economic policy from Gideon Gono, the Reserve Bank governor widely blamed for the profligate printing of money that drove inflation to astronomical levels.

"If Zimbabwe was a company, it would long ago have been liquidated," said Mr. Biti, a combative lawyer who was beaten and jailed on flimsy treason charges during his years in the political wilderness. "If it was a human being, it would be brain dead."

Looming over them all is the old man. Mr. Coltart has not quite figured out what to do with the portrait of Mr. Mugabe hanging behind his desk. "I'm thinking I'll find a more appropriate place," he said, "where he's not looking over my shoulder."

Equity in Representation for Women and Minorities

Wilma Rule and Joseph Zimmerman

The approach of the twenty-first century finds women and most minority groups grossly underrepresented in elective offices throughout the world because of cultural, legal, and political barriers. The token representation of women and minorities in elective offices that exists in many nations is little more than symbolic.

This underrepresentation has three major undesirable consequences. First, the lack of women and members of minority groups on governing bodies may mean that important issues receive little or no consideration during the policy-making process. Second, minorities may become alienated from the political system and display less respect for laws enacted without their direct input by legislative bodies they view as illegitimate.

Third, the electoral system in nations with several large minority groups can promote national unity or can encourage the splintering of a nation. If a sizeable minority group is able to elect only a few or no members to public offices, pressure for secession and establishment of a new nation may increase. One electoral system, proportional representation (PR), can guarantee a minority group direct representation in proportion to its voting strength, thereby helping to prevent the disintegration of a nation.

This chapter (1) identifies barriers to the election of women and members of minority groups to public offices, (2) describes the significance of cultural and socioeconomic factors in terms of their influence on election results, (3) offers alternatives among electoral systems to increase the number of women and minorities in elective offices based upon experience in various nations, and (4) presents criteria for determining the fairness of representation produced by various electoral systems.

Barriers to Election

Authors of chapters in this volume identify the following barriers to the election of women and members of minority groups to public offices: the dominant political culture, unequal education and employment opportunities, unfavorable electoral system, incumbents' advantages in seeking reelection to office, inadequate campaign funds for women and minority candidates, and election laws making it difficult for potential candidates or new parties to have their names included on the ballot. Each barrier may affect women or a specific minority group in a different manner, and two or more barriers may be interrelated in a particular nation.

Political Culture and Change

Every society over time develops dominant cultural norms governing the proper roles of individuals and groups. Failure of an individual or a group to follow assigned roles can cause society-at-large to discriminate against the offending individual or group.

Cultural norms are affected by changing economic and other societal conditions. The new or modified norms may be reflected in law, as in the United States, where the national Voting Rights Act offers protection to blacks and foreign-language minorities. On the other hand, it may be nearly impossible for a group such as the untouchables in India to have cultural practices changed other than very slowly, even though the law prohibits discrimination.

Cultural norms currently affect adversely the prospect for the election of women to public office in every nation. As'ad AbuKhalil describes the historical association between the Middle Eastern culture and the social and political oppression of women. However, changing political conditions have resulted in women's attaining voting rights in several Arab countries in recent years. Michelle A. Saint-Germain explains that the *machismo* culture emphasizes humility, passivity, and submissiveness as the proper behavior for women, thereby erecting major barriers to women interested in seeking election to public office. Similarly, traditional German culture delimited the roles of women as *kinder, kuche,* and *kirche* (children, kitchen, and church) and made it exceptionally difficult for a woman to be elected to public office. Traditional culture in both countries has been weakened in recent decades. Similarly, Avraham Brichta and Yael Brichta report that in Israel orthodox Jews reject women's participation in the political process and that Arabs also have a traditional negative attitude toward women's political activism.

Studies reveal that when women are first elected to parliament they are typically members of families long active in electoral politics. Fanny Tabak points out that Brazilian wives and daughters of deceased or retired public officials often replaced them. Today, many Brazilian women members of parliament (MPs) are professionals with personal prestige. Joan Rydon relates a similar pattern on Australian MPs. She also notes that older women years beyond their roles as wives and mothers were first elected, but currently young women also are being recruited as candidates.

The Nordic culture generally has been favorable to women's involvement in electoral politics. Jill M. Bystydzienski reports that Norway in 1986 became the first nation to have a government headed by a woman prime minister and a cabinet that was 44 percent women. She attributes women's electoral success in part to the Nordic values of equality and social justice.

Socioeconomic Opportunities

Socioeconomic conditions influence the opportunities for women and members of minority groups to become successful candidates for elective offices. If a nation has an educational system that is open to all young persons and prepares many students for professional careers, opportunities for election of women and minorities to public office will be enhanced.

Michelle A. Saint-Germain points out that the college graduation rate for women in Costa Rica is twice as high as the rate in Nicaragua and hence women in the latter nation do not have as many opportunities to become professionals, which would have improved prospects for women being elected to serve in the national legislature. Beate Hoecker, however, reports that many Germans harbor a strong prejudice against professionally and politically active women.

Feldblum and Lawson explain that changes in political attitudes and participation between first-generation and second-generation Franco-North Africans in France are attributable to the latter generation's education, which produced many professionals. Particularly striking is the sharp increase in the number of female Franco-North African candidates for election.

Opportunities for women to participate in local and national organizations can enhance their prospects for becoming elected public representatives. Jill Bystydzienski notes that in Norway men frequently were absent from fishing villages for long periods of time and women in these villages often organized various types of campaigns and also sought to promote the election of women to public office. Furthermore, Norwegians have a tradition of joining local and national organizations, and women's experiences in such organizations promote their opportunities to win elective offices.

Women in the former Soviet Union had open access to educational facilities, and many became professionals. Quotas were used to select approximately one-half of the members of the Supreme Soviet and women constituted one-third of its members. Constitutional changes in 1988–89 included replacement of the Supreme Soviet by the Congress of People's Deputies and the abandonment of quotas. Although democratic features were added to the single-member district system, it operates against the election of women, whose representation in the Congress declined to 15.7 percent in the 1989 election. Similarly, the single-member district system is a major barrier to the election of women to public office in the United States.

The Electoral System

Political scientists in recent years have studied the impact of different voting systems upon the election prospects of women and various minority groups. Experience with the single-member district system (known as the first-past-the-post system in the United Kingdom) reveals that it generally favors the election of candidates of the majority group in each district, with the exception of women. Argentina during the 1950s was an exception to the general finding that women are disadvantaged by the single-member district system.

As Enid Lakeman explains, the majority group in a district in the United Kingdom is a political party that cannot afford to offer voters a choice between a male and a female candidate or a black and a white candidate for fear of splitting the party's vote and defeating both candidates. She also explains that in local elections additional women candidates are nominated by parties in multimember districts and that voters are more apt to cast a ballot for a woman candidate when more than one candidate is to be elected.

Municipal reformers in the United States early in the 20th century launched a campaign to replace the single-member district system with an at-large system to elect a city council, on the grounds that the former system perpetuated boss control of the council.[1] By mid-century, the reformers had achieved success in changing the electoral system to at-large in numerous local governments. But by the 1960s several political scientists and black activists commenced to criticize the system by alleging it produced an overrepresentation of white middle-class values.[2]

Several cities incorporated a provision for a modified at-large system in the city charter to ensure neighborhood representation. The modified system employs district residency requirements for council members. If the two highest vote-getters in an election reside in the same district, only the top vote-getter is elected to the council. This system facilitates the election of a minority candidate if his or her group is concentrated in a district, but it does not guarantee the election of the candidate. Other United States cities have adopted a combination of the single-member and at-large electoral systems.

Limited voting is employed in a number of local governments to elect governing bodies. Each voter may cast a ballot for more than one candidate, but for fewer candidates than there are seats to be filled. This system, which can be employed on an at-large or multimember district basis, guarantees direct representation for members of the largest minority party or group.[3] As each voter gives the same support to the candidate least favored as to the candidate most favored, the voter may contribute to the defeat of his or her favorite candidate. Hence, this system encourages casting a ballot for only one candidate. Furthermore, limited voting does not ensure that each group or party will be represented in proportion to its voting strength. In addition, the system may allow a minority to elect a majority of council members if several strong slates of candidates divide the votes.

Cumulative voting has the same goal as limited voting, that is, enabling the largest minority group or party to elect one or more of its members to a governing body. Each elector has the same number of votes as there are seats to be filled on a governing body or in a multimember district. The elector may cast all votes for one candidate or apportion the votes among several candidates in accordance with the intensity of the elector's preferences. This system was employed to elect members of the Illinois House of Representatives in the period 1870 to 1980 and has been employed since 1988 in Alamogordo, New Mexico, and in Chilton County and three towns in Alabama.[4] In Norway, voters in several local governments may give a second vote to a candidate.

To ensure direct representation for minority parties, PR has been adopted by several nations for national and local elections. There are two types of PR, the list system and the single-transferable-vote system (STV). The former is more common and is designed to reward parties with seats on a governing body in accordance with their respective share of the total vote. Interestingly, the party-list PR system was employed in the United Nations—supervised election that marked the peaceful transition of Namibia from a colony of the Republic of South Africa to an independent nation and allocated seats in close approximation to the votes received by each party.

There are two variants of the list system. Under the fixed or rigid system, each party determines the order in which the names of its candidates appear on its list and the voter may cast a ballot only for that list of candidates. The other variant allows the voters to determine the place of each candidate on a party list. The list system can be combined with another system, such as the single-member district system, to elect members of a parliamentary body. A minimum vote threshold, such as 5 percent, also may be adopted for allocation of seats to political parties.

STV is employed in the Republic of Ireland to elect members of Dáil Eireann (the lower house of parliament) and members of local governing bodies. The system is used in the United States to elect the city council and school committee in Cambridge, Massachusetts, and thirty-two community school boards in New York City.[5]

STV is a type of preferential voting in a district that elects more than one representative. Each elector places a number next to the name of each candidate, with a number "1" indicating the first preference, number "2" second preference, and so on. Winning candidates are determined by a quota—the total number of valid ballots cast divided by the number of seats to be filled plus 1, with 1 added to the product of the division. If 100,000 valid ballots were cast to elect a nine-member governing body, the quota would be

$$\frac{100,000}{9 + 1} + 1 = 10,001$$

This formula always produces the smallest number of votes that ensures a candidate's election regardless of how the votes are distributed among the candidates.

The next step in the STV election involves sorting the ballots by first choices. Candidates receiving a total of number "1" votes equal to or exceeding the quota are declared elected. Ballots exceeding the quota are transferred to the other candidates according to the second choices indicated. Following this step, the candidate with the fewest number "1" votes is declared defeated and his or her votes are transferred to the remaining candidates according to the next choices marked on them. If a second choice already has been elected or defeated, the ballot is distributed to the third choice. A new count is conducted, and candidates are declared elected if they have a total of number "1" and transferred ballots exceeding the quota. Elected candidates' surplus ballots are transferred to the remaining candidates. The process of declaring defeated the lowest candidate and transferring his or her ballots to the other candidates as indicated by the next choice continues until the full governing body is elected. Most ballots, either on first choice or by transfer, help to elect a candidate.

Surplus ballots can be distributed by one of two methods. Under the first method, candidates are not allowed to exceed the quota. On reaching the quota, surplus ballots immediately are transferred to the next choices indicated. Under the second method, the ballots of a candidate receiving a surplus of number "1" votes are reexamined to determine the distribution of number "2" votes. The surplus ballots are distributed proportionately according to second choices. If candidate X received 12,000 number "1" votes and the quota is 10,000, the candidate has a surplus of 2,000 ballots. Assuming that candidate Y was the number "2" choice on 6,000 of candidate X's number "1" ballots, candidate Y would be given one-half of the surplus or 1,000 ballots.

In contrast to the single-member district system, STV allows a geographically dispersed minority to elect a candidate, as the constituency is based on interest and not on residence. In addition, the strength of a minority group is not dissipated whether the group gives most of its number "1" votes to one of its candidates or scatters its votes among several of its candidates. Furthermore, a minority group cannot elect a majority of the members of a governing body in the event of a split among opposition groups, as can occur under limited voting or cumulative voting. Joan Rydon notes that the adoption of STV with five members chosen in each district markedly increased the election of women candidates to the Australian Senate.

Direct representation of women and minorities on governing bodies can be increased without changing the voting system. The election law in Taiwan provides for reserved seats, thereby encouraging women to seek election and guaranteeing that a specific number of women will be elected. Similarly, political parties in several nations have decided to establish a quota of women candidates for public offices.

Incumbency

A major barrier to the election of women and minorities to public office is the incumbent advantage in seeking reelection. Unless an incumbent has been involved in a scandal or his or her party is blamed by the voters for an unpopular occurrence, an incumbent officeholder has many more political resources than a challenger in an election campaign, including name recognition because of media attention.

In the United States, incumbent state legislators in several states and members of the national Congress employ relatively large staffs that may devote part of their time and efforts to promoting legislators' reelection. Elected officials also communicate with constituents through newsletters prepared and posted at public expense and may make public-service announcements that generate or reinforce their name recognition. Although a number of state constitutions and city charters limit the number of terms a governor or a mayor may serve, no such restrictions were placed upon state legislators until 1990, when voters in California, Colorado, and Oklahoma approved constitutional amendments limiting the number of terms that state legislators may serve. Such limitations should facilitate the election of women to state legislatures.

Campaign Finance

That incumbents have a decided advantage over challengers in terms of campaign fund raising has been documented in many studies in the United States. If the term of office is only two years, as in the House of Representatives, incumbents may engage in fund-raising activities throughout the term of office and may not completely separate their fund-raising activities from their official activities.

In contrast to the United States, funds are raised in many nations primarily by the political parties and/or government. These funds help finance the reelection campaigns of incumbent public officers and party candidates. Women

and minorities in other countries usually have little access to campaign funds, which limits their opportunities for election to public offices.

Complex Election Rules

The election playing field for incumbents and challengers also may be uneven because of election regulations. In 1988, the New York State Commission on Government Integrity reported that complex requirements in the state's election law often necessitate that candidates who collect more than the required number of signatures must "participate in expensive, time-consuming litigation in order to defend their right to run for office."[6]

Technical failure to comply with all provisions of election laws may prevent women and minority candidates from qualifying to have their names on the ballot. In addition, the complex legal obstacles to ballot access may discourage other competent individuals from seeking election to public office.

The "threshold" rule in certain proportional representation counties—which may require, for example, 5 percent of the popular vote for a seat parliament—also discourages new parties from forming. Complex regulations in many states in the United States make it difficult for third parties to elect candidates, thereby limiting the election opportunity of women and minorities.

Six Criteria for Fair Representation

In a polity where no legal or other impediments prevent adult citizens from registering and voting in elections, the following six canons of a good electoral system can be employed to assess the equity of representation produced by various electoral systems. The canons, or criteria, are interrelated and overlapping rather than discrete.

Effectiveness of Ballots Cast

The effectiveness canon measures the potency of each ballot cast by a registered voter. A nondiscriminatory electoral system does not cancel or dilute invidiously the effectiveness of ballots cast by any citizen or group of citizens. In the eyes of a minority group, the election must be more than a type of periodic consultation ritual that is meaningless to the group because their ballots are rendered ineffective by the design of the electoral system. If a minority group perceives that the electoral system makes the group powerless, group participation in the political process will be low and the public interest will suffer accordingly.

Maximization of Participation

A fair electoral system encourages the registration of eligible voters because they can visualize that their exercise of the franchise will be effective in helping to determine one or more winners in an election contest. Logically, voter participation by members of a group in an election will be in direct relation to the possible influence that the group can exert. Low voter registration and turnout on election day may be the product of alienation—a sense of powerlessness—rather than apathy.

Representation of Competing Interests

An electoral system that guarantees direct representation on a legislative body for members of a minority group and women will facilitate the necessary political accommodation. Such a system will help to ensure responsiveness by the legislators to the special needs of the minority groups and women.

Maximization of Access to Decision Makers

A proper system of voting will result in the selection of legislators who are willing to listen to and to seek out the views of all groups in the polity. Consultation with constituents must be genuine and not pro forma, or alienation and cynicism will be promoted.

Equity in Group Members' Representation

Fairness in representation is the hallmark of a democratic political system. If members of a group are underrepresented grossly in terms of their population strength in a legislature or other elected offices, the election system should be changed to guarantee that they will be able to elect more members of their group to bring their direct representation closer to parity.

Legitimization of the Legislative Body

An important function of an electoral system is to legitimize the legislative body in the eyes of the citizenry, thereby facilitating the implementation of policy decision. The effectiveness of a government's policies depends in many instances on the active cooperation and support of citizens. A widespread view that the electoral system is designed deliberately to favor one group over another and that the legislators fail to represent citizens adequately will weaken seriously the perceived legitimacy of the policy-makers and their policies.

Summary and Conclusions

A review of elected legislative bodies in various nations reveals that women and members of minority groups tend to be grossly underrepresented. To increase the number of women and minority legislators, important barriers to their election will have to be removed or lowered. Changing a political culture that rejects women's participation in the political process will be a difficult task and may require

generations. The barriers created by the lack of socioeconomic opportunities for women and minorities potentially can be lessened in a much shorter period of time, but lack of resources may slow the pace of increasing educational opportunities.

The barrier created by use of the single-member district electoral system could be removed immediately with adoption of a proportional or semiproportional electoral system. There is, however, strong opposition in many nations to the abandonment of the single-member district system. In the United States, the system has been promoted by the national government to increase the number of blacks elected to public office, although proportional representation would achieve the same goal more effectively without the disadvantages associated with the single-member district system.

The advantages typically possessed by incumbent officials seeking reelection reduce the opportunities for women and minorities to be elected. In the United States, a growing anti-incumbent movement has resulted in voters in several states ratifying constitutional amendments placing limits on the number of terms members of the state legislature may serve. Non-incumbents' relative disadvantage in campaign funds can be offset by public financing of campaigns. Similarly, complex election laws and regulations that discourage non-incumbents from seeking office and forming new political parties could be repealed or simplified.

Direct representation for minorities and women, in approximate accordance with their respective proportions in the general population, should be a deliberate goal of the electoral system and not a product of happenstance. Such a system will ensure the election of public representatives who have a special sensitivity to the needs of minority groups and women and will also ensure that all citizens are treated fairly in the process of accommodating competing interests.

The major argument advanced by PR advocates is its ability to provide direct representation for minority parties or groups voting as blocs. It should be noted that PR also can provide the majority party or group with more seats than it would gain under the single-member district system if the party or group members are concentrated in only a few districts.

Notes

1. Richard S. Childs, *The First 50 Years of the Council-Manager Plan of Government* (New York: National Municipal League, 1965), p. 37.

2. See in particular Edward C. Banfield and James Q. Wilson, *City Politics* (Cambridge: Harvard University Press and M.I.T. Press, 1963), pp. 139–42.

3. See Edward Still, "Cumulative Voting and Limited Voting in Alabama," in Wilma Rule and Joseph F. Zimmerman, eds., *United*

States Electoral Systems: Their Impact on Women and Minorities (Westport, Conn.: Greenwood Press, 1992), pp. 183–96.

4. For details, see George S. Blair, *Cumulative Voting: An Effective Electoral Device in Illinois Politics* (Urbana: University of Illinois Press, 1960); and Edward Still, "Cumulative Voting and Limited Voting in Alabama."

5. Leon Weaver and Judith Baum, "Proportional Representation on New York City Community School Boards," in Rule and Zimmerman, eds., *United States Electoral Systems,* pp. 197–205.

6. *Access of the Ballot in Primary Elections: The Need for Fundamental Reform* (New York: New York State Commission on Government Integrity, 1988), p. 1.

Rwanda
Women Hold up Half the Parliament

ELIZABETH POWLEY[1]

In October 2003, women won 48.8 percent of seats in Rwanda's lower house of Parliament.[2] Having achieved near-parity in the representation of men and women its legislature, this small African country now ranks first among all countries of the world in terms of the number of women elected to parliament.

The percentage of women's participation is all the more noteworthy in the context of Rwanda's recent history. Rwandan women were fully enfranchised and granted the right to stand for election in 1961, with independence from Belgium. The first female parliamentarian began serving in 1965.[3] However, before its civil war in the early 1990s and the genocide in 1994, Rwandan women never held more than 18 percent of seats in the country's Parliament.[4]

The 1994 genocide in Rwanda, perpetrated by Hutu extremists against the Tutsi minority and Hutu moderates, killed an estimated 800,000 people (one-tenth of the population), traumatized survivors, and destroyed the country's infrastructure, including the Parliament building. Lasting approximately 100 days, the slaughter ended in July 1994 when the Tutsi-dominated Rwandan Patriotic Front (RPF), which had been engaged in a four-year civil war with the Hutu-dominated regime of President Juvenal Habyarimana, secured military victory. Once an opposition movement and guerilla army, the RPF is now a predominately (but not exclusively) Tutsi political party. It is in power in Rwanda today.

During the nine-year period of post-genocide transitional government, from 1994 to 2003, women's representation in Parliament (by appointment) reached 25.7 percent and a new gender-sensitive constitution was adopted. But it was the first post-genocide parliamentary elections of October 2003 that saw women achieve nearly 50 percent representation.

The dramatic gains for women are a result of specific mechanisms used to increase women's political participation, among them a constitutional guarantee, a quota system, and innovative electoral structures. This case study will describe those mechanisms and attempt to explain their origins, focusing in particular on the relationship between women's political representation and the organized women's movement, significant changes in gender roles in post-genocide Rwanda, and the commitment of Rwanda's ruling party, the RPF, to gender issues. It will also briefly introduce some of the achievements and challenges ahead for women in Rwanda's Parliament.

The Constitutional Framework

In 2000, nearing the end of its post-genocide transitional period, Rwanda undertook the drafting of a new constitution and established a 12-member Constitutional Commission. Three members of the commission were women, including one, Judith Kanakuze, who was also the only representative of civil society on the commission. She played an important role both as a "gender expert" within the commission ranks and as a liaison to her primary constituency, the women's movement in Rwanda.[5]

The commission was charged with drafting the constitution and with taking the draft to the population in a series of consultations designed to both solicit input and sensitize the population as to the significance and principal ideas of the document.[6] Although political elites controlled both the content and the process of the consultations with Rwanda's largely illiterate population, it was—at least on the face of it—a participatory process, and its participatory nature allowed for significant input by women and women's organizations.[7]

The women's movement mobilized actively around the drafting of the constitution to ensure that equality became a cornerstone of the new document. The umbrella organization, Collectifs Pro-Femmes/Twese Hamwe (Pro-Femmes) and its member NGOs brought pressure to bear on the process and carefully coordinated efforts with women parliamentarians and the Ministry of Gender and Women in Development.

Rwanda's new constitution was formally adopted in May 2003.[8] It enshrines a commitment to gender equality. The preamble, for instance, cites various international human rights instruments and conventions to which Rwanda is a signatory, including specific reference to the 1979 Convention on the Elimination of All Forms of Discrimination Against Women (CEDAW). It also states a commitment to "ensuring equal rights between Rwandans and between women and men without prejudice to the principles of gender equality and complementarity in national development." Title One of the constitution also establishes, as one of its "fundamental principles," the equality of Rwandans. This respect for equality is to be ensured in part by granting women "at least" 30 percent of posts "in all decision-making organs."

It is important to note, however, that, although Rwanda's constitution is progressive in terms of equal rights, gender equality and women's representation, it is limiting in other important ways; specific concerns have been raised about restrictions on freedom of speech around issues of ethnicity.

The Quota System and Innovative Electoral Structures

Since the genocide, several innovative electoral structures have been introduced to increase the numbers of women in elected office.[9] Towards the end of its transition period, Rwanda experimented with the representation of women in the Parliament. Two women were elected to the then unicameral legislature on the basis of descriptive representation, with a mandate to act on behalf of women's concerns. Those two women came not from political parties but from a parallel system of women's councils (described in more detail below) that had been established at the grass-roots level throughout the country.

The 2003 constitution increased exponentially the number of seats to be held by women in all structures of government.

The Senate

In the upper house of Rwanda's (now) bicameral legislature, the Senate, 26 members are elected or appointed for eight-year terms. Some members of the Senate are elected by provincial and sectoral councils, others are appointed by the president and other organs (e.g. the national university). Women, as mandated in the constitution, hold 30 percent of seats in the Senate.

The Chamber of Deputies

The lower house of the Rwandan Parliament is the Chambre des Députés (Chamber of Deputies). There are 80 members serving five-year terms, 53 of whom are directly elected by a proportional representation (PR) system. The additional seats are contested as follows: 24 deputies (30 percent) are elected by women from each province and the capital city, Kigali; two are elected by the National Youth Council; and one is elected by the Federation of the Associations of the Disabled.

The 24 seats that are reserved for women are contested in women-only elections, that is, only women can stand for election and only women can vote. The election for the women's seats was coordinated by the national system of women's councils and took place in the same week as the general election in September 2003. Notably, in addition to the 24 reserved seats in the Chamber of Deputies, the elections saw an additional 15 women elected in openly competed seats. Women thus had in total 39 out of 80 seats, or 48.8 percent.

The Women's Councils

The Ministry of Gender and Women in Development first established a national system of women's councils shortly after the genocide, and their role has since been expanded. The women's councils are grass-roots structures elected at the cell level (the smallest administrative unit) by women only, and then through indirect election at each successive administrative levels (sector, district, province). They operate in parallel to general local councils and represent women's concerns. The ten-member councils are involved in skills training at the local level and in awareness-raising about women's rights. The head of the women's council holds a reserved seat on the general local council, ensuring official representation of women's concerns and providing links between the two systems.

Berthe Mukamusoni, a parliamentarian elected through the women's councils, explains the importance of this system as follows:

> In the history of our country and society, women could not go in public with men. Where men were, women were not supposed to talk, to show their needs. Men were to talk and think for them. So with [the women's councils], it has been a mobilization tool, it has mobilized them, it has educated [women] . . . It has brought them to some [level of] self-confidence, such that when the general elections are approaching, it becomes a topic in the women's [councils]. 'Women as citizens, you are supposed to stand, to campaign, give candidates, support other women'. They have acquired a confidence of leadership.[10]

While the women's councils are important in terms of decentralization and grass-roots engagement, lack of resources prevents them from maximizing their impact and they are not consistently active throughout the country. Members of local women's councils are not paid, and because they have to volunteer in addition to performing their paid work and family responsibilities the councils are less effective than they could be. Nevertheless, women in these grass-roots councils have been successful in carving out new political space. And the 2003 constitution increased their importance by drawing on these structures to fill reserved seats for women in the Chamber of Deputies.

The Factors Giving Rise to Women's Increased Parliamentary Presence

The Women's Movement and Civil Society Mobilization

Immediately after the genocide, while society and government were in disarray, women's NGOs stepped in to fill the vacuum, providing a variety of much-needed services to the traumatized population. Women came together on a multi-ethnic basis to reconstitute the umbrella organization Pro-Femmes, which had been established in 1992. Pro-Femmes, which coordinated the activities of 13 women's NGOs in 1992, now coordinates more than 40 such organizations.[11] It has been particularly effective in organizing the activities of women, advising the government on issues of women's political participation, and promoting reconciliation.

Women in Rwanda's civil society have developed a three-pronged mechanism for coordinating their advocacy among civil society (represented by Pro-Femmes), the executive branch (Ministry of Gender and Women in Development), and the legislative branch (Forum of Women Parliamentarians).

An example of the effectiveness of this mechanism is the process the Rwandan women's movement initiated around the ratification of the new constitution. To elicit concerns, interests and suggestions regarding a new constitution, Pro-Femmes held consultations with its member NGOs and women at the grass-roots level. They then met with representatives of the Ministry of Gender and Women in Development and the Forum of Women Parliamentarians to report members' concerns. Together the three sectors contributed to a policy paper that recommended specific actions to make the constitution gender-sensitive and increase women's representation in government, which was submitted to the Constitutional Commission. Once the draft constitution sufficiently reflected their interests, Pro-Femmes engaged in a mobilization campaign encouraging women to support the adoption of the document in the country-wide referendum.

Through the coordination mechanism that Pro-Femmes has forged with women in the executive and legislative branches of government, the women's movement has an increasingly powerful voice. A 2002 report commissioned by the US Agency for International Development (USAID) recognized the significant challenges faced by Rwandan civil society, including limited capacity, problems of coordination, and excessive control by the government,[12] but commended the significant role Pro-Femmes plays in shaping public policy. The study concluded that women's NGOs are the "most vibrant sector" of civil society in Rwanda and that "Pro-Femmes is one of the few organizations in Rwandan civil society that has taken an effective public advocacy role."[13] Its effectiveness is a result of a highly cooperative and collaborative relationship forged with women in government. Unfortunately, the close relationship has also compromised Pro-Femmes' independence and ability to criticize the government.

Changing Gender Roles

In addition to an effective women's movement, the dramatic gains for women in Parliament can also be traced to the significant changes in gender roles in post-genocide Rwanda. Women were targeted during the genocide on the basis not only of their ethnicity, but also of their gender: they were subjected to sexual assault and torture, including rape, forced incest and breast oblation. Women who survived the genocide witnessed unspeakable cruelty and lost husbands, children, relatives and communities. In addition to this violence, women lost their livelihoods and property, were displaced from their homes, and saw their families separated. In the immediate aftermath, the population was 70 percent female (women and girls).[14] Given this demographic imbalance, women immediately assumed roles as heads of household, community leaders and financial providers, meeting the needs of devastated families and communities. The genocide forced women to think of themselves differently and in many cases develop skills they would not otherwise have acquired. Today, women remain a demographic majority in Rwanda, comprising 54 percent of the population

and contributing significantly to the productive capacity of the nation.

The overwhelming burdens on women and their extraordinary contributions are very much part of the public discourse in Rwanda. In April 2003, speaking about the parliamentary elections, President Paul Kagame said, "We shall continue to appeal to women to offer themselves as candidates and also to vote for gender sensitive men who will defend and protect their interests." He continued, "Women's under-representation distances elected representatives from a part of their constituency and, as such, affects the legitimacy of political decisions.... Increased participation of women in politics is, therefore, necessary for improved social, economic and political conditions of their families and the entire country."[15]

The Commitment of the Rwandan Patriotic Front

The Rwandan Government, specifically the ruling RPF, has made women's inclusion a hallmark of its programme for post-genocide recovery and reconstruction.[16] This approach is novel in both intent and scope; it deserves further study in part because it contradicts the notion that the inclusion of women is solely a "Western" value imposed upon developing countries.

The government's decision to include women in the governance of the country is based on a number of factors. The policy of inclusion owes much to the RPF's exposure to gender equality issues in Uganda, where many of its members spent years in exile. Uganda uses a system of reserved seats to guarantee women 20 percent of the seats in Parliament: one seat from each of the 56 electoral districts is reserved for a woman. Men and women in the RPF were familiar with this system, as they were with the contributions and successes of women in South Africa's African National Congress (ANC). Within its own ranks, too, women played a significant role in the success of the movement. They played critical roles from the RPF's early days as an exile movement through the years of armed struggle. Such involvement provided them with a platform from which to advocate for women's inclusion during the transitional phase and consolidate their gains in the new constitution.

The RPF's liberation rhetoric was embraced by its own members and was applied to the historic exclusion of women as well as the Tutsi minority; this gender-sensitivity is now government policy. As John Mutamba, an official at the Ministry of Gender and Women in Development explains, "Men who grew up in exile know the experience of discrimination. . . . Gender is now part of our political thinking. We appreciate all components of our population across all the social divides, because our country . . . [has] seen what it means to exclude a group."[17] RPF members who embraced notions of gender equality have informed the development of gender-sensitive governance structures in post-genocide Rwanda.

During the transitional period, before quotas were established in Rwanda, the RPF consistently appointed women to nearly 50 percent of the seats it controlled in Parliament. Other political parties lagged behind in their appointment of women, and therefore women never made up more than 25.7 percent of the Parliament during the transitional period.[18]

The RPF dominated the transitional government and consolidated its grip on power in the August 2003 post-transition election of President Paul Kagame and the installation of a new Parliament in October 2003. The RPF, together with its coalition, controls 73.8 percent of the openly contested seats in the Chamber of Deputies. The women's seats were not contested by political parties, but observers charge that a majority of the women in the reserved seats are also sympathetic to the RPF. Freedom House, in its most recent survey of nations, ranked Rwanda as "not free," with concern about political rights and civil liberties.[19] This puts Rwandan women and the women's movement in a precarious position, as they owe their ability to participate in democratic institutions to a political party that is less than fully democratic, and cannot be truly independent of the state.

Achievements and Challenges Ahead

In addition to performing all the functions their male counterparts do, women in Rwanda's Parliament have formed a caucus, the Forum of Women Parliamentarians, with international funding and support. This is the first such caucus in Rwanda, where members work together on a set of issues across party lines. Member of Parliament (MP) Connie Bwiza Sekamana explains, "When it comes to the Forum, we [unite] as women, irrespective of political parties. So we don't think of our parties, [we think of] the challenges that surround us as women."[20] The Forum has several roles: it reviews existing laws and introduces amendments to discriminatory legislation, examines proposed laws with an eye to gender sensitivity, liaises with the women's movement, and conducts meetings and training with women's organizations to sensitize the population to and advise about legal issues.

A key legislative achievement was the revoking of laws that prohibited women from inheriting land in 1999. Rwandan women parliamentarians, particularly the 24 who specifically represent the women's movement but also those who contested open seats and represent political parties, feel that it is their responsibility to bring a gender-sensitive perspective to legislating.

As elsewhere in the world, there are challenges related to descriptive representation. Many of the new parliamentarians are inexperienced legislators and have to overcome stereotypes about their (lack of) competence as leaders and their supposed naiveté, as well as some resistance to the fact that they owe their positions to the new quotas. There is an obvious status difference between those seats that are reserved for women and those that are gained in open competition with men, at both the local and the national levels.

It is also problematic, in the long term, to consider all Rwandan women a single constituency. Currently, the women's movement is represented most effectively by one organization, Pro-Femmes, and there is a great deal of consensus among women parliamentarians about the needs and priorities of women. In a mature democracy, however, women disagree on policies and desired political outcomes, even those, such as the use of quotas, which directly affect women's access to power. Perhaps because the quotas are so new and because the dominant voices in the women's movement supported their introduction so vigorously, there has not been public dissent within the movement about their utility.

There is, however, a sense, as in many other parts of the world, that quotas, reserved seats and descriptive representation are only a first step. Aloisea Inyumba, former women's minister, explains that at this point in Rwanda's development the new electoral mechanisms in Rwanda are needed to compensate for women's historic exclusion: "If you have a child who has been malnourished, you can't compare her to your other children. You have to give her a special feeding."[21]

It also remains to be seen what impact women will have, particularly on those issues that are not traditionally "women's issues." These women carry a double burden, as they must find ways to insert a gender perspective into a new range of issues—foreign affairs, for example—and yet remain loyal to their constituency of women in a country where the basic development needs are so great and women still lag behind men in terms of rights, status, and access to resources and education.

Conclusion

The representation of women in Rwanda's Parliament can be seen in the larger context of two trends: the use of quotas in Africa; and the post-conflict situation. The rate of increase of numbers of women in Parliament has been faster in sub-Saharan Africa in the last 40 years than in any other region of the world, primarily through the use of quotas.[22] And, according to the Inter-Parliamentary Union (IPU), in the last five years post-conflict countries have "featured prominently in the top 30 of the IPU's world ranking of women in national parliaments," and these countries have been effective at using quotas and reserved seats to 'ensure the presence and participation of women in [their] newly-created institutions'.[23]

The ten years since the Rwandan genocide have been ones of enormous change for all Rwandans, but most dramatically for women. Rwanda is still vastly underdeveloped and the great majority of Rwandan women are disadvantaged vis-à-vis men with regard to education, legal rights, health and access to resources. Furthermore, the nearly equal representation of men and women in Rwanda's Parliament has been achieved in a country that is less than democratic and where a single political party dominates the political landscape.

Despite these challenges, women are beginning to consolidate their dramatic gains, with the new gender-sensitive constitution of 2003 and parliamentary elections that saw them earn 48.8 percent of seats in the Chamber of Deputies. These successes were the result of the specific circumstances of Rwanda's genocide, the quota system, and a sustained campaign by the women's movement in Rwanda, in collaboration with women in government and with the explicit support of the Rwandan Patriotic Front. The Rwandan case provides us with examples of gender-sensitive policy making and innovative electoral mechanisms that could be models for other parts of the world.

Notes

1. This case study draws on and excerpts previously published material by the same author. Powley, Elizabeth, 2003. *Strengthening Governance: The Role of Women in Rwanda's Transition.* Washington, DC: Women Waging Peace; and Powley, Elizabeth, 2005. "Rwanda: La moitié des sièges pour les femmes au Parlement" [Rwanda: half the seats for women in Parliament], in Manon Tremblay (ed.). *Femmes et parlements: un regard international* [Women and parliaments: an international view]. Montreal: Remueménage.

2. Inter-Parliamentary Union (IPU), 2003. "Rwanda Leads World Ranking of Women in Parliament," 23 October. See <http://www.ipu.org/press-e/gen176.htm>.

3. "Africa: Rwanda: Government." Nationmaster, <http://www.nationmaster.com/country/rw/Government>.

4. Inter-Parliamentary Union (IPU), 1995. *Women in Parliaments 1945–1995: A World Statistical Survey.* Geneva: IPU.

5. Judith Kanakuze, personal interview, July 2003.

6. "Legal and Constitutional Commission," <http://www.cjcr.gov.rw/eng/index.htm>.

7. Hart, Vivien, 2003. "Democratic Constitution Making." United States Institute of Peace, Special Report 107, <http://www.usip.org/pubs/specialreports/sr107.html>.

8. Constitution of the Republic of Rwanda. <http://www.cjcr.gov.rw/eng/constitution_eng.doc>.

9. For a more complete description of electoral mechanisms designed to increase women's participation, including triple balloting in the 2001 district-level elections, see Powley 2003, op. cit.

10. Berte Mukamusoni, personal interview, translated in part by Connie Bwiza Sekamana, July 2002.

11. For more information on women's NGOs in Rwanda, see Newbury, Catharine, and Hannah Baldwin, 2001. "Confronting the Aftermath of Conflict: Women's Organizations in Postgenocide Rwanda," in Krishna Kumar (ed.). *Women and Civil War: Impact, Organizations, and Action.* Boulder, CO: Lynne Rienner Publishers, pp. 97–128.

12. "Rwanda Democracy and Governance Assessment," produced for USAID by Management Systems International, November 2002, p. 35.

13. Ibid., p. 37.

14. Women's Commission for Refugee Women and Children, 1997. *Rwanda's Women and Children: The Long Road to Reconciliation.* New York: Women's Commission, p. 6.

15. "Rwandan President Urges Women to Stand for Public Office." Xinhua News Agency, 23 April 2003, <http://www.xinhua.org/english/>.

16. Rwandan Government, "Good Governance Strategy Paper (2001)," <http://www.rwandal.com/government/president/speeches/2001/strategygov.htm>.

17. John Mutamba, personal interview, July 2003.

18. Powley 2003, op. cit.

19. Freedom House, *Freedom in the World 2004,* <http://www.freedomhouse.org/research/freeworld/2004/table2004.pdf>.

20. Connie Bwiza Sekamana, personal interview, July 2002.

21. Aloisea Inyumba, personal interview, July 2002.

22. Tripp, Aili Mari, 2004. "Quotas in Africa," in Julia Ballington (ed.). *The Implementation of Quotas: Africa Experiences,* Stockholm: International IDEA.

23. Inter-Parliamentary Union (IPU), 2004. "Women in Parliaments 2003: Nordic and Post-Conflict Countries in the Lead," <http://www.ipu.org/press-e/gen183.htm> (accessed 8 September 2004).

UNIT 5

The Bureaucracy and Judiciary: Unelected Policy Thugs or Expert Policymakers?

Unit Selections

Key Points to Consider

- What is administrative or bureaucratic oversight? What does it achieve?

- What is the problem of "many masters"? Why is this a problem?

- Should the judiciary be elected?

- What are the benefits of applying international law to domestic legislation?

- Should a judiciary apply international law? Why or why not?

- Can an elected judiciary apply international law? Why or why not?

- What measures prevent unelected officials from gaining too much influence on policies or lawmaking?

Student Website

www.mhhe.com/cls

Internet References

Carnegie Endowment for International Peace
   http://www.carnegieendowment.org
Central Intelligence Agency
   www.cia.gov
Research and Reference (Library of Congress)
   http://www.loc.gov/rr
U.S. Executive offices
   http://www.usa.gov/Agencies/Federal/Executive.shtml#vgn-executiveoffice-of-the-president-vgn
World Wide Web Virtual Library: International Affairs Resources
   http://www.etown.edu/vl

Unit 5 describes the workings of two unelected branches of the government—the judiciary and the bureaucracy—to show their impact on policy-making. The articles in the unit are quick to note the popular ambivalence regarding these two branches. Even though they are unelected, these officials are able to exert considerable influence as administrators or interpreters of if and how laws are carried out, as well as their effects. Given this ambivalence, why not remove the ability? Why continue the practice and possibility for unelected branches of government to challenge or even reverse the laws made by elected representatives?

The readings in this unit point out that there are at least three reasons why the unelected branches of government continue to have such policy-making influence. First, they fill in for government "failures" in representation. Thus, the article on judicial review reports that in countries where governments may not govern effectively, the judiciary has kept the state "up and running" by stepping in to provide the necessary laws and interpretation of laws, such as in Israel or India. It also points out that the judiciary often steps in to give voice to those unrepresented or poorly represented, such as following the Civil War in the United States and during the rise of fascism in Europe. The article on the national courts' application of foreign and international law shows how this may work in practice. For instance, the judiciary engages the other branches of government—the executive and the legislature—by applying the interpretation of foreign and international laws to cases. In doing so, the judiciary frees up a "policy space" for the other branches of government do deliberate and clarify legislation and how it is implemented.

Second, they have the expertise to evaluate, reveal, and remedy policy failures apolitically, that is, without a political bias. Generally, their influence does not derive from a political stake but, rather, is administratively motivated or justice-centered. Thus, the article on bureaucratic oversight points out that bureaucrats have a level of expertise on the policy issues greater than the legislature and the executive that compensates for overlooked or unconsidered aspects of policy-making. Likewise, the articles on the judiciary emphasize that the judiciary does not displace policy-making; in fact, the other branches of government may easily override the judiciary. In fact, the article on the national courts' application of foreign and international law shows that in the United States, the legislature has done so. What is remarkable, then, is how often the legislatures and executives allow the judicial decisions to stand. The evidence, then, suggests that it is not usually about "runaway" policy-making but, rather, the filling in of government failures.

Third, their influence on legislation largely relies on the support of, or at least, the lack of challenge from other branches of the government. Thus, the article on judicial review emphasizes that the judiciary is "the least dangerous branch of government" because it has no independent resource to enforce its ruling. To the contrary, its decisions may be overturned or simply ignored. Likewise, the article on bureaucratic oversight points out that there are multiple sources of challenge to the influence of the bureaucracy, including the executive, legislature, courts, and interest groups. Given the "many masters," the ability of

© Getty Images

the bureaucracy to exercise independent influence is severely limited. Indeed, both articles suggest that the influence of these unelected officials may be overrated.

Yet, the article on the KGB shows that bureaucratic influence and even the abuse of power is very real. In Russia, the abuse by the KGB's successor, the Federal Security Service (FSB) has deprived citizens of their businesses and even their lives, as in the case of Anna Politkovskaya, a renowned journalist, and Litvinenko, a former KGB officer. It is, thus, important that constraints are put in place to preempt and prevent such abuse. Similarly, the article on the Propaganda Department in China shows how the highly powerful "information police" department is able to end careers, even lives, in the name of public interest. Clearly, the consequences of such abuse are not trivial.

Which begs the question: Can unelected officials be constrained? The articles show that the answer is an unambiguous "yes." Thus, the articles on bureaucratic influence, the Propaganda Department in China, and the KGB point out that executive or legislative oversight of bureaucracies that carries penalties or rewards significantly constrain bureaucratic abuse or misuse. The penalties or rewards that are highly successful in conjunction with oversight—budget and reorganization—fundamentally affect how bureaucrats function. When this is contrasted with less effective techniques, such as congressional hearings or even executive or legislative vetoes, they suggest that the effectiveness stems from the possible penalties—akin to "carrying a big stick"—that bureaucrats may face if they overstep their roles. The article on the KGB corroborates the significance of budget or resources: It predicts that businesses seized by the FSB will not be run successfully and that this will turn out to be its undoing. Likewise, the articles on the judiciary show that the judiciary is constrained by the equivalent of the budget, that is, the lack of independent resources.

An important corollary to putting constraints on unelected officials is this question: When should these constraints be imposed? Is it is better to put them in place and tie their hands than respond to the abuses from the lack of restraints? The articles on the KGB and the Chinese Propaganda Department note that constraints may be reviewed and loosened, if necessary, later for smooth and efficient operations. However, imposing constraints in response to abuses—such as following the Propaganda Department's shutdown of journals or termination of journalists or the FSB's possible involvement in witness-intimidation or elimination—may focus on the effects of such abuses without addressing their sources. However, the articles on the judiciary point out that tying the hands of the judiciary ends up eliminating the "policy space" where legislators and executives deliberate on the finer points of policies that facilitates democratic development.

In reviewing the judiciary and bureaucracy, it is worthwhile to pay heed to the following argument on accountability:

"Horizontal accountability" (a concept developed by scholars such as Guillermo O'Donnell and Richard Sklar) refers to the capacity of governmental institutions—including such "agencies of restraint" as courts, independent electoral tribunals, anticorruption bodies, central banks, auditing agencies, and ombudsmen—to check abuses by other public agencies and branches of government. (It is distinguished from, and complements, "vertical accountability," through which public officials are held accountable by free elections, a free press, and an active civil society.)[1]

Clearly, democratic progress in any country must build on both vertical and horizontal accountability. In light of the need, perhaps the question is not why the judiciary or bureaucrats partake in policymaking but, rather, why not.

Note

1. Harald Waldrauch of the Institute for Advanced Studies (Vienna), and the editors of the International Forum for Democratic Studies's Report on the Third Vienna Dialogue on Democracy on "Institutionalizing Horizontal Accountability: How Democracies Can Fight Corruption and the Abuse of Power," 6-29 June 1997, co-sponsored by the Austrian Institute for Advanced Studies (Vienna) and the National Endowment for Democracy's International Forum for Democratic Studies (Washington, DC). Available at http://www.ned.org/forum/reports/accountability/report.html <last accessed July 30, 2009>

Judicial Review: The Gavel and the Robe

Established and emerging democracies display a puzzling taste in common: both have handed increasing amounts of power to unelected judges. Th[is] article examines the remarkable growth and many different forms of judicial review.

To some they are unaccountable elitists, old men (and the rare women) in robes who meddle in politics where they do not belong, thwarting the will of the people. To others they are bulwarks of liberty, champions of the individual against abuses of power by scheming politicians, arrogant bureaucrats and the emotional excesses of transient majorities.

Judges who sit on supreme courts must get used to the vilification as well as the praise. They often deal with the most contentious cases, involving issues which divide the electorate or concern the very rules by which their countries are governed. With so much at stake, losers are bound to question not only judges' particular decisions, but their right to decide at all. This is especially true when judges knock down as unconstitutional a law passed by a democratically elected legislature. How dare they?

Despite continued attacks on the legitimacy of judicial review, it has flourished in the past 50 years. All established democracies now have it in some form, and the standing of constitutional courts has grown almost everywhere. In an age when all political authority is supposed to derive from voters, and every passing mood of the electorate is measured by pollsters, the growing power of judges is a startling development.

The trend in western democracies has been followed by the new democracies of Eastern Europe with enthusiasm. Hungary's constitutional court may be the most active and powerful in the world. There have been failures. After a promising start, Russia's constitutional court was crushed in the conflict between Boris Yeltsin and his parliament. But in some countries where governments have long been riven by ideological divisions or crippled by corruption, such as Israel and India, constitutional courts have filled a political vacuum, coming to embody the legitimacy of the state.

In western democracies the growing role of constitutional review, in which judges rule on the constitutionality of laws and regulations, has been accompanied by a similar growth in what is known as administrative review, in which judges rule on the legality of government actions, usually those of the executive branch. This second type of review has also dragged judges into the political arena, frequently pitting them against elected politicians in controversial cases. But it is less problematic for democratic theorists than constitutional review for a number of reasons.

Democracy's Referees

The expansion of the modern state has seemed to make administrative review inevitable. The reach of government, for good or ill, now extends into every nook and cranny of life. As a result, individuals, groups and businesses all have more reason than ever before to challenge the legality of government decisions or the interpretation of laws. Such challenges naturally end up before the courts.

In France, Germany, Italy and most other European countries, special administrative tribunals, with their own hierarchies of appeal courts, have been established to handle such cases. In the United States, Britain, Canada and Australia, the ordinary courts, which handle criminal cases and private lawsuits, also deal with administrative law cases.

The growth of administrative review can be explained as a reaction to the growth of state power. But the parallel expansion of constitutional review is all the more remarkable in a democratic age because it was resisted for so long in the very name of democracy.

The idea was pioneered by the United States, the first modern democracy with a written constitution. In fact, the American constitution nowhere explicitly gives the Supreme Court the power to rule laws invalid because of their unconstitutionality. The court's right to do this was first asserted in *Marbury v Madison*, an 1803 case, and then quickly became accepted as proper. One reason for such ready acceptance may have been that a Supreme Court veto fitted so well with the whole design and spirit of the constitution itself, whose purpose was as much

135

to control the excesses of popular majorities as to give the people a voice in government decision-making.

In Europe this was the reason why the American precedent was not followed. As the voting franchise was expanded, the will of the voting majority became ever more sacrosanct, at least in theory. Parliamentary sovereignty reigned supreme. European democrats viewed the American experiment with constitutionalism as an unwarranted restraint on the popular will.

Even in the United States, judicial review was of little importance until the late 19th century, when the Supreme Court became more active, first nullifying laws passed after the civil war to give former slaves equal rights and then overturning laws regulating economic activity in the name of contractual and property rights.

After a showdown with Franklin Roosevelt over the New Deal, which the court lost, it abandoned its defence of laissez-faire economics. In the 1950s under Chief Justice Earl Warren it embarked on the active protection and expansion of civil rights. Controversially, this plunged the court into the mainstream of American politics, a position it retains today despite a retreat from Warren-style activism over the past two decades.

Attitudes towards judicial review also changed in Europe. The rise of fascism in the 1920s and 1930s, and then the destruction wrought by the second world war, made many European democrats reconsider the usefulness of judges. Elections alone no longer seemed a reliable obstacle to the rise of dangerously authoritarian governments. Fascist dictators had seized power by manipulating representative institutions.

The violence and oppression of the pre-war and war years also convinced many that individual rights and civil liberties needed special protection. The tyranny of the executive branch of government, acting in the name of the majority, became a real concern. (Britain remained an exception to this trend, sticking exclusively to the doctrine of parliamentary sovereignty. It is only now taking its first tentative steps towards establishing a constitutional court.)

While the goals of constitutional judicial review are similar almost everywhere, its form varies from country to country, reflecting national traditions. Some of the key differences:

• **Appointments.** The most famous method of appointment is that of the United States, largely because of a handful of televised and acrimonious confirmation hearings. The president appoints a Supreme Court judge, subject to Senate approval, whenever one of the court's nine seats falls vacant. Political horsetrading, and conflict, are part of the system. Judges are appointed for life, though very few cling to office to the end.

Other countries may appoint their constitutional judges with more decorum, but politics always plays some part in the process. France is the most explicitly political. The directly elected president and the heads of the Senate and the National Assembly each appoint three of the judges of the Constitutional Council, who serve non-renewable nine-year terms, one-third of them retiring every three years. Former presidents are awarded life membership on the council, although none has yet chosen to take his seat.

Half of the 16 members of Germany's Federal Constitutional Tribunal are chosen by the Bundestag, the lower house of parliament, and half by the Bundesrat, the upper house. Appointments are usually brokered between the two major parties. The procedure is similar in Italy, where one-third of the 15-strong Constitutional Court is chosen by the head of state, one-third by the two houses of parliament and one-third by the professional judiciary.

Senior politicians—both before and after serving in other government posts—have sat on all three constitutional courts, sometimes with unhappy results. In March Roland Dumas, the president of France's Constitutional Council, was forced to step down temporarily because of allegations of corruption during his earlier tenure as foreign minister. The trend in all three countries is towards the appointment of professional judges and legal scholars rather than politicians.

• **Powers.** Most constitutional courts have the power to nullify laws as unconstitutional, but how they do this, and receive cases, varies. Once again, the most anomalous is France's Constitutional Council which rules on the constitutionality of laws only before they go into effect and not, like all other courts, after.

The 1958 constitution of France's Fifth Republic allowed only four authorities to refer cases to the council: the president, the prime minister, and the heads of the two houses of parliament. In 1974, a constitutional amendment authorised 60 deputies or senators to lodge appeals with the council as well. Since then, the council has become more active, and most appeals now come from groups of legislators. Individuals have no right to appeal to the council.

French jurists argue that judicial review before a law goes into effect is simpler and faster than review after a law's promulgation. But it is also more explicitly political, and leaves no room for making a judgment in the light of a law's sometimes unanticipated effect.

No other major country has adopted prior review exclusively, but it is an option in Germany and Italy as well, usually at the request of the national or one of the regional governments. However, most of the work of the constitutional courts in both countries comes from genuine legal disputes, which are referred to them by other courts when a constitutional question is raised.

The Supreme Courts of the United States, Canada and Australia, by contrast, are the final courts of appeal for all cases, not just those dealing with constitutional issues. The United States Supreme Court does not give advisory or abstract opinions about the constitutionality of laws, but only deals with cases involving specific disputes. Moreover, lower courts in the United States can also rule on constitutional issues, although most important cases are appealed eventually to the Supreme Court.

Canada's Supreme Court can be barred from ruling a law unconstitutional if either the national or a provincial legislature has passed it with a special clause declaring that it should survive judicial review "notwithstanding" any breach of the country's Charter of Rights. If passed in this way, the law must be renewed every five years. In practice, this device has rarely been used.

• **Judgments.** The French and Italian constitutional courts deliver their judgments unanimously, without dissents. Germany abandoned this method in 1971, adopting the more transparent approach of the common-law supreme courts, which allow a tally of votes cast and dissenting opinions to be published alongside the court's judgment. Advocates of unanimity argue that it reinforces the court's authority and gives finality to the law. Opponents deride it as artificial, and claim that publishing dissents improves the technical quality of judgments, keeps the public better informed, and makes it easier for the law to evolve in the light of changing circumstances.

Also noteworthy is the growth in Europe of supra-national judicial review. The European Court of Justice in Luxembourg is the ultimate legal authority for the European Union. The court's primary task is to interpret the treaties upon which the EU is founded. Because EU law now takes precedence over national law in the 15 member states, the court's influence has grown considerably in recent years. The European Court of Human Rights in Strasbourg, the judicial arm of the 41-member Council of Europe, has, in effect, become the final court of appeal on human-rights issues for most of Europe. The judgments of both European courts carry great weight and have forced many countries to change their laws.

Despite the rapid growth of judicial review in recent decades, it still has plenty of critics. Like all institutions, supreme courts make mistakes, and their decisions are a proper topic of political debate. But some criticisms aimed at them are misconceived.

Unelected Legislators?

To criticise constitutional courts as political meddlers is to misunderstand their role, which is both judicial and political. If constitutions are to play any part in limiting government, then someone must decide when they have been breached and how they should be applied, especially when the relative powers of various branches or levels of government—a frequent issue in federal systems—are in question. When a court interprets a constitution, its decisions are political by definition—though they should not be party political.

Supreme courts also are not unaccountable, as some of their critics claim. Judges can be overruled by constitutional amendment, although this is rare. They must also justify their rulings to the public in written opinions. These are pored over by the media, lawyers, legal scholars and other judges. If unpersuasive, judgments are sometimes evaded by lower courts or legislatures, and the issue eventually returns to the constitutional court to be considered again.

Moreover, the appointment of judges is a political process, and the complexions of courts change as their membership changes, although appointees are sometimes unpredictable once on the bench. Nevertheless, new appointments can result in the reversal of earlier decisions which failed to win public support.

Constitutional courts have no direct power of their own. This is why Alexander Hamilton, who helped write America's constitution, called the judiciary "the least dangerous branch of government." Courts have no vast bureaucracy, revenue-raising ability, army or police force at their command—no way, in fact, to enforce their rulings. If other branches of government ignore them, they can do nothing. Their power and legitimacy, especially when they oppose the executive or legislature, depend largely on their moral authority and credibility.

Senior judges are acutely aware of their courts' limitations. Most tread warily, preferring to mould the law through interpretation of statutes rather than employing the crude instrument of complete nullification. Even the American Supreme Court, among the world's most activist, has ruled only sections of some 135 federal laws unconstitutional in 210 years, although it has struck down many more state laws.

Finally, it is worth remembering that judges are not the only public officials who exercise large amounts of power but do not answer directly to voters. Full-time officials and appointees actually perform most government business, and many of them have enormous discretion about how they do this. Even elected legislators and prime ministers are not perfect transmitters of the popular will, but enjoy great latitude when making decisions on any particular issue. Constitutional courts exist to ensure that everyone stays within the rules. Judges have the delicate, sometimes impossible, task of checking others' power without seeming to claim too much for themselves.

Political Influence on the Bureaucracy: The Bureaucracy Speaks

SCOTT R. FURLONG

Introduction

Scholars of political science and public policy have studied the bureaucracy and its relative power vis-a-vis other political institutions in the United States. The extent of Congress's delegation of authority to executive agencies has made the issue of bureaucratic power and discretion more topical. Some have argued that the power of the bureaucracy is too great and violates constitutional principles (Lowi 1979), while others see delegation as a necessity in modern American government (Bryner 1987).

Two veins of thought dominate the recent literature on this topic. The first, bureaucratic autonomy, emanates from the early history of the dichotomy between politics and administration (Wilson 1887; Goodnow 1900). This literature states that bureaucratic agencies have autonomy in policymaking due to factors such as expertise on issues, the agency's mission (Rourke 1984), and constituent support (Rourke 1984; M.A. Eisner and Meier 1990). These factors give agencies a great amount of discretion when they make policy. The second vein of thought, political influence, states that institutions in our system, beyond the bureaucracy, can significantly influence the bureaucracy and its policies. The influence literature focuses on constitutional issues regarding shared authority by Congress and the president over agencies, the role of the judiciary in such a system, and interest group influence on these agencies. Principal-agent theory (Mitnick 1980 and 1991) and oversight research (Gormley 1989; West 1995) also may be included with this vein by providing an understanding of the interaction between different institutions within our government system.

This study examines the political influence model from a different perspective. While most researchers have examined the mechanisms used by various institutions to influence bureaucratic behavior, very few have examined whether or not the bureaucrats themselves perceive this influence and respond to this pressure (see Waterman, Wright, and Rouse 1994). This exploratory study examines the bureaucratic agent's perception of influence from five other institutions in our system: Congress, the president, courts, interest groups, and the general public. How do agency officials perceive influence by these institutions? What mechanisms used by Congress, the president, and interest groups are used most often and which are seen as most effective? These questions were asked in a survey of bureaucratic managers. The instrument focused on the managers' perceptions of influence by these institutions and the different mechanisms used by Congress, the president, and interest groups. The study sheds additional light on political influence theory from the perspective of the executive agency personnel.

Literature Review

Research on influence, or control over bureaucratic agencies, has examined the ability of one or more institutions to participate and influence bureaucratic policy (Moe 1985; Kaufman 1981; Mitnick 1991; Krause 1994 and 1996). Kaufman's *The Administrative Behavior of Federal Bureau Chiefs* (1981) recognizes both the multiplicity of the external forces on an agency and the complexity of the relationship between bureaus and other institutions. According to Kaufman, "The relations were intricate, involving negotiations, exchanges of favors, accommodations, and endlessly shifting alliances and lines of conflict among the participants." Kaufman states that the congressional set, including committees, individuals, and offices, occupied the "center of the pattern of relationships for all the chiefs" and the external force to which the bureau chiefs were most sensitive. Within the executive branch set, Kaufman recognizes the partial independence of a bureau vis-a-vis the larger department or the presidency. Therefore, these "superiors" also qualify as external groups trying to influence the bureau. The nongovernmental set, typically interest groups, also represents important external actors to the bureau chief from substantive as well as political perspectives. Kaufman also discusses the role of other governmental actors, the general public, and the media and their relationship with the bureau. The courts are not given a major role in the bureau chief's environment. In general, Kaufman examines many of the external actors that may affect agency policymaking and provides information as to how the chiefs within the agencies perceive the influence on the agency.

Mitnick (1991), in his discussion of principal-agent theory, also recognizes the existence of multiple actors attempting to influence administrative agencies. His study addresses five components that are crucial to the regulatory environment: industry, public interest groups, legislators, chief executive, and the courts. These actors, along with the regulatory agency, interact under an incentive systems framework in order to achieve desired goals. The study attempts to model the relationships between the actors. Many of the actors discussed by Mitnick are included in this study as well. The following sections discuss other studies of external influence on the bureaucracy by different institutions.

Congress and the Bureaucracy

Political scientists have studied the relationship between Congress and the bureaucracy for many years. Since oversight of the bureaucracy is considered a major component of Congress's job, it is no wonder that researchers have explored the ability to engage in both oversight and the effects of that oversight (Ogul 1976; Foreman 1988; Aberbach 1990).

Many of these studies argue that Congress can influence bureaucratic policy through a variety of ex post controls including the use of the appropriation process, oversight hearings, and statutory changes (Weingast and Moran 1983; Bendor and Moe 1985; Aberbach 1990; Scholz and Wei 1986). Others argue that ex ante techniques—such as procedural requirements, agency structure, and requiring reports are also quite effective ways to influence bureaucratic policymaking (McCubbins 1985; McCubbins, Noll, and Weingast 1987; Calvert, McCubbins and Weingast 1989). Studies of oversight suggest that both ex post and ex ante techniques have some impact on bureaucratic policymaking.

Gormley (1989) classifies congressional oversight mechanisms as either prayers or muscles. Prayers are coercive controls such as legislative vetoes and legislative hammer provisions. A legislative hammer is a provision placed into a law that takes effect if the agency fails to meet the schedule. Muscles are catalytic controls that force the bureaucracy to perform a function but do not force a particular decision. An example might be the requirement to conduct an environmental impact statement. Based on this categorization, one might hypothesize that bureaucrats may perceive these techniques differently. For example, muscle strategies, due to their more forceful nature, may be perceived as more often used and more effective in influencing bureaucratic policy.

Congressional oversight also can be categorized in terms of formal versus informal methods of oversight (Ogul 1976; West 1995). Formal techniques include items such as committee hearings or changes in the enabling statutes, whereas informal methods include private meetings and telephone contacts. Once again, bureaucrats may perceive the frequency and effectiveness of these two forms of oversight differently. Information is available concerning who is testifying in front of a congressional committee, but most people do not know about phone calls and conversations that occur off the record.

President and the Bureaucracy

Increasingly, political scientists have explored the president's relationship to the bureaucracy. One would expect that the president, the constitutional head of the executive branch, would have influence over administrative policymaking. The president has mechanisms to influence bureaucratic policymaking, and research has begun to examine these as well. For example, the president has budgetary power (Bendor and Moe 1985), reorganization power (Wood 1988), and appointment power (Moe 1982; 1985; Ringquist 1995). All of these have been shown to have an impact on agency policymaking. Research has focused more specifically on the president's use of executive orders, the Office of Management and Budget (OMB), and other presidential offices to monitor and influence regulatory policy and rule making in the agencies (Cooper and West 1988; Durant 1992; Kerwin 1994; Furlong 1995). Executive Order 12291, instituted by President Reagan, provided the OMB with a mechanism to review agency regulations. The Council on Competitiveness, established by President Bush, provided yet another level of presidential review of agency actions. President Bush also instituted his regulatory moratorium as a way to limit agency actions. President Clinton continues to use executive orders and the OMB as a way to monitor and influence agency policies. Scholars have argued that all of these presidential mechanisms give the president significant influence over the bureaucracy.

The distinction between muscle and prayer techniques also may be relevant in presidential influence (Gormley 1989), and their perceived use and effectiveness may affect bureaucratic policymaking. In the case of presidential influence, muscle techniques may include reorganization, certain executive orders, or the strong use of OMB in policy review. On the other hand, prayers may include personnel appointments or the conducting of a cost-benefit analysis. Again, the more dominant muscle strategies seem to be more likely to get the attention of bureaucrats and potentially influence their decisions.

West's (1995) distinction in presidential influence is between what he deems personnel actions, such as appointment and removal power, and centralized management techniques such as reorganization, budgetary powers, executive orders, and the use of OMB as policy reviewers. In this case, the sheer number of techniques categorized under centralized management would seem to assure that bureaucrats would perceive them to be used more often and perhaps more effectively.

Courts and the Bureaucracy

Research has shown that courts have the ability to influence agency actions. The court systems have tremendous influence on executive agencies through their role of judicial review. The courts can make procedural rulings that may affect agency decision-making ability, or they can make substantive rulings that interpret statutory intent; both of these can influence the bureaucracy. In addition, the setting of judicial deadlines for issuing regulations often will set or change the priorities of an executive agency. Studies by Moe (1985) and Wood and Waterman (1993) conclude that courts play an active role in decision making within the bureaucracy. Likewise, in their study of EPA regional personnel, Waterman, Wright, and Rouse (1994) find that the judiciary has considerable influence over EPA enforcement activities.

Other studies have found the courts to have influence on agency policymaking. Melnick (1983) found that court decisions had major impacts on EPA rule-making programs. Likewise, O'Leary (1993) found that court actions influence EPA decisions. According to O'Leary, EPA often wins its cases in courts, but the simple action of filing the lawsuit appears to change EPA policy. As Kerwin states: "Our judges are full and active players in the rulemaking process and, in some instances, exert a degree of control that exceeds the reach and grasp of either the Congress or the president" (1994, 266).

Interest Groups and the Bureaucracy

Theories that discuss interest group influence on the bureaucracy mostly have centered around two not necessarily incompatible ideas. The first, capture theory (Bernstein 1955; Stigler 1971), posits that the agency is beholden to a certain industry that it is supposed to regulate. Capture theory has been associated primarily with economic regulation; it has been mostly dismissed because of its limitations in trying to explain interest group influence on current regulatory activity, particularly in the social regulatory arena.

The second idea revolves around the various theories associated with policy subsystems (Thurber 1991), issue networks (Heclo 1978), and advocacy coalitions (Sabatier and Jenkins-Smith 1993; Meier and Garman 1995). In all of these theories, interest groups from multiple perspectives of an issue participate in the decision-making process and attempt to influence the executive agencies through direct and indirect communication. While this study does not specifically explore these theories, it does examine the techniques used by interest groups attempting to influence agency decisions. Providing comments to proposed rule makings, participating in regulatory negotiations, and having informal contact with agency personnel can all help an interest group influence agency policy. While some have examined the indirect impact of interest groups (Bendor and Moe 1985), little research has examined the direct impact that these interest groups may have on agency policymaking (Golden 1995; Kerwin 1994; Furlong 1997; Hoefer 1994). One must assume that interest groups would not spend the resources to participate in this process without some perceived benefits.

Interest group participation in the bureaucratic process, as Gormley (1989) states, are limited to catalytic controls (prayers). This is because interest group techniques, in almost all cases of influence, are limited to providing information to the bureaucracy. Only rarely can an interest group actually force an action—a citizen suit may be one example. Interest group information may move a bureaucrat one way or another, but it does not predetermine the decision.

This study does not make a distinction between different types of interest groups (e.g., economic vs. noneconomic groups). While research suggests that influence by different group types may vary (Schattschneider 1960; Schlozman and Tierney 1986; Wright 1996), this study concerns itself with interest group influence compared to other institutions, not from a comparative interest group perspective. Saying this, one must recognize that the agencies surveyed in this study are influenced by different types of interest groups. Therefore they may perceive differing levels of influence depending on the particular interest groups involved with that agency. . . .

Discussion and Conclusions

The study . . . examines relative influence that a variety of institutions can have on agency policy . . . [I]t also examines the different methods used by these institutions in their pursuit of influence. Finally, the article explores the differences perceived by respondents who work in executive agencies and independent regulatory commissions.

The results of this study support much of the political influence research previously conducted by scholars using top-down approaches. That is, in general, the respondents of the survey perceive that Congress and the president have the greatest influence on agency policy. Yet, these results do support the general conclusions of the Waterman, Wright, and Rouse (1994) study in terms of the perceived importance of political principals in the making of agency policy. In addition, results of this study provide no significant proof that either branch of government dominates the bureaucracy. Rather, as the framers of the Constitution likely wanted, both Congress and the president share the ability and responsibility to make and influence policy, including agency policy. The issue is not one of congressional dominance or presidential control, but rather of shared authority and the ability to influence policy in one direction or another.

These results also suggest that further research dealing with political influence on the bureaucracy must include interest groups as a factor that can have an impact on executive policy. While little research has specifically compared the influence of interest groups with the influence of Congress on executive policymaking, interest groups' ability to access and shape policy both directly and indirectly is evident and must not be overlooked by researchers. Too often research that examines the role of Congress and the president in bureaucratic policymaking does not consider other important elements that may shape policy, such as interest groups. Interest group participation and influence can and do have relevance in agency policymaking and should not be overlooked.

Finally, the perceived effectiveness of the techniques used by the institutions provides supporting evidence, albeit from a different perspective, of much of the literature that examines executive agency relations with other institutions. Respondents from the agencies perceive certain congressional, presidential, and interest group techniques used to influence executive policy as particularly effective. Scholars have highlighted these techniques (e.g., budget changes, appointments, and participation on advisory committees) in their studies of the political influence on the executive branch as well. From the presidential perspective, it appears that bureaucratic managers are more aware of presidential management techniques, especially those associated with coercive controls (muscle), and consider them more effective. On the congressional side, formal congressional oversight mechanisms, again particularly those leaning toward muscle strategies, appear to be used more often and are more effective in influencing policy. The implication is that bureaucracies do respond to outside pressures, especially to those that speak loudly and carry a big stick.

The role of agencies and agency officials in policymaking is clear. Delegation of power has provided these agencies with the ability not only to implement policy but in many cases to develop policy as well. What is in question, though, is the amount of discretion these agencies have in policymaking. The debate between bureaucratic autonomy and political influence continues, but most scholars acknowledge that outside institutions have the ability to influence bureaucratic policy. Literature on bureaucratic influence mostly has examined these institutions and how they act upon the bureaucracy. This study has examined the perceptions of those within the bureaucracy so as to determine if they perceive pressure and make policy changes accordingly. Studies that examine this relationship from the top-down are important and necessary, but those within the agencies must first realize that this pressure exists and then react to it. This study provides some preliminary results suggesting that agency officials do perceive this pressure and react to it in much the same way as previous top-down studies conclude. The broader implications from a policy standpoint are that the bureaucracy serves many masters. Balancing the many and conflicting demands of these masters is a difficult task, made more problematic if they are unwilling to compromise. These many perspectives will continue to challenge the bureaucratic manager's ability to find an acceptable alternative and will frustrate the bureaucracy's development and implementation of policy.

References

Aberbach, Joel D. 1990. *Keeping a Watchful Eye: The Politics of Congressional Oversight.* Washington, D.C.: Brookings.

Bendor, Jonathan, and Moe, Terry M. 1985 "An Adaptive Model of Bureaucratic Politics." *American Political Science Review* 79:755–74.

Bernstein, Marver H. 1955. *Regulating Business by Independent Commission.* Princeton, N.J.: Princeton University Press.

Berry, Jeffrey M. 1977. *Lobbying for the People: The Political Behavior of Public Interest Groups.* Princeton, N.J.: Princeton University Press.

Brownson, Ann L. 1995. *Federal Staff Directory/I.* Staff Directories, LTD. Mount Vernon, Virginia.

Bryner, Gary C. 1987. *Bureaucratic Discretion: Law and Policy in Federal Regulatory Agencies.* New York: Pergamon.

Calvert, Randall; McCubbins, Matthew; and Weingast, Barry. 1989 "A Theory of Political Control of Agency Discretion." *American Journal of Political Science* 33:588–610.

Calvert, Randall; Moran, Mark J.; and Weingast, Barry. 1987 "Congressional Influence over Policymaking: The Case of the FTC." In Matthew D. McCubbins and Terry Sullivan, eds. *Congress: Structure and Policy.* New York: Cambridge University Press.

Coglianese, Cary. 1994 *Challenging the Rules: Litigation and Bargaining in the Administrative Process.* Ph.D. diss., University of Michigan.

Cooper, Joseph, and West, William F. 1988 "Presidential Power and Republican Government: The Theory and Practice of OMB Review of Agency Rules." *Journal of Politics* 50:864–95.

Durant, Robert F. 1992. *The Administrative Presidency Revisited: Public Lands, the BLM, and the Reagan Revolution.* Albany: State University of New York Press.

Eisner, Marc Allen, and Meier, Kenneth J. 1990 "Presidential Control versus Bureaucratic Power: Explaining the Reagan Revolution in Antitrust." *American Journal of Political Science* 34:269–87.

Eisner, Neil. 1989 "Agency Delay in Informal Rulemaking." *Administrative Law Journal* 3:7–52.

Fiorina, Morris. 1977. *Congress: Keystone of the Washington Establishment.* New Haven, Conn.: Yale University Press.

Foreman, Christopher H. 1988. *Signals from the Hill: Congressional Oversight and the Challenges of Social Regulation.* New Haven, Conn.: Yale University Press.

Furlong, Scott R. 1995 "The 1992 Regulatory Moratorium: Did it Make a Difference?" *Public Administration Review* 55:254–62.

_____. 1997 "Interest Group Influence on Rule Making." *Administration and Society* 29:213–35.

Golden, Marissa Martino. 1995. "Interest Groups in the Rulemaking Process: Who Participates? Whose Voices Get Heard?" Paper presented at the third national Public Management Research Conference, Lawrence, Kansas, October 5–7.

Gormley, William T. 1989. *Taming the Bureaucracy. Muscles, Prayers and Other Strategies.* Princeton, N.J.: Princeton University Press.

Goodnow, Frank J. 1900. *Politics and Administration.* New York: Macmillan.

Harter, Phillip. 1982 "Regulatory Negotiation: A Cure for the Malaise." *Georgetown Law Review* 71:1–113.

Heclo, Hugh. 1978. "Issue Networks and the Executive Establishment." In Anthony King, ed. *The New American Political System.* Washington, D.C.: American Enterprise Institute.

Hoefer, Richard. 1994 "Social Welfare Interest Groups' Advocacy Efforts on the Executive Branch." Paper presented at the annual meeting of the American Political Science Association, New York, Sept.

Kaufman, Herbert. 1981. *The Administrative Behavior of Federal Bureau Chiefs.* Washington, D.C.: Brookings.

Kerwin, Cornelius M. 1994. *Rulemaking: How Government Agencies Write Law and Make Policy.* Washington, D.C.: Congressional Quarterly.

Kerwin, Cornelius M., and Furlong, Scott R. 1992 "Time and Rulemaking: An Empirical Test of Theory." *Journal of Public Administration Research and Theory* 2:113–38.

Krause, George A. 1994 "Political Control, Bureaucratic Autonomy, or Somewhere in Between?: A Dynamic Systems Theory of Administrative Politics." Paper presented at the annual meeting of the Midwest Political Science Association, Chicago, April.

_____. 1996 "The Institutional Dynamics of Policy Administration: Bureaucratic Influence Over Securities Regulation." *American Journal of Political Science* 40:1083–1121.

Lowi, Theodore. 1979. *The End of Liberalism,* 2d ed. New York: Norton.

McCubbins, Matthew D. 1985 "The Legislative Design of Regulatory Structure." *American Journal of Political Science* 29:721–48.

McCubbins, Matthew D., and Schwartz, Thomas. 1984 "Congressional Oversight Overlooked: Police Patrols versus Fire Alarms." *American Journal of Political Science* 28:165–79.

McCubbins, Matthew D.; Noll, Roger G.; and Weingast, Barry R. 1987 "Administrative Procedures as Instruments of Political Control." *Journal of Law, Economics and Organization* 3:243–77.

_____. 1989 "Structure as Process as Solutions to the Politicians Principal-Agency Problems." *Virginia Law Review* 74:431–82.

Meier, Kenneth J. 1993. *Politics and the Bureaucracy: Policymaking in the Fourth Branch of Government.* Pacific Grove, Calif: Brooks/Cole.

Meier, Kenneth J., and Garman, E. Thomas. 1995. *Regulation and Consumer Protection.* Houston: Dame.

Melnick, R. Shep. 1983 *Regulation and the Courts.* Washington, D.C.: Brookings.

Mitnick, Barry M. 1980. *The Political Economy of Regulation.* New York: Columbia University Press.

_____. 1991 "An Incentive Systems Model of the Regulatory Environment." In Melvin J. Dubnick and Alan Gitelson, eds. *Public Policy and Economic Institutions,* volume 10 in Public Policy Studies: A Multi-Volume Treatise, Stuart S. Nagel, ed. Greenwich, Conn.: JAI.

Moe, Terry M. 1982 "Regulatory Performance and Presidential Administration." *American Journal of Political Science* 26:197–224.

_____. 1985 "Control and Feedback in Economic Regulation: The Case of the NLRB." *American Political Science Review* 79:1094–1116.

Ogul, Morris S. 1976. *Congress Oversees the Bureaucracy.* Pittsburgh: University of Pittsburgh Press.

O'Leary, Rosemary. 1993. *Environmental Change: Federal Courts and EPA.* Philadelphia: Temple University Press.

Reagan, Michael D. 1987. *Regulation: The Politics of Policy.* Boston: Little, Brown.

Ringquist, Evan J. 1995 "Political Control and Policy Impact in EPA's Office of Water Quality." *American Journal of Political Science* 39:336-63.

Rourke, Francis E. 1984. *Bureaucracy, Politics, and Public Policy.* Boston: Little, Brown.

Sabatier, Paul, and Jenkins-Smith, Hank. 1993. *Policy Change and Learning: An Advocacy Coalition Approach.* Boulder, Colo.: Westview.

Schattschneider, E.E. 1960. *The Semi-Sovereign People.* New York: Holt, Rinehart and Winston.

Schlozman, Kay L., and Tierey, John T. 1986. *Organized Interests and American Democracy.* New York: HarperCollins.

Scholz, John T., and Wei, Feng Heng. 1986 "Regulatory Enforcement in a Federalist System." *American Political Science Review* 80:1247–70.

Stigler, George J. 1971 "The Theory of Economic Regulation." *Bell Journal of Economics and Management Science* 2:3-21.

Thurber, James A. 1991 "Dynamics of Policy Subsystems in American Politics." In Alan Cigler and Burdette Loomis, eds. *Interest Group Politics,* 3d ed. Washington, D.C.: Congressional Quarterly.

Waterman, Richard W.; Wright, Robert; and Rouse, Amanda. 1994 "The Other Side of Political Control of the Bureaucracy: Agents' Perceptions of Influence and Control." Paper presented at the annual meeting of the American Political Science Association, New York, Sept.

Weingast, Barry R., and Moran, Mark J. 1983 "Bureaucratic Discretion or Congressional Control: Regulatory Policymaking by the Federal Trade Commission." *Journal of Political Economy* 91:765–80.

West, William F. 1995. *Controlling the Bureaucracy. Institutional Constraints in Theory and Practice.* Armonk, N.Y.: Sharpe.

Wilson, Woodrow. 1887 "The Study of Administration." *Political Science Quarterly* 2:197–222.

Wood, B. Dan. 1988 "Principals, Bureaucrats, and Responsiveness in Clean Air Enforcement." *American Political Science Review* 82:213–34.

Wood, B. Dan, and Waterman, Richard. 1991 "The Dynamics of Political Control of the Bureaucracy." *American Political Science Review* 85:801–28.

_____. 1993. "The Dynamics of PoliticalBureaucratic Adaptation." *American Journal of Political Science* 37:497–528.

Wright, John R. 1996. *Interest Groups and Congress: Lobbying, Contributions, and Influence.* Boston: Allyn and Bacon.

Wilson, James Q. 1989. *Bureaucracy: What Government Agencies Do and Why They Do It.* New York: Basic Books.

From *Journal of Public Administration Research and Theory,* January 1998, pp. 39–65. Copyright © 1998 by Oxford University Press Journals. Reprinted by permission.

Reclaiming Democracy: The Strategic Uses of Foreign and International Law by National Courts

EYAL BENVENISTI

Not so long ago the overwhelming majority of courts in democratic countries shared a reluctance to refer to foreign and international law. Their policy was to avoid any application of foreign sources of law that would clash with the position of their domestic governments. Many jurists find recourse to foreign and international law inappropriate. But even the supporters of reference to external sources of law hold this unexplored assumption that reliance on foreign and international law inevitably comes into tension with the value of national sovereignty. Hence, the scholarly debate is framed along the lines of the well-known broader debate on "the countermajoritarian difficulty." This article questions this assumption of tension. It argues that for courts in most democratic countries—even if not for U.S. courts at present—referring to foreign and international law has become an effective instrument for empowering the domestic democratic processes by shielding them from external economic, political, and even legal pressures. Citing international law therefore actually bolsters domestic democratic processes and reclaims national sovereignty from the diverse forces of globalization. Stated differently, most national courts, seeking to maintain the vitality of their national political institutions and to safeguard their own domestic status vis-à-vis the political branches, cannot afford to ignore foreign and international law.

In recent years, courts in several democracies have begun to engage seriously in the interpretation and application of international law and to heed the constitutional jurisprudence of other national courts. Most recently, this new tendency has been demonstrated by the judicial responses to the global counterterrorism effort since the events of September 11, 2001: national courts have been challenging executive unilateralism in what could perhaps be a globally coordinated move. In this article I describe and explain this shift, arguing that the chief motivation of the national courts is not to promote global justice, for they continue to regard themselves first and foremost as national agents. Rather, the new jurisprudence is part of a reaction to the forces of globalization, which are placing increasing pressure on the different domestic branches of government to conform to global standards. This reaction seeks to expand the space for domestic deliberation, to strengthen the ability of national governments to withstand the pressure brought to bear by interest groups and powerful foreign governments, and to insulate the national courts from intergovernmental pressures. For this strategy to succeed, courts need to forge a united judicial front, which entails coordinating their policies with equally positioned courts in other countries by developing common communication tools consisting of international law and comparative constitutional law. The analysis also explains why the U.S. Supreme Court, which does not need to protect the domestic political or judicial processes from external pressure, has still not joined this collective effort. On the basis of this insight into the driving force behind reliance on foreign law, the article proposes another outlook for assessing the legitimacy of national courts' resort to foreign and international legal sources. It asserts that recourse to these sources is perfectly legitimate from a democratic theory perspective, as it aims at reclaiming democracy from the debilitating grip of globalization. . . .

[The article begins with a theoretical explanation in part I of the motivation behind this new judicial assertiveness. Part II sets forth the evidence of the phenomenon of interjudicial cooperation in three areas in which it can now be discerned: counterterrorism, the environment, and migration. Part III discusses the potential, limits, and legitimacy of this evolving practice. Part IV concludes the article. . . .]

Judicial Cooperation— the Evidence

The strategic use of foreign and international law characterizes interjudicial cooperation that seeks to review and shape government policies. This collective empowerment process is not required in other areas of judicial cooperation, such as in transnational civil litigation, where governmental interests are not implicated. This part argues that so far this phenomenon is discernible in at least three areas: the judicial review of global counterterrorism measures, the protection of the environment in developing countries, and the status of asylum seekers in destination countries. In these three areas courts apparently reacted to governmental responses to external pressures that the courts regarded as either too weak (in the contexts of counterterrorism and the environment) or too strong (against asylum seekers). The following examination of the evolution of judicial cooperation as the courts seek to counterbalance their governments in these three areas can offer only a broad and sketchy outline of the emerging jurisprudence. It aims, of course, at demonstrating the probability of the thesis, rather than analyzing the specific areas in depth. Therefore, it focuses more on the means of communication—the increased use of comparative constitutional law and the creative use of international law—than on the specific content of the norms. Further and more intensive research is necessary to explore these and possibly other areas of judicial cooperation more deeply.

Reviewing Global Counterterrorism Measures

More than six years into the coordinated global effort against Al Qaeda and its associated groups, it has become increasingly clear that the persistent attempts by the executive and legislative branches of various democracies to curtail judicial review of counterterrorism policies have mostly failed. These governments have not succeeded in convincing their courts to defer judgment and, in fact, have generated a counterreaction by the judiciary. Hesitant at first, the courts regained their confidence and are asserting novel claims that bolster their judicial authority.

In the wake of the terrorist attack of September 11, 2001, national courts faced a major challenge to their authority. Alarmed over the potentially devastating effects of global terrorism, governments sought to intensify restrictions on rights and liberties perceived as facilitating terrorist acts or impeding counterterrorism measures. They insisted on broad, exclusive discretion to shape and implement these constraints as they saw fit, based on the claim that the executive holds a relative advantage over the other branches of government in assessing and managing the risks of terrorism. The post-9/11 global counterterrorism effort effectively united national security agencies in a common cause. They began acting both directly in collaboration with one another and indirectly through a web of formal and informal international institutions. The central formal collective effort was founded on the authority of the United Nations Security Council; the rather informal efforts ranged from the activities of such institutional entities as the Proliferation Security Initiative and the Financial Action Task Force, to government-to-government exchanges, to complicity in illegal practices such as "extraordinary renditions" and "secret prisons."

Most legislatures submitted to these measures without demur. Far-reaching legislative changes, hurriedly introduced in most democracies in the weeks and months following the Al Qaeda attack, sailed through legislatures with little public debate or scrutiny. The immediate shock of 9/11 led many to view basic principles of due process, shaped by democratic societies' preference to err in favor of liberty, as entailing unacceptable risks.

This wave of acquiescence in national political leaders' claims to absolute discretion in acting to guarantee national security swept the courts as well. Traditionally, conformity of this nature in times of war and national crisis has been a hallmark of judicial practice. Suffice it to recall the decisions rendered by the British and U.S. highest courts during the two world wars and the early Cold War era, in which they deferred to the executive's discretion, on the basis of the limited authority and institutional capacity of the judiciary to assess and manage the risks of war. Thus, in the weeks following September 11, the familiar rhetoric of judicial deference was repeated by an alarmed court. The 9/11 attacks in some inexplicable way "proved" more clearly than ever the case for judicial silence.

But three years later, the House of Lords found that the tragic events yielded a wholly different lesson. The Belmarsh Detainees decision of December 2004, which pronounced parts of the British Anti-terrorism Act incompatible with European human rights standards, was described by one of the Law Lords as countering "the public fear whipped up by the governments of the United States and the United Kingdom since September 11, 2001 and their determination to bend established international law to their will and to undermine its essential structures." The transformation in judicial approach evident in this decision was not limited to the UK context. In light of the similar, if not as dramatic, changes in the ways national courts have reacted to their executive's security-related claims since 9/11, it is possible now to speak of a new phase in the way democracies are addressing the threat of terrorism: national courts are challenging executive unilateralism in what could perhaps be a globally coordinated move. The bold House of Lords decision of 2004 was not the first sign of judicial resistance. This should be attributed to the (much criticized) decision by the Supreme Court of Canada of January 11, 2002. Although the Court found that, in principle, there is no prohibition on deportation to a country that may inflict torture on the deportee, it did require the minister to submit a written explanation for deporting a person to a country that is likely to torture him or her. This procedural requirement set a high enough bar to prevent such instances of deportation. The most recent decision of the Canadian Supreme Court in a terrorism-related matter, the Charkaoui decision of February 2007, significantly surpassed its 2002 judgment: the Court declared unanimously that the procedures allowing for the deportation of noncitizens suspected of terrorist activities on the basis of confidential information, as well as the denial of a prompt hearing to foreign nationals, are incompatible with the Canadian Charter of Rights and Freedoms. This bold decision was replete with comparative references to foreign and international statutory and case law. The Court referred specifically to the British Anti-terrorism Act as an example of hearing procedures for suspected terrorists that the Canadian legislature should consider adopting.

This emerging judicial dialogue has not been confined to the British and Canadian courts. It currently includes courts in several other jurisdictions, including France, Germany, Hong Kong, India, Israel, and New Zealand, all in the context of limiting counterterrorism measures. In their decisions these courts explore the international obligations of their respective states, making reference to the texts of treaties on human rights and the laws of armed conflict, and to customary international law. They learn from each other's constitutional law doctrines. They cite each other extensively in this process of interpretation. For example, in a House of Lords decision concerning the admissibility of evidence obtained through torture by foreign officials, the Law Lords engaged in a comparative analysis of the jurisprudence of foreign courts, including those of Canada, the Netherlands, France, Germany, and the United States. Moreover, they compare statutory arrangements in different countries as a way to determine the measures that minimally impair constitutional rights. They do so, fully aware of their own role in the global effort to curb terrorism. As the Indian Supreme Court has acknowledged: "Anti-terrorism activities in the global level are mainly carried out through bilateral and multilateral co-operation among nations. It has thus become our international obligation also to pass necessary laws to fight terrorism. [I]n the light of global terrorist threats, collective global action is necessary." The Indian Court supported this statement with a reference to Lord Woolf 's assertion that "[w]here international terrorists are operating globally. . . . a collective approach to terrorism is important."

This aggregation of defiant judicial decisions from various jurisdictions paints a distinct picture of an evolving pattern in national courts. The trend stands in clear contrast to the passivity of legislatures toward the executive and to previous judicial trends. National courts are refusing just to rubber-stamp the actions of the political branches of government. They have unmistakably signaled their intention to constrain counterterrorism measures they deem excessive. As reflected in the reasoning of the decisions of many courts, they are seriously monitoring other courts' jurisprudence, and their invocation of international law demonstrates knowledge and sophistication.

As opposed to the jurisprudence on migration policies, discussed below, the decisions on counterterrorism reveal a discernible effort by the courts to engage their political branches rather than have the final say on the issues under debate. What characterizes many of the decisions on the lawfulness of the counterterrorism measures is their attempt to avoid, to the extent possible, making a determination on the substance of the specific executive action and, instead, to clarify the considerations that the executive must take into account in exercising its discretion, or to invite the legislature to weigh in on the matter or reconsider a hasty or vague authorization it had granted. While focusing on these institutional levels, the courts have the opportunity to set higher barriers for legislative authorization by invoking the state's international obligations as relevant considerations for the legislature to consider. Direct limitation on the legislature based on constitutional grounds—the ultimate judicial sanction—has been used only sparingly.

An instructive example of carefully climbing up the ladder of judicial review can be found in the U.S. Supreme Court's jurisprudence on the treatment of post-9/11 detainees in Guantanamo and elsewhere. Referral back to the executive or legislature was the first stage of the Court's involvement in this matter. The Rasuland Hamdi decisions asserted the Court's jurisdiction to review executive action with respect to unlawful combatants

held on U.S. territory or territory under U.S. administration, and required the president to clarify the executive's authority to act. The second round came two years later with the Hamdan decision, which rejected the president's response to the previous judgments. In Hamdan, the majority relied on international law as the standard for assessing the legality of the military commissions established by the president to determine the status of Guantanamo detainees. In its judgment, the Court diverged from the executive's position in two important aspects: first, that common Article 3 of the 1949 Geneva Conventions applies to the conflict with Al Qaeda and, second, that the standards set by that article are not met by the commissions. The Justices continued to use the referral technique by indicating that the executive can still seek Congress's approval for derogating from those requirements, but four Justices hinted that the Court may eventually examine the constitutionality of Congress's intervention. The pending petition to the Supreme Court questioning the constitutionality of the Military Commissions Act of 200673 is the ultimate stage of review.

Whereas the U.S. Congress was not deterred from inflicting "a stinging rebuke to the Supreme Court" by stripping the courts of habeas corpus jurisdiction with respect to non-U.S. citizens determined by the executive to be enemy combatants, and immunizing the executive from judicial review based on the 1949 Geneva Conventions, other executive bodies and legislatures have demonstrated a stronger commitment to international standards as interpreted by their courts, despite the fact that if they wanted to, they could have the last word.

Environmental Protection in Developing Countries

One need not travel to India or Pakistan to realize the extent to which their environments are at risk. Indeed, it suffices to read the many court decisions rendered in those countries to get a sense of the health threats to their citizens posed by environmental degradation. The courts in several developing countries are responding to the deficient environmental laws and institutions, striving to ameliorate the situation as best they can. These courts are transforming themselves into lawmakers by opening their gates to potential petitioners with lenient standing requirements and by reading into the constitutional right to life a host of environmental obligations incumbent on the state. They even intervene proactively in the executive's sphere of discretion, establishing institutional mechanisms to assess and monitor environmental damage as a form of relief for petitioners. Judge Sabharwal of the Supreme Court of India hinted at this self-assigned role of the Indian courts, when he explained why the Supreme Court must depart from traditional common law doctrines of tort law to address contemporary environmental hazards:

> Law has to grow in order to satisfy the needs of the fast-changing society and keep abreast with the economic developments taking place in the country. Law cannot afford to remain static. The Court cannot allow judicial thinking to be constricted by reference to the law as it prevails in England or in any other foreign country. Though

the Court should be [open to enlightenment] from whatever source . . . it has to build up its own jurisprudence. It has to evolve new principles and lay down new norms which would adequately deal with the new problems which arise in a highly industrialized economy.

As this quote implies, aggressive judicial activism is not required in countries, particularly developed ones, where public awareness of environmental issues translates into effective political action and modern environmental legislation replaces ancient doctrines of tort law. Where public demand prompts legislators to enact legislation, courts can take a back seat. This factor may explain the distinction between the activism of the Indian Court in the environmental sphere, where existing legislation was viewed as "dysfunctional," and its passivity on employee rights, criticized for its narrow interpretation of statutes intended to expand those rights. This factor may also explain why courts in developed countries continue to defer to the domestic political process in the environmental context and refrain from implementing international standards. Indeed, the activist Indian Court declined to intervene in a petition against damming the Narmada River in view of the robust decision-making processes that led to the decision to do so.

In the absence of specific domestic legislation, courts in environmentally threatened jurisdictions can ground their formal authority to expand and enforce environment-related procedures and standards on two sources: their national constitutions and international law. These two sources enable communication with the courts of other nations, through cross-citing of one another's judgments; and, in fact, interjudicial communications have proved to be the hallmark of the jurisprudence of these courts, with the Indian Supreme Court leading the way. In 1994 the Pakistani Supreme Court made references to Indian cases. In 1996 Judge Rahman of the Bangladesh Appellate Division presented the Indian jurisprudence as a model for emulation. In 2000 the Sri Lanka Supreme Court referred to an Indian judgment with approval. The Indian Supreme Court itself referred to judgments of the courts of the Philippines, Colombia, and South Africa and of the European Court of Human Rights, as well as to a decision of the Inter-American Commission on Human Rights, noting with evident satisfaction that "the concept of a healthy environment as a part of the fundamental right to life, developed by our Supreme Court, is finding acceptance in various countries side by side with the right to development."

The absence of clear text relating to environmental protection in many constitutions has meant that courts must derive such protection from the basic right to life, which is anchored in all constitutions. The Supreme Court of India relied heavily on the constitutional right to life, holding that the right to enjoyment of pollution-free water and air is necessary for the full enjoyment of life. To develop the scope of this right, the Indian Court, as well as other courts, found inspiration and even authority in international law.

Recourse to international law, however, encounters tricky impediments. International environmental law is fragmented, many of the provisions being little more than hortatory declarations. The status of these norms in the domestic legal order often presents an additional obstacle to their judicial invocation. But faced with impending environmental disasters, courts in several countries have waived all doctrinal concerns and embraced whatever guidance they can derive from the diverse international documents dealing with the environment. The Supreme Court of India has taken the lead in tapping these international legal sources. Its decisions refer to the Declaration of the 1972 Stockholm Conference on the Human Environment as the "Magna-Carta of our environment" and import into domestic law concepts and principles such as "sustainable development," the "polluter pays" principle, and the "precautionary principle," all mentioned in international "soft law" instruments. The Court often does not explain the legal significance of these international documents, at times referring, for instance, to declarations such as the 1992 Rio Declaration on Environment and Development as "agreements" that were "enacted." The multiplicity of such nonbinding documents and their endorsement by a great number of governments at high-profile gatherings have been the apparent basis for the Court's reference to them as having been transformed into "Customary International Law though [their] salient feature[s] have yet to be finalised by the International Law Jurists." The Indian Court has grounded its decisions on standards set in unincorporated international agreements based on the premise that these conventions "elucidate and go to effectuate the fundamental rights guaranteed by our Constitution [and therefore] can be relied upon by Courts as facets of those fundamental rights and hence enforceable as such." Other courts in the region (in Pakistan, Sri Lanka, Nepal, and Bangladesh) have concurred in the Indian Supreme Court's jurisprudence by similarly invoking these principles in their judgments on the environment.

Clearly, these courts are fully aware of the potentially adverse economic implications of their pro-environment jurisprudence. Interjudicial cooperation must therefore be seen as a way to mitigate those adverse consequences. Given the grave environmental threat hovering over the Indian subcontinent, these national courts might just as doggedly have pushed for reform even without backing from their counterparts in neighboring nations. But lack of such cooperation might have made them much less resistant to pressure brought by domestic and foreign industry groups to whom lower environmental standards mean greater economic gain. These courts are not all-powerful in their quest to restrain the economic forces of globalization.

Coordinating the Migration into Destination Countries

Waves of asylum seekers from regions wasted by strife and poverty, especially since the early 1990s, have prompted developed countries to modify their migration policies by considerably restricting the access of refugees and limiting their rights. Such restrictions have increased the importance of the minimal obligations states owe to refugees under international law. The courts in destination countries have played an important role in shaping the policies regarding the various asylum seekers subject to *refoulementor* deportation. The migration policy adopted by one state had immediate effects in other states and many considered it essential to coordinate migration policies. The ways that national courts in destination countries have interpreted and applied international law on migration are therefore a key test of the thesis presented in this article.

As opposed to the two areas of judicial creativity discussed earlier in this part, the formulation of national migration policies has been high on the political agenda of many destination countries. The political branches expected the courts to respect domestic political processes and uphold both the results of sustained deliberation and public opinion. Defying the popular will by abiding by the demands of international law might incur more than heavy criticism. A court that "cooperated" with the strict requirements of international law would channel refugees to its country's shores if other courts "defected" by interpreting the international law concerning refugees less generously.

By and large, courts could not immediately reflect the transformation of national policies. The jurisprudence related to *refoulement* and expulsion to countries where torture could be committed against the expellee was too clear to be waived. Direct contact with individual refugees and their painful life stories, together with the judges' confidence in their ability to distinguish genuine from bogus claims, probably also moved courts to adopt a critical stance toward new executive and legislative policies. Decisions of courts in the majority of destination jurisdictions reflect this sentiment. Interjudicial cooperation is necessary in this area to enable the courts to stand up to the domestic political process without incurring the "costs" of increasing the numbers of refugees. The stakes, however, are high, and it would be ineffective, even irresponsible, for judges to rely only on the old practice of comparing decisions and engaging in intermittent exchanges. Perhaps such sentiments lay behind the establishment in 1995 of the International Association of Refugee Law Judges (IARLJ). In 2003 Dr. Hugo Storey, then a vice president of the UK Immigration Appeal Tribunal and a member of the IARLJ Council, explained the raison d'etre of the association: "[One] of IARLJ's principal objectives is the development of consistent and coherent refugee jurisprudence. Ideally a person who claims to be a refugee under the 1951 Convention should receive the same judicial assessment of his case whether he is in Germany, the USA, Japan or South Africa."

The constitution of the IARLJ reflects this ambitious program. Two of its preambular clauses describe the extent of the challenge:

Whereas the numbers of persons seeking protection outside of their countries of origin are significant and pose challenges that transcend national boundaries;

Whereas judges and quasi-judicial decision makers in all regions of the world have a special role to play in ensuring that persons seeking protection outside their country of origin find the 1951 Convention and its 1967 Protocol as well as other international and regional instruments applied fairly, consistently, and in accordance with the rule of law.

The IARLJ constitution also asserts that one of its objectives is "[t]o foster judicial independence and to facilitate the development within national legal systems of independent institutions applying judicial principles to refugee law issues." Membership in the IARLJ is open to judges or "quasi-judicial decision makers"; in August 2007, there were 332 members from fifty-two countries. The members can benefit from a Web-based database of court decisions applying the asylum law of different countries, and a members-only newsletter and forum. A leading expert in refugee law, James Hathaway, praised the association, viewing it as an alternative to the "more vigorously collaborative and formalized models" of international enforcement mechanisms in other areas of international human rights law, including international tribunals.

During the 1990s, national courts dealing with asylum seekers began citing each other's interpretation of the 1951 Convention Relating to the Status of Refugees, in particular its key provision regarding the definition of "refugee." This Convention provided a basis for coordinating a judicial position that often enabled these courts to strike down restrictive governmental policies without risking an influx of immigrants. This is not to suggest that the courts were always unanimous on each and every aspect of the elaborate qualifications of a "refugee." But what clearly emerges from several key decisions of the highest courts of the majority of destination states is the judicial effort to arrive at a contemporary meaning of the 1951 Convention that would expand the definition of "refugee" beyond the one envisioned in 1951, and to do so despite the concerns of contemporary governments. This effort is captured by the following statement of Lord Carswell:

The persecution of minorities and the migration of people seeking refuge from persecution have been unhappily enduring features, which did not end with the conclusion of the Second World War. . . . The vehicle [for balancing states' international obligations against their concerns] has been the [1951 Refugee Convention], which was the subject of agreement between states over 50 years ago, when the problems of the time inevitably differed in many respects from those prevailing today. That a means of reaching an accommodation suitable to cater for modern conditions has been achieved is a tribute to the wisdom and humanity of those who have had to construe the terms of the Convention and apply them to multifarious individual cases.

In their wisdom, the courts turned to construing the terms of the Convention collectively. This judicial dialogue can be traced to the early 1990s, when a 1993 judgment of the Canadian Supreme Court cited a 1985 decision of the United States Board of Immigration tribunal, to be cited itself later by the High Court of Australia in 1997, the New Zealand Refugee Status Authority in 1998, and the House of Lords in 1999. In the latter judgment, the Law Lords commend the New Zealand Refugee Status Authority for its "impressive judgment," which draws on "the case law and practice in Germany, The Netherlands, Sweden, Denmark, Canada, Australia and the U.S.A." In 2000 the U.S. Court of Appeals for the Ninth Circuit retreated from its prior interpretation, which these other courts had refused to follow, and endorsed the evolving common position, acknowledging that this position is also taken by the neighboring Canadian court. This ongoing interjudicial exchange has necessarily involved disagreements over particular aspects of the definition, but the dialogue has been conducted with the utmost respect and careful attention. "As evidenced by the Ninth Circuit's 2000 judgment in Hernandez-Montiel v. Immigration and Naturalization Service," such deliberation is ultimately capable of yielding general agreement.

In 2001 the House of Lords openly addressed the role of national courts in preventing "gross distortions" in the implementation of the 1951 Geneva Refugee Convention through "a uniformity of approach to the refugee problem." Lord Steyn insisted on a joint judicial effort to look beyond national peculiarities when interpreting a shared text:

> In principle therefore there can only be one true interpretation of a treaty. If there is disagreement on the meaning of the Geneva Convention, it can be resolved by the International Court of Justice (art 38 of the Geneva Convention). It has, however, never been asked to make such a ruling. The prospect of a reference to the International Court of Justice is remote. In practice it is left to national courts, faced with a material disagreement on an issue of interpretation, to resolve it. But in doing so it must search, untrammelled by notions of its national legal culture, for the true autonomous and international meaning of the treaty. And there can only be one true meaning.

But this very decision also demonstrated the limits of judicial independence, as well as the limited ability of the written word to withstand domestic political pressures. Some courts, most notably in France and Germany, have operated since the early 1990s in a political environment increasingly concerned about the influx of refugees. Restrictive policies were adopted in both countries by constitutional amendment. During the 1990s, many, if not most, refugees were fleeing countries affected by civil wars and intercommunal strife, and European courts were called upon to decide whether "persecution" in the sense of the 1951 Convention could be effected by nonstate agents. While the majority of the courts, including those of the United Kingdom, recognized that nonstate agents could be deemed "persecutors," some others, including those of Germany and France, refused to follow suit. As a result, German courts would not recognize as "refugees" asylum seekers from countries such as Afghanistan, Bosnia, Sri Lanka, and Somalia, who had suffered at the hands of nonstate actors, and French courts would similarly reject the applications of Algerians persecuted by militias, lacking evidence that the Algerian state had either encouraged or tolerated the persecution. The lesser protection afforded to such persons in these two countries prompted the House of Lords to quash the secretary of state's decision to send refugees from Somalia and Algeria to Germany and France, respectively, out of concern that they might be deported and face persecution.

The judicial "defections" by the French and German courts were based on the traditional justifications: the accordance of precedence to the peculiarities of national constitutions and laws implementing the international obligations; the narrow interpretation of the international obligations through the invocation of governmental practice rather than the jurisprudence of foreign courts; and the distinguishing of seemingly pertinent decisions of international courts. The French Constitutional Council and the German Federal Constitutional Court examined domestic legislation in light of the recently amended constitutions. The German Federal Administrative Court gave precedence to a domestic act that incorporated the international obligation to protect refugees, interpreting that act in light of the German Basic Law. The court did acknowledge that other courts had recognized the refugee status of those persecuted by nonstate agents (referring to the jurisprudence of the United States, the United Kingdom, France, Canada, and Australia). It even asserted that the interpretation of the same treaty by other courts usually carries "special weight," but not, it said, when the intention of the national legislator was as clear as it was in this case. Subsequently, the German court added that its understanding of international law reflected the understanding of most of the governments of the state parties to the 1951 Convention. In another decision handed down on the same day, the court refused to accept an "expansive" and "creative" conflicting interpretation by the European Court of Human Rights, noting that "[i]t is not the task of the courts to expand the boundaries of the member states' ability and willingness to absorb [refugees] through creative interpretation of treaties and thereby to disregard the constitutionally protected sovereignty of the national lawmaker and constitution maker." When the German Constitutional Court reviewed the constitutionality decisions of the Federal Administrative Court, it somewhat expanded the opportunities of asylum seekers who had fled persecution by nonstate agents. However, it did not refer to international law in its interpretation of the relevant provisions of the German law.

The coalition of courts determined to develop a consistent interpretation of the 1951 Convention and the opposing group of courts that insist on a different outcome are two sides of the same coin, the coin being the use of international law as a strategic tool by national courts. For courts that seek to establish a common front, a shared text is an asset they cultivate. At the same time, this story suggests that international law does not preempt courts' seeking to protect their domestic political process by deviating from an evolving standard. The German Federal Administrative Court serves as an example of a court that uses the language of international law to explain why the common standard should not apply in Germany.

As Gerald Neuman notes, a common interpretation of their status and rights may not always be beneficial to asylum seekers. Asylum seekers are likely to benefit from diversity of national policies. But in the trade-off between the common position of the governments and that of the courts, so far the latter has proved more beneficial to the refugees. . . .

Conclusion

This article has argued that the aspiration to "speak with one voice" is shared by a growing number of national courts across the globe. But, as opposed to what prevailed only a decade ago, these courts no longer wish to speak with the voice of their governments but, rather, to align their jurisprudence with that of other national courts. Comparative constitutional law and international law have proven to be the best tools for effectuating this strategy. The article explains this strategy as a reaction to the delegation of governmental authority to formal or informal international institutions and to the mounting economic pressures on governments and courts to conform to global standards. The judicial reaction, in turn, is designed to expand the domestic dialogue and bolster the national governments' ability to resist the attempts of interest groups and powerful foreign governments to influence them. Such motivation for transjurisdictional coordination is fully justified under democratic theories that conceive of the court as a facilitator of democratic deliberation.

As discussed, the coordination strategy is limited to situations in which courts observe that their government, their legislature, or they themselves have succumbed to, or are threatened by, economic or political powers that stifle the democratic process through coordinated supranational standards, be they formal (in treaties) or informal. This limitation suggests that courts might not be equally firm when only local dimensions mark a given dispute, as with those over conditions for detaining local criminals or the displacement of indigenous inhabitants due to dam construction.

It is too early to assess the success of this emerging trend. Every collective action depends on a sufficient number of contributors to the effort. Changes in the domestic rules protecting judicial independence could put a damper on the willingness of the courts in the relevant countries to take on an assertive role. In addition, governments may be pressured to submit to intergovernmental attempts to deprive courts of the authority or opportunity to act. But on the basis of the analysis in this article, it seems safe to assume that courts will not idly tolerate the erosion of their authority to review the actions of the political branches. In an era when governments are opting for alternatives to formal internal or international lawmaking, it is the national courts that are seriously resorting to comparative constitutional law and international law. This turn of events is a surprising mirror image of the state of affairs that prevailed only a decade ago.

EYAL BENVENISTI Professor of Law, Tel Aviv University. I thank Ziv Bohrer, Shai Dothan, George W. Downs, Alon Harel, Tally Kritzman, Ariel Porat, and Eran Shamir-Borer for their very helpful comments on previous versions, and Shay Gurion for excellent research assistance. This article is based partly on research conducted since September 11, 2001, on the ways that national courts cope with international terrorism, funded by the Israel Science Foundation and the Minerva Center for Human Rights at Tel Aviv University. The article was written during a sabbatical leave made possible by a Humboldt Research Award of the Alexander von Humboldt Foundation.

The Making of a Neo-KGB State

Political power in Russia now lies with the FSB, the KGB's successor.

On the evening of August 22nd 1991—16 years ago this week—Alexei Kondaurov, a KGB general, stood by the darkened window of his Moscow office and watched a jubilant crowd moving towards the KGB headquarters in Lubyanka Square. A coup against Mikhail Gorbachev had just been defeated. The head of the KGB who had helped to orchestrate it had been arrested, and Mr Kondaurov was now one of the most senior officers left in the fast-emptying building. For a moment the thronged masses seemed to be heading straight towards him.

Then their anger was diverted to the statue of Felix Dzerzhinsky, the KGB's founding father. A couple of men climbed up and slipped a rope round his neck. Then he was yanked up by a crane. Watching "Iron Felix" sway in mid-air, Mr Kondaurov, who had served in the KGB since 1972, felt betrayed "by Gorbachev, by Yeltsin, by the impotent coup leaders". He remembers thinking, "I will prove to you that your victory will be short-lived."

Those feelings of betrayal and humiliation were shared by 500,000 KGB operatives across Russia and beyond, including Vladimir Putin, whose resignation as a lieutenant-colonel in the service had been accepted only the day before. Eight years later, though, the KGB men seemed poised for revenge. Just before he became president, Mr Putin told his ex-colleagues at the Federal Security Service (FSB), the KGB's successor, "A group of FSB operatives, dispatched under cover to work in the government of the Russian federation, is successfully fulfilling its task." He was only half joking.

Over the two terms of Mr Putin's presidency, that "group of FSB operatives" has consolidated its political power and built a new sort of corporate state in the process. Men from the FSB and its sister organisations control the Kremlin, the government, the media and large parts of the economy—as well as the military and security forces. According to research by Olga Kryshtanovskaya, a sociologist at the Russian Academy of Sciences, a quarter of the country's senior bureaucrats are *siloviki*—a Russian word meaning, roughly, "power guys", which includes members of the armed forces and other security services, not just the FSB. The proportion rises to three-quarters if people simply affiliated to the security services are included. These people represent a psychologically homogeneous group, loyal to roots that go back to the Bolsheviks' first political police, the Cheka. As Mr Putin says repeatedly, "There is no such thing as a former Chekist."

By many indicators, today's security bosses enjoy a combination of power and money without precedent in Russia's history. The Soviet KGB and its pre-revolutionary ancestors did not care much about money; power was what mattered. Influential though it was, the KGB was a "combat division" of the Communist Party, and subordinate to it. As an outfit that was part intelligence organisation, part security agency and part secret political police, it was often better informed, but it could not act on its own authority; it could only make "recommendations". In the 1970s and 1980s it was not even allowed to spy on the party bosses and had to act within Soviet laws, however inhuman.

The KGB provided a crucial service of surveillance and suppression; it was a state within a state. Now, however, it has become the state itself. Apart from Mr Putin, "There is nobody today who can say no to the FSB," says Mr Kondaurov.

All important decisions in Russia, says Ms Kryshtanovskaya, are now taken by a tiny group of men who served alongside Mr Putin in the KGB and who come from his home town of St Petersburg. In the next few months this coterie may well decide the outcome of next year's presidential election. But whoever succeeds Mr Putin, real power is likely to remain in the organisation. Of all the Soviet institutions, the KGB withstood Russia's transformation to capitalism best and emerged strongest. "Communist ideology has gone, but the methods and psychology of its secret police have remained," says Mr Kondaurov, who is now a member of parliament.

Scotched, Not Killed

Mr Putin's ascent to the presidency of Russia was the result of a chain of events that started at least a quarter of a century earlier, when Yuri Andropov, a former head of the KGB, succeeded Leonid Brezhnev as general secretary of the Communist Party. Andropov's attempts to reform the stagnating Soviet economy in order to preserve the Soviet Union and its political system have served as a model for Mr Putin. Early in his presidency Mr Putin unveiled a plaque at the Lubyanka headquarters that paid tribute to Andropov as an "outstanding political figure".

Staffed by highly educated, pragmatic men recruited in the 1960s and 1970s, the KGB was well aware of the dire state of the Soviet economy and the antique state of the party bosses. It was therefore one of the main forces behind *perestroika*, the loose policy of restructuring started by Mr Gorbachev in the

1980s. *Perestroika*'s reforms were meant to give the Soviet Union a new lease of life. When they threatened its existence, the KGB mounted a coup against Mr Gorbachev. Ironically, this precipitated the Soviet collapse.

The defeat of the coup gave Russia an historic chance to liquidate the organisation. "If either Gorbachev or Yeltsin had been bold enough to dismantle the KGB during the autumn of 1991, he would have met little resistance," wrote Yevgenia Albats, a journalist who has courageously covered the grimmest chapters in the KGB's history. Instead, both Mr Gorbachev and Yeltsin tried to reform it.

The "blue blood" of the KGB—the First Chief Directorate, in charge of espionage—was spun off into a separate intelligence service. The rest of the agency was broken into several parts. Then, after a few short months of talk about openness, the doors of the agency slammed shut again and the man charged with trying to reform it, Vadim Bakatin, was ejected. His glum conclusion, delivered at a conference in 1993, was that although the myth about the KGB's invincibility had collapsed, the agency itself was very much alive.

Indeed it was. The newly named Ministry of Security continued to "delegate" the officers of the "active reserve" into state institutions and commercial firms. Soon KGB officers were staffing the tax police and customs services. As Boris Yeltsin himself admitted by the end of 1993, all attempts to reorganise the KGB were "superficial and cosmetic"; in fact, it could not be reformed. "The system of political police has been preserved," he said, "and could be resurrected."

Yet Mr Yeltsin, though he let the agency survive, did not use it as his power base. In fact, the KGB was cut off from the post-Soviet redistribution of assets. Worse still, it was upstaged and outwitted by a tiny group of opportunists, many of them Jews (not a people beloved by the KGB), who became known as the oligarchs. Between them, they grabbed most of the country's natural resources and other privatised assets. KGB officers watched the oligarchs get super-rich while they stayed cash-strapped and sometimes even unpaid.

Some officers did well enough, but only by offering their services to the oligarchs. To protect themselves from rampant crime and racketeering, the oligarchs tried to privatise parts of the KGB. Their large and costly security departments were staffed and run by ex-KGB officers. They also hired senior agency men as "consultants". Fillip Bobkov, the head of the Fifth Directorate (which dealt with dissidents), worked for a media magnate, Vladimir Gusinsky. Mr Kondaurov, a former spokesman for the KGB, worked for Mikhail Khodorkovsky, who ran and largely owned Yukos. "People who stayed in the FSB were B-list," says Mark Galeotti, a British analyst of the Russian special services.

Lower-ranking staff worked as bodyguards to Russia's rich. (Andrei Lugovoi, the chief suspect in the murder in London last year of Alexander Litvinenko, once guarded Boris Berezovsky, an oligarch who, facing arrest in Russia, now lives in Britain.) Hundreds of private security firms staffed by KGB veterans sprang up around the country and most of them, though not all, kept their ties to their *alma mater*. According to Igor Goloshchapov, a former KGB special-forces commando who is now a spokesman for almost 800,000 private security men,

In the 1990s we had one objective: to survive and preserve our skills. We did not consider ourselves to be separate from those who stayed in the FSB. We shared everything with them and we saw our work as just another form of serving the interests of the state. We knew that there would come a moment when we would be called upon.

That moment came on New Year's Eve 1999, when Mr Yeltsin resigned and, despite his views about the KGB, handed over the reins of power to Mr Putin, the man he had put in charge of the FSB in 1998 and made prime minister a year later.

The Inner Circle

As the new president saw things, his first task was to restore the management of the country, consolidate political power and neutralise alternative sources of influence: oligarchs, regional governors, the media, parliament, opposition parties and non-governmental organisations. His KGB buddies helped him with the task.

The most politically active oligarchs, Mr Berezovsky, who had helped Mr Putin come to power, and Mr Gusinsky, were pushed out of the country, and their television channels were taken back into state hands. Mr Khodorkovsky, Russia's richest man, was more stubborn. Despite several warnings, he continued to support opposition parties and NGOs and refused to leave Russia. In 2003 the FSB arrested him and, after a show trial, helped put him in jail.

To deal with unruly regional governors, Mr Putin appointed special envoys with powers of supervision and control. Most of them were KGB veterans. The governors lost their budgets and their seats in the upper house of the Russian parliament. Later the voters lost their right to elect them.

All the strategic decisions, according to Ms Kryshtanovskaya, were and still are made by the small group of people who have formed Mr Putin's informal politburo. They include two deputy heads of the presidential administration: Igor Sechin, who officially controls the flow of documents but also oversees economic matters, and Viktor Ivanov, responsible for personnel in the Kremlin and beyond. Then come Nikolai Patrushev, the head of the FSB, and Sergei Ivanov, a former defence minister and now the first deputy prime minister. All are from St Petersburg, and all served in intelligence or counter-intelligence. Mr Sechin is the only one who does not advertise his background.

That two of the most influential men, Mr Sechin and Viktor Ivanov, hold only fairly modest posts (each is a deputy head) and seldom appear in public is misleading. It was, after all, common Soviet practice to have a deputy, often linked to the KGB, who carried more weight than his notional boss. "These people feel more comfortable when they are in the shadows," explains Ms Kryshtanovskaya.

In any event, each of these KGB veterans has a plethora of followers in other state institutions. One of Mr Patrushev's former deputies, also from the KGB, is the minister of the interior, in charge of the police. Sergei Ivanov still commands authority within the army's headquarters. Mr Sechin has close family ties to the minister of justice. The prosecution service, which in Soviet times at least nominally controlled the KGB's work, has now become its instrument, along with the tax police.

The political clout of these *siloviki* is backed by (or has resulted in) state companies with enormous financial resources. Mr Sechin, for example, is the chairman of Rosneft, Russia's largest state-run oil company. Viktor Ivanov heads the board of directors of Almaz-Antei, the country's main producer of air-defence rockets, and of Aeroflot, the national airline. Sergei Ivanov oversees the military-industrial complex and is in charge of the newly created aircraft-industry monopoly.

But the *siloviki* reach farther, into all areas of Russian life. They can be found not just in the law-enforcement agencies but in the ministries of economy, transport, natural resources, telecoms and culture. Several KGB veterans occupy senior management posts in Gazprom, Russia's biggest company, and its pocket bank, Gazprombank (whose vice-president is the 26-year-old son of Sergei Ivanov).

Alexei Gromov, Mr Putin's trusted press secretary, sits on the board of Channel One, Russia's main television channel. The railway monopoly is headed by Vladimir Yakunin, a former diplomat who served his country at the United Nations in New York and is believed to have held a high rank in the KGB. Sergei Chemezov, Mr Putin's old KGB friend from his days in Dresden (where the president worked from 1985 to 1990), is in charge of Rosoboronexport, a state arms agency that has grown on his watch into a vast conglomerate. The list goes on.

Many officers of the active reserve have been seconded to Russia's big companies, both private and state-controlled, where they draw a salary while also remaining on the FSB payroll. "We must make sure that companies don't make decisions that are not in the interest of the state," one current FSB colonel explains. Being an active-reserve officer in a firm is, says another KGB veteran, a dream job: "You get a huge salary and you get to keep your FSB card." One such active-reserve officer is the 26-year-old son of Mr Patrushev who was last year seconded from the FSB to Rosneft, where he is now advising Mr Sechin. (After seven months at Rosneft, Mr Putin awarded Andrei Patrushev the Order of Honour, citing his professional successes and "many years of conscientious work".) Rosneft was the main recipient of Yukos's assets after the firm was destroyed.

The attack on Yukos, which entered its decisive stage just as Mr Sechin was appointed to Rosneft, was the first and most blatant example of property redistribution towards the *siloviki*, but not the only one. Mikhail Gutseriev, the owner of Russneft, a fast-growing oil company, was this month forced to give up his business after being accused of illegal activities. For a time, he had refused; but, as he explained, "they tightened the screws" and one state agency after another—the general prosecutor's office, the tax police, the interior ministry—began conducting checks on him.

From Oligarchy to Spookocracy

The transfer of financial wealth from the oligarchs to the *siloviki* was perhaps inevitable. It certainly met with no objection from most Russians, who have little sympathy for "robber barons".

It even earned the *siloviki* a certain popularity. But whether they will make a success of managing their newly acquired assets is doubtful. "They know how to break up a company or to confiscate something. But they don't know how to manage a business. They use force simply because they don't know any other method," says an ex-KGB spook who now works in business.

Curiously, the concentration of such power and economic resources in the hands of a small group of *siloviki*, who identify themselves with the state, has not alienated people in the lower ranks of the security services. There is trickle-down of a sort: the salary of an average FSB operative has gone up several times over the past decade, and a bit of freelancing is tolerated. Besides, many Russians inside and outside the ranks believe that the transfer of assets from private hands to the *siloviki* is in the interests of the state. "They are getting their own back and they have the right to do so," says Mr Goloshchapov.

The rights of the *siloviki*, however, have nothing to do with the formal kind that are spelled out in laws or in the constitution. What they are claiming is a special mission to restore the power of the state, save Russia from disintegration and frustrate the enemies that might weaken it. Such idealistic sentiments, says Mr Kondaurov, coexist with an opportunistic and cynical eagerness to seize the situation for personal or institutional gain.

The security servicemen present themselves as a tight brotherhood entitled to break any laws for the sake of their mission. Their high language is laced with profanity, and their nationalism is often combined with contempt for ordinary people. They are, however, loyal to each other.

Competition to enter the service is intense. The KGB picked its recruits carefully. Drawn from various institutes and universities, they then went to special KGB schools. Today the FSB Academy in Moscow attracts the children of senior *siloviki;* a vast new building will double its size. The point, says Mr Galeotti, the British analyst, "is not just what you learn, but who you meet there".

Graduates of the FSB Academy may well agree. "A Chekist is a breed," says a former FSB general. A good KGB heritage— a father or grandfather, say, who worked for the service—is highly valued by today's *siloviki*. Marriages between *siloviki* clans are also encouraged.

Viktor Cherkesov, the head of Russia's drug-control agency, who was still hunting dissidents in the late 1980s, has summed up the FSB psychology in an article that has become the manifesto of the *siloviki* and a call for consolidation.

We [*siloviki*] must understand that we are one whole. History ruled that the weight of supporting the Russian state should fall on our shoulders. I believe in our ability, when we feel danger, to put aside everything petty and to remain faithful to our oath.

As well as invoking secular patriotism, Russia's security bosses can readily find allies among the priesthood. Next to the FSB building in Lubyanka Square stands the 17th-century church of the Holy Wisdom, "restored in August 2001 with zealous help from the FSB," says a plaque. Inside, freshly painted icons gleam with gold. "Thank God there is the FSB. All power is from God and so is theirs," says Father Alexander, who leads the service. A former KGB general agrees: "They really believe that they were chosen and are guided by God and that even the high oil prices they have benefited from are God's will."

Sergei Grigoryants, who has often been interrogated and twice imprisoned (for anti-Soviet propaganda) by the KGB, says the security chiefs believe "that they are the only ones who have the real picture and understanding of the world." At the centre of this picture is an exaggerated sense of the enemy, which justifies their very existence: without enemies, what are they for? "They believe they can see enemies where ordinary people can't," says Ms Kryshtanovskaya.

"A few years ago, we succumbed to the illusion that we don't have enemies and we have paid dearly for that," Mr Putin told the FSB in 1999. It is a view shared by most KGB veterans and their successors. The greatest danger comes from the West, whose aim is supposedly to weaken Russia and create disorder. "They want to make Russia dependent on their technologies," says a current FSB staffer. "They have flooded our market with their goods. Thank God we still have nuclear arms." The siege mentality of the *siloviki* and their anti-Westernism have played well with the Russian public. Mr Goloshchapov, the private agents' spokesman, expresses the mood this way: "In Gorbachev's time Russia was liked by the West and what did we get for it? We have surrendered everything: eastern Europe, Ukraine, Georgia. NATO has moved to our borders."

From this perspective, anyone who plays into the West's hands at home is the internal enemy. In this category are the last free-thinking journalists, the last NGOs sponsored by the West and the few liberal politicians who still share Western values.

To sense the depth of these feelings, consider the response of one FSB officer to the killing of Anna Politkovskaya, a journalist whose books criticising Mr Putin and his brutal war in Chechnya are better known outside than inside Russia. "I don't know who killed her, but her articles were beneficial to the Western press. She deserved what she got." And so, by this token, did Litvinenko, the ex-KGB officer poisoned by polonium in London last year.

In such a climate, the idea that Russia's security services are entitled to deal ruthlessly with enemies of the state, wherever they may be, has gained wide acceptance and is supported by a new set of laws. One, aimed at "extremism", gives the FSB and other agencies ample scope to pursue anyone who acts or speaks against the Kremlin. It has already been invoked against independent analysts and journalists. A lawyer who complained to the Constitutional Court about the FSB's illegal tapping of his client's telephone has been accused of disclosing state secrets. Several scientists who collaborated with foreign firms are in jail for treason.

Despite their loyalty to old Soviet roots, today's security bosses differ from their predecessors. They do not want a return to communist ideology or an end to capitalism, whose fruits they enjoy. They have none of the asceticism of their forebears. Nor do they relish mass repression: in a country where fear runs deep, attacking selected individuals does the job. But the concentration of such power and money in the hands of the security services does not bode well for Russia.

And Not Very Good at Their Job

The creation of enemies may smooth over clan disagreements and fuel nationalism, but it does not make the country more secure or prosperous. While the FSB reports on the ever-rising numbers of foreign spies, accuses scientists of treason and hails its "brotherhood", Russia remains one of the most criminalised, corrupt and bureaucratic countries in the world.

During the crisis at a school in Beslan in 2004, the FSB was good at harassing journalists trying to find out the truth. But it could not even cordon off the school in which the hostages were held. Under the governorship of an ex-FSB colleague of Mr Putin, Ingushetia, the republic that borders Chechnya, has descended into a new theatre of war. The army is plagued by crime and bullying. Private businessmen are regularly hassled by law-enforcement agencies. Russia's foreign policy has turned out to be self-fulfilling: by perpetually denouncing enemies on every front, it has helped to turn many countries from potential friends into nervous adversaries.

The rise to power of the KGB veterans should not have been surprising. In many ways, argues Inna Solovyova, a Russian cultural historian, it had to do with the qualities that Russians find appealing in their rulers: firmness, reserve, authority and a degree of mystery. "The KGB fitted this description, or at least knew how to seem to fit it."

But are they doing the country any good? "People who come from the KGB are tacticians. We have never been taught to solve strategic tasks," says Mr Kondaurov. The biggest problem of all, he and a few others say, is the agency's loss of professionalism. He blushes when he talks about the polonium capers in London. "We never sank to this level," he sighs. "What a blow to the country's reputation!"

Beijing Censors Taken to Task in Party Circles

JOSEPH KAHN

A dozen former Communist Party officials and senior scholars, including a onetime secretary to Mao, a party propaganda chief and the retired bosses of some of the country's most powerful newspapers, have denounced the recent closing of a prominent news journal, helping to fuel a growing backlash against censorship.

A public letter issued by the prominent figures, dated Feb. 2 but circulated to journalists in Beijing on Tuesday, appeared to add momentum to a campaign by a few outspoken editors against micromanagement, personnel shuffles and an ever-expanding blacklist of banned topics imposed on China's newspapers, magazines, television stations and Web sites by the party's secretive Propaganda Department.

The letter criticized the department's order on Jan. 24 to shut down Freezing Point, a popular journal of news and opinion, as an example of "malignant management" and an "abuse of power" that violates China's constitutional guarantee of free speech.

The letter did not address Beijing's pressure on Web portals and search engines.

That issue gained attention abroad after Microsoft and Google acknowledged helping the government filter information and Yahoo was accused of providing information from its e-mail accounts that was used to jail dissident writers. The issue will be the subject of Congressional hearings in Washington on Wednesday.

In addition to shutting down Freezing Point, a weekly supplement to China Youth Daily, since late last year, officials responsible for managing the news media have replaced editors of three other publications that developed reputations for breaking news or exploring sensitive political and social issues.

The interventions amounted to the most extensive exertion of press control since President Hu Jintao assumed power three years ago.

But propaganda officials are also facing rare public challenges to their legal authority to take such actions, including a short strike and string of resignations at one newspaper and defiant open letters from two editors elsewhere who had been singled out for censure. Those protests have suggested that some people in China's increasingly market-driven media industry no longer fear the consequences of violating the party line.

The authors of the letter predicted that the country would have difficulty countering the recent surge of social unrest in the countryside unless it allowed the news media more leeway to expose problems that lead to violent protests.

"At the turning point in our history from a totalitarian to a constitutional system, depriving the public of freedom of speech will bring disaster for our social and political transition and give rise to group confrontation and social unrest," the letter said. "Experience has proved that allowing a free flow of ideas can improve stability and alleviate social problems."

Some of the signers held high official posts during the 1980's, when the political environment in China was becoming more open. Although they have long since retired or been eased from power, a collective letter from respected elder statesmen can often help mobilize opinion within the ruling party.

One of those people who signed the petition is Li Rui, Mao's secretary and biographer. Others include Hu Jiwei, a former editor of People's Daily, the party's leading official newspaper; Zhu Houze, who once ran the party's propaganda office; and Li Pu, a former deputy head of the New China News Agency, the main official press agency.

Party officials and political experts say President Hu, who was groomed to take over China's top posts for more than a decade, has often attended closely to the opinions of the party's elder statesmen.

Mr. Hu is widely thought to favor tighter media controls. Party officials said he referred approvingly to media management in Cuba and North Korea in a speech in late 2004.

But he has also solicited support from more liberal elements. Last year Mr. Hu organized high-profile official ceremonies to mark the 90th anniversary of the birth of Hu Yaobang, the reform-oriented party leader who lost his posts in a power struggle and whose death in 1989 was the initial cause of the student-led democracy demonstrations that year. Some of the officials who signed the petition were close associates of Hu Yaobang.

The reaction against the shutdown of Freezing Point was organized by its longtime editor, Li Datong, 53, a party member and senior official of the party-run China Youth Daily. Mr. Li broadcast news of the secret order on his personal blog moments after he received it and has since mobilized supporters to put pressure on the Propaganda Department to retract the decision.

Under his stewardship, Freezing Point became one of the most consistently provocative journals of news and public opinion. It published investigative articles on sensitive topics like the party's version of historical events, nationalism and the party-run education system. Freezing Point ran opinion articles on politics in Taiwan and rural unrest in mainland China that caused a stir in media circles in recent months.

The cause cited for closing Freezing Point was an opinion piece by a historian named Yuan Weishi. He argued that Chinese history textbooks tended to ignore mistakes and provocations by leaders of the Qing Dynasty that may have incited attacks by foreign powers in the late 19th century.

Mr. Li often tussled with his bosses at China Youth Daily and officials at the Propaganda Department. But he has also cultivated support among the party elite. He often speaks supportively of President Hu and quotes extensively from the writings of Marx, who he says favored a robust free press.

He has maintained that the Propaganda Department had overstepped its authority by ordering Freezing Point closed, and he filed a formal complaint to the party's disciplinary arm.

"The propaganda office is an illegal organization that has no power to shut down a publication," Mr. Li said in an interview. "Its power is informal, and it can only exercise it if people are afraid."

He added, "I am not afraid."

Mr. Li scored an initial victory last week, when propaganda officials told China Youth Daily to draft a plan to revive Freezing Point, which had been formally closed for "rectification," Mr. Li and another editor at the newspaper said. Some media experts had predicted that the authorities would not allow Freezing Point to reopen, and the new order was treated as a signal that officials had misjudged the reaction to its closing.

Shortly after the contretemps at China Youth Daily broke out, the former editor of another national publication attacked the bosses who had replaced him, saying they had exercised self-censorship in the face of pressure from propaganda officials.

Chen Jieren, who lost his position last week as the editor of Public Interest Times, posted a letter online entitled "Ridiculous Game, Despicable Intrigue." The letter disputed his bosses' statement that he had been dismissed for "bad management skills" and said he had a struggled constantly against senior officials for the right "to report the truth with a conscience."

One recent issue of Public Interest Times mocked the poor quality of English translations on official government websites.

In a separate incident earlier this year, a group of editors and reporters at the party-run Beijing News declined to report for work after the editor of the paper, known for breaking news stories on subjects the Propaganda Department has ruled off limits, was replaced. Many of the protesters have since resigned, reporters at the newspaper said.

The resistance against censorship could signal a decisive shift in China's news media controls, already under assault from the proliferation of e-mail, text messaging, Web sites, blogs and other new forums for news and opinion that the authorities have struggled to bring under their supervision.

Even most of the major party-run national publications in China, including China Youth Daily, no longer receive government subsidies and must depend mainly on income from circulation and advertising to survive.

That means providing more news or features that people want to pay for, including exclusive stories and provocative views that go well beyond the propaganda fare carried by the New China News Agency or People's Daily. Few serious publications survive for long without subsidies if they do not have popular content, editors say.

"Every serious publication in China faces tough choices," said Mr. Li of Freezing Point. "You can publish stories people want to read and risk offending the censors. Or you can publish only stories that the party wants published and risk going out of business."

UNIT 6

Public Policy: Defining Public, Effects and Trade-Offs

Unit Selections

Key Points to Consider

• What factors lead to policies to be adopted?

• If public policies generate losers and winners, should the government let the market address the issue? Why or why not?

• Is health coverage for the maternal care policy in Nepal the same or different from universal health policy in France? Why or why not?

• What are the considerations in health care policy or reform?

• Is it acceptable that some are given poorer health care if others have good coverage?

• Is it acceptable that wealth or income affects the quality of health care received? Why or why not?

Student Website

www.mhhe.com/cls

Internet References

International Institute for Sustainable Development
http://www.iisd.org/default.asp

The Commonwealth Fund
http://www.commonwealthfund.org

The World Health Organization
http://www.who.int/en

United Nations Environment Program
http://www.unep.ch

U.S. Information Agency
http://www.america.gov

World Bank
http://www.worldbank.org

The previous three units focused on how institutions in government affect political behavior and responses. This unit discusses the systematic treatment of the outcomes from government institutions, specifically, public policy. That is, the articles address the "why, what, and how" questions regarding public policy. In order to provide a truly comparative review of public policy, this Unit will showcase how different countries tackle the same public policy issue: health care policy.

Our first task is to clarify: "What is public policy?" Public policy refers to the government decisions and actions taken in response to social problems. Christopher Wlezien (2004) identifies nine public policy spending areas: environment, health, education, city development, social welfare, defense, space, foreign aid, and crime.[1] Francis and Weber (1980) describe 20 policy areas that include finance and economics, taxation, labor, business, civil rights, highways, and elections.[2] The lists are not exhaustive; this suggests that many social issues may fall within the scope of public concerns. Consequently, it means that few issues are beyond the purview of government response.

This speaks to a major debate in public policy: what is public and what private? That is, a major consideration regarding what is public policy lies with clarifying what are the limits to the public sphere and how to limit government authority so that it does not interfere with individual decisions. Few policy areas are free from this debate. As an example, one of the impediments to health-care reform is the concern that reforms will remove the individual's choice of medical providers or options.

Another area of debate regarding public policy is cost-efficiency. Many critics argue that government should minimize its policy presence to allow the free market, or the "invisible-hand," to work. As the article on CecilPigou and social economics notes, the free market does not always work. When it fails, what are the social costs? Who bears them? And, how are these costs borne? The article on Cecil Pigou and social economics shows that the social costs are considerable: from quality of health care to quality of life. And, the article on health care for American Indians underscores the significant social costs of continued neglect of health care.

Equally important, is the disparity between the haves- and have-nots an indicator of a failing health policy? That is certainly the case for South Africa, which had, under the presidency of Thabo Mbeki, adopted health policies on HIV-AIDs that were divergent with most other countries in the world as well as the World Health Organization. The policy has not only contributed to an estimated 330,000 premature deaths in 2008 but has led South Africa's birth mortality to rise—one of only four countries that defied the general downtrend in birth mortality in the world. The articles on the evolution of healthcare in Nepal, France, and in the United States for American Indians point out that one of the reasons that lead the government to step into policy-making is that the markets are unable to provide a satisfactory or equitable solution in the first place.

The apparent lack of resolution to these debates—what constitutes public policy and how efficient is it for the government to step into the fray—may lead to the temptation to stick

© William Ryall

to the status quo. Perhaps that is why in France, which has universal health care, it has proven a challenge to government to reform the system while in the United States, which has privatized health care, the option of reforming health care to be more extensive has proven just as challenging.

It behooves us to ask: Why pursue public policy and open that can of worms? We need public policy because many of the social issues that are of public concern—such as foreign aid, defense, health, and the environment—are not confined to a community. In these instances, government response provides the efficient and authoritative resolution. Thus, the article on state actor-social movement coalitions reveals that the turn-around in Japan's environment lies in the local government's enactment of anti-pollution policies in response to citizens' demands that calcified into national laws and the institutionalization of the Environment Agency in 1971. Similarly, the article on Nepal shows how political champions, the government's commitment, and accessible research expedited the implementation of a maternal health care policy.

Yet, public policy involves trade-offs. Indeed, it is probably realistic to consider that social issues are sometimes unsolvable within or between communities because there are trade-offs. Where there are clear winners and losers, disputes perpetuate over what is public policy or how it is pursued in order to over-turn the existing stance. As a result, the weight and enforcement of government authority is required to mediate the outcomes. Thus, the article on state actor-social movement coalitions shows that prior to the environmental turnaround in Japan, the citizens were on the losing side of the government's refusal to enact anti-pollution laws, while businesses benefited from the government's stance. More than a decade of mobilization passed before the hard-earned environmentally friendly laws were enacted, only to suffer from a backlash following Japan's economic slowdown in the 1970s. The articles on the health care among American Indians and in France show that the debates do not end with the implementation of universal health care. The quality of care and the problem of access continue to be debated, as well as the costs of administering the care.

Given the trade-offs, how is public policy evaluated? Largely, the evaluation of public policy may be boiled down to different values associated therewith: Is it about security or change? Is it about wealth or inequality? Is it about equal opportunities or equal outcomes? Is it acceptable if public health policy improves access for everyone, but leaves the quality of care a little worse off for everyone?

Such value-debates show that it is not often that there is an obvious "net gain" from public policy. Thus, the article on maternal health policy in Nepal shows that the costs of a maternal health care policy are justified by the reduction of maternity deaths. And, the articles on health care show that value-conflicts afflict the countries that adopt universal health care almost as much as those that do not. Thus, in France and in the United States, the questions of how much care to provide and at what costs dominates discussions about possible reforms. France was rated number 1 by the World Health Organization in an appraisal of health care systems in 191 countries in 2000; yet, since 1989, the health care system in that country has been operating at a deficit. In the same WHO appraisal, the United States came in 37th. It is no small irony that, as the United States is looking to France for possible health-care reform ideas, France is also looking to the United States for possible changes to their health care system.

The foregoing suggests that there are few easy answers related to policymaking. But, the juxtaposition of the article on environmental policy in Japan and maternal care policy in Nepal gives pause: perhaps piecemeal policies—like the maternal care policy in Nepal—may work better or, at the least, invite less challenge than a complete policy revamp—such as the environmental policy in Japan. Also, both articles underscore the importance of citizen- and interest group-participation to clarify their policy preferences and mobilize for their causes. And, finally, it emphasizes the need for executive accountability and responsiveness and the legislature's representation to ensure that policymaking captures the willingness of the citizenry to make the necessary trade-offs.

Notes

1. Christopher Wlezien. 2004. "Patterns of Representation: Dynamics of Public Preferences and Policy," *Journal of Politics,* vol. 66, no. 1 (Feb., 2004), pp. 1–24.
2. Wayne L. Francis and Ronald E. Weber. 1980. "Legislative Issues in the 50 States: Managing Complexity through Classification." *Legislative Studies Quarterly,* vol. 5, no. 3 (Aug., 1980), pp. 407–421.

The Formation of State Actor-Social Movement Coalitions and Favorable Policy Outcomes

LINDA BREWSTER STEARNS AND PAUL D. ALMEIDA

This study examines the role of loosely-coupled state actor-social movement coalitions in creating positive policy outcomes. It specifies the organizational locations within the state most conducive to state actor-social movement ties. Using the case of Japanese anti-pollution politics between 1956 and 1976, we demonstrate that favorable policy outcomes were the result of multiple coalitions between anti-pollution movements and state agencies, opposition political parties, local governments, and the courts.

In the 1960s Japan was internationally recognized with the notorious distinction of being the most polluted country in the advanced capitalist world. Literally, hundreds of people died (and thousands more chronically sickened) as a direct result of industrial pollution (Methyl Mercury poisoning, Cadmium poisoning, PCB poisoning, SMON disease, and various airborne pollutants). By the early 1970s, the Japanese state had made a rapid U-turn and implemented a series of environmental reforms viewed as a model for the industrialized world. This article aims to explain this dramatic shift in state policy-making priorities via the formation of multiple state-movement coalitions.

For social activists state policy reform happens too infrequently. Yet when it does, it can usually be accredited to two groups: 1) the actors external to the state that have made reform a political issue—social movement organizations, the mass media, and public opinion; and 2) the actors internal to the state that have ushered the reform through the state apparatus—politicians and state managers. Much has been written about social movements and the conditions that facilitate or hamper their success (Amenta and Young 1999b; Burstein, Einwohner, and Hollander 1995; Cress and Snow 2000; Gamson 1990; Giugni 1998; Piven and Cloward 1979). Less scholarly attention has focused on the relationship between social movements and state actors (Goldstone 2003; Wolfson 2001), specifically the organizational structures that give rise to the loosely-coupled

coalitions that form between these two groups and lead to favorable policy outcomes. In this article, we focus on this partnership between state actors and a social movement, rather than on the social movement itself.

Modern states are typically composed of nested and segmented administrative units that house many competing actors. Given this structural patterning, social movements can take advantage of the complex and decentralized nature of most democratic states to create state actor-social movement coalitions that represent potential venues for action. We define a state actor-social movement coalition broadly. A state-movement coalition comes into existence when state actors agree to apply their organizational resources and influence in ways that further the general aims of a social movement.

State actors participate in state-movement coalitions for a variety of reasons. Some state-movement coalitions involve institutional activists (i.e., "social movement participants who occupy formal statuses within the government and who pursue social movement goals through conventional bureaucratic channels" [Santoro and McGuire 1997:503]). These institutional activists are committed to the social movement's objectives and motivated by intrinsic rewards (Ganz 2000). While such coalitions have the potential to be ongoing, most state-movement coalitions are loosely coupled and temporary, consisting of state actors with shifting interests. Some state actors enter a state-movement coalition because they are ideologically predisposed to the movement's objectives. Other state actors participate in coalitions as a means of promoting their own agendas (Skocpol 1985). They enter state-movement coalitions primarily to pursue their own extrinsic rewards (i.e., further their careers and/or increase their status). Still other state actors, because of the location and function of their unit, take up the claims of a social movement to increase their unit's vitality and legitimacy within the state apparatus. State-movement coalitions, regardless of the state actors' motivations, increase the probability of producing positive outcomes for social movements. With the creation of state-movement coalitions, social movements are granted a level of legitimacy, and perhaps more important, indirect access to the state's decision-making structures.

In this article we examine the coalitions created between the Japanese environmental movement and four groups of state actors: 1) weak state agencies; 2) opposition political parties; 3) local governments; and 4) the courts. Initially, all five groups—the environmental movement and the four categories of state actors—had little influence in state policy-making and faced three powerful adversaries: 1) the industrial business establishment; 2) the entrenched Liberal Democratic Party (LDP); and 3) the more powerful state bureaucracies (in particular the most influential—the Ministry of International Trade and Industry [MITI] with its close relations to the business establishment). Building on recent developments in political sociology, we identify the institutional structures conducive to the formation of the state-movement coalitions that shaped policy reform. We also examine the policy impact of each state-movement coalition and show that the unprecedented change in state environmental policy that occurred in Japan depended on the creation of multiple state actor-movement coalitions.

Political Institutions and State Actor-Movement Coalitions

Once a social movement forms and is relatively unified, a state's reaction to a social movement might range from ignoring or repressing it, to addressing its demands either symbolically or with real change (Tilly 1978). The first choice of a democratic government is often to ignore a social movement with the expectation that it will defuse and disappear. In such a situation, a movement is likely to attempt to engage the state by influencing public opinion, employing disruptive actions, and creating electoral uncertainty (Almeida and Stearns 1998; Burstein 1979; Piven and Cloward 1979). Disruptive actions work to raise public awareness and increase the pressure on the state to address the issue. Changing public opinion catches the attention of state actors by increasing electoral uncertainty and raising the possibility that the distribution of status and power within the state will change. Because social movements threaten the status quo or the "rules of the game," few state actors have the incentive and/or the opportunity to enter into a state-movement coalition (Kriesi et al. 1995:54).

We argue that the political institutional structure of the state plays a key role in determining which state actors benefit or are receptive to forming state-movement coalitions. Specifically we discuss how the level of bureaucratic development, the electoral system, and the degree of fragmentation of authority within the state (Amenta 1998; McCarthy and Wolfson 1992) affect the prospects that a state-movement

coalition will form with the following state actors: 1) state agencies; 2) oppositional political parties; 3) local governments; and 4) courts.

State Agencies

When a social movement grows in size and public opinion support to where the state must acknowledge it as a political actor, the probability increases that the movement will form a coalition with an "in-house" state agency. State agencies in their roles as policy advocates and regulators have the potential to grant social movements important access into the state's policy-making apparatus.

A social movement introducing a new issue may find there is no agency to address its demands. Moreover, state-oriented social movements are often in conflict with agencies involved in promoting business confidence and supporting capital accumulation (Block 1987). Such agencies are often the larger, better-funded, and more politically influential members of the polity. Their agendas reflect the strong lobbying efforts of large corporations, and their staffs frequently come from the very groups the social movement opposes (Domhoff 2002). Hence, these agencies are not usually candidates for a state-movement coalition.

The more highly developed the democratic state bureaucracy (i.e., in terms of size and differentiation), however, the more likely there resides within it an agency favorable to the social movement's objectives (Amenta and Young 1999a). In most cases the agency is tied to the state's legitimation function and handles citizens' rights and quality of life programs (Faber and O'Connor 1989). Historically, such agencies are under-funded and politically weak. As a result, an agency might be receptive to forming a state-movement coalition if the movement's issue falls within the agency's policy domain, promotes its agenda, advances its status, and/or increases its budget.

When no appropriate agency exists, designate or otherwise, a social movement often pushes to have one established (Baumgartner and Jones 1993). If successful, the new agency in order to overcome the "liability of newness" and survive will seek internal and external support for its raison d'etre (Stinchcombe 1965). Internally, as part of its staff, the agency might appoint institutional activists or known movement supporters. Externally, as part of its constituency, the agency might foster an ongoing relationship with the social movement.

In cases where the social movement addresses an established issue, the designated agency might have been created in a past social struggle over a similar issue (Bourdieu 1998). In general, we expect such an agency to be amenable to forming a state-movement coalition. Even more so if its staff consists of insider institutional activists and, in addressing the issue, the agency stands to acquire greater resources and status (Amenta and Zylan 1991). Indeed, prior to the formation of the state-movement coalition, the agency might have attempted to realize some of the same kinds of policies as desired by the social movement but lacked the political capital to do so. Such was the situation of hazardous waste policymaking in the United States. Only in the late 1970s, with the rise of local movements against toxic waste (in particular Love Canal) and their exposure in the mass media, was the EPA strong enough to pass through Congress the Superfund in 1980 (Szasz 1994)—a nationally comprehensive hazardous waste remediation and disposal program.

The above discussion suggests that the more highly developed a democratic state's bureaucracy the greater the likelihood a social movement will form a coalition with an established or new state agency. Furthermore, this partnership most likely occurs when the agency's primary mission is the maintenance of the state's institutional credibility (e.g., healthcare, social welfare, anti-discrimination, environment, labor, housing, etc.).

Oppositional Political Parties

Looking at such things as the restrictions on political assembly, voting, and choices among leadership groups, Edwin Amenta (1998) argues, "where people count little in politics, money and access matter even more". As "people power" is the main resource of a social movement (not money or access to elite decision making) (Tarrow 1994), the level of democratic participation is key to its influence and the possibility of coalition formation. Under democratic conditions or during regime liberalization, it is often an oppositional political party that takes up the demands of a social movement (Almeida 2003; Kriesi et al. 1995).

An oppositional political party becomes a state actor when the following criteria are met: 1) the party has been granted (by the state) the legal recognition needed to run for and hold office; and 2) the party has successfully exercised that right. For it is in their role as elected officials that members of opposition parties provide social movements access to the state's policy-making apparatus.

The political party entering into a coalition will be determined in large part by the type of electoral system. One basic distinction in electoral systems is between winner-take-all and proportional representation (Amenta and Young 1999a). Proportional representation systems generally offer social movements a greater choice of parties (which translates into more ideological and policy options) from which to form a coalition (Dalton, Recchia, and Rohrschneider 2003). In addition, competition between oppositional parties increases the incentive of these parties to form a coalition with a social movement. For not only is the oppositional party competing against the dominant party for support and votes, but against other oppositional parties as well. In winner-take-all systems, on the other hand, there is less incentive for the out-of-power party to align itself with a social movement (especially one without much initial public support). Such systems also limit the social movements' options to

the ideology and policy agendas of a few (generally two) well-established parties.

In either system, all things being equal, a social movement would prefer to form a coalition with a powerful political party because such a party improves its chances of accomplishing its goals (i.e., more policy implementation capacity) (Burstein et al. 1995:289). This is often not possible, as entrenched powerful parties tend to view social movements as challengers to the status quo and routine politics (Kriesi et al. 1995). One exception might be in a perceived tight election if a political party views the social movement's sympathy pools as large enough to influence the election's outcome. Such was the case with the Social Democratic Party (SDP) in West Germany in the mid-1980s when the party took up the peace movement's cause of antinuclear energy and nuclear weapons deployment. Although in sharp contrast to the SDP's pro-nuclear stance of the late 1970s and early 1980s, this powerful party used the issue not only to take votes away from the increasingly successful Green Party, but also to win back their parliamentary majority by 1990 (Koopmans 1995:100–3).

Given political circumstances often the best a social movement can manage, however, is to create a coalition with a stable reform or minority party (Maguire 1995). For example, in recently democratized El Salvador, state employed medical workers and unionized physicians formed coalitions in 1999–2000 and 2002–2003 with the largest oppositional political party to prevent the privatization of the state-managed public healthcare system. Both times this oppositional party-movement coalition materialized during the months of the parliamentary election campaign and vote (Almeida 2002:179). On both occasions the movement achieved their stated goal of halting the privatization process, while the opposition party increased its number of parliamentary seats (Schuld 2003). The political and electoral weakness of opposition parties makes them more receptive to creating new coalitions and constituencies. For this reason, a social movement is more likely to form a coalition with a stable, ideologically similar, minority or reform opposition party.

Local Governments and Courts

We maintain that state-movement coalitions are more likely to develop in democratic nation states characterized by autonomous local governments and/or courts. Several studies (Amenta and Young 1999a; Andrews 2001:90; Baiocchi 2003; Kriesi and Wisler 1999) have shown that federalist political structures (e.g., Brazil, Canada, India, New Zealand, Switzerland, and the United States) delegate more power to local governments than top-down centralized governments (e.g., Austria, France, Norway, and Sweden). By increasing the number of "entree points," we expect the fragmentation of governmental authority to expand the potential for state-movement coalition formation (McCarthy and Wolfson 1992:287–92). Local governments offer social movements the potential for a more straightforward, hence quicker, path to policy channels (e.g., face-to-face interactions in publicly accessible city council meetings). Courts assist social movements by granting them a public forum for their views (with the cases themselves often eliciting important media coverage)." Courts also facilitate social movements by handing down decisions ordering changes (e.g., integrating schools). Finally courts can enjoin legislative action, rule on compensation settlements, and issue cease-and-desist orders.

That local government and court-movement coalitions can influence social policy has been effectively demonstrated in the United States in the case of the ban on same-sex marriages. During the late 1990s and early 2000s, the gay and lesbian movement took its case for equal access to marriage rights to the courts and local governments. It found support for its struggle in places such as Hawaii (courts), Vermont (courts), Massachusetts (courts), San Francisco (local government and courts), New Mexico (local government), and Oregon (local government). In 2004, San Francisco Mayor Gavin Newsom announced that the city would issue marriage licenses to same-sex couples. On four separate occasions, judges have refused to stop San Francisco from issuing marriage licenses to same-sex couples. When California Governor Schwarzenegger declared the licenses illegal, San Francisco city and county officials, with the help of such groups as Lambda Legal (a gay rights legal organization), went on the offensive and filed a lawsuit against the state. So successful has the gay and lesbian movement's tactic to change social policy at the local government and court levels been that President Bush announced his support for a Constitutional amendment to define marriage as the legal union between one man and one woman. In a February 2004 press speech, the President referred several times to "activist judges and local authorities" and stated that, "unless action is taken, we can expect more arbitrary court decisions, more litigation, more defiance of the law by local officials" (CNN.com 2004). Below, we specify the mechanisms that bring local governments and courts into coalitions with social movements.

Local Government. Municipal governments are generally more likely to enter coalitions with social movements than national governments because of the more volatile nature of local elections. At the local level, a social movement needs to mobilize fewer voters to have an electoral impact. In addition, campaign financing by more powerful lobbying groups is less common at the local level, providing a relatively more balanced playing field for reform-minded movements (Pollin and Luce 1998; Wolfson 2001:173–6).

The likelihood that a social movement will form a coalition with a local government is greatest when the social movement's cause has a widespread, direct, and negative effect on the locality, as in the case of toxic dumps and plant layoffs. The greater the consensus within the community that a problem exists, the more likely the social movement will form a state-movement coalition (Lofland 1989; McCarthy and Wolfson 1992) with an established local political party (Swarts 2003). If the established party refuses to take up its cause, a social movement will align itself with a reform party or run their own candidates. This was the strategy of the Chicano civil rights movement in south Texas in the 1960s and 1970s. Mexican Americans created their own slates of candidates and political parties (e.g., PASSO and La Raza Unida) to compete in city council and school board elections long held by white minorities (Navarro 1998).

If a local government-movement coalition is successful implementing reform (and this is never easy given the embeddedness of political and economic power and the outsider status of challenger movements), it provides a commanding example. Success imparts a template for change and a sense of efficacy—"it can be done!" Both strengthen a social movement's mobilization efforts (Klandermans 1997) and encourage further local government-movement coalitions. For example, Robert Pollin and Stephanie Luce (1998) show in the United States that campaigns for a living wage have rapidly multiplied as a result of local government-movement coalition victories. In 1999 only five years after the passage of the first local living wage ordinance in Baltimore, 22 other major cities had implemented similar statutes, including New York and Los Angeles (Martin 2001). By 2003, 112 cities, towns, and school districts had enacted such laws. Hanspeter Kriesi and Dominique Wisler (1999) also demonstrated that the movement for direct democracy laws (e.g., direct legislation and popular referendum) in Switzerland spread rapidly across cantons in the late nineteenth century once they were adopted in the canton of Zurich. The actual practice of direct democracy laws at the local level gave them "empirical credibility" for national diffusion and eventual enactment at the federal level.

Courts. Social movements often try to engage the court system. Social movement-court coalitions differ from state agency-, opposition party-, or local government-coalitions in that courts do not, nor can they, seek out or maintain an ongoing relation with a social movement. Because courts must maintain an appearance of neutrality, if a social movement-court coalition is to form, it is the social movement that must initiate and set the agenda for the relation. Nevertheless, courts are very important coalition partners for furthering the claims of social movements. This is demonstrated by the fact that mature social movements maintain their own legal organization(s) (e.g., abortion rights: National Abortion Rights Action League; environmental movement: National Resources Defense Council; etc.).

While the rationale of lifetime appointments is to guarantee impartial judicial officials, judges vary in their ability and desire to be neutral. The political intensity surrounding judicial appointments attests to this. For example, in the United States, the Republican and Democratic Parties consistently battle over the selection of judges. Furthermore, U.S.

presidents have on occasion taken control over the process to guarantee the assignment of their selected candidates. In 2004, during a congressional recess, President Bush did an end run around the "advise and consent" clause of the Constitution by appointing two conservative judges the Senate failed to confirm—Charles Pickering and William Pryor.

By initiating cases, social movements attempt to address immediate grievances, receive monetary compensation, and most importantly set legal precedent (Burstein 1991; McCammon and Kane 1997). For example, Lambda Legal litigated a case for marriage equality in Hawaii in the mid-1990s. In the first ruling of its kind, a Hawaii judge ordered that civil marriage licenses could not be restricted to heterosexual couples. Although a voter initiative later quashed the ruling, Lambda Legal (2004) went on to serve as a "friend of the court" in similar lawsuits in Vermont and Massachusetts. These actions led to civil unions for same-sex couples in Vermont and the order for the issuance of marriage licenses to applicants of the same gender by May 2004 in Massachusetts.

The acceptance by a court to address a case brought by a social movement creates the opportunity for a court-movement coalition to develop. While it is unlikely that any judge or court would openly acknowledge an ideological leaning, historical accounts (e.g., the liberal Warren court) and present day events (e.g., the Supreme Court's involvement in the 2000 Florida election decision) led social scientists to question otherwise. Once a social movement's case is accepted by a court, it can expect at minimum to have its claims given public voice, and at maximum, if successful, some action granted (Kane 2003).

In sum, the relative autonomy and greater access of court systems and local governments increase the likelihood for coalitions to form between these units and a social movement. Furthermore, the formation of a successful local government-movement coalition can lead to other local government-movement coalitions (Martin 2001).

Power in Numbers

Finally, by creating as many state-movement coalitions as possible, a social movement increases its probability of having its demands addressed. For example, recent cross-national work on environmental organizations suggests that environmental movements try to influence public opinion and to establish on-going relations with multiple state actors including state agencies, political parties, local governments, and courts. According to Russell Dalton and associates (2003:751) in a study of 248 environmental groups in 59 nations, they report: 1) 64 percent of environment groups claimed that they had made efforts to mobilize public opinion; 2) 51 percent had informal meetings with civil servants or government ministers while 39 percent had formal meetings; 3) 44 percent participated in government advisory commissions; 4) 45 percent reported contact with local government

authorities; 5) 15 percent acknowledged having contact with officials of political parties; and 6) 15 percent reported taking legal action through the courts or other judicial bodies.

We contend that there is power in numbers. First, with more than one coalition, a social movement cannot be relegated to a single "institutional home" or ineffectual state agency (Bonastia 2000). Second, the more coalitions formed across different state structures, the more entree points a social movement has to strategically apply and sustain pressure. Third, a greater number of coalitions helps to decrease the impact of a veto or unfavorable ruling by state actors in political structures where authoritative power is fragmented. Finally, multiple coalitions can have an additive effect, increasing the potential impact of each individual coalition.

Although we believe that a coordinated effort among coalitions increases their political impact, such an effort is not always possible. State-movement coalitions are not only loosely coupled within themselves but between themselves as well. Often the only common denominator among coalitions is the social movement and its goals. This is because each group of state actors enters into a coalition with its own interests and agenda.

It is also not necessary for all four types of coalitions to be present for positive national policy outcomes to occur. At minimum a state-movement coalition must exist with a national level state actor (state agency, opposition political party, or national court). The reason being, there has to be within the national state apparatus a coalition member with access to the organizational resources, legitimacy, and most important, authority required to usher through (state agency and/or opposition party) or decree (courts) national policy reforms (Burstein et al. 1995:284). Local coalition partners (government, opposition party, or court), while important as examples of change, are ultimately limited by the geographical scope of their authority.

The more entrenched the in-power party, however, the greater the need for multiple coalitions. In such cases, court and local government-movement coalitions help to chip away at the hold of the ruling party. Court-movement coalitions increase the costs (in terms of dollars, mass-media coverage, and public opinion) of government inaction; local government-movement coalitions provide a blueprint for change (in terms of electoral shifts and models of policy reform).

It should also be noted that state actors in general have more direct access to the media, and are more likely to be perceived as authorities regarding a policy conflict, than are social movement activists by themselves (Best 1989). Hence, social movements that form coalitions with state actors can expect to reach a much wider audience via the mass media, as the media is more willing to listen to sympathetic governmental authorities, especially when public policy is being debated.

In summary, we believe state agency-, oppositional party-, local government-, and court-movement coalitions all play key roles in bringing about shifts in social policy that favorably address the demands of social movements. We expect the greater the number of state-movement coalitions (i.e., state agency, oppositional party, local government, and court) present, the more likely policy change will occur. . . .

Conclusion

Even into the late 1990s and early 2000s several notable review, empirical, and theoretical articles on movement impacts and consequences concurred that the study of movement outcomes is much more underdeveloped than studies focusing on movement emergence, recruitment, tactical choices, and the mobilization process (see Amenta and Young 1999b:22; Andrews 2002:105; Burstein et al. 1995:276; Cress and Snow 2000:1063–4; Giugni 1998:373; Giugni 1999:xiv–xv; Meyer 2002:6). We believe the kinds of state actor-social movement coalitions found in this case provide a useful framework to advance the study of policy outcomes of state-oriented social movements. Political process models of social movements have long noted the importance of influential and elite allies (e.g., scientific and legal experts, mass media, other social movements, celebrities, etc.) for explaining movement outcomes. Indeed, as Edwin Amenta and Michael Young (1999b) note, "challengers are rarely alone in pressing for collective benefits for a group".

This study suggests that a focus on state-centered allies may be the most fruitful avenue for understanding the variation in the level of policy reform achieved by national social movements. The most successful movements of the past few decades (e.g., civil rights, women's rights, environmental, and anti-nuclear/peace movements) seem to have generated similar kinds of multiple state actor-social movement relations as observed in Japan in the late 1960s and early 1970s. That is, they entered into loose coalitions with the courts, local governments, state agencies, and political parties to enact policy change (Burstein 1991; Costain 1992; Meyer and Marullo 1992; Sawyers and Meyer 1999). Along these lines, scholars are increasingly examining the relationship between social movements and state actors (e.g., courts, political parties, legislatures, and institutional activists) to explain the variation in policy outcomes (see Burstein 1991; Goldstone 2003; Kane 2003; McCammon and Kane 1997; Santoro and McGuire 1997; Wolfson 2001). Not only do we concur with this recent trend of analyzing the intersection of specific state actors and social movements to understand differential levels of policy change, but also propose that the existence of multiple coalitions between state actors and social movements greatly raises the probability that favorable policy implementation occurs.

Favorable policy outcomes range from the state's acceptance of demands, placing them on the policy agenda to adopting new policies and finally implementing them (Burstein et al. 1995:283–5). The present study suggests that state actor-movement coalitions may be indispensable at each stage of the policy reform process as well as increasing the likelihood of more substantive enactment—beyond mere symbolic gestures.

Courts, political parties, and sympathetic state agencies all have the capacity to place social movement policy issues on the political agenda for further political debate/deliberation. Political parties and state agencies have the bureaucratic power to get new laws passed. State agencies are the primary sources for policy implementation. At the local level, city councils and regional governments have the ability to push through all stages of the policy process within their delimited jurisdictions. Local policy enactment and implementation provide both viable models (Martin 2001) and increasing pressure for national level state actors to move in the same direction for policy reform on the issue in question (Kriesi and Wisler 1999:53–6). Courts have the ability to order changes as well as issue cease-and-desist orders, award compensation settlements, and call for legislative action. Furthermore court actions establish legal precedents.

Although the cultural context of policymaking and the strong and enduring presence of the LDP are unique to Japan, we believe our framework may be useful to help explain policy outcomes in other democratic settings. Variation among democratic state structures would obviously have important implications for the kinds of state actor-social movement coalitions likely to form, and which coalitions would be most efficacious in terms of policy change. For example, parliamentary systems with multi-party competition provide greater potential for the establishment of opposition party-movement coalitions (Kitschelt 1986; Kriesi et al. 1995), as is the case for several European and Latin American polities in the contemporary period. Furthermore, democratic states integrated into the world system of emerging global standards (e.g., environmental quality, health, human rights, and labor protections) with large bureaucracies are more likely to house state agencies that specialize in institutional credibility and legitimacy (Meyer et al. 1997). It is precisely such state agencies where reform-minded social movements may find receptive allies to push forward policy changes.

Legal systems also vary across democratic polities in terms of their autonomy and political strength. The fact that Japan's court system was relatively marginal demonstrates the potential power (symbolic and real) of courts even in states where they have historically been weak. Lastly, the power of local and regional governments depends on the level of national government centralization. We expect federalist political structures (e.g., Brazil, Canada, India, New Zealand, Switzerland, and the United States) that give more power to local governments than top-down centralized governments (e.g., Austria, France, Norway, and Sweden) would supply greater potential for social movements to form coalitions with them (Amenta and Young 1999a; Andrews 2001:90; Baiocchi 2003; Martin 2001).

Besides variations in national political structures, the pattern of state actor-movement coalitions and policy reform will also vary by the type of state-oriented social movement under consideration. Once a movement is relatively powerful with widespread mass media and public opinion support, it will more likely find sympathetic state actors that fall within its issue domain. Thus labor-based movements will more likely coalesce with ministries of labor and/or occupational health agencies, gender and ethnic-based movements will find more support within anti-discrimination offices of the modern state, while environmental movements form coalitional relations with environmental and public health agencies. Opposition political parties are also more prone to align with movements closer to their ideological platforms (Rucht 1999) (e.g., green parties with environmental movements; labor parties with labor-based movements). Courts and local governments, on the other hand, are more catholic and potentially penetrable by a variety of state-oriented social movements.

The claims made in the present analysis regarding the efficacy of state actor-movement coalitions require further study in other polities and with different kinds of state-oriented social movements. Comparative and quantitative designs may be especially informative when they include cases of both successful and failed social movements in terms of achieving policy reform (Cress and Snow 2000; Giugni 1999:xxiv). Analysts should give special attention to the kinds of state actor-movement coalitions that form (courts, local governments, political parties, and state agencies) as well as the overall number of state actor-movement coalitions for each of the compared cases in order to decipher if these variations result in differential rates of movement success. Additionally, scholars may want to expand the theoretical scope of state actor-movement coalitions to incorporate cases in which the policy conflict includes a well-organized countermovement (Meyer and Staggenborg 1996) that also forges ties to state actors. Such settings may include coalitions between economic elites and state actors that shape policy-making.

Finally, while this article has introduced the cumulative effect of multiple state actor-social movement coalitions with regards to promoting new policy reforms, the same thesis might be useful in analyzing the ability of coalitions to prevent unwanted policy retrenchments (Reese 1996) (e.g., welfare state cutbacks, pension system economizing, and public sector privatization schemes). Political conflicts involving policy retrenchments increasingly characterize the period of neo-liberal economic reform around the globe (Almeida 2002; Korpi and Palme 2003). Analyzing the kinds of defensive state actor-social movement partnerships that coalesce to prevent such "reforms" may help to explain the variation in the pace of such policy changes within and between countries in democratic polities in the late twentieth and early twenty-first centuries.

References

Almeida, Paul D. 2003. "Opportunity Organizations and Threat Induced Contention: Protest Waves in Authoritarian Settings." *American Journal of Sociology* 109:345–400.

_____. 2002. "Los Movimientos Populares contra las Politicas de Austeridad Economica en America Latina entre 1996 y 2001."

Realidad: Revista de Ciencias Sociales y Humanidades 86:177–89.

Almeida, Paul and Linda Brewster Stearns. 1998. "Political Opportunities and Local Grassroots Environmental Movements: The Case of Minamata." *Social Problems* 45:37–60.

Amenta, Edwin. 1991. "Making the Most of a Case Study: Theories of the Welfare State and the American Experience." *International Journal of Comparative Sociology* 32: 172–94.

_____. 1998. *Bold Relief: Institutional Politics and the Origins of Modern American Policy.* Princeton, NJ: Princeton University Press.

Amenta, Edwin, Kathleen Dunleavy, and Mary Bernstein. 1994. "Stolen Thunder? Huey Long's 'Share Our Wealth,' Political Mediation, and the Second New Deal." *American Sociological Review* 59:678–702.

Amenta, Edwin and Michael Young. 1999a. "Democratic States and Social Movements: Theoretical Arguments and Hypotheses." *Social Problems* 46:153–68.

_____. 1999b. "Making an Impact: Conceptual and Methodological Implications of the Collective Goods Criterion." pp. 22–41 in *How Social Movements Matter,* edited by Marco Giugni, Doug McAdam, and Charles Tilly. Minneapolis: University of Minnesota Press.

Amenta, Edwin and Yvonne Zylan. 1991. "It Happened Here: Political Opportunity, the New Institutionalism, and the Townsend Movement." *American Sociological Review* 56:250–65.

Andrews, Kenneth. 2001. "Social Movements and Policy Implementation: The Mississippi Civil Rights Movement and the War on Poverty." *American Sociological Review* 66:71–95.

_____. 2002. "Creating Social Change: Lessons from the Civil Rights Movement." pp. 105–17 in *Social Movements: Identity, Culture, and the State,* edited by David S. Meyer, Nancy Whittier, and Belinda Robnett. Oxford: Oxford University Press.

Apter, David and Nagayo Sawa. 1984. *Against the State: Politics and Social Protest in Japan.* Cambridge, MA: Harvard University Press.

Baiocchi, Gianpaolo. 2003. "Emergent Public Spheres: Talking Politics in Participatory Governance." *American Sociological Review* 68:52–74.

Barrett, Brendan and Riki Therivel. 1991. *Environmental Policy and Impact Assessment in Japan.* London: Routledge.

Baumgartner, Frank R. and Bryan D. Jones. 1993. *Agendas and Instability in American Politics.* Chicago: University of Chicago Press.

Best, Joel. 1989. "Secondary Claims-Making: Claims about Threats to Children on the Network News." *Perspectives on Social Problems* 1:259–82.

Block, Fred. 1987. *Revising State Theory.* Philadelphia: Temple University Press.

Bonastia, Chris. 2000. "Why Did Affirmative Action in Housing Fail during the Nixon Era? Exploring the 'Institutional Homes' of Social Policies." *Social Problems* 47:523–42.

Bourdieu, Pierre. 1998. *Acts of Resistance: Against the Tyranny of the Market.* New York: New Press.

Bradshaw, York and Michael Wallace. 1991. "Informing Generality and Explaining Uniqueness: The Place of Case Studies in Comparative Research." *International Journal of Comparative Sociology* 32:154–71.

Broadbent, Jeffrey. 1998. *Environmental Politics in Japan: Networks of Power and Protest.* Cambridge: Cambridge University Press.

Burstein, Paul. 1979. "Public Opinion, Demonstrations, and the Passage of Anti-Discrimination Legislation." *Public Opinion Quarterly* 43:157–72.

_____. 1991. "Legal Mobilization as a Social Movement Tactic: The Struggle for Equal Employment Opportunity." *American Journal of Sociology* 96:1202–25.

Burstein, Paul, Rachel Einwohner, and Jocelyn A. Hollander. 1995. "The Success of Political Movements: A Bargaining Perspective." pp. 275–95 in *The Politics of Social Protest: Comparative Perspectives on States and Social Movements,* edited by J. Craig Jenkins and Bert Klandermans. Minneapolis: University of Minnesota Press.

CNN.com. 2004. "Transcript of Bush Statement." CNN.com. February 24. Retrieved April 17, 2004 (http://www.cnn.com/2004/ALLPOLITICS/02/24/elecO4.prez.bush.transcript/).

Costain, Anne N. 1992. *Inviting Women's Rebellion: A Political Process Interpretation of the Women's Movement.* Baltimore: Johns Hopkins University Press.

Cress, Daniel and David Snow. 2000. "The Outcomes of Homeless Mobilization: The Influence of Organization, Disruption, Political Mediation, and Framing." *American Journal of Sociology* 105:1063–104.

Dalton, Russell J., Steve Recchia, and Robert Rohrschneider. 2003. "The Environmental Movement and the Modes of Political Action." *Comparative Political Studies* 36:743–71.

Diamond, Larry. 1999. *Developing Democracy: Toward Consolidation.* Baltimore, MD: Johns Hopkins University Press.

Domhoff, G. William. 2002. *Who Rules America?* 4th ed. Columbus, OH: McGraw-Hill.

Environment Agency. 1974. *Quality of the Environment in Japan.* Tokyo: Ministry of Finance.

_____. 1977. *Quality of the Environment in Japan.* Tokyo: Ministry of Finance.

_____. 1978. *Quality of the Environment in Japan.* Tokyo: Ministry of Finance.

Faber, Daniel and James O'Connor. 1989. "The Struggle for Nature: Environmental Crises and the Crisis of Environmentalism in the United States." *Capitalism Nature Socialism* 2:12–39.

Frank, David John, Ann Hironaka, and Evan Schofer. 2000. "The Nation-State and the Natural Environment over the Twentieth Century." *American Sociological Review* 65:96–116.

Gamson, William A. 1990. *Strategy of Social Protest.* 2d ed. Belmont, CA: Wadsworth Publishing.

Ganz, Marshall. 2000. "Resources and Resourcefulness: Strategic Capacity in the Unionization of California Agriculture, 1959–1966." *American Journal of Sociology* 105:1003–62.

Giugni, Marco. 1998. "Was It Worth the Effort? The Outcomes and Consequences of Social Movements." *Annual Review of Sociology* 24:371–93.

_____. 1999. "How Social Movements Matter: Past Research, Present Problems, Future Developments." pp. xiii–xxxiii in How Social Movements Matter, edited by Marco Giugni, Doug McAdam, and Charles Tilly. Minneapolis: University of Minnesota Press.

Goldstone, Jack A. 2003. "Introduction: Bridging Institutionalized and Noninstitutionalized Politics." pp. 1–24 in *States, Parties, and Social Movements,* edited by Jack Goldstone. Cambridge: Cambridge University Press.

Gresser, Julian, Koichiro Fujikara and Akio Morishima. 1981. *Environmental Law in Japan.* Cambridge, MA: MIT Press.

Huddle, Norrie and Michael Reich. 1975. *Island of Dreams: Environmental Crisis in Japan.* New York: Autumn Press.

Iijima, Nobuko. 1979. *Pollution Japan: Historical Chronology.* Tokyo: Asahi Evening News.

Kane, Melinda D. 2003. "Social Movement Policy Success: Decriminalizing State Sodomy Laws, 1969–1998." *Mobilization* 8:313–34.

Kitschelt, Herbert P. 1986. "Political Opportunity Structures and Political Protest: Anti-Nuclear Movements in Four Democracies." *British Journal of Political Science* 16:57–85.

Klandermans, Bert. 1997. *The Social Psychology of Protest.* Oxford: Blackwell Publishers.

Kondo, Shozo. 1981. "Summary Procedures for the Settlement of Pollution Cases." pp. 103–12 in *Environmental Law and Policy in the Pacific Basin Area,* edited by Ichiro Kato, Nobio Kumamoto, and William H. Mathews. Tokyo: University of Tokyo Press.

Koopmans, Ruud. 1995. *Democracy from Below: New Social Movements and the Political System in Germany.* Boulder, CO: Westview Press.

Korpi, Walter and Joakim Palme. 2003. "New Politics and Class Politics in the Context of Austerity and Globalization: Welfare State Regress in 18 Countries, 1975–1995." *American Political Science Review* 97:425–46.

Krauss, Ellis and Bradford Simcock. 1980. "Citizens' Movements: The Growth and Impact of Environmental Protest in Japan." pp. 187–227 in *Political Opposition and Local Politics in Japan,* edited by Kurt Steiner, Ellis S. Krauss, and Scott C. Flanagan. Princeton, NJ: Princeton University Press.

Kriesi, Hanspeter, Ruud Koopmans, Jan-Willem Duyvendak, and Marco G. Giugni. 1995. *The Politics of New Social Movements in Western Europe: A Comparative Analysis.* Minneapolis: University of Minnesota Press.

Kriesi, Hanspeter and Dominique Wisler. 1999. "The Impact of Social Movements on Political Institutions: A Comparison of the Introduction of Direct Legislation in Switzerland and the United States." pp. 42–65 in *How Social Movements Matter,* edited by Marco Giugni, Doug McAdam, and Charles Tilly. Minneapolis: University of Minnesota Press.

Lambda Legal Defense Fund. 2004. "Background and Pending Cases Seeking Full Equity for Gay Couples." Lambda Legal. Retrieved June 8, 2004 (http://www.lambdalegal.org/cgi-bin/iowa/documents/record?record= 1459).

Lewis, Jack G. 1980. "Civic Protest in Mishima: Citizens' Movements and the Politics of the Environment in Contemporary Japan." pp. 274–313 in *Political Opposition and Local Politics in Japan,* edited by Kurt Steiner, Ellis S. Krauss, and Scott C. Flanagan. Princeton, NJ: Princeton University Press.

Lofland, John. 1989. "Consensus Movements: City Twinning and Derailed Dissent in the American Eighties." *Research in Social Movements, Conflict and Change* 11:163–96.

MacDougall, Terry E. 1976. "Japanese Urban Local Politics: Toward a Viable Progressive Political Opposition." pp. 31–56 in *Japan: The Paradox of Power,* edited by Lewis Austin. New Haven, CT: Yale University Press.

Maguire, Diarmuid. 1995. "Opposition Movements and Opposition Parties: Equal Partners or Dependent Relations in the Struggle for Power and Reform." pp. 199–228 in *The Politics of Social*

Protest: Comparative Perspectives on States and Social Movements, edited by J. Craig Jenkins and Bert Klandermans. Minneapolis: University of Minnesota Press.

Martin, Isaac. 2001. "Dawn of the Living Wage: The Diffusion of a Redistributive Municipal Policy." *Urban Affairs Review* 36:470–96.

Matsui, Saburo. 1992. *Industrial Pollution Control in Japan: A Historical Perspective.* Tokyo: Asian Productivity Organization.

McAdam, Doug. 1996. "Conceptual Origins, Current Problems, Future Directions." pp. 23–40 in *Comparative Perspectives on Social Movements: Political Opportunities, Mobilizing Structures, and Cultural Framings,* edited by Doug McAdam, John D. McCarthy, and Mayer N. Zald. Cambridge: Cambridge University Press.

McCammon, Holly and Melinda Kane. 1997. "Shaping Judicial Law in the Post-World War II Period: When Is Labor's Legal Mobilization Successful." *Sociological Inquiry* 67:27 5–98.

McCarthy, John D. and Mark Wolfson. 1992. "Consensus Movements, Conflict Movements, and the Cooptation of Civic and State Infrastructures." pp. 273–97 in *Frontiers in Social Movement Theory,* edited by Aldon D. Morris and Carol M. Mueller. New Haven, CT: Yale University Press.

McKean, Margaret. 1977. "Pollution and Policymaking." pp. 201–38 in *Policymaking in Contemporary Japan,* edited by T. J. Pempel. Ithaca, NY: Cornell University Press.

_____. 1981. *Environmental Protest in Japan.* Berkeley, CA: University of California Press.

Meyer, David S. 2002. "Opportunities and Identities: Bridge-Building in the Study of Social Movements." pp. 3–21 in *Social Movements: Identity, Culture, and the State,* edited by David S. Meyer, Nancy Whittier, and Belinda Robnett. Oxford: Oxford University Press.

Meyer, David S. and Suzanne Staggenborg. 1996. "Movements, Countermovements, and the Structure of Political Opportunity." *American Journal of Sociology* 101:1628–60.

Meyer, David S. and Sam Marullo. 1992. "Grassroots Mobilization and International Politics: Peace Protest and the End of the Cold War." *Research in Social Movements, Conflicts, and Change* 14:99–140.

Meyer, John W., John Boli, George M. Thomas, and Francisco O. Ramirez. 1997. "World Society and the NationState." *American Journal of Sociology* 103:144–81.

Miyamoto, Keiichi. 1991. "Japanese Environmental Policies Since World War II." *Capitalism Nature Socialism* 2:71–100.

Morishima, Akio. 1981. "Japanese Environmental Policy and Law." pp. 77–84 in *Environmental Law and Policy in the Pacific Basin Area,* edited by Ichiro Kato, Nobio Kumamoto, and W.H. Mathews. Tokyo: University of Tokyo Press.

Navarro, Armando. 1998. *The Cristal Experiment: A Chicano Struggle for Community Control.* Madison: University of Wisconsin Press.

Organization for Economic Co-operation and Development (OECD). 1977. *Environmental Policies in Japan.* Paris: OECD.

_____. 1994. *OECD Performance Reviews: Japan.* Paris: OECD.

Piven, Frances Fox and Richard A. Cloward. 1979. *Poor People's Movements: Why They Succeed, How They Fail.* New York: Vintage.

Pollin, Robert and Stephanie Luce. 1998. *The Living Wage: Building a Fair Economy.* New York: The New Press.

Reed, Steven. 1981. "Environmental Politics: Some Reflections Based on the Japanese Case." *Comparative Politics* 13:253–70.

Reese, Ellen. 1996. "Maternalism and Political Mobilization: How California's Postwar Childcare Campaign was Won." *Gender and Society* 10:566–89.

Reich, Michael. 1983. "Environmental Policy and Japanese Society: Part II, Lessons about Japan and about Policy." *International Journal of Environmental Policy* 20:199–207.

_____. 1984a. "Mobilizing for Environmental Policy in Italy and Japan." *Comparative Politics* 16:379–402.

_____. 1984b. "Crisis and Routine: Pollution Reporting by the Japanese Press." pp. 148–65 in *Institutions for Change in Japanese Society,* edited by George De Vos. Berkeley, CA: Institute for East Asian Studies.

_____. 1991. *Toxic Politics: Responding to Chemical Disasters.* Ithaca, NY: Cornell University Press.

Reischauer, Edwin O. 1988. *The Japanese Today: Change and Continuity.* Cambridge, MA: Belknap Press.

Rucht, Dieter. 1999. "The Impact of Environmental Movements in Western Societies." pp. 204–24 in *How Social Movements Matter,* edited by Marco Giugni, Doug McAdam, and Charles Tilly. Minneapolis: University of Minnesota Press.

Santoro, Wayne A. and Gail M. McGuire. 1997. "Social Movement Insiders: The Impact of Institutional Activists on Affirmative Action and Comparable Worth Policies." Social Problems 44:503–19.

Sawyers, Traci M. and David S. Meyer. 1999. "Missed Opportunities: Social Movement Abeyance and Public Policy." *Social Problems* 46:187–206.

Schuld, Leslie. 2003. "El Salvador: Who Will Save the Hospitals?" *NACLA Report on the Americas* 21:42–5.

Skocpol, Theda. 1985. "Bringing the State Back In: Strategies of Analysis in Current Research." pp. 3–37 in *Bringing the State Back In,* edited by Peter B. Evans, Dietrich Rueschemeyer, and Theda Skocpol. New York: Cambridge University Press.

Snow, David and Robert Benford. 1992. "Master Frames and Cycles of Protest." pp. 133–55 in *Frontiers in Social Movement Theory,* edited by Aldon D. Morris and Carol M. Mueller. New Haven, CT: Yale University Press.

Steiner, Kurt. 1980. "Progressive Local Administrations: Local Public Policy and Local-National Relations." pp. 317–52 in *Political Opposition and Local Politics in Japan,* edited by Kurt Steiner, Ellis S. Krauss, and Scott C. Flanagan. Princeton, NJ: Princeton University Press.

Stinchcombe, Arthur. 1965. "Social Structure and Organizations." pp. 142–93 in *Handbook of Organizations,* edited by James G. March. Chicago: Rand-McNally.

Sumisato, Arima and Imazu Hiroshi. 1977. "The Opposition Parties: Organizations and Policies." *Japan Quarterly* 24:148–84.

Swarts, Heidi J. 2003. "Setting the State's Agenda: Church-Based Community Organizations in American Urban Politics." pp. 78–106 in *States, Parties, and Social Movements, edited by Jack Goldstone.* Cambridge: Cambridge University Press.

Szasz, Andrew. 1994. *Ecopopulism: Toxic Waste and the Movement for Environmental Justice.* Minneapolis: University of Minnesota Press.

Tarrow, Sidney. 1994. *Power in Movement.* Cambridge: Cambridge University Press.

Tilly, Charles. 1978. *From Mobilization to Revolution.* Reading, MA: Addison-Wesley.

Tsuru, Shigeto. 1970. *International Symposium on Environmental Disruption in the Modern World.* Tokyo: International Social Science Council.

Tsurutani, Taketsugu. 1977. *Political Change in Japan.* New York: David McKay.

Upham, Frank. 1976. "Litigation and Moral Consciousness in Japan: An Interpretive Analysis of Four Japanese Pollution Suits." *Law and Society Review* 10:579–619.

_____. 1987. *Law and Social Change in Postwar Japan.* Cambridge, MA: Harvard University Press.

Vogel, Ezra. 1980. *Japan as Number One: Lessons for America.* New York: Harper Colophon Books.

Weidner, Helmut. 1986. "Japan: The Success and Limitations of Technocratic Environmental Policy." *Policy and Politics* 14:43–70.

Wolfson, Mark. 2001. *The Fight Against Big Tobacco: The Movement, the State, and the Public's Health.* Hawthorne, NY: Aldine de Gruyter.

What Drives Health Policy Formulation: Insights from the Nepal Maternity Incentive Scheme?

TIM ENSOR, SUSAN CLAPHAM, AND DEVI PRASAD PRASAI

1. Introduction and Background

Maternal health remains a central policy concern in Nepal. A recently published 3 year interim plan embeds within overall development, advancement of the status of women including improvement of women's health and a target for a reduction in the national maternal mortality ratio (MMR) [1]. Over the last decade Nepal has made substantial progress in improving maternal health. The recent DHS suggested that the maternal mortality ratio has fallen from 539 to 281 per 100,000 live births [2]. Although a welcome decline, this still equates to an estimated six women a day dying from pregnancy related causes. In addition, debate continues over the true extent of the decline since wide (95%) confidence intervals means that the upper bound of earlier (1989–1995) estimates almost overlap with more recent (1999–2005) study. The size and determinants of the decline are now the subject of further exploration. Although improving, maternal service delivery utilisation remains low: skilled birth attendance is only 19% (although a 70% increase over 5 years), 18% of women delivered in a facility (this has doubled in 5 years) while 31% received post-natal and 44% received antenatal care [2], Recent estimates put skilled attendance rates at just 7% in mountainous areas [3].

It is generally thought that high financial cost is a major barrier in seeking and utilising delivery care, particularly in remote areas. To measure the importance of this barrier and to generate evidence to inform the national skilled attendance strategy that was at the time being developed by the Ministry of Health and Population (MOHP), Nepal Safer Motherhood Project (1997–2004) commissioned a study on the financial implications of skilled attendance at delivery.

Since the publication of the study, policy interest in the area moved swiftly. Skilled birth attendance became a major issue in 2001, the research on financing was commissioned in 2003 and a policy was implemented across the country in the middle of 2005. This paper does not focus on the research itself which is described elsewhere [4]. Rather it attempts to analyse why the results of the research appeared to influence policy so rapidly. Following a brief review of the literature on policy impact of research, we describe the main events that led to the adoption of the Safe Delivery Incentive Programme (SDIP) (it was given this name late in 2007, previously it was known the Maternity Incentives Scheme). In subsequent sections we attempt to analyse the main factors that appeared to influence policy based on a series of key informant interviews. The discussion section highlights implications of these findings for the way research is used in Nepal and elsewhere.

2. Literature Review: The Role of Research in Policy Development

The issue of how best to get research evidence to influence policy is one that has for long vexed bureaucrats, donors and, perhaps belatedly, researchers. Too often the experience of research is to find long reports consigned to dusty shelves in government and donor offices. A recent article juxtaposed two stereotypical images: the researcher as independent scientist with a focus on the production of robust evidence in a narrow field with publication as the ultimate verification of achievement, versus the policy maker as a Mr/Ms "Fix it" with a wide mandate to seek quick, workable solutions to current problems often based on compromise [5]. These are polar stereotypes with many in both groups sitting somewhere in between but they do help to explain how the incentives of each 'profession' might work to produce quite different results.

Studying the factors that help to facilitate the use of research findings into policy tends to be an imprecise endeavour, requiring a dialogue with key informants that attempt to identify and, if possible, weight the main reasons that lead to the research being used or abandoned. Among the constellation of factors that can assist or hinder the use of research findings a small number have been identified as particularly important. A recent systematic review of articles exploring the attitudes of policy makers to research highlighted the timeliness and relevance of research findings to problem policy areas, the importance of continuous and personal communication of results with key policy makers and a clear and simple explanation of findings and implications for policy [6]. The ODI Research and Policy in Development project (RAPID) and a recent review for DFID arrived at similar conclusions [7,8].

Much research is pre-planned and can take a substantial period to initiate. This does not necessarily fit well with policy and political calendars that usually require results that address current issues in a timely way. Although focusing too much on the political agenda runs the risk of discarding the important in favour of the urgent, all recent analyses suggest that more attention is paid to research that is stimulated by policy needs.

The Mwanza RCT in Tanzania is frequently cited as an important example of the impact of striking research on policy. The RCT reported a substantial reduction in HIV incidence from improved case management of STIs; although subsequent study of the impact of an expanded programme has shed doubt on this initial finding. The RCT results were quickly accepted by policy makers to form the basis of the national strategy. Subsequent policy analysis suggested three factors that were important in the rapid conversion of research results into policy: a favourable policy environment, effective strategic alliances between researchers and policy makers and the presentation of results in an easily digestible format [9]. Commentators suggest that the research experience of Mwanza 'fell into a ready made bed'. Donors were able to mobilise flexible funding for a national roll out while both donors and policy makers were looking for positive ways to stem rapidly rising HIV prevalence.

The importance of communication by researchers with policy makers is reflected in the literature in a number of different ways. For some the key is to ensure that researchers are based in country and have regular dialogue with policy makers [9]. The danger of researcher capture is the obverse of this when policy makers and researchers are so closely associated that it is not clear who is leading the production of results. Sometimes research that actively challenges an existing consensus may have substantial impact [8].

Problems also occur where scientists involved in the research fail to speak in the same 'language' as policy makers. In this case there may be a role for an intermediary or knowledge broker to facilitate communication [5]. Internal communication and advocacy within the policy-making apparatus is also vital. Shiffman highlights the importance of political entrepreneurship—a policy maker or someone close to policy making who is a respected and articulate proponent of a particular policy [10]. Such an entrepreneur will recognise how best to ensure that the political interests of policy makers (political expediency) are met through the development of policy.

Other experience suggests that an emphasis on one striking indicator can make a lasting impression on policy audiences. Continually publicising the high level of maternal mortality based in Indonesia helped to ensure that attention moved beyond one or two lone voices in government to a policy that was strongly supported and advocated at the highest level [10]. Similarly, the Mwanza experience was helped to prominence by offering evidence based on a single indicator of project effectiveness [9].

The importance of complementing 'pure research' evidence with best practice on the practical implementation of policy is highlighted in the case of impregnated bed-nets. Although good biomedical evidence had been available for years on the efficacy of utilising chemically treated bed-nets to reduce malaria, research projects were not scaled up largely due to practical problems of supplying nets and persuading people to use them. Further research focused not on the medical evidence but on implementation issues involved in ensuring that bed-nets were affordable, used and accessible to vulnerable groups [11]. This research helped to fill the gap between identification of efficacy and ensuring that this could be converted into an effective intervention.

The importance of backing evidence with strong intuitive ideas was emphasised by a noted macroeconomist (Lord Desai) who suggested that evidence is far less important than good ideas [12]. Desai uses the examples of the acceptance of Keynesian economic concepts and his own involvement in the development of the human development index, both of which were primarily 'ideas' based innovations without (initially) strong empirical evidence. This suggests that health researchers must be prepared to back up empirical evidence with strong, lucid and preferably simple theories to lead or justify empirical findings. This is particularly important where the findings are initially counter-intuitive to accepted wisdom.

Evidence on the impact of research on policy demonstrates that the association between cause and impact is not easy to isolate. Nevertheless a number of core messages are apparent among them the need to present clear results preferably based around a message or figure that resonates with current policy questions and recognises political expediency, to think through problems associated with implementation or at least develop a strategy for dealing with them and the need to identify potential 'champions' for the policy change.

3. The Development of the Safe Delivery Incentive Programme in Nepal

The priority placed on maternal health status by the Nepalese Government and donors led to investment in a 7 year DFID funded project managed by Options [13]. A consultation exercise was initiated to explore the reasons for inadequate access to services: cost was identified as one of five main barriers to care identified through participatory social analysis [14]. Despite the recognition of the importance of financial barriers, adequate evidence on the significance of costs compared to other barriers was lacking. Literature reviews showed that 75% of health care costs is borne by individuals [15-17]. A World Bank study demonstrated that the cost of emergency obstetric care is a major barrier to access, and concluded that most women would only seek care on their own accord if services were free [18]. An earlier study undertaken by the National Planning Commission showed that transport cost for safe delivery could be as high as NRs 1000 (US $13.3), a delivery without complications NRs 400 (US $5.3) and with complications NRs 800 (US $10.7) [19]. More recently, review work to generate data on the overall cost of essential services estimated a total cost of normal delivery of NS 1799 (US $3.8) based on publicly financed inputs [20]. An exit survey was carried out in 2003 which focused in particular on differences in the cost of services between private and public providers. The small sample size (60 interviews) meant that it was not possible to provide an estimate of costs of complicated delivery [21]. Thus while some evidence was available on the costs of care, small sample size, old data and lack of a consistent approach to valuing both facility and non-facility costs to households meant there was a need for a fresh look at the financial burden.

Study terms of reference and protocol were developed by NSMP in collaboration with the Health Economics and Financing Unit (HEFU) and Family Health Division (FHD) of Department of Health Services, MOHP. Findings were shared in early 2004 with the MOHP followed by dissemination to a wider audience of safe motherhood partners. This included the production of four topic based, "snappy" briefing papers aimed at policy makers (Appendix A).

The results, which showed the high cost (Box 1) particularly of transport, of obtaining delivery care alarmed the MOHP. Examining the cost from the point of view of the household presented a different and novel perspective to many health planners.

In June 2004 a new coalition government headed by the National Congress—Democratic party made the United Marxist Leninist (UML) party responsible for the a number of ministries including Health [22]. The UML had pledged a commitment to advancing the status of women in their manifesto and was seeking an early opportunity to fulfil this promise. In addition the then Prime Minister also committed to assisting the poor and in particular women. His wife was a women's activist and chaired the Safe Motherhood Network Federation Nepal (SMNF)—an organisation supporting 488 NGOs—which plays a critical role in the advocacy of women's health and rights [23].

Box 1: Key Findings from 'Coping with the Burden of the Costs of Maternal Health'

Objective: To measure facility and non-facility costs to households in 8 districts of Nepal and use the results to estimate the national cost of reducing the financial.
Methodology: A survey of women who had recently delivered both in the community and in facilities, based, for facility deliveries on a review of records, and, for all deliveries, a survey of facility and non-facility costs incurred.
Findings: The study found that the average cost to a household of a home delivery ranged from NR 410 (US $5.4) (with a friend or relative attending) to NR 879 (US $11.63) (with a health worker). While the facility costs of a normal delivery were not found to be significantly higher (around NR 678 or US $9), these are increased substantially when additional charges, opportunity and transport costs are added. Total costs to the household rise to more than NR 5000 (US $70). For a caesarean section the total household cost was more than 11 400 NR (US $150). The cost of a normal delivery in a facility for the poorest group is equal to more than 3 months of their household income, and more than 6 months for a caesarean section.
The study suggested that a policy of universal institutional delivery would cost NR 238 (US $3.15) per capita while a policy of skilled attendance at home with early referral of cases from remote areas would cost around NR 117 (US $1.55) per capita. These are significant sums in the context of a health budget of about NR 400 (US $5) per capita.
The study also included a review of health financing schemes in Nepal together with an international review of experience with different financing mechanisms in mitigating the costs of maternal health care [4].

Box 2: The Safe Delivery Incentive Programme

The policy is made up of three elements:

1. Cash incentives to women for attending a facility for delivery—Rs. 1500 (US $19.7) Mountainous districts, Rs. 1000 (US $13.1) Hill, Rs. 500 (US $6.6) Terai. This is paid to women at the time of delivery. Crucially facilities must have the capability to handle the amounts of cash required. Women continue to pay charges for delivery at the facility.
   The study found that the average transport cost in the Terai was just over NRS 1000 while for the Hill and Mountain area it was over NRS 3000. A principle of the scheme was cost sharing rather than full subsidy. The mountain cost is only similar to hill areas because women do not obtain the care they need and so do not travel to service providers. As a consequence the level of met need is very low in mountain areas and actual expenditure does not properly reflect the high cost. Hence the graduated amounts of 500, 1000 and 1500 that assume cost recovery and also increased utilisation particularly in mountainous areas.
2. Free delivery in the 25 poorest districts. No facility charges are made for any women delivering at the registered facilities. This benefit is given in addition to the cash incentives in these districts.
3. Incentive NR 300 to skilled birth attendants for delivery. Skilled birth attendants at facilities and in the community keep a record of deliveries attended and are reimbursed according to this record on a monthly basis.

The UML Health Minister asked senior officials to explore ways of improving women's health and a national committee was established. Following internal consultations the Committee, consisting of senior civil servants and economists in the MOHP, focused on reducing maternal costs. Maternal health interest groups were aware that a policy on maternal health costs was being discussed and increased their lobbying activity. The Finance Minister, for example, was invited to the Nursing Association of Nepal's annual conference and asked to prioritise the policy.

Work of the Committee was informed by a series of four briefing papers that were derived from the cost study. One of these presented the costs of potential delivery strategies [24]. Using this information, the Committee considered four options (i) free facility delivery care for the poor, (ii) free facility delivery services for all, (iii) provision of a matching funds to community based maternal and child health emergency funds[1] and (iv) cash-in-hand to all women who have a skilled birth at a facility. Based on an evaluation of management requirements, sustainability and ease of monitoring a decision was taken to support option (iv) which was initially termed the "transportation cost sharing approach" [25]. While option (ii) was favoured, this was deemed unaffordable while option (i) was rejected because it was felt public hospitals were not sufficiently attractive and transport costs were not addressed.

Given that emergency funds were not linked to a government financing mechanisms, option (iii) was determined impractical. The MOHP and Ministry of Finance (MOF) rejected a pilot or phased approach arguing that in the interests of equity the policy should be implemented nationwide, although political expediency to ensure that a policy was adopted as quickly as possible may have influenced this decision.

In December 2004 HEFU, in consultation with the principal investigator of the research study, undertook a costing for a 5-year period. It was estimated that the cost of the policy would be between Rs. 1.3 and Rs 0.95 billion (GBP 7.3–9.9 million). MOHP requested DFID to fund this through the successor programme to NSMP, the Support to the Safer Motherhood Programme (SSMP). Since this policy was not developed at the time of the programme negotiations it was not agreed to in the bilateral agreement. The Government, however, considered that this was such an important priority that it requested DFID that budget support for equipment and infrastructure be reassigned to be used to implement the policy. This was agreed.

The policy (Box 2) was presented to the Minister of Finance who took immediate action and included an instruction in the mid-year budget ordinance in December 2004 to introduce the scheme in the following fiscal year (commencing in July 2005) to commence in 6 months. Information on the scheme was communicated to the general public through national newspapers and radio. Roll out of the policy

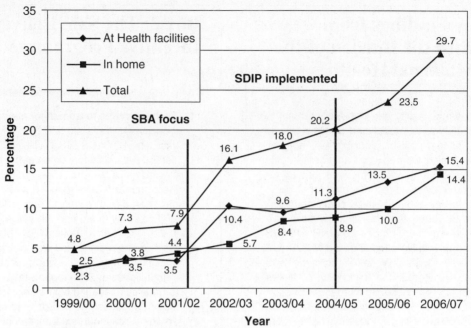

Figure 1 Delivery by trained health worker: 1999/2000–2006/2007.

Note: The sudden increase in attended deliveries, particularly at facilities, between 2001/2002 and 2002/2003 can be attributed to an improvement in reporting from central, regional and maternity hospitals.

Source: MOHP HMIS data.

began in July 2005 (initially called the Maternity Incentives Scheme and now the Skilled Delivery Incentive Programme). Local speed of implementation was determined by the readiness and interest of district health officers.

Since the launch of the SDIP in 2005, attendance of trained health workers (THWs) at deliveries has increased from 20% to nearly 30%.[2] In 2006–2007 there has been an increase of 6% on the 2005–2006 level—institutional deliveries have increased from 14% to 15%, and home deliveries with support of a THW at an accelerating rate from 10% to 15%. This trend is repeated across each of the ecological areas (mountain, hill and terai) with slightly more rapid growth reported in mountain and terai areas (Figure 1).

Forty eight percent of the SDIP budget has gone to mothers, 47% to service providers and 5% to health institutions. More than 200,000 mothers and families have benefited directly from the scheme at a total cost of £1.15 million. It should be noted, however, that the increase in uptake in health workers' delivery is building on a historic trend and appears to be occurring in all areas of the country. An evaluation to examine to what extent the policy has caused the increase in skilled attendance is ongoing.

4. Proximate Factors Influencing Policy Adoption

The development of policy on maternal costs was developed and approved by Government within about a year of the completion of the earlier research on burden of household costs of delivery care. Implementation began 6 months later. In this section we examine some of the factors behind this rapid policy adoption.

The brief review of the literature in Section 2 emphasises a series of factors that are likely to be important in promoting particular policies as a result of and, sometimes, in the absence of empirical research.

The importance of these factors was examined through a series of key informant interviews conducted with senior stakeholders involved in the development of the policy. Interviews were conducted with senior officials and partners who were central to the policy formulation process. These included: the then Minister of Finance, the then Minister for Health and Population and the State Minister for Health and Population, the wife of the then Prime Minister, the former Head of the Finance Section in the Ministry of Health and Population and senior maternal health advocates. The interviews focused on a series of influences including political and personal interests in the issue, public concern about maternal health, importance of maternal mortality as a health priority, impact of international health agendas and influence of donors as well as the conduct of the research itself. The interviews also examined why the particular policy of incentives was chosen, why the policy was not piloted and the importance of other political and international influences on policy development.

4.1. Research Dissemination

There is no doubt that the research was driven by a policy agenda rather than being undertaken 'out of the blue'. The principal investigator had already established a strong link with the MOHP through an existing relationship. This made it more likely that the work would be accepted. The ground was well prepared before and after fieldwork and was undertaken as a part of the NSMP which was already well integrated with the work of the Department of Health Services, MOHP. Senior staff in the project had built up a strong working relationship with government counterparts. Although the research provided evidence of the size and nature of the financial barriers, suggesting it took a larger proportion of household income and that much of the cost was incurred on items outside the health facility, the general findings were not unexpected. Considerable effort was made to ensure that findings were well disseminated. Initial workshops were held to discuss the findings. This was followed up by a number of consultation meetings to discuss the findings with senior health officials. Finally, the research was condensed into a series of policy briefs which synthesised the findings.

The relatively straightforward message of the research backed by quantified effects on households appears to have had a powerful effect on policy makers. The head of the Finance Section of the MOHP suggested that 'hard data talks', that the figures had a profound effect on the Ministries of Health and Finance. In contrast, the State Minister mentioned a series of other factors including political interests, personal concern (for maternal health issues) as being key and only when pressed on other influences was the research mentioned. An interlocutor from the Ministry of Finance suggested that the ideas behind the policy were his alone although the MOHP briefings on cost were good.

The study included a review of Nepalese exemption schemes and a systematic international review of mechanisms used to mitigate the financial burden of obstetric care. The latter included a review of loan funds, revolving drugs funds and insurance mechanisms. Although this background was considered an important basis for study by researchers it does not appear to have been particularly influential to policy makers. An alternative perspective is that the study suggested a negative lesson that very few scaled publicly run interventions have really addressed the issue of demand-side costs—in many ways the Nepalese scheme is innovative.

4.2. Donor Support and Funding

National policies are often influenced by international policy concerns and funding. The MOHP and the National Planning Commission have been focused on maternal health for a decade. Knowing that achievement of the child mortality MDG was on course shifted attention to the underachieving maternal mortality MDG. This focus was part of a nationally driven agenda which donors supported.

The period around the time of the research and policy development coincided with the start of Nepal's first sector wide approach in health. Donors were in the process of renegotiating their support for the sector including sector budget support which commenced in July 2005. In addition, SSMP commenced with over half the budget allocated to earmarked sector budget support. There was good reason to think that this timing could have had a positive impact on the policy in making it easier to obtain funding for implementation and therefore could have been an important factor in adopting the policy.

There is little evidence from the interviews that donors had a strong impact on the decision to implement the policy. Respondents said they would have financed the scheme domestically if donor funding was not forthcoming since it was such an important and high profile policy. If anything causation appeared to be reversed: Government exerted pressure on donors to finance the new scheme as part of their overall financial commitment to the sector. Notwithstanding this commitment, the timing of the policy before the start of a new 5 year cross-donor financial commitment (part of a SWAP arrangement) is likely to have made it easier for Government to push for swift commitment to policy implementation.

4.3. A Political Champion

The then Prime Minister's wife is a women's activist and the organisation SMF which she supports has a long history of championing women's rights. While a strong advocate for access to maternal services, the lack of other concrete policy ideas meant that the proposed SDIP when drawn to her attention seemed particularly attractive although she had no direct knowledge of the research study. The policy was seen as one that could easily be advocated for. Cash given to women was seen by her as having more direct appeal to women than a (vague) promise that care would be free at the often poor quality public health facilities.

4.4. Convergence of Political Interests

The issue of women's rights and maternal appeared to unite party and personal political interests across the coalition government. One of the two political parties in government, the UML, was committed to addressing the needs of the poor but the entire Government was being heavily criticised by Maoists for their lack of progress in meeting these needs. Both Ministers of Health and Finance were from the UML and the issue, in addressing the financial concerns of women at delivery, fitted well with the pro-poor agenda. Additionally, advancing women's development formed part of the UML manifesto and the National Planning Commission (responsible for strategic development in Nepal) was actively seeking innovative means to promote this commitment. By 2004 the coalition was planning for elections and so was looking for vote catching new policies.

Although there was some discussion during policy development to target poorer areas only with the incentive scheme, the government took the decision to provide a universal benefit albeit one that varies according to geographic area. It was felt, on equity grounds that all women should benefit. This decision itself has a political dimension in that it ensures that a more politically vocal and influential urban population will benefit as well those living in poorer rural areas. A cash incentive for delivery was seen as an attractive and relatively simple policy that could secure widespread support.

Yet the speedy acceptance of the SDIP was driven by more than a conventional desire to secure votes. By the time the policy was being developed the likelihood of elections was fading as the coalition government became ever more fragile. In a bid to survive the government was looking not simply for populist policies but policies based on a sound development strategy for the country. Policies such as the SDIP are relatively un-contentious receiving broad approval within the country and also amongst the international community. It appeared, therefore, that the need to survive led a fragile coalition to work together to produce a policy that was politically popular and socially progressive.

5. Conclusion

The development of the SDIP provides a striking example of how the convergence of political interests underpinned by solid research evidence enabled rapid development and implementation of health policy. Credible research, supported by clear dissemination by respected project staff already close to government, was certainly important in preparing the ground for policy advocacy. At the same time, however, it was the convergence of political interests in implementing a policy that helped demonstrate the effectiveness of a (beleaguered) government in appealing to a broad constituency that ultimately ensured that the research was translated into policy in a short period of time.

The process also helps demonstrate how researchers can increase the likelihood that their research will be noticed but recognising inevitable limitations. It appeared to help considerably that the research led to results that supported previous work while at the same time providing relatively easy to grasp numbers demonstrating potential gains from intervention. Yet even researchers that produce controversial findings can increase potential policy-maker receptiveness by ensuring early involvement of projects that are known and respected and by involving potential champions for the results from within the senior policy and academic community. Presenting the research through a variety of channels including punchy policy briefs, presentations and one to one dialogues with key decision makers helped to increase the profile of the results.

In the experience of the authors, for every one study that has 'impact' perhaps half a dozen will be disregarded completely or only used partially. Even in the current example in Nepal, political considerations often overrode technical economic or clinical advice. Ultimately researchers can adapt the process of research to increase likelihood of policy impact but they cannot guarantee acceptance.

Appendix A. Policy Briefing Papers

Based on the original report, four policy briefing papers were produced as follows:

- Summary: Actual Costs of Care and Willingness-to-Pay
- Summary Paper Two: Coping Strategies
- Summary Paper Three: Resource Scenarios
- Summary Paper Four: Policy Recommendations

Notes

1. But most emergency funds were still on a small scale, supported by projects such as NSMP.

2. Trained health workers include both skilled birth attendants—doctors and midwives—as well as health workers not included in the skilled birth attendant definition such as maternal and child health workers and paramedics.

References

1. National Planning Commission. Nepal interim plan (2008–2011). Kathmandu: Government of Nepal/National Planning Commission; 2007.
2. Ministry of Health and Population, New ERA, & Macro International Inc. Nepal demographic and health survey 2006. Kathmandu, Nepal: Ministry of Health and Population, New ERA, and Macro International Inc.; 2007.
3. Barker CE, Bird CE, Pradhan A, Shakya G. Support to the Safe Motherhood Programme in Nepal: an integrated approach. Reproductive Health Matters 2007;15(30):81–90.
4. Borghi J, Ensor T, Neupane BD, Tiwari S. Financial implications of skilled attendance at delivery in Nepal. Tropical Medicine & International Health 2006;11(2):228–37.
5. Choi BCK, Pang T, Lin V, Puska P, Sherman G, Goddard M, et al. Can scientists and policy makers work together? Journal of Epidemiology and Community Health 2005;59(8):632–7, doi:10.1136/jech.2004.031765.
6. Innvaer S, Vist G, M T, A O. Health policy-makers perceptions of their use of evidence: a systematic review. Journal of Health Services Research and Policy 2002:239–44.
7. Court J. Bridging research and policy on HIV/AIDS in developing countries. London: Overseas Development Institute; 2004.
8. Spray P. Research and policy in DFID, research and policy in development: does evidence matter? London: Overseas Development Institute; 2004.
9. Philpott A, Maher D, Grosskurth H. Translating HIV/AIDS research findings into policy: lessons from a case study of 'the Mwanza trial'. Health Policy and Planning 2002;17:196–201.
10. Shiffman J. Generating political will for safe motherhood in Indonesia. Social Science & Medicine 2003;56:1197–207.
11. Surr M, Barnett A, Duncan A, Bradley D, Rew A, Toye J. Research for poverty reduction: DFID research policy paper. London: DFID; 2002.
12. ODI. In: Young J, editor. Research and Policy in Development: Does Evidence Matter? Meeting Series. London: Overseas Development Institute; 2004.
13. NSMP. Summary Report on Hospital Needs Assessment, Nepal Safer Motherhood Project 1997–2004. Kathmandu: Options/DFID; 1999.
14. Hawkins K. Review and Documentation of NSMP's Increasing Access Component. Kathmandu: NSMP, Options; 1998.
15. Al-Nahi Q, May P. Health seeking behaviour study of women in five safe motherhood districts. UNICEF/Nepal: Kathmandu; 1998.
16. Carlough M, LeMaster J. How can motherhood be made safer in Nepal? More than hospitals are needed. Journal of the Institute of Medicine 1998;20(1):20–8.
17. Hotchkiss D, Rous JJ, Karmacharya K, Sangraula P. Household health expenditures in Nepal: implications for health financing reform. Health Policy and Planning 1998;13(4):371–83.
18. The World Bank. Understanding the access, demand and utilization of health services, by rural women in Nepal. Kathmandu: The World Bank; 2002.
19. National Planning Commission. Care during pregnancy and delivery: implications for protecting the health of mothers and their babies. In: Nepal multiple indicator surveillance, fifth cycle. Kathmandu His Majesty's Government/Nepal National Planning Commission Secretariat in Collaboration with UNICEF—Nepal; 1998.
20. Alban A. Economic assessment of the health sector strategy, Nepal an agenda for reform. Kathmandu: Short term consultancy for World Bank; 2003 [UPI no. 54614].
21. MacDonagh S, Neupane R. Private for profit maternity services, Nepal case study, final report, ref AG 3128. London: Options & Kings College London for DFID, UK and Department of Health Services, HMGN; 2003.
22. Nepal Home Page. http://www.nepalhomepage.com/politics/cabinet/050704.html. Kathmandu; 2007.
23. Safe Motherhood Network Federation Nepal. Safe Motherhood Network Federation Nepal (SMNF), Profile. Kathmandu; 2007.
24. Borghi J, Ensor T, Neupane BD, Tiwari S. Coping with the burden of the costs of maternal health. London: NSMP/Options; 2004.
25. HEFU. Ministry of Health Transportation Cost Sharing Approach for Safe Delivery Services, Information Sheet (9th December). Kathmandu: Ministry of Health; 2004

Acknowledgements—We are extremely grateful to current and former policy makers and civil servants for making time to speak to use during the preparation of this paper.

The findings, interpretations, and conclusions expressed in this paper are those of the authors and do not necessarily reflect the views of the organisations they represent.

An Economist's Invisible Hand

Arthur Cecil Pigou, overlooked for decades, provides a guide to the financial crisis.

JOHN CASSIDY

At the Heavenly Models home for deceased economists, an award is being presented to the resident whose work best explains financial crises, global warming, and other pressing issues of today. The favored candidates include John Maynard Keynes, the patron saint of stimulus programs; Hyman Minsky, an American disciple of Mr. Keynes who warned about the dangers of financial deregulation; and Milton Friedman, the late Chicago economist. (Mr. Friedman's free market principles are out of vogue, but Federal Reserve Chairman Ben Bernanke recently took his advice on how to prevent depressions by pumping money into the economy.)

The winner's name, however, turns out to be much less familiar: Arthur Cecil Pigou (pronounced "Arthur See-sil Pig-oo"). Stepping from the wings, a strapping Englishman with fair, wavy hair and a luxuriant moustache, smiles awkwardly and accepts his prize. A contemporary of Mr. Keynes at Cambridge University, Mr. Pigou was, for a long time, the forgotten man of economics. In the years leading up to his death, in 1959, he was a reclusive figure, rarely venturing from his rooms at King's College. His novel ideas on taxing polluters and making health insurance compulsory were met with indifference: Keynesianism was all the rage.

Today Mr. Pigou's intellectual legacy is being rediscovered, and, unlike those of Messrs. Keynes and Friedman, it enjoys bipartisan appeal. Leading Republican-leaning economists such as Greg Mankiw and Gary Becker have joined Democrats such as Paul Krugman and Amartya Sen in recommending a Pigovian approach to policy. Much of President Barack Obama's agenda—financial regulation, cap and trade, health care reform—is an application of Mr. Pigou's principles. Whether the president knows it or not, he is a Pigovian.

Mr. Pigou pioneered the study of market failure—the branch of economics that explores why free enterprise sometimes fails. During the 1930s, Mr. Keynes lampooned him as a reactionary because of his suggestion that the economic slump would eventually recover of its own accord.

But while Mr. Pigou believed capitalism works tolerably most of the time, he also demonstrated how, on occasion, it

---

Other Voices

'The great advances of civilization, whether in architecture or painting, in science or literature, in industry or agriculture, have never come from centralized government.'

—Milton Friedman, 1912–2006

'Our desire to hold money as a store of wealth is a barometer of the degree of our distrust of our own calculations and conventions concerning the future.'

—John Maynard Keynes, 1883–1946

'If investors are confident that they will be "bailed out" by a lender of last resort their selfreliance may be weakened.'

—Charles Kindleberger, 1910–2003

'The final outcome of the credit expansion is general impoverishment.'

—Ludwig von Mises, 1881–1973

---

malfunctions. His key insight was that actions in one part of the economy can have unintended consequences in others.

Thus, for example, a blow-up in a relatively obscure part of the credit markets—the subprime mortgage industry—can undermine the entire banking system, which, in turn, can drag the entire economy into a recession, as banks refuse to lend. "The actual occurrence of business failures will be more or less widespread according (to whether) bankers' loans . . . are more or less readily available," Mr. Pigou wrote in 1929. Today, that might seem obvious. But just two and a half years ago, when the subprime crisis began, most economists, Mr. Bernanke included, believed it would have only modest consequences.

The son of an army officer, Mr. Pigou was raised on the Isle of Wight. After attending Harrow, an exclusive private school, he went to King's College, Cambridge. His tutor was Alfred Marshall, the great late-Victorian economist, who regarded him as a budding genius and helped him get a chair in economics—the one Mr. Marshall vacated in 1908. Until the Great Depression brought Mr. Keynes to international prominence, Mr. Pigou was probably the most eminent English economist.

Like many contemporary economic commentators, Mr. Pigou was reacting against laissez faire—the hands-off approach to policy that free market economists, from Adam Smith onwards, had recommended. Such thinkers had tended to view the market economy as a perfectly balanced, self-regulating machine. But "even in the most advanced States there are failures and imperfections" that "prevent a community's resources from being distributed . . . in the most efficient way," Mr. Pigou wrote in 1920. His goal, he said, was to explore ways in which "it now is, or eventually may become, feasible for governments to . . . promote the economic welfare, and through that, the total welfare, of their citizens as a whole."

Mr. Pigou drew an important distinction between the private and social value of economic activities, such as the opening of a new railway line. The savings in time and effort that users of the railway enjoy are private benefits, which will be reflected in the prices they are willing to pay for tickets. Similarly, the railroad's expenditures on tracks, rolling stock, and employee wages are private costs, which will help to determine the prices it charges. But the opening of the railway may also create costs for "people not directly concerned, through, say, uncompensated damage done to surrounding woods by sparks from railway engines," Mr. Pigou pointed out.

Such social costs—modern economists call them "externalities"—don't enter the calculations of the railroads or its customers, but in tallying up the ultimate worth of any economic activity, "[a]ll such effects must be included," Mr. Pigou insisted. In focusing exclusively on private costs and private benefits, the traditional defense of the free market misses out on a vital element of reality.

To correct the problems that spillovers created, Mr. Pigou advocated government intervention. Where the social value of an activity was lower than its private value, as in the case of a railroad setting ablaze the surrounding woodland, the authorities should introduce "extraordinary restraints" in the form of user taxes, he said. Conversely, some activities have a social value that exceeds their private value. The providers of recreational parks, street lamps, and other "public goods" have difficulty charging people to use them, which means the free market may fail to ensure their adequate supply. To rectify this shortcoming, Mr. Pigou advocated "extraordinary encouragements" in the form of government subsidies.

Economics textbooks have long contained sections on how free markets fail to deal with negative spillovers such as pollution, traffic congestion and the like. Since August 2007, however, we have learned that negative spillovers occur in other sectors of the economy, especially banking. "The financial system failed to perform its function as a reducer and distributor of risk," Treasury Secretary Timothy Geithner and Lawrence Summers, the head of the National Economic Council, wrote in the *Washington Post* earlier this year. "Instead, it magnified risks, precipitating an economic contraction that has hurt families and businesses around the world."

The mere existence of negative spillovers doesn't necessarily justify government intervention, Mr. Pigou conceded. In some cases, the parties concerned might be able to come to a voluntary agreement about how to compensate innocent bystanders. A landlord, for instance, may reduce the rents for tenants who have to live over a noisy bar.

With spillovers from the financial industry, however, too many parties are involved for private bargaining to provide a practical solution. During the credit bubble of 2002–2006, the entire housing market turned into a speculative bazaar. Mortgage companies that were supposed to apportion credit on the basis of ability to pay distributed it willy-nilly. And banks and other financial intermediaries, which exist to channel capital to its most productive uses, misallocated resources on a vast scale.

When other industries do a bad job, the fallout is usually limited. If Budweiser and Miller marketed undrinkable beers, it would be bad news for those companies and their customers, but the rest of the economy would be largely unscathed.

In banking, the negative spillover can be catastrophic. Many millions of households and firms rely on credit to finance their expenditures. If this credit is suddenly curtailed, spending can fall precipitously throughout the economy. That is what we witnessed at the end of last year.

Even if policy makers have been tardy about citing the influence of Mr. Pigou's analytical framework, they are working within it. Raising capital requirements on banks, urging Wall Street firms to pay bonuses in stock, and forcing investment banks to keep some of the securities they issue on their own books are all efforts to mitigate the spillovers from irresponsible risk-taking.

Although it is rarely presented in such terms, reforming health care can also be viewed as a counter-spillover policy. Sick people who don't have health insurance often end up using emergency rooms, which imposes a cost on the insured, perhaps as much as $1,000 per person per year. A successful reform package would eliminate these social costs, and it could also generate some positive spillovers. Improvements in public health can make employees more productive, Mr. Pigou pointed out, which increases the gross domestic product.

If the administration ends up partly financing health-care reform by increasing taxes on the rich, a proposal contained in a bill that the House of Representatives recently passed, it will be enacting yet another Pigovian policy. "[I]t is evident that the transference of income from a relatively rich man to a relatively poor man of similar temperament, since it enables more intense wants to be satisfied at the expense of less intense wants, must increase the aggregate sum of satisfactions," he wrote.

Global warming presents perhaps the most dramatic example of what can happen if spillovers are ignored. It was the growing public concern over global warming that resurrected Mr. Pigou from obscurity. In 2006, the British government published an official report on climate change by Sir Nicholas Stern, a well-known English economist, which relied extensively on Mr. Pigou's analytical framework. "In common with many other environmental problems, human-induced climate change is at its most basic level an externality," Mr. Stern wrote. And he went on: "It is the greatest and widest-ranging market failure ever seen."

In addition to referencing Mr. Pigou's work directly several times, Mr. Stern recommended the imposition of one of his extraordinary restraints: a substantial carbon tax. This proposal remains controversial, but a number of Republican economists have endorsed it. Harvard's Greg Mankiw has founded an informal Pigou Club for economists and pundits that support a carbon tax.

During the 1930s and 1940s, many economists were pessimistic about the market system's long-term prospects. Mr. Pigou's message, on the other hand, was optimistic, and, in some ways, very American. He believed in progress, the power of rational analysis, and the ability of well-intentioned people, such as himself, to effect meaningful reforms.

He didn't put much store in elaborate mathematical theories. Above all else, he was practical. "We shall endeavor to elucidate, not any generalized system of possible worlds," he wrote in his greatest book, *The Economics of Welfare*, "but the actual world of men and women as they are found in experience to be."

JOHN CASSIDY is a staff writer at the *New Yorker*. His book *How Markets Fail: The Logic of Economic Calamities* was recently published by Farrar, Straus & Giroux.

New Hopes on Health Care for American Indians

PAM BELLUCK

The meeting last month was a watershed: the leaders of 564 American Indian tribes were invited to Washington to talk with cabinet members and President Obama, who called it "the largest and most widely attended gathering of tribal leaders in our history."

Topping the list of their needs was better health care.

"Native Americans die of illnesses like tuberculosis, alcoholism, diabetes, pneumonia and influenza at far higher rates," Mr. Obama said. "We're going to have to do more to address disparities in health care delivery."

The health care overhaul now being debated in Congress appears poised to bring the most significant improvements to the Indian health system in decades. After months of negotiations, provisions under consideration could, over time, direct streams of money to the Indian health care system and give Indians more treatment options.

Some proposals, like exempting Indians from penalties for not obtaining insurance, may meet resistance from lawmakers opposed to expanding benefits for Indians, many of whom receive free medical care.

But advocates say the changes recognize Indians' unique status and could ease what Senator Byron L. Dorgan, Democrat of North Dakota, calls "full-scale health care rationing going on on Indian reservations."

"We've got the 'first Americans' living in third world conditions," Mr. Dorgan said.

Mr. Obama has emphasized Indian issues more than most presidents. He campaigned on reservations, created a senior policy adviser for Native American affairs and appointed Kimberly Teehee, a Cherokee, to the post, and gave Indians other high-ranking positions.

He has proposed a budget increase of 13 percent for the federal Indian Health Service, which provides free care to 1.9 million Indians who belong to federally recognized tribes, most of whom live on tribally owned land. The service, which had a budget this year of $3.3 billion, has also received $500 million in stimulus money for construction, repairs and equipment.

"This new administration has been much more positive," said W. Ron Allen, chairman of the Jamestown S'Klallam tribe in Washington State and treasurer of the National Congress of American Indians, adding that the Congressional proposals provide "a very impressive opportunity to close the gap in Indian health care."

On Thursday, the Senate Indian Affairs Committee is scheduled to discuss other Indian health issues that could end up in the overhaul bill.

Indians could benefit from broader overhaul programs for low-income and uninsured citizens, but they do not want to relinquish the health care they claim as a historical right.

"Indian people have given up a lot," said Dr. Yvette Roubideaux, director of the Indian Health Service. "They really feel like they have, in a sense, prepaid for this health care with loss of land, natural resources, loss of culture."

'List Goes On and On'

In the vast, varied territory called Indian Country, health care is stung with struggle.

Too few doctors. Too little equipment. Hospitals and clinics miles of hardscrabble road away.

In cities, where over half of the country's roughly 3 million Indians now live (and nearly 5 million including part-Indians), only 34 programs get Indian Health Service funding, providing mostly basic care and arranging more advanced care and coverage elsewhere.

While some Indians have private insurance, often through employers or tribal businesses like casinos, a third are uninsured and a quarter live in poverty. By all accounts, the Indian Health Service is substantially underfunded.

Money shortages, bureaucracy and distance can delay treatment of even serious conditions for months, even years.

Many Indians face multiple roadblocks.

Joanna Quotskuyva's breast cancer did not require a mastectomy, but she chose to have surgery because radiation would mean months of driving five hours round-trip from her home on the Hopi reservation in Kykotsmovi, Ariz.

Many make similar choices, because "unfortunately, we don't have the capability," said Dr. Joachim Chino, chief of surgery at the nearest hospital, the Tuba City Regional Health Care Corporation. Treating large swaths of the Hopi and Navajo reservations—the Navajo alone is the size of West Virginia—is inherently difficult.

Despite its dedicated medical staff, the hospital struggles "to bring, right here, appropriate state-of-the-art, specialty, critical-care medicine," said Joseph Engelken, the hospital's chief executive.

While the Indian health system has improved nationally and Indians are living longer, Dr. Roubideaux acknowledged problems, not all from underfunding, saying, "The list goes on and on in terms of areas that need improvement."

Sometimes urgent "life or limb" cases get attention, while others, some serious, must wait.

Dr. David Yost, clinical director at the White Mountain Apache reservation in Arizona, cited "piles of care we have to put on the back burner," including 150 cases this summer, some "waiting a year and a half." This budget year, he said, 40 patients are still waiting, and about "10 people a month" are added to the list.

Ronnye Manuelito, 56, a Navajo in Naschitti, N.M., said he "almost felt like giving up" after waiting for brain surgery to quell blackouts, seizures and headaches experienced over three years from a shifting metal plate in his head from a childhood carousel injury.

One time he "left the stove on in the kitchen and passed out," and another he had a seizure in a car, said his sister, Brenda. His Indian Health Service doctor "was trying to get him a referral to a specialist in Albuquerque, but they weren't approving it because it wasn't life-or-limb," she said.

Ultimately, two surgical procedures helped him.

Dr. Roubideaux, speaking generally, said, "There are some places where funding is so short and there are so few health care providers, unfortunately people may have to wait quite a long time."

A former reservation doctor herself, Dr. Roubideaux said she would see "someone who maybe had chronic knee pain and a little bit of surgery would help, yet the person was still walking," making it non-life-threatening. "It's really heartbreaking," she said.

In cities, scarce Indian facilities and patchwork insurance can mean "a woman with a lump in her breast—we can't guarantee we can get her into treatment in a reasonable period," said Ralph Forquera, the executive director of the nonprofit Seattle Indian Health Board. "A cardiac problem? We can't guarantee that person can get to see a specialist."

Sometimes, Mr. Forquera said, when that woman is treated, "the lump has metastasized." He added, "We've had people actually die on waiting lists."

Jackie BirdChief, 46, a single mother with thyroid cancer, did not have to wait. She just had to move 200 miles from Phoenix to the Apache reservation she left in 1983, leaving her city, her job and, for months, her daughter, then 14. She moved because cost containment rules link coverage for care to establishing residency on reservations.

Ms. BirdChief, a secretary, was lucky because the Indian Health Service, her employer, "manipulated the system to make it work out for her," Dr. Yost said. It found her jobs on the reservation, he said, "whereas someone working in a grocery store would have had to quit their job—or decide if they wanted to have the procedure."

Still, Dr. Yost said, Ms. BirdChief "was a victim of our system, and ironically, she worked for the Indian health system."

Living on a reservation, however, does not ensure accessible care.

Ruby Biakeddy's six-sided hogan, a traditional Navajo home, without running water or a phone, is an hour's drive on a dirt road from drinking water, and even farther from diabetes and blood pressure medication. Since her truck got swept away in a rain-swollen ditch five years ago, Ms. Biakeddy, 67, who tends sheep, must borrow her children's vehicles.

"I recently ran out of the medicine I inject for a week," she said in Navajo through a translator.

Serious cases, where getting care within the "golden hour" after problems start is critical, can also suffer. "For many of our patients," said Dr. Anne Newland, acting clinical director of a clinic in Kayenta, Ariz., "that hour is gone by the time they get to us."

Ciara Antone, 4, died on the Navajo reservation outside Tuba City from an apparent bowel obstruction. Her mother, Genita Yazzie, called 911, but said that with the distance and road conditions, the ambulance was two hours away.

"I kept telling the dispatcher, 'My daughter's coding, she's *not breathing*,'" Ms. Yazzie said. Desperate, she drove to the closer Hopi reservation to get an ambulance, but by then, "they couldn't bring her back."

Whether a closer ambulance could have saved her daughter is unclear (the family has sued the non-Indian hospital that treated her). Henry Wallace, director of Navajo Emergency Medical Services, which Ms. Yazzie called first for an ambulance, declined to discuss the case, but said, "the geographic area is so large that the time factor is probably the biggest problem we have."

"We really don't have a golden hour," he said. "Ours could be the golden three hours."

Staffing shortages exacerbate things. Recently, Kayenta began closing its emergency room overnight, making Tuba City, at 90 minutes away, the closest hospital. At Indian hospitals and clinics nationally, a fifth of physician positions and a quarter of the nursing slots are unfilled.

Patients contribute to the frustrations. Nearly a third do not show up for scheduled surgery at Tuba City, often citing distance or cost.

Richard White, 61, acknowledged taking his medicine sporadically and drinking, aggravating his diabetes. He went blind, lost a toe and, during a Navajo medicine-man ceremony that he hoped would restore his vision, burned his other foot, which was then amputated.

"Stare at these incredible statistics, you become overwhelmed," Dr. Yost said. "It's like drinking out of a fire hydrant."

Keeping a Promise

Congress's goal, in using penalty and co-payment exemptions, is to encourage Indians to enroll in proposed programs like subsidized private insurance or expanded Medicaid, while respecting their sovereignty and the conviction that they are owed health care.

That conviction and bureaucratic hurdles have kept many eligible Indians from enrolling in Medicaid. But getting insurance allows Indians to receive care from more providers and allows the Indian system to get reimbursed from Medicaid or other insurers.

That would generate "an influx of capital," said Jim Roberts, policy analyst for Northwest Portland Area Indian Health Board, that "you can use to improve Indian health care."

Some disagree. Senator Tom Coburn, Republican of Oklahoma, said exemptions could discourage insurance enrollment, raise premiums for insured people and further stress the Indian health care system, which he called "poorly managed" and in need of billions of dollars to "keep the promise to Native Americans."

Even if more Indians become insured, it will not end the problems, especially if providers and insurers, daunted by the alarming health problems, continue avoiding Indian Country.

Proposed legislation would not give Indians everything they want, but the overhaul does include grants for preventive care and research. And the Indian Health Care Improvement Act, which stands a good chance of being reauthorized by Congress for the first time since 2001, would enhance programs, physician recruitment and hospital construction. Although it approves no funding, advocates hope it will prompt additional money.

Representative Frank Pallone Jr., Democrat of New Jersey, said that with the current climate in Congress, and "particularly the president, it's definitely going to be easier to get Indian provisions in the health care bills."

Easier, but no sure thing.

With expansions in public coverage or subsidies to buy private coverage, some lawmakers may question whether Indian Country should "still be getting direct payments to run I.H.S. clinics," said Stephen Zuckerman, a health economist at the Urban Institute, a research group.

"Some people are saying, 'We can't make all these adjustments for you guys,'" Mr. Allen said, adding that some Indians reply: "Make us pay for health care, then the deal is off. Give us the land back, and we're good."

Breaking with Past, South Africa Issues Broad AIDS Policy

Celia W. Dugger

Johannesburg—President Jacob Zuma, taking a concrete step away from the South African government's previous delays in providing drugs to treat AIDS and prevent women from infecting their newborns, declared Tuesday in a national address on World AIDS Day that drug therapy for H.I.V.-positive pregnant women and babies would be broadened and start earlier.

The new policy on pregnant women, aimed at ensuring that babies are born healthy, is in line with the new treatment guidelines issued by the World Health Organization just a day before. Treating infected babies earlier is expected to help South Africa, one of only four countries where child mortality has worsened since 1990, improve the survival odds of its youngest citizens.

The alacrity with which the government adopted the health organization's advice and extended access to AIDS drugs gives substance to Mr. Zuma's break with the views of his predecessor, Thabo Mbeki, who during almost a decade in office had questioned whether H.I.V. causes AIDS and suggested that antiretroviral drugs could be harmful.

More people are H.I.V. positive here than in any other nation, and Mr. Zuma called on South Africans to struggle against AIDS as they had against apartheid. "We have no choice but to deploy every effort, mobilize every resource and utilize every skill our nation possesses," he said.

The policy changes he announced will expand access to treatment. Mr. Zuma said that by April the government would start treating H.I.V.-positive people with tuberculosis earlier, when their immune systems are stronger—a step the World Health Organization said would reduce death rates. Tuberculosis is the leading killer of South Africans with H.I.V., the virus that causes AIDS, and deaths from tuberculosis have more than tripled here since 1997.

"What does this all mean?" Mr. Zuma asked in his address, broadcast on public television. "It means that we will be treating significantly larger numbers of H.I.V.-positive patients. It means that people will live longer and more fulfilling lives."

Mr. Zuma's emergence as the first South African president to seize center stage on AIDS comes with its own subplots. Just three years ago, he admitted while on trial for rape that he knowingly had had sex with a woman infected with H.I.V.

without using a condom, saying he showered afterward to minimize his risk of infection. Though acquitted, his words became fodder for cartoonists and critics.

That tarnished personal record served as a backdrop to his speech Tuesday, as he rallied his fellow South Africans to learn their H.I.V. status, promised to get another H.I.V. test himself and urged the nation to "use condoms consistently and correctly during every sexual encounter."

Harvard researchers estimated last year that the delay by Mr. Mbeki's government in using antiretroviral drugs to prevent women from infecting their newborns earlier this decade led to the deaths of 35,000 babies, and that 330,000 people died prematurely for lack of treatment.

Despite Mr. Zuma's break with Mr. Mbeki on AIDS, he has apparently rejected a rising public clamor here, even among some of his party's allies, for an accounting of Mr. Mbeki's culpability.

The Congress of South African Trade Unions said Monday that Mr. Mbeki should apologize to the nation for his failures in fighting an epidemic it has described as "destroying more lives than any invading army in history." The Young Communist League has demanded that Mr. Mbeki be prosecuted for genocide.

Business Day, a newspaper, editorialized on Nov. 20 that a murder trial and cross-examination of witnesses offered the possibility of extracting some truth. "The prospect of having a bite at understanding the Mbeki madness beckons," the paper wrote, "even if legal charges might not ultimately stick."

Mr. Mbeki, asked in a rare interview with the newspaper *The Sunday Independent* published on Nov. 1 if he had any regrets about his nine years as president, made no mention of AIDS.

Mr. Zuma and his party clearly have no desire to open an inquiry into the government's record on AIDS. Mr. Zuma was Mr. Mbeki's deputy president until Mr. Mbeki fired him in 2005. And like virtually all the leaders of the African National Congress, Mr. Zuma did not publicly oppose Mr. Mbeki on AIDS.

In an article published Tuesday in *The Star,* a daily newspaper, Mr. Zuma defended the government's record and said that under past presidents from his party, specifically mentioning Mr. Mbeki, the government had put in place "strategies to comprehensively deal with H.I.V./AIDS." He argued that as the government seeks to do still more, "We should avoid being drawn into an agenda of blame and recrimination."

Still, Mr. Zuma's approach on Tuesday—to speak frankly to the nation about each individual's responsibility to prevent the spread of AIDS by changing his or her sexual behavior and to lay out new policies on life-saving treatment—won him wide praise from the advocates who had despaired under Mr. Mbeki.

In another significant vote of confidence, Donald Gips, the American ambassador to South Africa, announced that the United States would give South Africa $120 million over the coming two years to help meet the growing demand for antiretroviral drugs. That comes on top of the $560 million the United States was already planning to give South Africa in the 2010 fiscal year to fight AIDS.

But South Africans may best remember Mr. Zuma's speech for his embrace of those who have suffered because of the epidemic or been shunned by society and their families. Among those listening Tuesday at the Pretoria show grounds was the daughter of Gugu Dlamini, a woman stoned and stabbed to death in 1998 near Durban after she said on the radio that she was H.I.V. positive.

While Mr. Mbeki once said he had never known anyone who died of AIDS, Mr. Zuma offered his sympathy.

"To families looking after sick relatives, we wish you strength," he said. "We understand what you are going through. To those who have lost their loved ones to the epidemic, we share your pain and extend our deepest condolences."

France Fights Universal Care's High Cost

DAVID GAUTHIER-VILLARS

When Laure Cuccarolo went into early labor on a recent Sunday night in a village in southern France, her only choice was to ask the local fire brigade to whisk her to a hospital 30 miles away. A closer one had been shuttered by cost cuts in France's universal health system.

Ms. Cuccarolo's little girl was born in a firetruck.

France claims it long ago achieved much of what today's U.S. health-care overhaul is seeking: It covers everyone, and provides what supporters say is high-quality care. But soaring costs are pushing the system into crisis. The result: As Congress fights over whether America should be more like France, the French government is trying to borrow U.S. tactics.

In recent months, France imposed American-style "co-pays" on patients to try to throttle back prescription-drug costs and forced state hospitals to crack down on expenses. "A hospital doesn't need to be money-losing to provide good-quality treatment," President Nicolas Sarkozy thundered in a recent speech to doctors.

And service cuts—such as the closure of a maternity ward near Ms. Cuccarolo's home—are prompting complaints from patients, doctors and nurses that care is being rationed. That concern echos worries among some Americans that the U.S. changes could lead to rationing.

The French system's fragile solvency shows how tough it is to provide universal coverage while controlling costs, the professed twin goals of President Barack Obama's proposed overhaul.

French taxpayers fund a state health insurer, Assurance Maladie, proportionally to their income, and patients get treatment even if they can't pay for it. France spends 11% of national output on health services, compared with 17% in the U.S., and routinely outranks the U.S. in infant mortality and some other health measures.

The problem is that Assurance Maladie has been in the red since 1989. This year the annual shortfall is expected to reach 9.4 billion euros ($13.5 billion), and 15 billion euros in 2010, or roughly 10% of its budget.

France's woes provide grist to critics of Mr. Obama and the Democrats' vision of a new public health plan to compete with private health insurers. Republicans argue that tens of millions of Americans would leave their employer-provided coverage for the cheaper, public option, bankrupting the federal government.

Despite the structural differences between the U.S. and French systems, both face similar root problems: rising drug costs, aging populations and growing unemployment, albeit for slightly different reasons. In the U.S., being unemployed means you might lose your coverage; in France, it means less tax money flowing into Assurance Maladie's coffers.

France faces a major obstacle to its reforms: French people consider access to health care a societal right, and any effort to cut coverage can lead to a big fight.

For instance, in France, people with long-term diseases get 100% coverage (similar to, say, Medicare for patients with end-stage kidney diseases). The government proposed trimming coverage not directly related to a patient's primary illness—a sore throat for someone with diabetes, for example. The proposal created such public outcry that French Health Minister Roselyne Bachelot later said the 100% coverage rule was "set in stone."

"French people are so attached to their health-insurance system that they almost never support changes," says Frederic Van Roekeghem, Assurance Maladie's director.

Both patients and doctors say they feel the effects of Mr. Sarkozy's cuts. They certainly had an impact on Ms. Cuccarolo of the firetruck birth.

She lives near the medieval town of Figeac, in southern France. The maternity ward of the public hospital there was closed in June as part of a nationwide effort to close smaller, less efficient units. In 2008, fewer than 270 babies were born at the Figeac maternity ward, below the annual minimum required of 300, says Fabien Chanabas, deputy director of the local public hospital.

"We were providing good-quality obstetric services," he says. "But at a very high cost." Since the maternity closed, he says, the hospital narrowed its deficit and began reallocating resources toward geriatric services, which are in high demand.

In the Figeac region, however, people feel short-changed. "Until the 1960s, many women delivered their babies at home," says Michel Delpech, mayor of the village where Ms. Cuccarolo lives. "The opening of the Figeac maternity was big progress. Its closure is perceived as a regression."

For Ms. Cuccarolo, it meant she would have to drive to Cahors, about 30 miles away. "That's fine when you can plan in advance," she says. "But my little girl came a month earlier than expected."

France launched its first national health-care system in 1945. World War II had left the country in ruins, and private insurers were weak. The idea: Create a single health insurer and make it compulsory for all companies and workers to pay premiums to it based on a percentage of salaries. Patients can choose their own doctors, and—unlike the U.S., where private health insurers can have a say—doctors can prescribe any therapy or drug without approval of the national health insurance.

Private insurers, both for-profit and not-for-profit, continued to exist, providing optional benefits such as prescription sunglasses, orthodontics care or individual hospital rooms.

At a time when the U.S. is considering ways of providing coverage for its entire population, France's blending of public and private medical structures offers important lessons, says Victor Rodwin, professor of health policy and management at New York University's Wagner School. The French managed to design a universal system incorporating physician choice and a mix of public and private service providers, without it being "a monolithic system of Soviet variety," he says.

It took decades before the pieces fell into place. Only in 1999 did legislation mandate that anyone with a regular residence permit is entitled to health benefits with no strings attached. Also that year, France clarified rules for illegal residents: Those who can justify more than three months of presence on French territory, and don't have financial resources, can receive full coverage.

That made the system universal.

In the U.S., health-overhaul bills don't attempt to cover illegal immigrants. Doing so would increase costs and is considered politically difficult.

Today, Assurance Maladie covers about 88% of France's population of 65 million. The remaining 12%, mainly farmers and shop owners, get coverage through other mandatory insurance plans, some of which are heavily government-subsidized. About 90% of the population subscribes to supplemental private health-care plans.

Proponents of the private-based U.S. health system argue that competition between insurers helps provide patients with the best possible service. In France, however, Assurance Maladie says its dominant position is its best asset to manage risks and keep doctors in check.

"Here, we spread health risks on a very large base," says Mr. Van Roekeghem of Assurance Maladie.

The quasi-monopoly of Assurance Maladie makes it the country's largest buyer of medical services. That gives it clout to keep the fees charged by doctors low. About 90% of general practitioners in France have an agreement with Assurance Maladie specifying that they can't charge more than 22 euros (about $32) for a consultation. For house calls they can add 3.50 euros to the bill.

By comparison, under Medicare, doctors are paid $91.97 for a first visit and $124.97 for a moderately complex consultation, according to the American College of Physicians.

In France, "If you are in medical care for the money, you'd better change jobs," says Marc Lanfranchi, a general practitioner from Nancy, an eastern town. On the other hand, medical school is paid for by the government, and malpractice insurance is much cheaper.

In 2000, the World Health Organization ranked France first in a one-time study of the health-care services of 191 countries. The U.S. placed 37th.

Financial pain has long dogged the French plan. As in the U.S., demand for care is growing faster than the economy as people take better care of themselves and new treatments become available.

Since the 1970s, almost all successive French health ministers have tried to reduce expenses, but mostly managed to push through only minor cost cuts. For instance, in 1987, patients were required to put a stamp on letters they mailed to the national health insurer. Previously, postage was government-subsidized.

In 2004, France introduced a system under which patients must select a "preferred" general practitioner who then sends them onward to specialists when necessary. Under that policy—similar to one used by many private U.S. health-care plans—France's national health insurance reimburses only 30% of the bill, instead of the standard 70%, if patients consult a doctor other than the one they chose.

At the start, patients balked, saying it infringed on their right to consult the doctors of their choice. But the system is now credited for helping improve the coordination between primary and specialty care, which remains one of the main weakness in the U.S. health-care system.

In recent years, Assurance Maladie has focused on reducing high medicine bills. Just like U.S. insurers and pharmacy-benefit managers, France's national health insurer is promoting the use of cheaper generic drugs, penalizing patients when they don't use them by basing reimbursements on generic-drug prices.

The most important aspect of Mr. Sarkozy's latest health-care legislation, passed this summer, focuses on reducing costs at state hospitals. About two-thirds of France's hospitals are state-run, and they are seen as ripe for efficiency savings. Among other things, Mr. Sarkozy has asked them to hire more business managers and behave more like private companies, for instance, by balancing their budgets.

The proposals didn't go down well.

In April, some of France's most famous doctors signed a petition saying they feared Mr. Sarkozy would turn health care into a "lucrative business" rather than a public service.

In the U.S., hospitals are paid for each individual procedure. This system, called fee-for-service, is suspected of contributing to runaway costs because it doesn't give hospitals an incentive to limit the number of tests or procedures.

Ironically, France is actually in the midst of shifting to a fee-for-service system for its state-run hospitals. The hope is that it will be easier for the government to track if the money is being spent efficiently, compared with the old system of simply giving hospitals an annual lump-sum payment.

France's private hospitals are more cost-efficient. But state hospitals say it is unfair to compare the two, because state hospitals often handle complex cases that private hospitals can't.

"When a private hospital has trouble with a newborn baby, we are here to help, night and day," says Pascal Le Roux, a pediatrician at the state hospital in Le Havre, an industrial city in northern France. "Having people standing by costs money."

In theory, Assurance Maladie should be able to contain hospital costs the same way it does with doctors: by harnessing its position as the dominant payer in the health-care system. In practice, it doesn't work that way.

The state hospital of Le Havre, called Groupement Hospitalier du Havre, or GHH, has nearly 2,000 beds and is one of the most financially strapped in France. A 2002 report by France's health-inspection authority found that the hospital had a track record of falsifying accounts in order to obtain more state funds.

Philippe Paris was hired about two years ago to help fix the hospital's spiraling costs. He is cutting 173 jobs out of the staff of 3,543.

And he is trying to enforce working hours. "People don't work enough," he said. "If consultations are scheduled to begin at 8 A.M., that means 8 A.M. and not 11 A.M."

Yet even the smallest budget moves are proving controversial. Local residents are up in arms over a cost-cutting measure that makes patients pay 1.10 euros an hour to park at the hospital. "It's a scandal," says retired local Communist politician Gerard Eude. "It goes against the very idea of universal health care."

UNIT 7

Trends and Challenges: Institutional Change through Capitalism, Globalization or Supra-National Government?

Unit Selections

Key Points to Consider

- How is capitalism related to democratization?

- How is democratization related to capitalism?

- How does globalization lead to institutional changes?

- Is the EU important?

- How is negative opinion different from value-bias in expressing anti-Americanism?

- How does culture explain value changes?

- What explains value changes?

Student Website
www.mhhe.com/cls

Internet References

Carnegie Endowment for International Peace
http://www.ceip.org
Europa: European Union
http://europa.eu/index_en.htm
Freedom House
http://freedomhouse.org/template.cfm?page=1

ISN International Relations and Security Network
http://www.isn.ethz.ch
NATO Integrated Data Service (NIDS)
http://www.nato.int/structur/nids/nids.htm

Units 1 through 6 describe the systematic treatment of the political behaviors of citizens, interest groups, parties, the executive, legislature, bureaucracy, and the judiciary in government. The discussions make clear the relevance of institutions in providing formal venues to regulate and regularize political behaviors so that they are clear-cut, comprehensible, constant and, thus, predictable. But, if institutions affect political behaviors, it is also indisputable that political behaviors shape institutions. In this unit, we examine the "what, how, and why" of institutional changes. In the process, we consider the extent to which political behaviors shape institutions.

What are institutional changes? Institutional changes refer to the creation or alteration of political organizations, conventions, or participation. They include modifications in political or legal processes, such as reported in the article on China's institutional changes. They may be radical or gradual, which is also suggested in the article. They may involve the creation of new political organizations, as indicated by the article on the EU. Or they may capture a change in values and conventions, as described in the article on anti-Americanism and "Clash of Civilizations."

How do institutional changes occur? Institutional changes are brought on by a combination of the following: domestic demand, such as by citizens, interest groups, and the government; or new pressures, such as the need for political, social, and economic integration in response to globalization. Thus, the article on institutional change in China points out that the need to transform the Chinese economy impelled the government to engage in the global economy, which, in turn, fostered China's institutional transformation. The discussion reveals the potency of market forces, particularly in the form of capital, as a viable means to bring about political or institutional change.

Does this mean that capitalism is the conduit to institutional change? Gabriel Almond notes in his article on "Capitalism and Democracy" that there is no clear relationship between capitalism and democracy to support an advocacy of capitalism as the means to institutional change. Indeed, this is corroborated by the article on China: China's institutional change may be possible only because it adopted some, but not all, aspects of capitalism.

There is also a criticism about market forces from the perspective of a culture clash. In particular, the article on anti-Americanism notes that some have speculated that anti-Americanism actually represents a "globalization backlash" against the role of capitalism or market forces in changing societies and political traditions. But the international scholars Peter Katzenstein and Robert Keohane and Ronald Inglehart and Pippa Norris go on to assert that this speculation is baseless. Instead, they conclude that "economic development generates changed attitudes" that fundamentally fuel institutional changes.

Of course, culture is not irrelevant to institutional changes. The problem lies not with the irrelevance of culture but, rather, the imprecise use of the term. In particular, the article by Inglehart and Norris concludes that the term is imprecise and hinges on stereotypes rather than on realistic information. Thus, Inglehart and Norris note that survey results show that, contrary to Huntington's assertion that "individualism, liberalism, constitutionalism, and human rights" are uniquely Western values, survey results show that in Albania, Azerbaijan, Bangladesh, Egypt, Indonesia, Iran, Morroco, and Turkey, "92 to 99 percent of the public endorsed democratic institutions—a higher proportion than in the U.S. (89 percent)."

Rather than a broad brush such as culture, the articles by Katzenstein and Keohane and Inglehart and Norris emphasize the relevance of value or attitude changes to undergird institutional

© The McGraw-Hill Companies, Inc./Christopher Kerrigan, photographer

changes. Thus, Inglehart and Norris point out that democratization in the Muslim world is supported or hampered by values over self-expression rather than on its cultural aptitude for democracy. Likewise, Katzenstein and Keohane argue that the anti-Americanism is most problematic when it goes beyond negative opinions and is, instead, based on value-bias against the U.S. This seems to be reiterated in the article by Alberta Sbragia: Her proposal that the EU constitution will likely be accepted if framed as a geopolitical or geoeconomics project that maximizes European influence shows that it is an issue of values rather than a fundamental rejection of EU institutionalization.

Professor Sbragia's article on the EU constitution also notes another way to elicit institutional changes: in response to new pressures. Thus, the article notes that the economic, social, and political regional integration of European nations has been institutionalized in the past 50 years in response to political, economic, and social pressures from a changing world. She names several EU policies that are in place that have benefited those in and out of Europe, including development aid to poor countries, peacekeeping troops in Bosnia and Herzegovina, and a lower cost of living and travel for Europeans. Given the situation, one is pressed to ask: Why was the EU constitution rejected? According to Alberta Sbragia, the rejection is from the public, whose reaction to the EU is largely from a domestic economic perspective rather than a supra-national, geopolitical, or geoeconomics argument. While her article deals with the setback posed by the rejection of the EU constitution in France and the Netherlands, it is provocative primarily in its conclusion of the inevitability of such regional integration, rather than how such integration is achieved.

Our survey of political behaviors and institutions across a wide net of countries returns full circle to this: Institutional changes occur in response to demands for better or more representative venues within which citizens and government may interact. While onlookers may fault institutions or even countries for failing to be more accountable, representative, or just, it is primarily the demands of domestic constituents—the citizens—that will usher in and support changes. How the international community nurtures and supports such demands, without imposing our own preferences and impatience, is key to promoting stability in inter-nation relations.

China: The Quiet Revolution
The Emergence of Capitalism

DOUG GUTHRIE

When Deng Xiaoping unveiled his vision of economic reform to the Third Plenum of the 11th Central Committee of the Chinese Communist Party in December 1978, the Chinese economy was faltering. Reeling from a decade of stagnation during the Cultural Revolution and already falling short of the projections set forth in the 1976 10-year plan, China needed more than a new plan and the Soviet-style economic vision of Deng's political rival, Hua Guofeng, to improve the economy. Deng's plan was to lead the country down a road of gradual and incremental economic reform, leaving the state apparatus intact, while slowly unleashing market forces. Since that time, the most common image of China, promulgated by members of the US Congress and media, is of an unbending authoritarian regime that has grown economically but seen little substantive change.

There is often a sense that China remains an entrenched and decaying authoritarian government run by corrupt Party officials; extreme accounts depict it as an economy on the verge of collapse. However, this vision simply does not square with reality. While it is true that China remains an authoritarian one-party system, it is also the most successful case of economic reform among communist planned economy in the 20th century. Today, it is fast emerging as one of the most dynamic market economies and has grown to be the world's sixth largest. Understanding how this change has come about requires an examination of three broad changes that have come together to shape China's transition to capitalism: the state's gradual recession from control over the economy, which caused a shift in economic control without privatization; the steady growth of foreign investment; and the gradual emergence of a legal-rational system to support these economic changes.

Reform without Privatization

During the 1980s and 1990s, economists and institutional advisors from the West advocated a rapid transition to market institutions as the necessary medicine for transforming communist societies. Scholars argued that private property provides the institutional foundation of a market economy and that, therefore, communist societies making the transition to a market economy must privatize industry and other public goods. The radical members of this school argued that rapid privatization—the so-called "shock therapy" or "big bang" approach to economic reforms—was the only way to avoid costly abuses in these transitional systems.

The Chinese path has been very different. While countries like Russia have followed Western advice, such as rapidly constructing market institutions, immediately removing the state from control over the economy, and hastily privatizing property, China has taken its time in implementing institutional change. The state has gradually receded from control over the economy, cautiously experimenting with new institutions and implementing them incrementally within existing institutional arrangements. Through this gradual process of reform, China has achieved in 20 years what many developing states have taken over 50 to accomplish.

The success of gradual reform in China can be attributed to two factors. First, the gradual reforms allowed the government to retain its role as a stabilizing force in the midst of the turbulence accompanying the transition from a planned to a market economy. Institutions such as the "dual-track" system kept large state-owned enterprises partially on the plan and gave them incentives to generate extra income by selling what they could produce above the plan in China's nascent markets. Over time, as market economic practices became more successful, the "plan" part of an enterprise's portfolio was reduced and the "market" part grew. Enterprises were thus given the stability of a continued but gradually diminishing planned economy system as well as the time to learn to set prices, compete for contracts, and produce efficiently. Second, the government has gradually promoted ownership-like control down the government administrative hierarchy to the localities. As a result, the central government was able to give economic control to local administrators without privatization. But with economic control came accountability, and local administrators became very invested in the successful economic reform of the villages, townships, and municipalities under their jurisdictions. In a sense, as Professor Andrew Walder of Stanford University has argued, pushing economic responsibilities onto local administrators created an incentive structure much like those experienced by managers of large industrial firms.

Change from Above

Even as economic reform has proceeded gradually, the cumulative changes over two decades have been nothing short of radical. These reforms have proceeded on four levels: institutional changes instigated by the highest levels of government; firm-level institutions that reflect the legal-rational system emerging at the state level; a budding legal system that allows workers institutional backing outside of the factory and is heavily influenced by relationships with foreign investors; and the emergence of new labor markets, which allow workers the freedom and mobility to find new employment when necessary. The result of these changes has been the emergence of a legal-rational regime of labor, where the economy increasingly rests upon an infrastructure of ordered laws that workers can invoke when necessary.

Under Deng Xiaoping, Zhao Ziyang brought about radical change in China by pushing the country toward constitutionality and the rule of law to create rational economic processes. These changes, set forth ideologically as a package of reforms necessary for economic development, fundamentally altered the role of politics and the Communist Party in Chinese society. The early years of reform not only gave a great deal of autonomy to enterprise managers and small-scale entrepreneurs, but also emphasized the legal reforms that would undergird this process of change. However, by creating a body of civil and economic law, such as the 1994 Labor Law and Company Law and the 1995 National Compensation Law upon which the transforming economy would be based, the Party elites held themselves to the standards of these legal changes. Thus the rationalization of the economy led to a decline in the Party's ability to rule over the working population.

In recent years, this process has been continued by global integration and the tendency to adopt the norms of the international community. While championing global integration and the Rule of Law, Zhu Rongji also brought about broader political and social change, just as Zhao Ziyang did in China's first decade of economic reform.

Zhu's strategy has been to ignore questions of political reform and concentrate instead on the need to adopt economic and legal systems that will allow the country to integrate smoothly into the international community. From rhetoric on "linking up with the international community" to laws such as the 2000 Patent Law to institutions such as the State Intellectual Property Office and the Chinese International Economic Trade and Arbitration Commission, this phase of reform has been oriented toward enforcing the standards and norms of the international investment community. Thus, Zhu's objective is to deepen all of the reforms that have been discussed above, while holding these changes to the standards of the international community.

After two decades of transition, the architects of the reforms have established about 700 new national laws and more than 2,000 new local laws. These legal changes, added regulations, and experiments with new economic institutions have driven the reform process. A number of laws and policies in the 1980s laid the groundwork for a new set of policies that would redefine labor relations in fundamental ways. For example, the policies that set in motion the emergence of labor contracts in China were first introduced in an experimental way in 1983, further codified in 1986, and eventually institutionalized with the Labor Law in 1994. While there are economic incentives behind Chinese firms' willingness to embrace labor contracts, including the end of lifetime employment, these institutional changes have gradually rationalized the labor relationship, eventually providing a guarantee of due process in the event of unfair treatment and placing workers' rights at the center of the labor relationship. Incremental changes such as these have been crucial to the evolution of individual rights in China.

The obvious and most common response to these changes is that they are symbolic rather than substantive, that a changing legal and policy framework has little meaning when an authoritarian government still sits at the helm. Yet the scholarship that has looked extensively at the impact of these legal changes largely belies this view. Workers and managers take the new institutions seriously and recognize that the institutions have had a dramatic impact on the structure of authority relations and on the conception of rights within the workplace.

Other research shows that legal and policy changes that emphasize individual civil liberties are also significant. In the most systematic and exhaustive study to date of the prison system, research shows that changes in the treatment of prisoners have indeed resulted in the wake of the Prison Reform Law. And although no scholarship has been completed on the National Compensation Law, it is noteworthy that 97,569 suits were filed under this law against the government in 1999, a proportional increase of over 12,000 percent since the beginning of the economic reforms. These institutions guarantee that, for the first time in the history of the People's Republic of China, individuals can have their day in court, even at the government's expense.

The 1994 Labor Law and the Labor Arbitration Commission (LAC), which has branches in every urban district, work hand-in-hand to guarantee workers their individual rights as laborers. Chapter 10 of the Labor Law, entitled "Labor Disputes," is specifically devoted to articulating due process, which laborers are legally guaranteed, should a dispute arise in the workplace. The law explicitly explains the rights of the worker to take disputes to outside arbitration (the district's LAC) should the resolution in the workplace be unsatisfactory to the worker. Further, many state-owned enterprises have placed all of their workers on fixed-term labor contracts, which significantly rationalize the labor relationships beyond the personalized labor relations of the past. This bundle of changes has fundamentally altered the nature of the labor relationship and the mechanisms through which authority can be challenged. For more than a decade, it has been possible for workers to file grievances against superiors and have those grievances heard at the LACs. In 1999, 52 percent of the 120,191 labor disputes settled by arbitration or mediation were decided wholly in favor of the workers filing the suits. These are official statistics from the Chinese government, and therefore should be viewed skeptically. However, even if the magnitude is incorrect, these numbers illuminate an important trend toward legal activity regarding workers' rights.

Many of these changes in labor practices were not originally adopted with workers' rights in mind, but the unintended consequence of the changes has been the construction of a regime of labor relations that emphasizes the rights of workers. For instance, extending the example of labor contracts that were being experimented with as early as 1983, these were originally intended as a form of economic protection for ailing enterprises, allowing a formal method of ending lifetime employment. However, workers began using the terms of employment codified in the contracts as the vehicle for filing grievances when contractual agreements were not honored. With the emergence of the LACs in the late 1980s and the further codification of these institutions in the Labor Law, the changes that were in progress became formalized in a set of institutions that ultimately benefited workers in the realm of rights. In a similar way, workers' representative committees were formed in the state's interest, but became an institution workers claimed as their own. These institutions, which many managers refer to as "our own little democracy," were adopted early in the reforms to co-opt the agitation for independent labor unions. These committees do not have the same power or status as independent labor unions in the West, but workers have made them much more significant in factories today than they were originally intended to be.

Foreign Investment's Impact

At the firm level, there is a process of rationalization in which firms are adopting a number of rational bureaucratic systems, such as grievance filing procedures, mediation

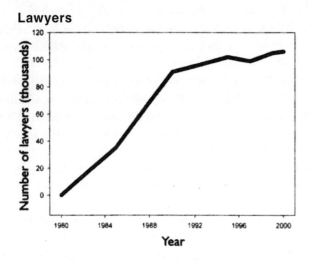 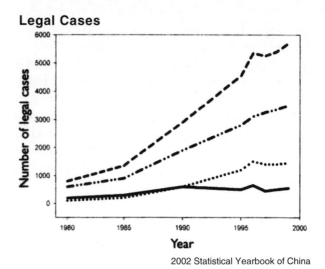

2002 Statistical Yearbook of China

Figure 1 An Age of Jurisprudence.

The above graphs depict two recent trends in China: a growing body of lawyers and an increasing number of legal cases. As the graph at left indicates, the number of lawyers in China has increased dramatically in the past 20 years, rising from fewer than 10,000 in 1980 to over 100,000 in 2000. The graph at right shows the growth in various types of legal cases over the same period. In particular, there have been significant increases in civil, economic, and first-trial cases.

committees, and formal organizational processes, that are more often found in Western organizations. In my own work on these issues, I have found that joint venture relationships encourage foreign joint ventures to push their partner organizations to adopt stable legal-rational structures and systems in their organizations. These stable, legal-rational systems are adopted to attract foreign investors, but have radical implications for the structure of authority relations and the lives of individual Chinese citizens. Chinese factories that have formal relationships with foreign, and particularly Western, firms are significantly more likely to have institutionalized formal organizational rules, 20 times more likely to have formal grievance filing procedures, five times more likely to have worker representative committee meetings, and about two times more likely to have institutionalized formal hiring procedures. They also pay about 50 percent higher wages than other factories and are more likely to adopt China's new Company Law, which binds them to abide by the norms of the international community and to respect international legal institutions such as the Chinese International Economic Arbitration and Trade Commission. Many managers openly acknowledge that the changes they have set in place have little to do with their own ideas of efficient business practices and much more to do with pressure brought on them by their foreign partners. Thus, there is strong evidence that foreign investment matters for on-the-ground change in China.

Foreign investors and Chinese firms are not interested in human rights per se, but the negotiations in the marketplace lead to transformed workplaces, which affect millions of Chinese citizens on a daily basis.

Given the common image of multinational corporations seeking weak institutional environments to capitalize on cheap labor, why would joint venture relationships with Western multinationals have a more positive impact in the Chinese case? The answer has to do with the complex reasons for foreign investment there. Corporations are rarely the leading advocates of civil liberties and labor reform, but many foreign investors in China are more interested in long-term investments that position them to capture market share than they are in cheap labor. They generally seek Chinese partners that are predictable, stable, and knowledgeable about Western-style business practices and negotiations. Chinese factories desperately want to land

these partnerships and position themselves as suitable investment partners by adopting a number of the practices that Western partners will recognize as stable and reform-minded. Among the basic reforms they adopt to show their fitness for "linking up" with the international community are labor reforms. Thus, the signaling of a commitment to stable Western-style business practices through commitments to labor reform has led to fundamental changes in Chinese workplace labor relations. Foreign investors and Chinese firms are not interested in human rights per se, but the negotiations in the marketplace lead to transformed workplaces, which affect millions of Chinese citizens on a daily basis.

However, changes at the firm level are not meaningful if they lack the legal infrastructure upon which a legal-rational system of labor is built. The construction of a legal system is a process that takes time; it requires the training of lawyers and judges, and the emergence of a culture in which individuals who are part of the legal system come to process claims. This process of change is difficult to assess because it relies on soft variables about the reform process, such as, for example, how judges think about suits and whether a legal-rational culture is emerging. But we can look at some aspects of fundamental shifts in society. All of these changes, in turn, rest upon a legal-rational system that is slowly but surely emerging in China.

Finally, beyond the legal and institutional changes that have begun to transform Chinese society fundamentally, workers are no longer tied to workplaces in the way that they once were. In the pre-reform system, there was very little mobility of labor, because workers were generally bound to their "work units" for life. The system created a great deal of stability for workers, but it also became one of the primary means through which citizens were controlled. Individuals were members of their work units, which they were dependent on for a variety of fundamental goods and services.

This manufactured dependence was one of the basic ways that the Party exercised control over the population. Writing about the social uprisings that occurred in 1989, Walder points out that the erosion of this system is what allowed citizens to protest with impunity on a scale never before observed in communist China: "[W]hat changed in these regimes in the last decade was not their economic difficulties, widespread cynicism or corruption, but that the institutional mechanisms that served to promote order in the past—despite these long-standing problems—lost their capacity to do so." It is precisely because labor markets have opened up that workers are no longer absolutely dependent upon the government for job placements; they now have much more leverage to assert the importance of their own rights in the workplace. And while the private sector was nonexistent when the economic reforms began, the country has seen this sector, which includes both private enterprises and household businesses, grow to more than 30 million individuals. With the growth of the private sector, there is much greater movement and autonomy among laborers in the economy. This change has afforded workers alternative paths to status attainment, paths that were once solely controlled by the government.

Quiet Revolution

Much like the advocates of rapid economic reform, those demanding immediate political and social reform often take for granted the learning that must occur in the face of new institutions. The assumption most often seems that, given certain institutional arrangements, individuals will naturally know how to carry out the practices of capitalism. Yet these assumptions reflect a neoclassical view of human nature in which rational man will thrive in his natural environment—free markets. Completely absent from this view are the roles of history, culture, and pre-existing institutions; it is a vision that is far too simplistic to comprehend the challenge of making rational economic and legal systems work in the absence of stable institutions and a history to which they can be linked. The transition from a command economy to a market economy can be a wrenching experience, not only at the institutional level but also at the level of individual practice. Individuals must learn the rules of the market and new institutions must be in place long enough to gain stability and legitimacy.

The PRC government's methodical experimentation with different institutional forms and the Party's gradual relinquishing of control over the economy has brought about a "quiet revolution." It is impossible to create a history of a legal-rational economic system in a dramatic moment of institutional change. The architects of China's transition to capitalism have had success in reforming the economy because they have recognized that the transition to a radically different type of economic system must occur gradually, allowing for the maximum possible institutional stability as economic actors slowly learn the rules of capitalism. Capitalism has indeed arrived in China, and it has done so via gradual institutional reform under the communist mantle.

Doug Guthrie is Associate Professor of Sociology at New York University.

From *Harvard International Review*, Summer 2003, pp. 48–53. Copyright © 2003 by the President of Harvard College. Reprinted by permission.

Capitalism and Democracy*

GABRIEL A. ALMOND

Joseph Schumpeter, a great economist and social scientist of the last generation, whose career was almost equally divided between Central European and American universities, and who lived close to the crises of the 1930s and '40s, published a book in 1942 under the title, *Capitalism, Socialism, and Democracy*. The book has had great influence, and can be read today with profit. It was written in the aftergloom of the great depression, during the early triumphs of Fascism and Nazism in 1940 and 1941, when the future of capitalism, socialism, and democracy all were in doubt. Schumpeter projected a future of declining capitalism, and rising socialism. He thought that democracy under socialism might be no more impaired and problematic than it was under capitalism.

He wrote a concluding chapter in the second edition which appeared in 1946, and which took into account the political-economic situation at the end of the war, with the Soviet Union then astride a devastated Europe. In this last chapter he argues that we should not identify the future of socialism with that of the Soviet Union, that what we had observed and were observing in the first three decades of Soviet existence was not a necessary expression of socialism. There was a lot of Czarist Russia in the mix. If Schumpeter were writing today, I don't believe he would argue that socialism has a brighter future than capitalism. The relationship between the two has turned out to be a good deal more complex and intertwined than Schumpeter anticipated. But I am sure that he would still urge us to separate the future of socialism from that of Soviet and Eastern European Communism.

Unlike Schumpeter I do not include Socialism in my title, since its future as a distinct ideology and program of action is unclear at best. Western Marxism and the moderate socialist movements seem to have settled for social democratic solutions, for adaptations of both capitalism and democracy producing acceptable mixes of market competition, political pluralism, participation, and welfare. I deal with these modifications of capitalism, as a consequence of the impact of democracy on capitalism in the last half century.

At the time that Adam Smith wrote *The Wealth of Nations*, the world of government, politics and the state that he knew—pre-Reform Act England, the French government of Louis XV and XVI—was riddled with special privileges, monopolies, interferences with trade. With my tongue only half way in my check

I believe the discipline of economics may have been traumatized by this condition of political life at its birth. Typically, economists speak of the state and government instrumentally, as a kind of secondary service mechanism.

I do not believe that politics can be treated in this purely instrumental and reductive way without losing our analytic grip on the social and historical process. The economy and the polity are the main problem solving mechanisms of human society. They each have their distinctive means, and they each have their "goods" or ends. They necessarily interact with each other, and transform each other in the process. Democracy in particular generates goals and programs. You cannot give people the suffrage, and let them form organizations, run for office, and the like, without their developing all kinds of ideas as to how to improve things. And sometimes some of these ideas are adopted, implemented and are productive, and improve our lives, although many economists are reluctant to concede this much to the state.

My lecture deals with this interaction of politics and economics in the Western World in the course of the last couple of centuries, in the era during which capitalism and democracy emerged as the dominant problem solving institutions of modern civilization. I am going to discuss some of the theoretical and empirical literature dealing with the themes of the positive and negative interaction between capitalism and democracy. There are those who say that capitalism supports democracy, and those who say that capitalism subverts democracy. And there are those who say that democracy subverts capitalism, and those who say that it supports it.

The relation between capitalism and democracy dominates the political theory of the last two centuries. All the logically possible points of view are represented in a rich literature. It is this ambivalence and dialectic, this tension between the two major problem solving sectors of modern society—the political and the economic—that is the topic of my lecture.

Capitalism Supports Democracy

Let me begin with the argument that capitalism is positively linked with democracy, shares its values and culture, and facilitates its development. This case has been made in historical, logical, and statistical terms.

*Lecture presented at Seminar on the Market, sponsored by the Ford Foundation and the Research Institute on International Change of Columbia University, Moscow, October 29—November 2.

Albert Hirschman in his *Rival Views of Market Society* (1986) examines the values, manners and morals of capitalism, and their effects on the larger society and culture as these have been described by the philosophers of the 17th, 18th, and 19th centuries. He shows how the interpretation of the impact of capitalism has changed from the enlightenment view of Montesquieu, Condorcet, Adam Smith and others, who stressed the *douceur* of commerce, its "gentling," civilizing effect on behavior and interpersonal relations, to that of the 19th and 20th century conservative and radical writers who described the culture of capitalism as crassly materialistic, destructively competitive, corrosive of morality, and hence self-destructive. This sharp almost 180-degree shift in point of view among political theorists is partly explained by the transformation from the commerce and small-scale industry of early capitalism, to the smoke blackened industrial districts, the demonic and exploitive entrepreneurs, and exploited laboring classes of the second half of the nineteenth century. Unfortunately for our purposes, Hirschman doesn't deal explicitly with the capitalism–democracy connection, but rather with culture and with manners. His argument, however, implies an early positive connection and a later negative one.

Joseph Schumpeter in *Capitalism, Socialism, and Democracy* (1942) states flatly, "History clearly confirms . . . [that] . . . modern democracy rose along with capitalism, and in causal connection with it . . . modern democracy is a product of the capitalist process." He has a whole chapter entitled "The Civilization of Capitalism," democracy being a part of that civilization. Schumpeter also makes the point that democracy was historically supportive of capitalism. He states, ". . . the bourgeoisie reshaped, and from its own point of view rationalized, the social and political structure that preceded its ascendancy . . ." (that is to say, feudalism). "The democratic method was the political tool of that reconstruction." According to Schumpeter capitalism and democracy were mutually causal historically, mutually supportive parts of a rising modern civilization, although as we shall show below, he also recognized their antagonisms.

Barrington Moore's historical investigation (1966) with its long title, *The Social Origins of Dictatorship and Democracy; Lord and Peasant in the Making of the Modern World*, argues that there have been three historical routes to industrial modernization. The first of these followed by Britain, France, and the United States, involved the subordination and transformation of the agricultural sector by the rising commercial bourgeoisie, producing the democratic capitalism of the 19th and 20th centuries. The second route followed by Germany and Japan, where the landed aristocracy was able to contain and dominate the rising commercial classes, produced an authoritarian and fascist version of industrial modernization, a system of capitalism encased in a feudal authoritarian framework, dominated by a military aristocracy, and an authoritarian monarchy. The third route, followed in Russia where the commercial bourgeoisie was too weak to give content and direction to the modernizing process, took the form of a revolutionary process drawing on the frustration and resources of the peasantry, and created a mobilized authoritarian Communist regime along with a state-controlled industrialized economy. Successful capitalism dominating and transforming the rural agricultural sector, according

to Barrington Moore, is the creator and sustainer of the emerging democracies of the nineteenth century.

Robert A. Dahl, the leading American democratic theorist, in the new edition of his book (1990) *After the Revolution? Authority in a Good Society*, has included a new chapter entitled "Democracy and Markets." In the opening paragraph of that chapter, he says:

> It is an historical fact that modern democratic institutions . . . have existed only in countries with predominantly privately owned, market-oriented economies, or capitalism if you prefer that name. It is also a fact that all "socialist" countries with predominantly state-owned centrally directed economic orders—command economies—have not enjoyed democratic governments, but have in fact been ruled by authoritarian dictatorships. It is also an historical fact that some "capitalist" countries have also been, and are, ruled by authoritarian dictatorships.

> To put it more formally, it looks to be the case that market-oriented economies are necessary (in the logical sense) to democratic institutions, though they are certainly not sufficient. And it looks to be the case that state-owned centrally directed economic orders are strictly associated with authoritarian regimes, though authoritarianism definitely does not require them. We have something very much like an historical experiment, so it would appear, that leaves these conclusions in no great doubt. (Dahl 1990)

Peter Berger in his book *The Capitalist Revolution* (1986) presents four propositions on the relation between capitalism and democracy:

> Capitalism is a necessary but not sufficient condition of democracy under modern conditions.

> If a capitalist economy is subjected to increasing degrees of state control, a point (not precisely specifiable at this time) will be reached at which democratic governance becomes impossible.

> If a socialist economy is opened up to increasing degrees of market forces, a point (not precisely specifiable at this time) will be reached at which democratic governance becomes a possibility.

> If capitalist development is successful in generating economic growth from which a sizable proportion of the population benefits, pressures toward democracy are likely to appear.

This positive relationship between capitalism and democracy has also been sustained by statistical studies. The "Social Mobilization" theorists of the 1950s and 1960s which included Daniel Lerner (1958), Karl Deutsch (1961), S. M. Lipset (1959) among others, demonstrated a strong statistical association between GNP per capita and democratic political institutions. This is more than simple statistical association. There is a logic in the relation between level of economic development and democratic institutions. Level of economic development has been shown to be associated with education and literacy, exposure to mass media, and democratic psychological propensities such as subjective efficacy, participatory aspirations and skills. In a major investigation of the social psychology of industrialization and modernization, a research team led by the sociologist Alex Inkeles (1974) interviewed several thousand workers in the modern industrial and the traditional economic sectors of six countries of differing culture. Inkeles found empathetic, efficacious, participatory and activist propensities much more frequently among the modern industrial workers, and to a much lesser extent in the traditional sector in each one of these countries regardless of cultural differences.

The historical, the logical, and the statistical evidence for this positive relation between capitalism and democracy is quite persuasive.

Capitalism Subverts Democracy

But the opposite case is also made, that capitalism subverts or undermines democracy. Already in John Stuart Mill (1848) we encounter a view of existing systems of private property as unjust, and of the free market as destructively competitive—aesthetically and morally repugnant. The case he was making was a normative rather than a political one. He wanted a less competitive society, ultimately socialist, which would still respect individuality. He advocated limitations on the inheritance of property and the improvement of the property system so that everyone shared in its benefits, the limitation of population growth, and the improvement of the quality of the labor force through the provision of high quality education for all by the state. On the eve of the emergence of the modern democratic capitalist order John Staurt Mill wanted to control the excesses of both the market economy and the majoritarian polity, by the education of consumers and producers, citizens and politicians, in the interest of producing morally improved free market and democratic orders. But in contrast to Marx, he did not thoroughly discount the possibilities of improving the capitalist and democratic order.

Marx argued that as long as capitalism and private property existed there could be no genuine democracy, that democracy under capitalism was bourgeois democracy, which is to say not democracy at all. While it would be in the interest of the working classes to enter a coalition with the bourgeoisie in supporting this form of democracy in order to eliminate feudalism, this would be a tactical maneuver. Capitalist democracy could only result in the increasing exploitation of the working classes. Only the elimination of capitalism and private property could result in the emancipation of the working classes and the attainment of true democracy. Once socialism was attained the basic political problems of humanity would have been solved through the elimination of classes. Under socialism there would be no distinctive democratic organization, no need for institutions to resolve conflicts, since there would be no conflicts. There is not much democratic or political theory to be found in Marx's writings. The basic reality is the mode of economic production and the consequent class structure from which other institutions follow.

For the followers of Marx up to the present day there continues to be a negative tension between capitalism, however reformed, and democracy. But the integral Marxist and Leninist rejection of the possibility of an autonomous, bourgeois democratic state has been left behind for most Western Marxists. In the thinking of Poulantzas, Offe, Bobbio, Habermas and others, the bourgeois democratic state is now viewed as a class struggle state, rather than an unambiguously bourgeois state. The working class has access to it; it can struggle for its interests, and can attain partial benefits from it. The state is now viewed as autonomous, or as relatively autonomous, and it can be reformed in a progressive direction by working class and other popular movements. The bourgeois democratic state can be moved in the direction of a socialist state by political action short of violence and institutional destruction.

Schumpeter (1942) appreciated the tension between capitalism and democracy. While he saw a causal connection between competition in the economic and the political order, he points out ". . . that there are some deviations from the principle of democracy which link up with the presence of organized capitalist interests. . . . [T]he statement is true both from the standpoint of the classical and from the standpoint of our own theory of democracy. From the first standpoint, the result reads that the means at the disposal of private interests are often used in order to thwart the will of the people. From the second standpoint, the result reads that those private means are often used in order to interfere with the working of the mechanism of competitive leadership." He refers to some countries and situations in which ". . . political life all but resolved itself into a struggle of pressure groups and in many cases practices that failed to conform to the spirit of the democratic method." But he rejects the notion that there cannot be political democracy in a capitalist society. For Schumpeter full democracy in the sense of the informed participation of all adults in the selection of political leaders and consequently the making of public policy, was an impossibility because of the number and complexity of the issues confronting modern electorates. The democracy which was realistically possible was one in which people could choose among competing leaders, and consequently exercise some direction over political decisions. This kind of democracy was possible in a capitalist society, though some of its propensities impaired its performance. Writing in the early years of World War II, when the future of democracy and of capitalism were uncertain, he leaves unresolved the questions of ". . . Whether or not democracy is one of those products of capitalism which are to die out with it . . ." or ". . . how well or ill capitalist society qualifies for the task of working the democratic method it evolved."

Non-Marxist political theorists have contributed to this questioning of the reconcilability of capitalism and democracy. Robert A. Dahl, who makes the point that capitalism historically has been a necessary precondition of democracy, views contemporary democracy in the United States as seriously compromised, impaired by the inequality in resources among the citizens. But Dahl stresses the variety in distributive patterns, and in politico-economic relations among contemporary democracies. "The category of capitalist democracies" he writes, "includes an extraordinary variety . . . from nineteenth century, laissez faire, early industrial systems to twentieth century, highly regulated, social welfare, late or postindustrial systems. Even late twentieth century 'welfare state' orders vary all the way from the Scandinavian systems, which are redistributive, heavily taxed, comprehensive in their social security, and neocorporatist in their collective bargaining arrangements to the faintly redistributive, moderately taxed, limited social security, weak collective bargaining systems of the United States and Japan" (1989).

In *Democracy and Its Critics* (1989) Dahl argues that the normative growth of democracy to what he calls its "third transformation" (the first being the direct city-state democracy of classic times, and the second, the indirect, representative inegalitarian democracy of the contemporary world) will require democratization of the economic order. In other words, modern corporate capitalism needs to be transformed. Since government control and/or ownership of the economy would be destructive of the pluralism which is an essential requirement of democracy, his preferred solution to the problem of the mega-corporation is employee control of corporate industry. An economy so organized, according to Dahl, would improve the distribution of political resources without at the same time destroying the pluralism which democratic competition requires. To those who question the realism of Dahl's solution to the problem of inequality, he replies that history is full of surprises.

Charles E. Lindblom in his book, *Politics and Markets* (1977), concludes his comparative analysis of the political economy of modern capitalism and socialism, with an essentially pessimistic conclusion about contemporary market-oriented democracy. He says

> We therefore come back to the corporation. It is possible that the rise of the corporation has offset or more than offset the decline of class as an instrument of indoctrination. . . . That it creates a new core of wealth and power for a newly constructed upper class, as well as an overpowering loud voice, is also reasonably clear. The executive of the large corporation is, on many counts, the contemporary counterpart to the landed gentry of an earlier era, his voice amplified by the technology of mass communication. . . . [T]he major institutional barrier to fuller democracy may therefore be the autonomy of the private corporation.

Lindblom concludes, "The large private corporation fits oddly into democratic theory and vision. Indeed it does not fit.

There is then a widely shared agreement, from the Marxists and neo-Marxists, to Schumpeter, Dahl, Lindblom, and other liberal political theorists, that modern capitalism with the dominance of the large corporation, produces a defective or an impaired form of democracy.

Democracy Subverts Capitalism

If we change our perspective now and look at the way democracy is said to affect capitalism, one of the dominant traditions of economics from Adam Smith until the present day stresses the importance for productivity and welfare of an economy that is relatively free of intervention by the state. In this doctrine of minimal government there is still a place for a framework of rules and services essential to the productive and efficient performance of the economy. In part the government has to protect the market from itself. Left to their own devices, according to

Smith, businessmen were prone to corner the market in order to exact the highest possible price. And according to Smith businessmen were prone to bribe public officials in order to gain special privileges, and legal monopolies. For Smith good capitalism was competitive capitalism, and good government provided just those goods and services which the market needed to flourish, could not itself provide, or would not provide. A good government according to Adam Smith was a minimal government, providing for the national defense, and domestic order. Particularly important for the economy were the rules pertaining to commercial life such as the regulation of weights and measures, setting and enforcing building standards, providing for the protection of persons and property, and the like.

For Milton Friedman (1961, 1981), the leading contemporary advocate of the free market and free government, and of the interdependence of the two, the principal threat to the survival of capitalism and democracy is the assumption of the responsibility for welfare on the part of the modern democratic state. He lays down a set of functions appropriate to government in the positive interplay between economy and polity, and then enumerates many of the ways in which the modern welfare, regulatory state has deviated from these criteria.

A good Friedmanesque, democratic government would be one ". . . which maintained law and order, defended property rights, served as a means whereby we could modify property rights and other rules of the economic game, adjudicated disputes about the interpretation of the rules, enforced contracts, promoted competition, provided a monetary framework, engaged in activities to counter technical monopolies and to overcome neighborhood effects widely regarded as sufficiently important to justify government intervention, and which supplemented private charity and the private family in protecting the irresponsible, whether madman or child. . . ." Against this list of proper activities for a free government, Friedman pinpointed more than a dozen activities of contemporary democratic governments which might better be performed through the private sector, or not at all. These included setting and maintaining price supports, tariffs, import and export quotas and controls, rents, interest rates, wage rates, and the like, regulating industries and banking, radio and television, licensing professions and occupations, providing social security and medical care programs, providing public housing, national parks, guaranteeing mortgages, and much else.

Friedman concludes that this steady encroachment on the private sector has been slowly but surely converting our free government and market system into a collective monster, compromising both freedom and productivity in the outcome. The tax and expenditure revolts and regulatory rebellions of the 1980s have temporarily stemmed this trend, but the threat continues. "It is the internal threat coming from men of good intentions and good will who wish to reform us. Impatient with the slowness of persuasion and example to achieve the great social changes they envision, they are anxious to use the power of the state to achieve their ends, and confident of their own ability to do so." The threat to political and economic freedom, according to Milton Friedman and others who argue the same position, arises out of democratic politics. It may only be defeated by political action.

In the last decades a school, or rather several schools, of economists and political scientists have turned the theoretical models of economics to use in analyzing political processes. Variously called public choice theorists, rational choice theorists, or positive political theorists, and employing such models as market exchange and bargaining, rational self interest, game theory, and the like, these theorists have produced a substantial literature throwing new and often controversial light on democratic political phenomena such as elections, decisions of political party leaders, interest group behavior, legislative and committee decisions, bureaucratic, and judicial behavior, lobbying activity, and substantive public policy areas such as constitutional arrangements, health and environment policy, regulatory policy, national security and foreign policy, and the like. Hardly a field of politics and public policy has been left untouched by this inventive and productive group of scholars.

The institutions and names with which this movement is associated in the United States include Virginia State University, the University of Virginia, the George Mason University, the University of Rochester, the University of Chicago, the California Institute of Technology, the Carnegie Mellon University, among others. And the most prominent names are those of the leaders of the two principal schools: James Buchanan, the Nobel Laureate leader of the Virginia "Public Choice" school, and William Riker, the leader of the Rochester "Positive Theory" school. Other prominent scholars associated with this work are Gary Becker of the University of Chicago, Kenneth Shepsle and Morris Fiorina of Harvard, John Ferejohn of Stanford, Charles Plott of the California Institute of Technology, and many others.

One writer summarizing the ideological bent of much of this work, but by no means all of it (William Mitchell of the University of Washington), describes it as fiscally conservative, sharing a conviction that the ". . . private economy is far more robust, efficient, and perhaps, equitable than other economies, and much more successful than political processes in efficiently allocating resources. . . ." Much of what has been produced ". . . by James Buchanan and the leaders of this school can best be described as contributions to a theory of the failure of political processes." These failures of political performance are said to be inherent properties of the democratic political process. "Inequity, inefficiency, and coercion are the most general results of democratic policy formation." In a democracy the demand for publicly provided services seems to be insatiable. It ultimately turns into a special interest, "rent seeking" society. Their remedies take the form of proposed constitutional limits on spending power and checks and balances to limit legislative majorities.

One of the most visible products of this pessimistic economic analysis of democratic politics is the book by Mancur Olson, *The Rise and Decline of Nations* (1982). He makes a strong argument for the negative democracy–capitalism connection. His thesis is that the behavior of individuals and firms in stable societies inevitably leads to the formation of dense networks of collusive, cartelistic, and lobbying organizations that make economies less efficient and dynamic and polities less governable. "The longer a society goes without an upheaval, the more powerful such organizations become and the more they slow down economic expansion. Societies in which these narrow interest groups have been destroyed, by war or revolution, for example, enjoy the greatest gains in growth." His prize cases are Britain on the one hand and Germany and Japan on the other.

> The logic of the argument implies that countries that have had democratic freedom of organization without upheaval or invasion the longest will suffer the most from growth-repressing organizations and combinations. This helps explain why Great Britain, the major nation with the longest immunity from dictatorship, invasion, and revolution, has had in this century a lower rate of growth than other large, developed democracies. Britain has precisely the powerful network of special interest organization that the argument developed here would lead us to expect in a country with its record of military security and democratic stability. The number and power of its trade unions need no description. The venerability and power of its professional associations is also striking. . . . In short, with age British society has acquired so many strong organizations and collusions that it suffers from an institutional sclerosis that slows its adaptation to changing circumstances and technologies. (Olson 1982)

By contrast, post-World War II Germany and Japan started organizationally from scratch. The organizations that led them to defeat were all dissolved, and under the occupation inclusive organizations like the general trade union movement and general organizations of the industrial and commercial community were first formed. These inclusive organizations had more regard for the general national interest and exercised some discipline on the narrower interest organizations. And both countries in the post-war decades experienced "miracles" of economic growth under democratic conditions.

The Olson theory of the subversion of capitalism through the propensities of democratic societies to foster special interest groups has not gone without challenge. There can be little question that there is logic in his argument. But empirical research testing this pressure group hypothesis thus far has produced mixed findings. Olson has hopes that a public educated to the harmful consequences of special interests to economic growth, full employment, coherent government, equal opportunity, and social mobility will resist special interest behavior, and enact legislation imposing anti-trust, and anti-monopoly controls to mitigate and contain these threats. It is somewhat of an irony that the solution to this special interest disease of democracy, according to Olson, is a democratic state with sufficient regulatory authority to control the growth of special interest organizations.

Democracy Fosters Capitalism

My fourth theme, democracy as fostering and sustaining capitalism, is not as straightforward as the first three. Historically there can be little doubt that as the suffrage was extended in the last century, and as mass political parties developed, democratic development impinged significantly on capitalist institutions and practices. Since successful capitalism requires risk-taking entrepreneurs with access to investment capital, the democratic propensity for redistributive and regulative policy tends to reduce the incentives and the resources available for risk-taking and creativity. Thus it can be argued that propensities inevitably resulting from democratic politics, as Friedman, Olson and many others argue, tend to reduce productivity, and hence welfare.

But precisely the opposite argument can be made on the basis of the historical experience of literally all of the advanced capitalist democracies in existence. All of them without exception are now welfare states with some form and degree of social insurance, health and welfare nets, and regulatory frameworks designed to mitigate the harmful impacts and shortfalls of capitalism. Indeed, the welfare state is accepted all across the political spectrum. Controversy takes place around the edges. One might make the argument that had capitalism not been modified in this welfare direction, it is doubtful that it would have survived.

This history of the interplay between democracy and capitalism is clearly laid out in a major study involving European and American scholars, entitled *The Development of Welfare States in Western Europe and America* (Flora and Heidenheimer 1981). The book lays out the relationship between the development and spread of capitalist industry, democratization in the sense of an expanding suffrage and the emergence of trade unions and left-wing political parties, and the gradual introduction of the institutions and practices of the welfare state. The early adoption of the institutions of the welfare state in Bismarck Germany, Sweden, and Great Britain were all associated with the rise of trade unions and socialist parties in those countries. The decisions made by the upper and middle class leaders and political movements to introduce welfare measures such as accident, old age, and unemployment insurance, were strategic decisions. They were increasingly confronted by trade union movements with the capacity of bringing industrial production to a halt, and by political parties with growing parliamentary representation favoring fundamental modifications in, or the abolition of capitalism. As the calculations of the upper and middle class leaders led them to conclude that the costs of suppression exceeded the costs of concession, the various parts of the welfare state began to be put in place—accident, sickness, unemployment insurance, old age insurance, and the like. The problem of maintaining the loyalty of the working classes through two world wars resulted in additional concessions to working class demands: the filling out of the social security system, free public education to higher levels, family allowances, housing benefits, and the like.

Social conditions, historical factors, political processes and decisions produced different versions of the welfare state. In the United States, manhood suffrage came quite early, the later bargaining process emphasized free land and free education to the secondary level, an equality of opportunity version of the welfare state. The Disraeli bargain in Britain resulted in relatively early manhood suffrage and the full attainment of parliamentary government, while the Lloyd George bargain on the eve of World War I brought the beginnings of a welfare system to Britain. The Bismarck bargain in Germany produced an early welfare state, a postponement of electoral equality and parliamentary government. While there were all of these differences in historical encounters with democratization and "welfarization," the important outcome was that little more than a century after the process began all of the advanced capitalist democracies had similar versions of the welfare state, smaller in scale in the case of the United States and Japan, more substantial in Britain and the continental European countries.

We can consequently make out a strong case for the argument that democracy has been supportive of capitalism in this strategic sense. Without this welfare adaptation it is doubtful that capitalism would have survived, or rather, its survival, "unwelfarized," would have required a substantial repressive apparatus. The choice then would seem to have been between democratic welfare capitalism, and repressive undemocratic capitalism. I am inclined to believe that capitalism as such thrives more with the democratic welfare adaptation than with the repressive one. It is in that sense that we can argue that there is a clear positive impact of democracy on capitalism.

We have to recognize, in conclusion, that democracy and capitalism are both positively and negatively related, that they both support and subvert each other. My colleague, Moses Abramovitz, described this dialectic more surely than most in his presidential address to the American Economic Association in 1980, on the eve of the "Reagan Revolution." Noting the decline in productivity in the American economy during the latter 1960s and '70s, and recognizing that this decline might in part be attributable to the "tax, transfer, and regulatory" tendencies of the welfare state, he observes,

> The rationale supporting the development of our mixed economy sees it as a pragmatic compromise between the competing virtues and defects of decentralized market capitalism and encompassing socialism. Its goal is to obtain a measure of distributive justice, security, and social guidance of economic life without losing too much of the allocative efficiency and dynamism of private enterprise and market organization. And it is a pragmatic compromise in another sense. It seeks to retain for most people that measure of personal protection from the state which private property and a private job market confer, while obtaining for the disadvantaged minority of people through the state that measure of support without which their lack of property or personal endowment would amount to a denial of individual freedom and capacity to function as full members of the community. (Abramovitz 1981)

Democratic welfare capitalism produces that reconciliation of opposing and complementary elements which makes possible the survival, even enhancement of both of these sets of institutions. It is not a static accommodation, but rather one which fluctuates over time, with capitalism being compromised by the tax-transfer-regulatory action of the state at one point, and then correcting in the direction of the reduction of the intervention of the state at another point, and with a learning process over time that may reduce the amplitude of the curves.

The case for this resolution of the capitalism-democracy quandary is made quite movingly by Jacob Viner who is quoted in the concluding paragraph of Abramovitz's paper, "... If ... I nevertheless conclude that I believe that the welfare state, like old Siwash, is really worth fighting for and even dying for as compared to any rival system, it is because, despite its imperfection in theory and practice, in the aggregate it provides more promise of preserving and enlarging human freedoms, temporal prosperity, the extinction of mass misery, and the dignity of man and his moral improvement than any other social system which has previously prevailed, which prevails elsewhere today or which outside Utopia, the mind of man has been able to provide a blueprint for" (Abramovitz 1981).

References

Abramovitz, Moses. 1981. "Welfare Quandaries and Productivity Concerns." *American Economic Review*, March.

Berger, Peter. 1986. *The Capitalist Revolution*. New York: Basic Books.

Dahl, Robert A. 1989. *Democracy and Its Critics*. New Haven: Yale University Press.

_____. 1990. *After the Revolution: Authority in a Good Society*. New Haven: Yale University Press.

Deutsch, Karl. 1961. "Social Mobilization and Political Development." *American Political Science Review*, 55 (Sept.).

Flora, Peter, and Arnold Heidenheimer. 1981. *The Development of Welfare States in Western Europe and America*. New Brunswick, NJ: Transaction Press.

Friedman, Milton. 1981. *Capitalism and Freedom*. Chicago: University of Chicago Press.

Hirschman, Albert. 1986. *Rival Views of Market Society*. New York: Viking.

Inkeles, Alex, and David Smith. 1974. *Becoming Modern: Individual Change in Six Developing Countries*. Cambridge, MA: Harvard University Press.

Lerner, Daniel. 1958. *The Passing of Traditional Society*. New York: Free Press.

Lindblom, Charles E. 1977. *Politics and Markets*. New York: Basic Books.

Lipset, Seymour M. 1959. "Some Social Requisites of Democracy." *American Political Science Review*, 53 (September).

Mill, John Stuart. 1848, 1965. *Principles of Political Economy*, 2 vols. Toronto: University of Toronto Press.

Mitchell, William. 1988. "Virginia, Rochester, and Bloomington: Twenty-Five Years of Public Choice and Political Science." *Public Choice*, 56: 101–119.

Moore, Barrington. 1966. *The Social Origins of Dictatorship and Democracy*. New York: Beacon Press.

Olson, Mancur. 1982. *The Rise and Decline of Nations*. New Haven: Yale University Press.

Schumpeter, Joseph. 1946. *Capitalism, Socialism, and Democracy*. New York: Harper.

GABRIEL A. ALMOND, professor of political science emeritus at Stanford University, is a former president of the American Political Science Association.

From *PS: Political Science and Politics,* September 1991, pp. 467–474. Copyright © 1991 by American Political Science Association—APSA. Reprinted by permission.

Anti-Americanisms

Biases as Diverse as the Country Itself

Peter J. Katzenstein and Robert O. Keohane

Arab reactions to American support for Israel in its recent conflict with Hezbollah have put anti-Americanism in the headlines once again. Around the world, not just in the Middle East, when bad things happen there is a widespread tendency to blame America for its sins, either of commission or omission. When its Belgrade embassy is bombed, Chinese people believe it was a deliberate act of the United States government; terror plots by native British subjects are viewed as reflecting British support for American policy; when AIDS devastates much of Africa, the United States is faulted for not doing enough to stop it.

These outbursts of anti-Americanism can be seen simply as a way of protesting American foreign policy. Is "anti-Americanism" really just a common phrase for such opposition, or does it go deeper? If anti-American expressions were simply ways to protest policies of the hegemonic power, only the label would be new. Before World War I Americans reacted to British hegemony by opposing "John Bull." Yet there is a widespread feeling that anti-Americanism is more than simply opposition to what the United States *does,* but extends to opposition to what the United States *is*—what it stands for. Critiques of the United States often extend far beyond its foreign policy: to its social and economic practices, including the public role of women; to its social policies, including the death penalty; and to its popular culture, including the flaunting of sex. Globalization is often seen as Americanization and resented as such. Furthermore, in France, which has had long-standing relations with the United States, anti-Americanism extends to the decades before the founding of the American republic.

With several colleagues we recently completed a book, *Anti-Americanisms in World Politics,*[1] exploring these issues, and in this short article we discuss four of its themes. First, we distinguish between anti-Americanisms that are rooted in opinion or bias. Second, as our book's title suggests, there are many varieties of anti-Americanism. The beginning of wisdom is to recognize that what is called anti-Americanism varies, depending on who is reacting to America. In our book, we describe several different types of anti-Americanism and indicate where each type is concentrated. The variety of anti-Americanism helps us to see, third, the futility of grand explanations for anti-Americanism. It is accounted for better as the result of particular sets of forces.

Finally, the persistence of anti-Americanism, as well as the great variety of forms that it takes, reflects what we call the *polyvalence* of a complex and kaleidoscopic American society in which observers can find whatever they don't like—from Protestantism to porn. The complexity of anti-Americanism reflects the polyvalence of America itself.

Opinion and Bias

Basic to our argument is a distinction between *opinion* and *bias.* Some expressions of unfavorable attitudes merely reflect opinion: unfavorable judgments about the United States or its policies. Others, however, reflect *bias:* a predisposition to believe negative reports about the United States and to discount positive ones. Bias implies a distortion of information processing, while adverse opinion is consistent with maintaining openness to new information that will change one's views. The long-term consequences of bias for American foreign policy are much greater than the consequences of opinion.

The distinction between opinion and bias has implications for policy, and particularly for the debate between left and right on its significance. Indeed, our findings suggest that the positions on anti-Americanism of both left and right are internally inconsistent. Broadly speaking, the American left focuses on opinion rather than bias—opposition, in the left's view largely justified, to American foreign policy. The left also frequently suggests that anti-Americanism poses a serious long-term problem for U.S. diplomacy. Yet insofar as anti-Americanism reflects ephemeral opinion, why should it have long-lasting effects? Policy changes would remove the basis for criticism and solve the problem. Conversely, the American right argues that anti-Americanism reflects a deep bias against the United States: People who hate freedom hate us for what we are. Yet the right also tends to argue that anti-Americanism can be ignored: If the United States follows effective policies, views will follow. But the essence of bias is the rejection of information inconsistent with one's prior view: Biased people do not change their views in response to new information. Hence, if bias is the problem, it poses a major long-term problem for the United States. Both left and right need to rethink their positions.

The view we take in the volume is that much of what is called anti-Americanism, especially outside of the Middle East, indeed is largely opinion. As such, it is volatile and would diminish in response to different policies, as it has in the past. The left is correct on this score, while the right overestimates resentment toward American power and hatred of American values. If the right were correct, anti-Americanism would have been high at the beginning of the new millennium. To the contrary, 2002 Pew polls show that outside the Middle East and Argentina, pluralities in every country polled were favorably disposed toward the United States. Yet with respect to the consequences of anti-American views, the right seems to be on stronger ground. It is difficult to identify big problems for American foreign policy created by anti-Americanism as such, as opposed to American policy. This should perhaps not be surprising, since prior to the Iraq war public opinion toward the United States was largely favorable. The right is therefore broadly on target in its claim that much anti-Americanism—reflecting criticisms of what the United States does rather than what it is—does not pose serious short-term problems for American foreign policy. However, if opinion were to harden into bias, as may be occurring in the Middle East, the consequences for the United States would be much more severe.

Anti-Americanisms

Since we are interested in attitudes that go beyond negative opinions of American foreign policy, we define anti-Americanism as *a psychological tendency to hold negative views of the United States and of American society in general.* Such negative views, which can be more or less intense, can be classified into four major types of anti-Americanism, based on the identities and values of the observers. From least to most intense, we designate these types of anti-Americanism as liberal, social, sovereign-nationalist, and radical. Other forms of anti-Americanism are more historically specific. We discuss them under a separate rubric.

Liberal anti-Americanism. Liberals often criticize the United States bitterly for not living up to its own ideals. A country dedicated to democracy and self-determination supported dictatorships around the world during the Cold War and continued to do so in the Middle East after the Cold War had ended. The war against terrorism has led the United States to begin supporting a variety of otherwise unattractive, even repugnant, regimes and political practices. On economic issues, the United States claims to favor freedom of trade but protects its own agriculture from competition stemming from developing countries and seeks extensive patent and copyright protection for American drug firms and owners of intellectual property. Such behavior opens the United States to charges of hypocrisy from people who share its professed ideals but lament its actions.

Liberal anti-Americanism is prevalent in the liberal societies of advanced industrialized countries, especially those colonized or influenced by Great Britain. No liberal anti-American ever detonated a bomb against Americans or planned an attack on the United States. The potential impact of liberal anti-Americanism would be not to generate attacks on the United States but to reduce support for American policy. The more the United States

is seen as a self-interested power parading under the banners of democracy and human rights rather than as a true proponent of those values, the less willing other liberals may be to defend it with words or deeds.

Since liberal anti-Americanism feeds on perceptions of hypocrisy, a less hypocritical set of United States policies could presumably reduce it. Hypocrisy, however, is inherent in the situation of a superpower that professes universalistic ideals. It afflicted the Soviet Union even more than the United States. Furthermore, a prominent feature of pluralist democracy is that its leaders find it necessary to claim that they are acting consistently with democratic ideals while they have to respond to groups seeking to pursue their own self-interests, usually narrowly defined. When the interests of politically strong groups imply policies that do not reflect democratic ideals, the ideals are typically compromised. Hypocrisy routinely results. It is criticized not only in liberal but also in nonliberal states: for instance, Chinese public discourse overwhelmingly associates the United States with adherence to a double standard in its foreign policy in general and in its conduct of the war on terror specifically.

Hypocrisy in American foreign policy is not so much the result of the ethical failings of American leaders as a byproduct of the role played by the United States in world politics and of democratic politics at home.

It will not, therefore, be eradicated. As long as political hypocrisy persists, abundant material will be available for liberal anti-Americanism.

Social anti-Americanism. Since democracy comes in many stripes, we are wrong to mistake the American tree for the democratic forest. Many democratic societies do not share the peculiar combination of respect for individual liberty, reliance on personal responsibility, and distrust of government characteristic of the United States. People in other democratic societies may therefore react negatively to America's political institutions and its social and political arrangements that rely heavily on market processes. They favor deeper state involvement in social programs than is politically feasible or socially acceptable in the United States. Social democratic welfare states in Scandinavia, Christian democratic welfare states on the European continent, and developmental industrial states in Asia, such as Japan, are prime examples of democracies whose institutions and practices contrast in many ways with those of the United States.

Social anti-Americanism is based on value conflicts that reflect relevant differences in many spheres of life that are touching on "life, liberty and the pursuit of happiness." The injustice embedded in American policies that favor the rich over the poor is often decried. The sting is different here than for liberals who resent American hypocrisy. Genuine value conflicts exist on issues such as the death penalty, the desirability of generous social protections, preference for multilateral approaches over unilateral ones, and the sanctity of international treaties. Still, these value conflicts are smaller than those with radical anti-Americanism, since social anti-Americanism shares in core American values.

Sovereign-nationalist anti-Americanism. A third form of anti-Americanism focuses not on correcting domestic market outcomes but on political power. Sovereign nationalists focus on two values: the importance of not losing control over the terms by which polities are inserted in world politics and the inherent importance and value of collective national identities. These identities often embody values that are at odds with America's. State sovereignty thus becomes a shield against unwanted intrusions from America.

The emphasis placed by different sovereign nationalists can vary in three ways. First, it can be on *nationalism:* on collective national identities that offer a source of positive identification. National identity is one of the most important political values in contemporary world politics, and there is little evidence suggesting that this is about to change. Such identities create the potential for anti-Americanism, both when they are strong (since they provide positive countervalues) and when they are weak (since anti-Americanism can become a substitute for the absence of positive values).

Second, sovereign nationalists can emphasize *sovereignty.* In the many parts of Asia, the Middle East, and Africa where state sovereignty came only after hard-fought wars of national liberation, sovereignty is a much-cherished good that is to be defended. And in Latin America, with its very different history, the unquestioned preeminence of the U.S. has reinforced the perceived value of sovereignty. Anti-Americanism rooted in sovereignty is less common in Europe than in other parts of the world for one simple reason: European politics over the past half-century has been devoted to a common project—the partial pooling of sovereignty in an emerging European polity.

A third variant of sovereign-nationalist anti-Americanism appears where people see their states as potential great powers. Such societies may define their own situations partly in opposition to dominant states. Some Germans came to strongly dislike Britain before World War I as blocking what they believed was Germany's rightful "place in the sun." The British-German rivalry before the First World War was particularly striking in view of the similarities between these highly industrialized and partially democratic societies and the fact that their royal families were related by blood ties. Their political rivalry was systemic, pitting the dominant naval power of the nineteenth century against a rapidly rising land power. Rivalry bred animosity rather than vice versa.

Sovereign-nationalist anti-Americanism resonates well in polities that have strong state traditions. Encroachments on state sovereignty are particularly resented when the state has the capacity and a tradition of directing domestic affairs. This is true in particular of the states of East Asia. The issues of "respect" and saving "face" in international politics can make anti-Americanism especially virulent, since they stir nationalist passions in a way that social anti-Americanism rarely does.

China is particularly interesting for this category, since all three elements of sovereign-nationalist anti-Americanism are present there. The Chinese elites and public are highly nationalistic and very sensitive to threats to Chinese sovereignty. Furthermore, China is already a great power and has aspirations to become more powerful. Yet it is still weaker than the United States. Hence, the superior military capacity of the United States and its expressed willingness to use that capacity (for instance, against an attack

by China on Taiwan) create latent anti-Americanism. When the United States attacks China (as it did with the bombing of the Chinese embassy in Belgrade in 1999) or seems to threaten it (as in the episode of the EC–3 spy plane in 2001), explicit anti-Americanism appears quickly.

Radical anti-Americanism. We characterize a fourth form of anti-Americanism as radical. It is built around the belief that America's identity, as reflected in the internal economic and political power relations and institutional practices of the United States, ensures that its actions will be hostile to the furtherance of good values, practices, and institutions elsewhere in the world. For progress toward a better world to take place, the American economy and society will have to be transformed, either from within or from without.

Radical anti-Americanism was characteristic of Marxist-Leninist states such as the Soviet Union until its last few years and is still defining Cuba and North Korea today. When Marxist revolutionary zeal was great, radical anti-Americanism was associated with violent revolution against U.S.-sponsored regimes, if not the United States itself. Its Marxist-Leninist adherents are now so weak, however, that it is mostly confined to the realm of rhetoric. For the United States to satisfy adherents of this brand of radical anti-Americanism, it would need to change the nature of its political-economic system.

The most extreme form of contemporary radical anti-Americanism holds that Western values are so abhorrent that people holding them should be destroyed. The United States is the leading state of the West and therefore the central source of evil. This perceived evil may take various forms, from equality for women, to public displays of the human body, to belief in the superiority of Christianity. For those holding extreme versions of Occidentalist ideas, the central conclusion is that the West, and the United States in particular, are so incorrigibly bad that they must be destroyed. And since the people who live in these societies have renounced the path of righteousness and truth, they must be attacked and exterminated.

Religiously inspired and secular radical anti-Americanism argue for the weakening, destruction, or transformation of the political and economic institutions of the United States. The distinctive mark of both strands of anti-Americanism is the demand for revolutionary changes in the nature of American society.

It should be clear that these four different types of anti-Americanism are not simply variants of the same schema, emotions, or set of norms with only slight variations at the margin. On the contrary, adherents of different types of anti-Americanism can express antithetical attitudes. Radical Muslims oppose a popular culture that commercializes sex and portrays women as liberated from the control of men and are also critical of secular liberal values. Social and Christian democratic Europeans, by contrast, may love American popular culture but criticize the United States for the death penalty and for not living up to secular values they share with liberals. Liberal anti-Americanism exists because its proponents regard the United States as failing to live up to its professed values—which are entirely opposed to those of religious radicals and are largely embraced by liberals. Secular radical anti-Americans may oppose the American embrace of capitalism but may accept scientific rationalism, gender egalitarianism, and secularism—as Marxists have done. Anti-Americanism can be fostered by Islamic fundamentalism, idealistic liberalism, or Marxism. And it can be embraced by people who, not accepting any of these sets of beliefs, fear the practices or deplore the policies of the United States.

Historically Specific Anti-Americanisms

Two other forms of anti-Americanism, which do not fit within our general typology, are both historically sensitive and particularistic: elitist anti-Americanism and legacy anti-Americanism.

Elitist anti-Americanism arises in countries in which the elite has a long history of looking down on American culture. In France, for example, discussions of anti-Americanism date back to the eighteenth century, when some European writers held that everything in the Americas was degenerate.[2] The climate was enervating; plants and animals did not grow to the same size; people were uncouth. In France and in much of Western Europe, the tradition of disparaging America has continued ever since. Americans are often seen as uncultured materialists seeking individual personal advancement without concern for the arts, music, or other finer things of life. Or they are viewed as excessively religious and therefore insufficiently rational. French intellectuals are the European epicenter of anti-Americanism, and some of their disdain spills over to the public. However, as our book shows, French anti-Americanism is largely an elite phenomenon. Indeed, polls of the French public between the 1960s and 2002 indicated majority pro-Americanism in France, with favorable ratings that were only somewhat lower than levels observed elsewhere in Europe.

Legacy anti-Americanism stems from resentment of past wrongs committed by the United States toward another society. Mexican anti-Americanism is prompted by the experiences of U.S. military attack and various forms of imperialism during the past 200 years. The Iranian revolution of 1979 and the subsequent hostage crisis were fueled by memories of American intervention in Iranian politics in the 1950s, and Iranian hostility to the United States now reflects the hostile relations between the countries during the revolution and hostage crisis. Between the late 1960s and the end of the twentieth century, the highest levels of anti-Americanism recorded in Western Europe were found in Spain and especially Greece—both countries that had experienced civil wars; in the case of Spain the United States supported for decades a repressive dictator. Legacy anti-Americanism can be explosive, but it is not unalterable. As the Philippines and Vietnam—both highly pro-American countries today—show, history can ameliorate or reverse negative views of the United States as well as reinforce them.

The Futility of Grand Explanations

Often Anti-Americanism is explained as the result of some master set of forces—for example, of hegemony or globalization. The United States is hated because it is "Mr. Big" or because

of its neoliberalism. However, all of these broad explanations founder on the variety of anti-Americanisms.

Consider first the "Mr. Big" hypothesis. Since the end of the Cold War, the United States has been by far the most powerful state in the world, without any serious rivals. The collapse of the Soviet bloc means that countries formerly requiring American protection from the Soviet Union no longer need such support, so their publics feel free to be more critical. In this view, it is no accident that American political power is at its zenith while American standing is at its nadir. Resentment at the negative effects of others' exercise of power is hardly surprising. Yet this explanation runs up against some inconvenient facts. If it were correct, anti-Americanism would have increased sharply during the 1990s; but we have seen that outside the Middle East, the United States was almost universally popular as late as 2002. The Mr. Big hypothesis could help account for certain forms of liberal and sovereign-nationalist anti-Americanism: Liberals criticize the United States for hypocrisy (and sometimes for being too reluctant to intervene to right wrongs), while sovereign nationalists fear the imposition of American power on their own societies. But it could hardly account for social, radical, elitist, or legacy anti-Americanism, each of which reacts to features of American society, or its behavior in the past, that are quite distinct from contemporary hegemony.

A second overarching explanation focuses on *globalization backlash*. The expansion of capitalism—often labeled globalization—generates what Joseph Schumpeter called "creative destruction." Those who are adversely affected can be expected to resist such change. In Benjamin Barber's clever phrase, the spread of American practices and popular culture creates "McWorld," which is widely resented even by people who find some aspects of it very attractive.[3] The anti-Americanism generated by McWorld is diffuse and widely distributed in world politics. But some societies most affected by economic globalization—such as India—are among the most pro-American. Even among the Chinese, whose reactions to the United States are decidedly mixed, America's wealth and its role in globalization are not objects of distrust or resentment as much as of envy and emulation. In terms of our typology, only social anti-Americanism and some forms of sovereign-nationalist anti-Americanism could be generated by the role of the United States in economic globalization—not the liberal, radical, elitist, or legacy forms.

A third argument ascribes anti-Americanism to cultural and religious identities that are antithetical to the values being generated and exported by American culture—from Christianity to the commercialization of sex. The globalization of the media has made sexual images not only available to but also unavoidable for people around the world. One reaction is admiration and emulation, captured by Joseph Nye's concept of soft power. But another reaction is antipathy and resistance. The products of secular mass culture are a source of international value conflict. They bring images of sexual freedom and decadence, female emancipation, and equality among the sexes into the homes of patriarchal and authoritarian communities, Muslim and otherwise. For others, it is American religiosity, not its sex-oriented commercialized culture, that generates negative reactions. Like the other arguments, the cultural identity argument has some resonance, but only for certain audiences. It may provide an explanation of some aspects of social, radical, and elitist anti-Americanism, but does not explain the liberal, sovereign-nationalist, or legacy varieties.

Each of the grand explanations probably contains at least a grain of truth, but none constitutes a general explanation of anti-Americanism.

The Polyvalence of American Society

American symbols are *polyvalent*. They embody a variety of values with different meanings to different people and indeed even to the same individual. Elites and ordinary folks abroad are deeply ambivalent about the United States. Visitors, such as Bernard-Henri Lévy, are impressed, repelled, and fascinated in about equal measure. Lévy dislikes what he calls America's "obesity"—in shopping malls, churches, and automobiles—and its marginalization of the poor; but he is impressed by its openness, vitality, and patriotism.[4] As David Laitin has noted, the World Trade Center was a symbol not only of capitalism and America but of New York's cosmopolitan culture, so often scorned by middle America. The Statue of Liberty symbolizes not only America and its conception of freedom. A gift of France, it has become an American symbol of welcome to the world's "huddled masses" that expresses a basic belief in America as a land of unlimited opportunity.

The United States has a vigorous and expressive popular culture, which is enormously appealing both to Americans and to many people elsewhere in the world. This popular culture is quite hedonistic, oriented toward material possessions and sensual pleasure. At the same time, however, the U.S. is today much more religious than most other societies. One important root of America's polyvalence is the tension between these two characteristics. Furthermore, both American popular culture and American religious practices are subject to rapid change, expanding further the varieties of expression in the society and continually opening new options. The dynamism and heterogeneity of American society create a vast set of choices: of values, institutions, and practices.

America's openness to the rest of the world is reflected in its food and popular culture. The American fast-food industry has imported its products from France (fries), Germany (hamburgers and frankfurters) and Italy (pizza). What it added was brilliant marketing and efficient distribution. In many ways the same is true also for the American movie industry, especially in the past two decades. Hollywood is a brand name held by Americans and non-Americans alike. In the 1990s only three of the seven major Hollywood studios were controlled by U.S. corporations. Many of Hollywood's most celebrated directors and actors are non-American. And many of Hollywood's movies about America, both admiring and critical, are made by non-Americans. Like the United Nations, Hollywood is both in America and of the world. And so is America itself—a product of the rest of the world as well as of its own internal characteristics.

"Americanization," therefore, does not describe a simple extension of American products and processes to other parts of the world. On the contrary, it refers to the selective appropriation of American symbols and values by individuals and groups in other societies—symbols and values that may well have had their origins elsewhere. Americanization thus is a profoundly interactive process between America and all parts of the world. And, we argue here, it is deeply intertwined with anti-American views. The interactions that generate Americanization may involve markets, informal networks, or the exercise of corporate or governmental power—often in various combinations. They reflect and reinforce the polyvalent nature of American society as expressed in the activities of Americans, who freely export and import products and practices. But they also reflect the variations in attitudes and interests of people in other societies, seeking to use, resist, and recast symbols that are associated with the United States. Similar patterns of interaction generate pro-Americanism and anti-Americanism, since both pro- and anti-Americanism provide an idiom to debate American and local concerns. Anti- and pro-Americanism have as much to do with the conceptual lenses through which individuals living in very different societies view America as with America itself. In our volume, Iain Johnston and Dani Stockmann report that when residents of Beijing in 1999 were asked simply to compare on an identity-difference scale their perceptions of Americans with their views of Chinese, they placed them very far apart. But when, in the following year, Japanese, the antithesis of the Chinese, were added to the comparison, respondents reduced the perceived identity difference between Americans and Chinese. In other parts of the world, bilateral perceptions of regional enemies can also displace, to some extent, negative evaluations of the United States. For instance, in sharp contrast to the European continent, the British press and public continue to view Germany and Germans primarily through the lens of German militarism, Nazi Germany, and World War II.

Because there is so much in America to dislike as well as to admire, polyvalence makes anti-Americanism persistent. American society is both extremely secular and deeply religious. This is played out in the tensions between blue "metro" and red "retro" America and the strong overtones of self-righteousness and moralism this conflict helps generate. If a society veers toward secularism, as much of Europe has, American religiosity is likely to become salient—odd, disturbing, and, due to American power, vaguely threatening. How can a people who believe more strongly in the Virgin Birth than in the theory of evolution be trusted to lead an alliance of liberal societies? If a society adopts more fervently Islamic religious doctrine and practices, as has occurred throughout much of the Islamic world during the past quarter-century, the prominence of women in American society and the vulgarity and emphasis on sexuality that pervades much of American popular culture are likely to evoke loathing, even fear. Thus, anti-Americanism is closely linked to the polyvalence of American society.

In 1941 Henry Luce wrote a prescient article on "the American Century." The American Century—at least its first 65 years—created enormous changes, some sought by the United States and others unsought and unanticipated. Resentment and anti-Americanism were among the undesired results of American power and engagement with the world. Our own cacophony projects itself onto others and can be amplified as it reverberates, via other societies, around the world.

Perhaps the most puzzling thing about anti-Americanism is that we Americans seem to care so much about it. Americans want to know about anti-Americanism: to understand ourselves better and, perhaps above all, to be reassured. This is one of our enduring traits. Americans' reaction to anti-Americanism in the twenty-first century thus is not very different from what Alexis de Tocqueville encountered in 1835:

The Americans, in their intercourse with strangers, appear impatient of the smallest censure and insatiable of praise. ... They unceasingly harass you to extort praise, and if you resist their entreaties they fall to praising themselves. It would seem as if, doubting their own merit, they wished to have it constantly exhibited before their eyes.[5]

Perhaps we care because we lack self-confidence, because we are uncertain whether to be proud of our role in the world or dismayed by it. Like people in many other societies, we look outside, as if into a mirror, in order to see our own reflections with a better perspective than we can provide on our own. Anti-Americanism is important for what it tells us about United States foreign policy and America's impact on the world. It is also important for what it tells us about ourselves.

Notes

1. Peter J. Katzenstein and Robert O. Keohane, eds., *Anti-Americanisms in World Politics* (Cornell University Press, *2007*).

2. Philippe Roger, *The American Enemy: The History of French Anti-Americanism* (University of Chicago Press, *2005*).

3. Benjamin Barber, *Jihad vs. McWorld* (Crown, *1995*).

4. Bernard-Henri Lévy, *American Vertigo: Traveling America in the Footsteps of Tocqueville* (Random House, 2006).

5. Alexis de Tocqueville, *Democracy in America* (*1835*), *1965* edition, *252*.

The True Clash of Civilizations

Samuel Huntington was only half right. The cultural fault line that divides the West and the Muslim world is not about democracy but sex. According to a new survey, Muslims and their Western counterparts want democracy, yet they are worlds apart when it comes to attitudes toward divorce, abortion, gender equality, and gay rights—which may not bode well for democracy's future in the Middle East.

RONALD INGLEHART AND PIPPA NORRIS

Democracy promotion in Islamic countries is now one of the Bush administration's most popular talking points. "We reject the condescending notion that freedom will not grow in the Middle East," Secretary of State Colin Powell declared last December as he unveiled the White House's new Middle East Partnership Initiative to encourage political and economic reform in Arab countries. Likewise, Condoleezza Rice, President George W. Bush's national security advisor, promised last September that the United States is committed to "the march of freedom in the Muslim world."

> **Republican Rep. Christopher Shays of Connecticut: "Why doesn't democracy grab hold in the Middle East? What is there about the culture and the people and so on where democracy just doesn't seem to be something they strive for and work for?"**

But does the Muslim world march to the beat of a different drummer? Despite Bush's optimistic pronouncement that there is "no clash of civilizations" when it comes to "the common rights and needs of men and women," others are not so sure. Samuel Huntington's controversial 1993 thesis—that the cultural division between "Western Christianity" and "Orthodox Christianity and Islam" is the new fault line for conflict—resonates more loudly than ever since September 11. Echoing Huntington, columnist Polly Toynbee argued in the British *Guardian* last November, "What binds together a globalized force of some extremists from many continents is a united hatred of Western values that seems to them to spring

from Judeo-Christianity." Meanwhile, on the other side of the Atlantic, Republican Rep. Christopher Shays of Connecticut, after sitting through hours of testimony on U.S.-Islamic relations on Capitol Hill last October, testily blurted, "Why doesn't democracy grab hold in the Middle East? What is there about the culture and the people and so on where democracy just doesn't seem to be something they strive for and work for?"

Huntington's response would be that the Muslim world lacks the core political values that gave birth to representative democracy in Western civilization: separation of religious and secular authority, rule of law and social pluralism, parliamentary institutions of representative government, and protection of individual rights and civil liberties as the buffer between citizens and the power of the state. This claim seems all too plausible given the failure of electoral democracy to take root throughout the Middle East and North Africa. According to the latest Freedom House rankings, almost two thirds of the 192 countries around the world are now electoral democracies. But among the 47 countries with a Muslim majority, only one fourth are electoral democracies—and none of the core Arabic-speaking societies falls into this category.

> **. . . the real fault line between the West and Islam. . . concerns gender equality and sexual liberation. . . the values separating the two cultures have much more to do with eros than demos.**

Yet this circumstantial evidence does little to prove Huntington correct, since it reveals nothing about the underlying

The Cultural Divide

Approval of Political and Social Values in Western and Muslim Societies

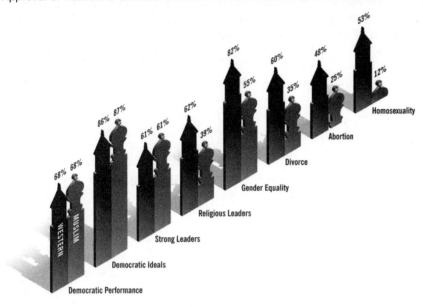

Source: World Values Survey, Pooled Sample 1995-2001; Charts (3) By Jared Schneidman for FP

The chart above draws on responses to various political and social issues in the World Values Survey. The percentages indicate the extent to which respondents agree/disagree with or approved/disapproved of the following statements and questions:

Democratic Performance

- Democracies are indecisive and have too much quibbling. (Strongly disagree.)
- Democracies aren't good at maintaining order. (Strongly disagree.)

Democratic Ideals

- Democracy may have problems, but it's better than any other form of government. (Strongly agree.)
- Approve of having a democratic political system. (Strongly agree.)

Strong Leaders

- Approve of having experts, not government, make decisions according to what they think is best for the country. (Strongly disagree.)
- Approve of having a strong leader who does not have to bother with parliament and elections. (Strongly disagree.)

Religious Leaders

- Politicians who do not believe in God are unfit for public office. (Strongly disagree.)
- It would be better for [this country] if more people with strong religious beliefs held public office. (Strongly disagree.)

Gender Equality

- On the whole, men make better political leaders than women do. (Strongly disagree.)
- When jobs are scarce, men should have more right to a job than women. (Strongly disagree.)
- A university education is more important for a boy than for a girl. (Strongly disagree.)
- A woman has to have children in order to be fulfilled. (Strongly disagree.)
- If a woman wants to have a child as a single parent but she doesn't want to have a stable relationship with a man, do you approve or disapprove? (Strongly approve.)

Divorce

- Divorce can always be justified, never be justified, or something in between. (High level of tolerance for divorce.)

Abortion

- Abortion can always be justified, never be justified, or something in between. (High level of tolerance for abortion.)

Homosexuality

- Homosexuality can always be justified, never be justified, or something in between. (High level of tolerance for homosexuality.)

beliefs of Muslim publics. Indeed, there has been scant empirical evidence whether Western and Muslim societies exhibit deeply divergent values—that is, until now. The cumulative results of the two most recent waves of the World Values Survey (wvs), conducted in 1995–96 and 2000–2002, provide an extensive body of relevant evidence. Based on questionnaires that explore values and beliefs in more than 70 countries, the wvs is an investigation of sociocultural and political change that encompasses over 80 percent of the world's population.

A comparison of the data yielded by these surveys in Muslim and non-Muslim societies around the globe confirms the first claim in Huntington's thesis: Culture does matter—indeed, it matters a lot. Historical religious traditions have left an enduring imprint on contemporary values. However, Huntington is mistaken in assuming that the core clash between the West and Islam is over political values. At this point in history, societies throughout the world (Muslim and Judeo-Christian alike) see democracy as the best form of government. Instead, the real fault line between the West and Islam, which Huntington's theory completely overlooks, concerns gender equality and sexual liberalization. In other words, the values separating the two cultures have much more to do with eros than demos. As younger generations in the West have gradually become more liberal on these issues, Muslim nations have remained the most traditional societies in the world.

This gap in values mirrors the widening economic divide between the West and the Muslim world. Commenting on the disenfranchisement of women throughout the Middle East, the United Nations Development Programme observed last summer that "no society can achieve the desired state of well-being and human development, or compete in a globalizing world, if half its people remain marginalized and disempowered." But this "sexual clash of civilizations" taps into far deeper issues than how Muslim countries treat women. A society's commitment to gender equality and sexual liberalization proves time and again to be the most reliable indicator of how strongly that society supports principles of tolerance and egalitarianism. Thus, the people of the Muslim world overwhelmingly want democracy, but democracy may not be sustainable in their societies.

Testing Huntington

Huntington argues that "ideas of individualism, liberalism, constitutionalism, human rights, equality, liberty, the rule of law, democracy, free markets, [and] the separation of church and state" often have little resonance outside the West. Moreover, he holds that Western efforts to promote these ideas provoke a violent backlash against "human rights imperialism." To test these propositions, we categorized the countries included in the wvs according to the nine major contemporary civilizations, based largely on the historical religious legacy of each society. The survey includes 22 countries representing Western Christianity (a West European culture that also encompasses North America, Australia, and New Zealand), 10 Central European nations (sharing a Western Christian heritage, but which also lived under Communist rule), 11 societies with a

Muslim majority (Albania, Algeria, Azerbaijan, Bangladesh, Egypt, Indonesia, Iran, Jordan, Morocco, Pakistan, and Turkey), 12 traditionally Orthodox societies (such as Russia and Greece), 11 predominately Catholic Latin American countries, 4 East Asian societies shaped by Sino-Confucian values, 5 sub-Saharan Africa countries, plus Japan and India.

Despite Huntington's claim of a clash of civilizations between the West and the rest, the wvs reveals that, at this point in history, democracy has an overwhelmingly positive image throughout the world. In country after country, a clear majority of the population describes "having a democratic political system" as either "good" or "very good." These results represent a dramatic change from the 1930s and 1940s, when fascist regimes won overwhelming mass approval in many societies; and for many decades, Communist regimes had widespread support. But in the last decade, democracy became virtually the only political model with global appeal, no matter what the culture. With the exception of Pakistan, most of the Muslim countries surveyed think highly of democracy: In Albania, Egypt, Bangladesh, Azerbaijan, Indonesia, Morocco, and Turkey, 92 to 99 percent of the public endorsed democratic institutions—a higher proportion than in the United States (89 percent).

Yet, as heartening as these results may be, paying lip service to democracy does not necessarily prove that people genuinely support basic democratic norms—or that their leaders will allow them to have democratic institutions. Although constitutions of authoritarian states such as China profess to embrace democratic ideals such as freedom of religion, the rulers deny it in practice. In Iran's 2000 elections, reformist candidates captured nearly three quarters of the seats in parliament, but a theocratic elite still holds the reins of power. Certainly, it's a step in the right direction if most people in a country endorse the idea of democracy. But this sentiment needs to be complemented by deeper underlying attitudes such as interpersonal trust and tolerance of unpopular groups—and these values must ultimately be accepted by those who control the army and secret police.

The wvs reveals that, even after taking into account differences in economic and political development, support for democratic institutions is just as strong among those living in Muslim societies as in Western (or other) societies [see box, The Cultural Divide]. For instance, a solid majority of people living in Western and Muslim countries gives democracy high marks as the most efficient form of government, with 68 percent disagreeing with assertions that "democracies are indecisive" and "democracies aren't good at maintaining order." (All other cultural regions and countries, except East Asia and Japan, are far more critical.) And an equal number of respondents on both sides of the civilizational divide (61 percent) firmly reject authoritarian governance, expressing disapproval of "strong leaders" who do not "bother with parliament and elections." Muslim societies display greater support for religious authorities playing an active societal role than do Western societies. Yet this preference for religious authorities is less a cultural division between the West and Islam than it is a gap between the West and many other less secular societies around the

A Barometer of Tolerance

Gender Equality and Democracy

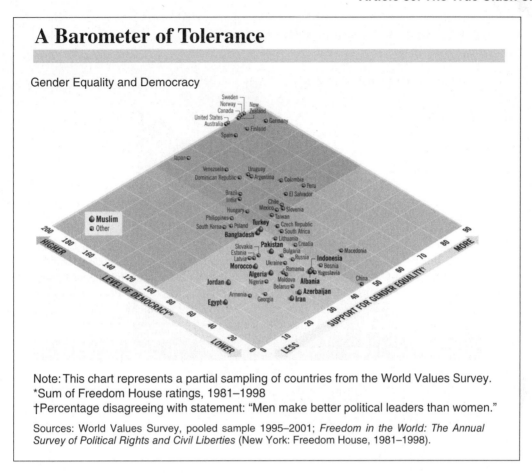

Note: This chart represents a partial sampling of countries from the World Values Survey.
*Sum of Freedom House ratings, 1981–1998
†Percentage disagreeing with statement: "Men make better political leaders than women."

Sources: World Values Survey, pooled sample 1995–2001; *Freedom in the World: The Annual Survey of Political Rights and Civil Liberties* (New York: Freedom House, 1981–1998).

globe, especially in sub-Saharan Africa and Latin America. For instance, citizens in some Muslim societies agree overwhelmingly with the statement that "politicians who do not believe in God are unfit for public office" (88 percent in Egypt, 83 percent in Iran, and 71 percent in Bangladesh), but this statement also garners strong support in the Philippines (71 percent), Uganda (60 percent), and Venezuela (52 percent). Even in the United States, about two fifths of the public believes that atheists are unfit for public office.

Today, relatively few people express overt hostility toward other classes, races, or religions, but rejection of homosexuals is widespread. About half of the world's populations say that homosexuality is "never" justifiable.

However, when it comes to attitudes toward gender equality and sexual liberalization, the cultural gap between Islam and the West widens into a chasm. On the matter of equal rights and opportunities for women—measured by such questions as whether men make better political leaders than women or whether university education is more important for boys than for girls—Western and Muslim countries score 82 percent and

55 percent, respectively. Muslim societies are also distinctively less permissive toward homosexuality, abortion, and divorce.

These issues are part of a broader syndrome of tolerance, trust, political activism, and emphasis on individual autonomy that constitutes "self-expression values." The extent to which a society emphasizes these self-expression values has a surprisingly strong bearing on the emergence and survival of democratic institutions. Among all the countries included in the wvs, support for gender equality—a key indicator of tolerance and personal freedom—is closely linked with a society's level of democracy [see box, A Barometer of Tolerance].

Muslim societies are neither uniquely nor monolithically low on tolerance toward sexual orientation and gender equality. . . . However, on the whole, Muslim countries not only lag behind the West but behind all other societies as well.

In every stable democracy, a majority of the public disagrees with the statement that "men make better political leaders than women." None of the societies in which less than 30 percent of the public rejects this statement (such as Jordan, Nigeria, and Belarus) is a true democracy. In China, one of the world's least

209

A Widening Generation Gap

Support for Gender Equality, by Age and Type of Society

*The 100-point Gender Equality Scale is based on responses to the following five statements and questions: "If a woman wants to have a child as a single parent but she doesn't want to have a stable relationship with a man, do you approve or disapprove?"; "When jobs are scarce, men should have more right to a job than women"; "A university education is more important for a boy than a girl"; "Do you think that a woman has to have children in order to be fulfilled or is this not necessary?"; and "On the whole, men make better political leaders than women do." The scale was constructed so that if all respondents show high scores on all five items (representing strong support for gender equality), it produces a score of 100, while low scores on all five items produce a score of 0.

Source: World Values Surveys, pooled 1995–2001.

democratic countries, a majority of the public agrees that men make better political leaders than women, despite a party line that has long emphasized gender equality (Mao Zedong once declared, "women hold up half the sky"). In practice, Chinese women occupy few positions of real power and face widespread discrimination in the workplace. India is a borderline case. The country is a long-standing parliamentary democracy with an independent judiciary and civilian control of the armed forces, yet it is also marred by a weak rule of law, arbitrary arrests, and

extra-judicial killings. The status of Indian women reflects this duality. Women's rights are guaranteed in the constitution, and Indira Gandhi led the nation for 15 years. Yet domestic violence and forced prostitution remain prevalent throughout the country, and, according to the wvs, almost 50 percent of the Indian populace believes only men should run the government.

The way a society views homosexuality constitutes another good litmus test of its commitment to equality. Tolerance of well-liked groups is never a problem. But if someone wants

Want to Know More?

Samuel Huntington expanded his controversial 1993 article into a book, *The Clash of Civilizations and the Remaking of World Order* (New York: Simon and Schuster, 1996). Among the authors who have disputed Huntington's claim that Islam is incompatible with democratic values are Edward Said, who decries the clash of civilizations thesis as an attempt to revive the "good vs. evil" world dichotomy prevalent during the Cold War ("**A Clash of Ignorance,**" *The Nation*, October 22, 2001); John Voll and John Esposito, who argue that "The Muslim heritage. . . contains concepts that provide a foundation for contemporary Muslims to develop authentically Muslim programs of democracy" ("**Islam's Democratic Essence,**" *Middle East Quarterly*, September 1994); and Ray Takeyh, who recounts the efforts of contemporary Muslim scholars to legitimize democratic concepts through the reinterpretation of Muslim texts and traditions ("**Faith-Based Initiatives,**" FOREIGN POLICY, November/December 2001).

An overview of the Bush administration's **Middle East Partnership Initiative**, including the complete transcript of Secretary of State Colin Powell's speech on political and economic reform in the Arab world, can be found on the Web site of the U.S. Department of State. Marina Ottaway, Thomas Carothers, Amy Hawthorne, and Daniel Brumberg offer a stinging critique of those who believe that toppling the Iraqi regime could unleash a democratic tsunami in the Arab world in "**Democratic Mirage in the Middle East**" (Washington: Carnegie Endowment for International Peace, 2002).

In a poll of nearly 4,000 Arabs, James Zogby found that the issue of "civil and personal rights" earned the overall highest score when people were asked to rank their personal priorities (*What Arabs Think: Values, Beliefs and Concerns*, Washington: Zogby International, 2002). A poll available on the Web site of the Pew Research Center for the People and the Press ("**Among Wealthy Nations . . . U.S. Stands Alone in Its Embrace of Religion,**" December 19, 2002) reveals that Americans' views on religion and faith are closer to those living in developing nations than in developed countries.

The Web site of the **World Values Survey** (WVS) provides considerable information on the survey, including background on methodology, key findings, and the text of the questionnaires. The second iteration of the A.T. Kearney/Foreign Policy Magazine Globalization Index ("**Globalization's Last Hurrah?**" Foreign Policy, January/February 2002) found a strong correlation between the WVS measure of "subjective well-being" and a society's level of global integration.

For links to relevant Web sites, access to the FP Archive, and a comprehensive index of related Foreign Policy articles, go to www.foreignpolicy.com.

---

to gauge how tolerant a nation really is, find out which group is the most disliked, and then ask whether members of that group should be allowed to hold public meetings, teach in schools, and work in government. Today, relatively few people express overt hostility toward other classes, races, or religions, but rejection of homosexuals is widespread. In response to a WVS question about whether homosexuality is justifiable, about half of the world's population say "never." But, as is the case with gender equality, this attitude is directly proportional to a country's level of democracy. Among authoritarian and quasi-democratic states, rejection of homosexuality is deeply entrenched: 99 percent in both Egypt and Bangladesh, 94 percent in Iran, 92 percent in China, and 71 percent in India. By contrast, these figures are much lower among respondents in stable democracies: 32 percent in the United States, 26 percent in Canada, 25 percent in Britain, and 19 percent in Germany.

Muslim societies are neither uniquely nor monolithically low on tolerance toward sexual orientation and gender equality. Many of the Soviet successor states rank as low as most Muslim societies. However, on the whole, Muslim countries not only lag behind the West but behind all other societies as well [see box, A Widening Generation Gap]. Perhaps more significant, the figures reveal the gap between the West and Islam is even wider among younger age groups. This pattern suggests that the younger generations in Western societies have become progressively more egalitarian than their elders, but the younger generations in Muslim societies have remained almost as traditional as their parents and grandparents, producing an expanding cultural gap.

Clash of Conclusions

"The peoples of the Islamic nations want and deserve the same freedoms and opportunities as people in every nation," President Bush declared in a commencement speech at West Point last summer. He's right. Any claim of a "clash of civilizations" based on fundamentally different political goals held by Western and Muslim societies represents an oversimplification of the evidence. Support for the goal of democracy is surprisingly widespread among Muslim publics, even among those living in authoritarian societies. Yet Huntington is correct when he argues that cultural differences have taken on a new importance, forming the fault lines for future conflict. Although nearly the entire world pays lip service to democracy, there is still no global consensus on the self-expression values—such as social tolerance, gender equality, freedom of speech, and interpersonal trust—that are crucial to democracy. Today, these divergent values constitute the real clash between Muslim societies and the West.

But economic development generates changed attitudes in virtually any society. In particular, modernization compels systematic, predictable changes in gender roles: Industrialization brings women into the paid work force and dramatically reduces fertility rates. Women become literate and begin to participate in representative government but still have far less power than men. Then, the postindustrial phase brings a shift toward greater gender equality as women move into higher-status economic roles in management and gain political influence within elected and appointed bodies. Thus, relatively industrialized Muslim societies such as Turkey share the same views on gender equality and sexual liberalization as other new democracies.

Even in established democracies, changes in cultural attitudes—and eventually, attitudes toward democracy—seem to be closely linked with modernization. Women did not attain the right to vote in most historically Protestant societies until about 1920, and in much of Roman Catholic Europe until after World War II. In 1945, only 3 percent of the members of parliaments

around the world were women. In 1965, the figure rose to 8 percent, in 1985 to 12 percent, and in 2002 to 15 percent.

The United States cannot expect to foster democracy in the Muslim world simply by getting countries to adopt the trappings of democratic governance, such as holding elections and having a parliament. Nor is it realistic to expect that nascent democracies in the Middle East will inspire a wave of reforms reminiscent of the velvet revolutions that swept Eastern Europe in the final days of the Cold War. A real commitment to democratic reform will be measured by the willingness to commit the resources necessary to foster human development in the Muslim world. Culture has a lasting impact on how societies evolve. But culture does not have to be destiny.

From *Foreign Policy*, March/April 2003, pp. 63–70. Copyright © 2003 by the Carnegie Endowment for International Peace. Reprinted with permission. www.foreignpolicy.com

The EU and Its "Constitution"

Public Opinion, Political Elites, and Their International Context

ALBERTA SBRAGIA

The European Union is going about its regular business. It is putting forth proposals to keep the Doha Round alive, continuing to negotiate a major trade agreement with Mercosur in South America, keeping peace-keeping troops in Bosnia and Herzegovina, spending development aid in numerous poor countries, financially supporting the Palestine Authority while giving Israel preferential access to the EU market, investigating Microsoft's business practices, and battling over the reach and scope of an ambitious new legislative attempt to regulate the chemical industry. The EU Greenhouse Trading Scheme, the largest greenhouse emissions trading scheme in the world, is up and running. The European Central Bank is making monetary policy decisions while the euro makes up almost 20% of central banks' foreign currency holdings. The European Medicines Agency (EMEA) has called for suspending the sale of the children's vaccine Hexavac. The European Court of Justice, for its part, has recently declared illegal a high profile Italian law designed to prevent foreign take-over of Italian energy companies. And the commissioner for Health and Consumer Protection is playing a leading role in the EU's response to the threat of a pandemic of avian bird flu.

Meanwhile, EU citizens are enjoying the benefits of the EU in very direct ways—when they fly on a low cost airline, make a phone call which is far cheaper than it otherwise would have been, study abroad while receiving credit back at their home institution, cross national boundaries without passport or customs control, or use the euro in any one of the 12 EU member-states which have adopted it. Although the EU is often characterized as a regulatory rather than a welfare state (Majone 1996), it is responsible for many policy outputs which are generally popular.

The defeat of the EU Constitution[1] in French and Dutch referenda held in mid-2005 has not blocked the EU from carrying out its usual activities. Those are currently subject to the Treaty of Nice as well as the other treaties which have been ratified since 1958 and are still in force. Nor has it affected the kinds of benefits to which EU citizens have become accustomed. While there is angst and confusion about the future direction of the Union among political elites, it is important to note that the institutionalized machinery of governance which has evolved over nearly 50 years is in place and functioning. The fact that the Constitution's defeat did not alter the by now routine operations of policymaking highlights how embedded such policymaking is in the political life of an integrating Europe. The institutions of the European Union—the European Commission, the European Court of Justice, the European Parliament, the Council of Ministers, and the European Central Bank—are in place and doing the kind of substantive work they did before the Constitution was drafted.

Nonetheless, the Constitution's defeat is clearly an important moment in the history of European integration. For the first time, an agreement designed to further integration has been resoundingly defeated in two of the original six founding members of the European Union. Although supporters of the Constitution argue that the use of the referendum is an inappropriate mechanism for the approval of treaties, the referendum does enjoy a legitimacy which is difficult to negate. The impact of the "no" votes has been so great that many analysts argue the days of further integration in Europe are finished.

The medium to long-term impact of the Constitution's rejection, however, is far from clear. Even without the contingency endemic to international affairs, the Constitution's defeat very probably will have unanticipated consequences. And those consequences, in turn, may actually run counter to the predictions of those who argue that the future looks bleak for European integration.

Two basic arguments can be made regarding the implications for European integration of the Constitution's defeat. The first argues that the political context has changed so fundamentally that policymaking and the trajectory of further integration will be affected in irreversible ways. In that sense, the defeat is a strategic defeat for those who wish for Europe to move toward ever greater integration.

The second argues that, by contrast, this defeat will simply encourage Europe's political elites to continue the process of integration through means other than treaties put to a referendum. That process could include a new treaty focused on the institutional changes incorporated in the Constitution which would be submitted to parliamentary ratification only. More interestingly, however, it could also involve moving toward further integration by using the institutional instruments currently available under the Treaty of Nice—in spite of the fact that political elites supported the Constitution because they viewed those instruments as too weak to allow further integration. Both arguments can be justified.

The Constitution

The Constitution was clearly meant to drive integration forward. Although the "Constitution" was actually a constitutional treaty since it had to be ratified unanimously and could only be amended unanimously, it was viewed as the next major agreement which would lead both to more integration among the EU-25 and pave the way for further enlargement. It was written in a less intergovernmental fashion than had been previous treaties. Although national governments negotiating in an intergovernmental forum had the last word, national and (especially) European parliamentarians had an important role in shaping its content and direction.

The comparatively diverse group of participants in the Constitution-drafting process highlighted the Constitution's symbolic value. That symbolic value was in fact far greater than its actual substantive content would have warranted. And the question now stands—how much does its defeat matter?

Much of the EU Constitution was not new. It included "old" treaties which had been approved (at times in referenda in selected countries) and had been in effect for years. Those treaties will remain in effect. The defeat primarily affects proposed new institutional arrangements. Those included increasing the power of the European Parliament, establishing new voting weights for the various member-states, and strengthening the Union's external relations. It may, therefore, become more difficult, at the institutional level, to construct a more cohesive European Union in the global arena. Finally, enlargement will become more problematic, as the proposed institutional changes were designed to accommodate new members.

A Strategic Defeat?

There is no doubt that the defeats have re-framed the process of European integration in the minds of Europe's political class. There is currently a sense of indirection, of confusion, and of doubt as to where the grand project that the Six began with the Treaty of Paris in 1951 is going. The current climate is reminiscent of that which emerged after the Maastricht Treaty was approved by a margin of 1% in France in September 1992 and was only approved by the Danes in a second referendum in May 1993. At that time, too, the Commission was weakened, political elites were shaken, and the process of integration seemed much frailer than it had appeared only a few months earlier. The calls for full EU membership by the post-communist countries undergoing often difficult transitions to democracy added a kind of pressure which national leaders were at times reluctant to accept. Terms such as "a multi-speed Europe," "variable geometry," and

a "Europe a la Carte" entered the political as well as academic discourse about future paths which European integration might follow (Stubb 1996).

Of course, the EU recovered in a spectacular fashion from the Maastricht crisis. Although a great deal was written at the time about the caution that elites would need to demonstrate given the French public's reluctance to whole-heartedly endorse the next stage of integration, the European Union in 2005 looks very different from its pre-Maastricht incarnation. It created the new institutions called for in the Treaty and continued to become more important as a global actor. The European Central Bank was established, the euro was accepted by 12 of the 15 members, and, on the international stage, the EU was critical to the establishment of an important new international institution—the International Criminal Court—as well as to the successful conclusion of the Uruguay Round. It even began developing a European Security and Defense Policy. Thus, the question arises of whether the long-term implications of the Constitution's defeat will be as transient as were those of the narrow margin of victory in France (and the necessity of holding a second referendum in Denmark) during the Maastricht process.

The difference between Maastricht and the Constitution lies in the clear and unequivocal distinction between approval (however slim the margin) and defeat. Maastricht became the treaty in force—with its commitment to a single currency and a more united European Union acting on the global stage. Furthermore, it was a much smaller EU that had to deal with the aftershocks of the Maastricht debate—the then EU-12 could more easily regroup than the current EU-25 (soon to be 27).

The consequences of defeat could in fact be far more damaging than the consequences of a razor-thin ratification. The political momentum which has traditionally been so important for the movement toward further integration could be absent, for political leaders would be unwilling to act against public opinion. The lack of a "permissive consensus" on the part of electorates could lead to a protracted stalemate, paralysis, and a gradual drift away from the kind of goals and aspirations which are traditionally associated with further integration. In particular, the attempt to create a stronger global presence would be stymied, and the move toward bringing ever more policy areas under the EU umbrella would be stopped or even reversed. The role of the so-called Community method—which involves a key policymaking role for the supranational European Commission, the European Parliament, and the European Court of Justice—would be at best frozen. And further enlargement—beyond the accession of Romania and Bulgaria—would become impossible.

In a worst case scenario, the lack of commitment by political leaders to the European Union would gradually infect the EU's institutions, for the latter's effectiveness is in fact anchored in the willingness of national institutions and elites to support the overall project of integration by supporting its supranational institutions.

The view that the defeat of the Constitution will sap the political momentum from the Union privileges the role of public opinion in the process of European integration. It implicitly argues that the hitherto elite-driven process of integration has been fundamentally transformed. The role of a majoritarian representative institution—the national parliament—in ratifying treaties which advance European integration would have been diminished by the expression of voters engaged in direct democracy through the referendum. In fact, given the role of party government and party discipline in national parliamentary systems, the role of political parties would have been diminished.

Since the major political parties in Europe (whether in government or in opposition) have supported treaty ratification since 1958 and supported the ratification of the Constitution, the view that European integration will stall privileges public opinion *vis a vis* the opinions of governmental and party elites. In brief, the key support for integration—elite consensus—would become less powerful as an effective driving force.

The role of public opinion in European integration over the past 50 years has been ambiguous. The scholarly literature has come to varied conclusions, and in general scholars of European integration have focused on the role of elites in driving integration forward. Yet it is fair to ask how such an elite-driven process could sustain itself over so many decades. The liberalization of markets in particular would have been expected to lead to more contentious politics directed specifically against the EU than has been evident (Imig and Tarrow 2001; Gabel 1998; Sbragia 2000). Perhaps the underlying assumption of those who assume that public opinion should be expected to play a central role in the integration process was most pungently expressed by Herbert Morrison, deputy prime minister of Britain at the time when the British Cabinet rejected the invitation to join the European Coal and Steel Community. As Morrison summed up the issue, "It's no good. We can't do it. The Durham miners would never wear it" (cited in Gilbert 2003, 42).

If public opinion were indeed to significantly slow the pace of integration or re-shape its nature in the post-Constitution phase, it would have entered the stage as a significant factor relatively late in the process of integration. Given that elections to the European Parliament have been viewed as "second order elections"—based far more on national issues and political cleavages as opposed to EU-wide political debate—and that elites have enjoyed a "permissive consensus" which they have used to deepen integration, the strengthening of the role of public opinion in determining the course of European integration would represent a major new phase in this project.

The EU: A Geo-Economic/Political Project?

Europe's political elites, however, may well continue the process of European integration, enlargement, and global integration *even if* key aspects of the Constitution are not ultimately resurrected in some fashion. This argument views the European Union as a key geo-economic/political project as well as a complex variant of a (con) or (semi) or (crypto) federation/federalism-constructing exercise (Sbragia 1993; Majone 2006).

It is quite possible that the EU's international dimension may well override the kinds of constraints imposed by public opinion. If the EU is viewed only or primarily as a domestic political system, the defeat of the Constitution would in fact be a strategic defeat. If the EU is also conceptualized as a geo-economic/political project, however, the defeat might well have unanticipated consequences which are far more conducive to further integration than might be evident in the short-term.

The beginning of the accession negotiations with Turkey in October in the face of widespread public hostility to Turkish membership symbolizes the determination of governments to carry out the promises they have already made to other international actors. Although governments opened the accession negotiations with Turkey after a good deal of conflict with each other and down-to-the-wire negotiations with the Austrian government (which wanted to leave open the possibility of a privileged partnership for Turkey rather than accession), what stands out is the fact that accession negotiations actually went forward as planned. A mere four months after the Constitution's defeat, the EU was not only back in business, but back in a very difficult kind of business. Although many analysts argue that Turkey will never actually join, the very fact of opening negotiations has triggered a process of long-term change within Turkey that makes the outcome less predictable than the skeptics admit.

In a similar vein, the active engagement of the EU in the Doha Round symbolizes the understanding by elites that Europe's economic well-being is nested within a larger—global—economic reality. Although French voters fear economic liberalization of the services sector, it is quite possible that at least some such liberalization will occur due to pressure from the Doha negotiations. The EU is enmeshed in a larger multilateral trading system, and the decisions made at that level affect it in ways which have not been well understood by either publics or political scientists.

I would argue that external challenges, although understudied in the EU literature, have always been very significant in influencing the evolution of European integration.[2] The Soviet threat and the evolution of the GATT in the 1950s, the impact of de-colonization on states' commercial interests in the 1960s, the changes in economic competitiveness in the 1980s, and the perceived need for greater military and political power during the Balkan crises of the 1990s have all been influential in the process. The dynamics of European integration have been embedded in the larger international environment, and that environment cannot be ignored in explaining the extraordinary depth of European integration.

More specifically, the implementation of the customs union in goods was supported by the GATT negotiations in the Kennedy and Dillon rounds (Langhammer 2005). The Single European Act which brought the single market to the EU was motivated in great part by the sense that European firms were falling behind their Japanese and American counterparts (Sandholtz and Zysman 1992) while the Maastricht Treaty was shaped in significant ways by the fall of the Berlin Wall and the end of the division of Europe. The restructuring of the Common Agricultural Policy was partially driven by the Uruguay Round negotiations (Patterson 1997). The movement toward a European Security and Defense Policy was at least partially a response to pressure from Washington (Howorth 2005) as well as to Europe's failures in addressing the tragedy of the wars in the Balkans.

ANNUAL EDITIONS

External economic and security pressures will continue to exert a deep influence. While some of the most immediate pressures have been addressed by extending membership to the EU-15's neighbors, the enlargement process cannot keep meeting that challenge indefinitely. The WTO, the rise of China, changes in American grand strategy, and new security threats on the periphery of the Union will unavoidably push the European project in new directions as elites attempt to deal with emerging situations in world politics.

Some of the most significant institutional changes that the Constitution would have made were in fact designed to help the EU address foreign policy challenges in a more cohesive and effective way. Ironically, public opinion across the EU seems to favor a more unified global posture on the part of Brussels (German Marshall Fund 2005). Europe does not exist in a vacuum, and both elites and publics are aware of that basic fact. A more cohesive Euro-level foreign policy may therefore emerge even in the absence of the institutional changes that the Constitution would have produced. It is very likely that elites can pull mass publics with them in the area of foreign policy. In fact, the effort to strengthen the Union as a global actor can serve to link elites and publics more firmly than have economic policies of liberalization and regulation.

Economic integration, inevitably involving economic liberalization, is not as intuitively attractive as is a "stronger Europe on the world stage." Whether such liberalization can be successfully presented to voters as necessary for the strengthening of the EU as a geo-economic project is unclear, but it is possible that the "twinning" of European economic and foreign policy integration would help make economic liberalization more appealing.

The argument that an elite-driven process of integration—which incorporates party, governmental, and many business elites as well as national parliamentarians—has suffered a disruption but neither a strategic change of direction nor a strategic defeat downplays the role of public opinion as expressed in the defeat of the Constitution. It assumes that elites will in fact be able to move toward further integration. External events will provide support for further integration—such as recent events in the area of energy have demonstrated.

One of the unanticipated consequences of the Constitution's defeat in France and the Netherlands may be that integration will proceed in new ways. Just as the defeat of the European Defence Community in 1954 led to the European Economic Community, so too the need to circumvent public opinion (or at least not consult it directly) may lead to new forms of integration. The American executive, for example, has developed a host of ways to deal with international affairs which essentially circumvent or limit the role of Congress. Executive agreements and "fast track authority" for trade agreements (now known as trade promotion authority) both have been designed to allow the executive to have more flexibility in international than domestic affairs.

Second, cohesion in the foreign policy arena may develop more quickly than it has heretofore. Integration in foreign policy has lagged integration in "domestic" affairs given the member-states' concern with sovereignty. However, elites' desire to continue the process of integration coupled with the need to matter in a world in which not only the U.S. but also such countries as China and

India will be important actors may provide the impetus for moving forward in that area. The role that the EU has played since 1958 in the GATT/WTO provides a useful precedent.

The defeat of the Constitution ironically may lead national leaders to move forward, develop new mechanisms to forge agreements without creating a context in which referenda are called, and actually become far more cohesive in foreign policy than would have been expected. One of the motivating forces for the Constitution was the desire on the part of national elites that the European Union should become a more effective global actor. The defeat of the Constitution will not necessarily defeat that desire, and external pressures will continue to entice national leaders to follow that road. Geo-economics and geo-politics have always provided a rationale within domestic politics for the insulation of representative institutions from direct constituency pressures. It is very possible that they will provide the same kind of rationale for the European Union.

If the EU is in fact framed or presented by elites as a geo-economic and geo-political project which will maximize European influence on the world stage and thereby help it respond to external events, it is quite possible that mass publics will become more supportive and that integration will move relatively rapidly in the one area that has been most resistant to Europeanization—that of foreign policy. Furthermore "sensitive" domestic areas clearly subject to external influences, such as energy, will become Europeanized far more quickly than one would expect.

The lack of institutional efficiency which the Constitution was supposed to remedy will undoubtedly make this process messier and more convoluted than the Constitution's backers would have liked. That same inefficiency will, however, allow the new accession states to play a role more similar to that which the EU-15 have played and give them a chance to make their mark in the shaping of the EU-25. If external pressures do indeed allow political elites to move integration forward, convince public opinion that such integration is acceptable, and help integrate the new accession states politically rather than simply institutionally, the defeat of the Constitution may be viewed quite differently 20 years from now than it is at present.

References

Gabel, Matthew J. 1998. *Interest and Integration: Market Liberalization, Public Opinion, and European Union.* Ann Arbor: University of Michigan Press.

German Marshall Fund of the United States et al. 2005. *Transatlantic Trends: Key Findings 2005.* Washington, D.C.: German Marshal Fund of the United States.

Gilbert, Mark. 2003. *Surpassing Realism: The Politics of European Integration since 1945.* New York: Rowman and Littlefield.

Howorth, Jolyon. 2005. "Transatlantic Perspectives on European Security in the Coming Decade." *Yale Journal of International Affairs* (summer/fall): 8–22.

Imig, Doug, and Sidney Tarrow, eds. 2001. *Contentious Europeans: Protest and Politics in the New Europe.* Lanham, MD: Rowman and Littlefield.

Langhammer, Rolf J. 2005. "The EU Offer of Service Trade Liberalization in the Doha Round: Evidence of a Not-Yet-Perfect Customs Union." *Journal of Common Market Studies* 51 (2): 311–325.

Majone, Giandomenico. 1996. *Regulating Europe.* New York: Routledge.

———. 2006. "The Common Sense of European Integration." Presented at the Princeton International Relations Faculty Colloquium, March 13.

Mayhew, David R. 2005. "Wars and American Politics." *Perspectives on Politics* 3 (September): 473–493.

Patterson, Lee Ann. 1997. "Agricultural Policy Reform in the European Community: A Three-Level Game Analysis." *International Organization* 51 (1): 135–165.

Sandholtz, Wayne, and John Zysman. 1989. "1992: Recasting the European Bargain." *World Politics* 42: 95–128.

Sbragia, Alberta. 1993. "The European Community: A Balancing Act." *Publius: The Journal of Federalism* 23 (summer): 23–38.

———. 2000. "Governance, the State, and the Market: What Is Going On?" *Governance* 13 (April): 243–250.

Stubb, Alexander C-G. 1996. "A Categorization of Differentiated Integration." *Journal of Common Market Studies* 13 (2): 283–295.

Notes

1. The "Constitution" was actually a constitutional treaty rather than a constitution as traditionally understood. However, the political debate in most countries used the term "Constitution" rather than "constitutional treaty," and I therefore shall use the term "Constitution" as well.

2. For a similar perspective on American politics, see Mayhew 2005.

ALBERTA SBRAGIA is director of the European Union Center of Excellence and a Jean Monnet Professor of Political Science at the University of Pittsburgh. She has chaired the European Union Studies Association and is particularly interested in EU-U.S. comparisons. Her current work focuses on the role of the EU in the field of commercial diplomacy and the global emergence of economic regionalism.

Test-Your-Knowledge Form

We encourage you to photocopy and use this page as a tool to assess how the articles in *Annual Editions* expand on the information in your textbook. By reflecting on the articles you will gain enhanced text information. You can also access this useful form on a product's book support website at *http://www.mhhe.com/cls*.

NAME: DATE:

_____

TITLE AND NUMBER OF ARTICLE:

_____

BRIEFLY STATE THE MAIN IDEA OF THIS ARTICLE:

_____

LIST THREE IMPORTANT FACTS THAT THE AUTHOR USES TO SUPPORT THE MAIN IDEA:

_____

WHAT INFORMATION OR IDEAS DISCUSSED IN THIS ARTICLE ARE ALSO DISCUSSED IN YOUR TEXTBOOK OR OTHER READINGS THAT YOU HAVE DONE? LIST THE TEXTBOOK CHAPTERS AND PAGE NUMBERS:

_____

LIST ANY EXAMPLES OF BIAS OR FAULTY REASONING THAT YOU FOUND IN THE ARTICLE:

_____

LIST ANY NEW TERMS/CONCEPTS THAT WERE DISCUSSED IN THE ARTICLE, AND WRITE A SHORT DEFINITION:

We Want Your Advice

ANNUAL EDITIONS revisions depend on two major opinion sources: one is our Advisory Board, listed in the front of this volume, which works with us in scanning the thousands of articles published in the public press each year; the other is you—the person actually using the book. Please help us and the users of the next edition by completing the prepaid article rating form on this page and returning it to us. Thank you for your help!

ANNUAL EDITIONS: Comparative Politics 10/11

ARTICLE RATING FORM

Here is an opportunity for you to have direct input into the next revision of this volume.
We would like you to rate each of the articles listed below, using the following scale:

1. **Excellent: should definitely be retained**
2. **Above average: should probably be retained**
3. **Below average: should probably be deleted**
4. **Poor: should definitely be deleted**

Your ratings will play a vital part in the next revision.
Please mail this prepaid form to us as soon as possible.
Thanks for your help!

RATING	ARTICLE	RATING	ARTICLE
	1. What Democracy Is . . . and Is Not		22. Fragile Signs of Hope Emerging in the Gloom of Mugabe's Rule
	2. Public Opinion: Is There a Crisis?		23. Equity in Representation for Women and Minorities
	3. Advanced Democracies and the New Politics		
	4. Referendums: The People's Voice		24. Rwanda: Women Hold up Half the Parliament
	5. Facing the Challenge of Semi-Authoritarian States		25. Judicial Review: The Gavel and the Robe
	6. People Power: In Africa, Democracy Gains Amid Turmoil		26. Political Influence on the Bureaucracy: The Bureaucracy Speaks
	7. Bin Laden, the Arab "Street," and the Middle East's Democracy Deficit		27. Reclaiming Democracy: The Strategic Uses of Foreign and International Law by National Courts
	8. What Political Institutions Does Large-Scale Democracy Require?		28. The Making of a Neo-KGB State
	9. Interest Groups: Ex Uno, Plures		29. Beijing Censors Taken to Task in Party Circles
	10. Political Parties: Empty Vessels?		30. The Formation of State Actor-Social Movement Coalitions and Favorable Policy Outcomes
	11. Asia's Democracy Backlash		
	12. Civil Society, Youth and Societal Mobilization in Democratic Revolutions		31. What Drives Health Policy Formulation: Insights from the Nepal Maternity Incentive Scheme?
	13. Angela Merkel's Germany		32. An Economist's Invisible Hand
	14. Russia's Transition to Autocracy		33. New Hopes on Health Care for American Indians
	15. How Did We Get Here?: Mexican Democracy after the 2006 Elections		34. Breaking with Past, South Africa Issues Broad AIDS Policy
	16. Behind the Honduran Mutiny		35. France Fights Universal Care's High Cost
	17. Thailand in 2008: Crises Continued		36. China: The Quiet Revolution: The Emergence of Capitalism
	18. Iranian Infighting Leaves Mahmoud Ahmadinejad Isolated		
	19. Discipline, Accountability, and Legislative Voting in Latin America		37. Capitalism and Democracy
			38. Anti-Americanisms: Biases as Diverse as the Country Itself
	20. The Case for a Multi-Party U.S. Parliament?: American Politics in Comparative Perspective		39. The True Clash of Civilizations
	21. India's Election: Singh When You're Winning		40. The EU and Its "Constitution": Public Opinion, Political Elites, and Their International Context

ABOUT YOU

Name

Date

Are you a teacher? ☐ A student? ☐
Your school's name

Department

Address   City   State   Zip

School telephone #

YOUR COMMENTS ARE IMPORTANT TO US!

Please fill in the following information:
For which course did you use this book?

Did you use a text with this ANNUAL EDITION? ☐ yes ☐ no
What was the title of the text?

What are your general reactions to the Annual Editions concept?

Have you read any pertinent articles recently that you think should be included in the next edition? Explain.

Are there any articles that you feel should be replaced in the next edition? Why?

Are there any World Wide Websites that you feel should be included in the next edition? Please annotate.

May we contact you for editorial input? ☐ yes ☐ no
May we quote your comments? ☐ yes ☐ no